# Criminal Judges

# Criminal Judges
Legitimacy, Courts and State-Induced Guilty Pleas in Britain

Mike McConville

*Emeritus Professor, The Chinese University of Hong Kong*

Luke Marsh

*Assistant Professor, The Chinese University of Hong Kong*

**Edward Elgar**
Cheltenham, UK • Northampton, MA, USA

© Mike McConville and Luke Marsh 2014

All rights reserved. No part of this publication may be reproduced, stored in a retrieval system or transmitted in any form or by any means, electronic, mechanical or photocopying, recording, or otherwise without the prior permission of the publisher.

Published by
Edward Elgar Publishing Limited
The Lypiatts
15 Lansdown Road
Cheltenham
Glos GL50 2JA
UK

Edward Elgar Publishing, Inc.
William Pratt House
9 Dewey Court
Northampton
Massachusetts 01060
USA

A catalogue record for this book
is available from the British Library

Library of Congress Control Number: 2014932530

This book is available electronically in the ElgarOnline.com Law Subject Collection, E-ISBN 978 1 78254 892 8

ISBN 978 1 78254 891 1

Typeset by Servis Filmsetting Ltd, Stockport, Cheshire
Printed and bound in Great Britain by T.J. International Ltd, Padstow

# Contents

| | | |
|---|---|---|
| *Preface and acknowledgements* | | vi |
| *Table of cases* | | viii |
| *Table of legislation* | | xvi |
| 1 | Criminal justice: system, process and legitimacy | 1 |
| 2 | Helping the police with their inquiries | 27 |
| 3 | State-induced guilty pleas and legitimacy | 62 |
| 4 | Lowering the Bar | 87 |
| 5 | Institutional distress: the State | 127 |
| 6 | Institutional distress: the defence | 156 |
| 7 | Scotland: coercion and discourse | 190 |
| 8 | Conclusion | 216 |
| *Bibliography* | | 255 |
| *Index* | | 287 |

# Preface and acknowledgements

This book is an attempt to examine the roots and context of the British criminal justice system and challenge basic assumptions about the roles of institutions and participants within it. In our discussion, a critical, at times acerbic edge is evident. This simply reflects what we see as a fundamental shift that has taken place in criminal justice, not only through the sentencing bandwagon with its official inducements to plead guilty, but more especially in the language of the law, the antipathy towards individuals (suspects and defendants) caught up in the system increasingly being matched by an open disrespect for criminal defence lawyers and contempt for the conventional understanding that the actions of State officials (including judges) should be justified. It is one aim of the book to puncture the dogmatic and high-handed (often, unintelligible and unintelligent) manner in which this 'sea-change' is being brought about. If it succeeds at all in this regard, then our task has been greatly facilitated by many individuals who generously helped to make the publication of this book possible.

We have been supported throughout by all of our colleagues at the Centre for Rights and Justice at The Chinese University of Hong Kong as well as by our other colleagues at the Faculty of Law. Professor Eva Pils was especially supportive with her early guidance and belief in the project. The University Law Librarian, John Bahrij and his assistant Lily Ko excelled in chasing down arcane and obscure references for us and both were always ready to give advice and assistance. Similarly, Sarah Wheeler of the library at Lincoln's Inn and James Woolf and Emma Pateman at the Bar Council provided help in digging up various works almost forgotten.

We would like to further record our appreciation to Professor John Jackson and Professor Gary Edmond whose comments helped us to explore some of the themes contained within the book's analysis. The research and writing of this book was also assisted as a result of time spent by one of its authors as a Visiting Scholar at Columbia Law School, New York during the winter term of 2013, where Professor Barbara Schatz and Edwin Rekosh were especially supportive.

Appropriate expressions of gratitude must also go to the many excellent criminal law practitioners in London who offered lasting insight into the difficulties facing the profession as a whole; notably, the leading figures HHJ Anuja Dhir QC, Denis Barry and Ben Douglas-Jones, who were all a source of unfailing support, encouragement and patience (perhaps in unequal measure). The usual disclaimer applies: the views, and any errors, contained within this book are entirely our own.

More generally, we owe an enormous debt to those scholars who have written about plea bargaining over the last fifty or more years. As always, we have drawn wisdom and insights from their endeavours and hope that, as a result, we have added to the already great stock of knowledge about the practices of State officials in criminal justice.

We owe a further great debt to Tim Williams at Edward Elgar for having faith in the project and to his colleagues, John-Paul McDonald and Victoria Nicols for guiding us through the publication process – without whom this project would not have become a reality.

Above all, we must thank our friends (particularly Erica McPherson, Nigel Perfect and Deepali Joshi for their forgiveness in missing their respective weddings when the enormity of tasks got in the way) and families who have shown unswerving support and encouragement throughout the genesis of this book: Sonia McConville for always being there and helping at critical stages, and Caspar McConville and Victoria Wang for the uplifting visits; Kim Wiles for her endeavour, and Michael Marsh and Margaret McGee for providing timely doses of equanimity.

# Table of cases

## UNITED KINGDOM CASES

*A v Secretary of State* [2005] 2 AC 68 .................................................59
*Abdalla Mohammed v R et al.* [2010] EWCA Crim
  2400 ..........................................................................................164
*A-G Ref No 17 of 1998 (R v Stokes)* [1999] 1 Cr. App.
  R. (S.) 357, *The Times*, 12 October 1998 ...............................74
*A-G Ref No 3 of 1999* [2001] 2 AC 91.........................................169
*A-G Ref Nos 80 and 81 of 1999 (Thompson and Rodgers)*
  [2000] 2 Cr. App. R. (S.) 138 113,.............................................147
*A-G Ref No 44 of 2000 (Peverett)* [2001] 1 Cr. App.
  R. 416 136,.................................................................................141
*A-G Ref No 58 of 2000 (R v Wynne)* (2001) 2 Cr. App.
  R. (S) 19, CA .............................................................................113
*A-G Ref No 81 of 2000 (R v Jacobs)* (2001) 2 Cr. App.
  R. (S) 16, CA .............................................................................113
*A-G Ref Nos 8, 9 and 10 of 2002 (R v Mohammed,
  R v Habib, R v. Hussain)* [2003] 1 Cr. App.
  R. (S.) 57............................................................................ 149-150
*A-G Ref No 19 of 2004* [2004] EWCA Crim
  1239 ...........................................................................................147
*A-G Ref No 19 of 2004 (Brett Charlton)* [2005] 1
  Cr. App. R. (S.) 18....................................................................113
*A-G Ref No 80 of 2005* [2005] EWCA Crim 3367.....................97
*A-G Ref Nos 119 and 120 of 2005* [2006] EWCA
  Crim 1501 .............................................................................145-6
*A-G Ref Nos 14 and 15 of 2006 (French and Webster)*
  [2006] EWCA Crim 1335 ........................................................114
*A-G Ref No 48 of 2006 (R v Farrow)* [2007] 1 Cr.
  App. R. (S.) 558 114,.................................................................134
*A-G Ref No 44 of 2007* [2007] EWCA Crim 1530....................135
*A-G Refs 25–26 of 2008* [2008] EWCA Crim 2665...................135
*A-G Ref No 49 of 2008 (Blake)* [2009] 1 Cr. App.
  R. (S.) 109..................................................................................135
*A-G Ref No 6 of 2009* [2009] EWCA Crim 132................... 134-5
*A-G Ref No 50 of 2010* [2010] EWCA Crim
  2872 135, 144-5, .......................................................................163
*A-G Ref Nos 82 to 96 and 104 to 111 of 2011* [2012]
  EWCA Crim155 .......................................................................153
*A-G Ref No 6 of 2011* [2012] EWCA Crim 86 .........................113

*A-G Ref Nos 11 and 12 of 2012* [2012] EWCA
   Crim 1119 113, ...................................................................................................... 145
*A-G Ref Nos 21 and 22 of 2012 (Benjamin Pugh;*
   *Jordan Naaif)* [2012] EWCA Crim 1806 145, .............................................. 153-4
*A-G Ref Nos 26, 27 & 28 of 2012* [2012] EWCA
   Crim 2290 ................................................................................................. 135
*A-G Ref No 44 of 2012* [2012] EWCA Crim 2562 ................................................ 135
*A-G Ref Nos 50–53 2012* [2012] EWCA Crim 2558 ....................................... 139-40
*A-G Ref Nos 61 and 62 of 2012* [2012] EWCA Crim ............................................ 153
*A-G Ref No 71 of 2012* [2012] EWCA Crim 3071 ................................................ 153
*A-G Ref Nos 73 & 74 of 2012* [2013] EWCA Crim 23 ......................................... 228
*Ali Reza Sadighpour v R* [2012] EWCA Crim 2669
   (CA).............................................................................................................. 62
*Asmeron v R* [2013] EWCA Crim 435 ................................................................ 152
*Balogun v DPP* [2010] EWHC 799 (Admin) ....................................................... 175
*C v R* [2012] EWCA Crim 1478 ......................................................................... 151
*CF v R* [2008] EWCA Crim 994 ......................................................................... 133
*Cadder v HM Advocate* [2010] UKSC 43 ............................................................ 191
*Caetano v Commissioner of Police for the Metropolis*
   [2013] EWHC 375 (Admin)....................................................................... 163
*Cairns & Others v R* [2013] EWCA Crim 467
   146, ............................................................................................................ 225
*Caley & Others v R* [2012] EWCA Crim 2821 ............................... 115, 146-7,225
*Carter (Sentencing Remarks)* [2001] EW
   Misc 12 (Crown Ct) ..................................................................................... 22
*Chic Fashions v Jones* [1968] 2 QB 299 ................................................... 41-42, 55
*Ghani v Jones* [1970] 1 QB 693.................................................................. 41, 55, 57
*Hallam v R* [2012] EWCA Crim 1158 ................................................................. 232
*Holmes v SGB Services* [2001] EWCA Civ 354 ................................................. 170
*Hughes v DPP* [2012] EWHC 606 ...................................................................... 138
*Jeffrey v Black* (1978) 1 QB 490 ........................................................................... 41
*Ludlow v Shelton* (1938) *The Times*, 3 and 4
   February 1938.............................................................................................. 49
*Malcolm v DPP [*2007] EWHC 363 (Admin)................................................... 177-8
*McFadden* (1975) 62 Cr App R 187 .................................................................... 168
*McMenemy* [1962] Crim. L.R. 44........................................................................... 71
*Millberry v R* [2002] EWCA Crim 2891 ............................................................... 97
*Miranda v Secretary of State for the Home*
   *Department and The Commissioner of the Police of*
   *the Metropolis* [2014] EWHC 255 ............................................................. 250
*Mohammed-Holgate v Duke* (1983) 3 All ER 526,
   CA ................................................................................................................ 54
*Moss v McLachlan* (1938) *The Times*,
   29 November 1984 ...................................................................................... 14
*Nightingale* (13 March 2013, CA No 1206575 D5) ............................................ 124
*Nolan and Howard v R* [2012] EWCA Crim 671 ......................................... 93, 133
*Nunn v Chief Constable of Suffolk* [2012] EWHC
   1186 (Admin)............................................................................................... 59
*P Foster (Haulage) Ltd v Roberts* [1978] 2 All ER 751 ........................................ 62
*R v A* [2010] EWCA Crim 2913........................................................................... 227

*R v Alagago, Patel and Khanom (Sentencing Remarks)*
 (25 August 2011) (Crown Ct) ..................................................................... 23
*R v Alladice* (1988) 87 Cr. App. R. 380 ........................................................ 46-47
*R v Allen* [1977] Crim. L.R. 163 .................................................................. 40
*R v Anne McGee* [2012] EWCA Crim 613 ................................................... 150
*R v Anouar Bouhaddou* [2012] EWCA Crim 1006 ...................................... 135
*R v Anthony Pearce, Andrew Daniel William*
 *Galloway* [2013] EWCA Crim 808 ............................................................ 4
*R v Applied Language Solutions Ltd* [2013] EWCA
 Crim 326 ..................................................................................................... 102
*R v Auguste* [2003] EWCA Crim 3329 ......................................................... 150
*R v Atkinson* (1978) 2 All ER 460 ................................................................ 76-7, 83-4
*R v Austin* [2013] EWCA Crim 1028 ........................................................... 243
*R v Banfield & Banfield* [2013] EWCA Crim 1394 ..................................... 132-3
*R v Banks* (1917) 12 Cr. App. R. 74 ............................................................. 220
*R v Barkshire & Ors* [2011] EWCA Crim 1885, CA ................................... 93, 226, 239
*R v Barnes* (1970) 55 Cr. App. R. 100 .......................................................... 121
*R v Bass* (1953) 37 Cr. App. R. 51 ............................................................... 43, 56, 218
*R v Bathurst* [1968] 2 QB 99 ........................................................................ 46
*R v Behman* (1938) *The Times*, 28 July 1967 ............................................. 70
*R v Bentley* [1998] EWCA Crim 2516 ......................................................... 48
*R v Berens & Others* (1865) 176 E. R. 815 ................................................. 128
*R v Beswick* (1996) 1 Cr. App. R. (S.) 343, CA .......................................... 113, 136, 143-4
*R v Bhatti* [2000] All ER (D) 2353 ............................................................... 62
*R v Bird* [1978] Crim. L.R. 237 .................................................................... 74, 79, 83
*R v Blackshaw* [2011] EWCA Crim 2312 .................................................... 18, 21, 23-4
*R v Boal* (1992) 95 Cr. App. R. 272 ............................................................. 62, 163-4
*R v Bodkin* (1863) 9 Cox CC 403 ................................................................ 230
*R v Booth and Jones* (1910) 5 Cr. App. R. 177 ............................................ 37, 55, 150
*R v Boyd* (1980) 2 Cr. App. R. (S.) 234 ....................................................... 84
*R v Brackenbury* (1893) 17 Cox C.C. 628 ................................................... 37
*R v Brereton* [2012] EWCA Crim 85 ........................................................... 140
*R v Brook* [1970] Crim. L.R. 601 ................................................................. 74
*R v Brown* [1994] 1 AC 212 ......................................................................... 176
*R v Brown* [2006] EWCA Crim 141 ............................................................ 241
*R v Bryant* [2005] EWCA Crim 2079 .......................................................... 177
*R v C* [2005] EWCA Crim 3533 .................................................................. 133
*R v Cain* [1976] Crim. L.R. 464; (1976) *The Times*,
 23 February 1976 ....................................................................................... 74, 79, 82-3, 121
*R v Carter & Others (Sentencing Remarks)* [2011] EW
 Misc 12 (16 August 2011) (Crown Ct) ...................................................... 22-23
*R v CCRC ex parte Pearson* [2000] 1 Cr. App. R. 1414 .............................. 3-4
*R v Chaaban* [2003] EWCA Crim 1012 95, ................................................. 169-170
*R v Chandler* [1976] 3 All ER 105 ............................................................... 39
*R v Chaney* [2009] EWCA Crim 52 ............................................................ 133
*R v Chaytors* [2012] EWCA Crim 1810 ...................................................... 115
*R (on the application of the DPP) v Chorley Justices* [2006]
 EWHC 175 ................................................................................................. 167
*R v Coe* (1969) 1 All ER 65 ......................................................................... 104
*R v Cole* [2008] EWCA Crim 3234 ............................................................. 149

*R v Cole* [2013] EWCA Crim 1149 .................................................................. 243
*R v Cordingley* (2007) EWCA Crim 2174 ........................................................ 149
*R v Cornelius* [2012] EWCA Crim 500 ............................................................ 133
*R v Costen* (1989) 11 Cr. App. R. (S.) 182 ............................................... 84, 114
*R v Court and Gu* [2012] EWCA Crim 133 ..................................................... 135
*R v Cullen* [1985] Crim. L.R. 107 ..................................................................... 74
*R v Day* [2003] EWCA Crim 1060 .................................................................. 174
*R v Delay* (2006) 170 JP 581; [2006] EWCA 1110 ......................................... 178
*R v Director of the Serious Fraud Office, ex parte Smith* [1993] AC 1 ................ 229
*R v Dowty* [2011] EWCA Crim 3138 ............................................................... 140
*R v Dudley (Stephen Paul)* [2012] *C.L.R.* 230 ................................................. 113
*R v Eccles* [1978] Crim. L.R. 757 ..................................................................... 74
*R v Edwards* (1991) 1 WLR 207 ..................................................................... 243
*R v Ellis* [2013] EWCA Crim 213 ..................................................................... 19
*R v Ensor* [2009] EWCA Crim 2519; [2010] 1 Cr App R 18 ............................. 179
*R (Firth) v Epping Justices* [2011] EWHC 388 (Admin); [2011]
    1WLR 1818 .................................................................................................. 179
*R v Gavin* (1885) 15 Cox C.C. 656 ................................................................... 37
*R (Gillan) v Commissioner of Police of the Metropolis* [2003]
    EWHC 2545 (Admin)
*R (Gillan) v Commissioner of Police of the Metropolis* [2004]
    EWCA Civ 1067; [2005] QB 388 ............................................................ 30-31
*R (Gillan) v Commissioner of Police of the Metropolis* [2006]
    UKHL 12; [2006] 2 AC 307 28, ................................................................... 32
*R v Gilbert* (1978) 66 Cr. App. R. 237 ............................................................... 49
*R v Gleeson* [2003] EWCA Crim 3357 ........................................................... 173
*R v Goodings* [2012] EWCA Crim 2392 ......................................................... 139
*R v Goodyear* (2005) EWCA Crim 888 ............... 94-101, 110, 116, 120-26, 205, 225
*R v Grafton* (1993) 96 Cr. App. R. 156 ............................................................ 220
*R v Grice* (1977) 66 Cr. App. R. 167 ......................................................... 74, 77
*R v H* [2010] EWCA Crim 1931 ................................................................. 147-8
*R v Hackney* [2013] EWCA Crim 1156 ........................................................... 225
*R v Hall* (1968) 52 Cr. App. R. 528 66, .............................................................. 78
*R v Harper* (1967) *The Times*, 7 October 1967 ........................................... 70, 72
*R v Harper-Taylor* (1991) R.T.R. 76 ................................................... 76, 79-80, 83
*R v Harper-Taylor and Bakker* (1988)138 NJL 80 ....................................... 79-80
*R v Hastings* (1996) 1 Cr. App. R. (S.) 167 ....................................................... 84
*R v Holchester & Others* (1868) Cox C.C. 226 ................................................ 128
*R v Hollington and Emmens* [1986] Crim. L.R. 270 .......................................... 85
*R v Houghton and Franciosy* (1979) 68 Cr. App. R. 197 ......................... 39, 50, 55
*R v Howell* (1981) 73 Cr. App. R. 31, CA ......................................................... 13
*R v Howell* [1978] Crim. L.R. 239 .................................................................... 74
*R v Ibori* [2013] EWCA Crim 815 ................................................................... 225
*R v Inns* (1974) 60 Cr. App. R. 231 ................................................ 74, 79-81, 83, 121
*R v JA* [2012] EWCA Crim 1156 .................................................................... 225
*R v James* (1990) Crim. L.R. 815 ..................................................................... 75
*R v Jarvis* [2008] EWCA Crim 488 ................................................................. 179
*R v Jenkins* (1986) 83 Cr. App. R. 152 ............................................................ 128
*R v Jisl* [2004] EWCA Crim 696 ..................................................................... 170
*R v Jonathan Dodd* [2013] EWCA Crim 660 .................................................. 133

*R v Jones* [2003] 1 AC 1 .................................................................................... 150
*R v Joof & Others* [2012] EWCA Crim 1475 ............................................ 93, 237-8
*R v Keily* [1990] Crim. L.R. 204 ......................................................................... 74
*R v Kerrigan* (1993) 14 Cr. App. R. (S.) 179, CA ............................................. 113
*R v Kinnaird* [2013] EWCA Crim 715 ............................................................. 243
*R v Knight and Thayre* (1905) 20 Cox C.C. 711 ................................................ 37
*R v Kulah* [2007] EWCA Crim 1701 ............................................................... 113
*R v Landy* (1995) 16 Cr. App. R. (S.) 908 ..................................................... 84-5
*R v Lawrence* [2013] EWCA Crim 1054 ......................................................... 134
*R v Lemsatef* (1977) 2 All ER 835; [1997] 1 WLR 812 ............................... 40, 56
*R v Llewellyn* (1978) 67 Cr. App. R. 149 ........................................... 74-7, 79, 83
*R v Lopez* [2013] All ER (D) 193 (Sep) ............................... 102-103, 150-51
*R v Mansfield Justices* [1985] QB 613 ......................................................... 14-15
*R v March* (2002) EWCA Crim 551 ............................................................ 137-8
*R v Mateta et al.* [2013] EWCA Crim 1372 .................................................. 164-5
*R v Maxwell* (2010) UKSC 48 ........................................................ 58, 236-7, 239
*R v McIlkenny & Ors* (1991) 93 Cr. App. R. 287 ........................................... 176
*R v McFadden* (1975) 62 Cr. App. R. 187 ....................................................... 168
*R v Mick* (1863) 3 F. & F. 322 ............................................................................ 37
*R v Mirza* [2004] 1 AC 1118 ............................................................................. 59
*R v Musone* [2007] 1 WLR 2467; [2007] EWCA Crim 1237 ...................... 178-9
*R v Myers* (1996) 1 Cr. App. R. (S.) 187, CA .................................................. 113
*R v Nelson* [1967] 1 All ER 358 .............................................................. 121, 124
*R v Newell* [2012] EWCA Crim 650 ............................................................... 250
*R v Newman* [2010] EWCA Crim 1566 .......................................................... 113
*R v Newton* (1983) 77 Cr. App. R. 13, CA ...................................................... 113
*R v Northam* (1968) 52 Cr. App. R. 97 .............................................................. 49
*R (on the application of Crown Prosecution Service)*
    *v Norwich Magistrates' Court* [2011] EWHC 82 (Admin) ......................... 175
*R v Peace* [1976] Crim. L.R. 119; *The Times*, 28 November
    1975, CA ................................................................................................... 80, 121
*R v Pelletier* [2012] EWCA Crim 1060 ........................................................... 133
*R v Penner* [2010] EWCA Crim 1155 .............................................................. 175
*R v Pitman* (1990) R. T. R. 70 ............................................................. 74, 76, 80
*R v Plimmer* (1975) 61 Cr. App. R. 264 .......................................................... 74-5
*R v Prager* (1972) 1 All ER 933 ......................................................................... 38
*R v Puddick* (1865) 176 ER 662 ....................................................................... 220
*R v Quartey* (1975) Crim. L.R. 592 ................................................................... 74
*Regina v R (a Juvenile)* (1992) *The Times*, 16 January 1992 ............................ 85
*Randall v R* (2002) 2 Cr App R 17 (PC) ................................................... 220, 250
*R v Rawson* [2013] EWCA Crim 9 .................................................................. 115
*R (on the application of Tinnion) v Reading Crown Court*
    [2009] EWHC 2930 (Admin) (DC) .............................................................. 178
*R v Rochford* [2010] EWCA Crim 1928 .................................................. 175, 177
*R v Rollings* [2012] EWCA Crim 86 ................................................................ 150
*R v Ryan* (1978) 67 Cr. App. R. 177 .................................................................. 77
*R v Sang* [1979] 2 All ER 1222 .......................................................................... 55
*R v Sanghera and Takhar* [2012] EWCA Crim 16 ........................................... 177
*R v Seddon* [2007] EWCA Crim 3022 ............................................................. 113
*R v Shields* [2011] EWCA 2343 ............................................................... 133, 163

*R v Simpson (Dean)* [2009] EWCA 423 .................................................................. 114
*R v Sina Jaddi* [2012] EWCA Crim 2565 ................................................................ 164
*R v Smith* (1990) 90 Cr. App. R. 413; [1990] Criminal
   L. R. 354 ........................................................................................................ 76, 149
*R v Smith (PA)* (1986) 8 Cr. App. R. (S.) 169 ........................................................ 113
*R v Smith* (2011) EWCA Crim 1098 ...................................................................... 149
*R (on the application of Lawson) v Stafford Magistrates'*
   *Court* [2007] EWHC 2490 ............................................................................... 168
*R (on the application of Payne) v South Lakeland Magistrates'*
   *Court* [2011] EWHC 1802 (Admin) ................................................................. 175
*R v Stephen King* [1978] Crim. L.R. 632 ................................................................. 40
*R v Stocker* [2013] EWCA Crim 1993 .................................................................... 132
*R (Robinson) v Sutton Coldfield Magistrates' Court* [2006]
   4 All ER 1029 ................................................................................................... 178
*R v SVS Solicitors* [2012] EWCA Crim 319 .......................................................... 178
*R v Talbot* (2013) CLW/13/3/3 ............................................................................... 152
*R v Tolera* (1999) 1 Cr App R 29, CA ............................................................. 113, 134
*R v Tougher* [2001] 3 All ER 463 ............................................................................. 62
*R v Turner* (1970) 54 Cr. App. R. 352; (1970) 2 QB 321 ..................................
   66-73, 121, 125-126, 156-7, 205, 218-20, 249, 251
*R v Twemlow* (Sentencing Remarks) [2011] EW Misc 14
   (Crown Ct) ......................................................................................................... 23
*R v Unah* [2011] EWCA Crim 1837 .................................................................. 151-2
*R v Underwood* (2005) 1 Cr. App. R. (S.) 13, CA .................................................. 113
*R v Voisin* (1918) 13 Cr. App. R. 89 ......................................................................... 55
*R (Kelly) v Warley Magistrates' Court* [2008] 1 Cr. App. R. .............................. 179
*R v White* CLW/12/20/17 ........................................................................................ 152
*R v William* [2013] EWCA Crim 1262 .................................................................. 243
*R v Wilson* [2011] EWCA Crim 16 .......................................................................... 93
*R v Wilson (Paul Anthony)* [2012] Criminal L. R. 560 ......................................... 114
*R v Winterflood* (1979) 68 Cr. App. R. 291 ..................................................... 74-5, 77
*R v Warth* (1991) 93 Cr. App. R. 187 ....................................................................... 78
*R v Wattam* (1952) 36 Cr. App. R. 72 ...................................................................... 49
*Rondel v Worsley* [1969] 1 AC 191 ........................................................................ 166
*Smith* (1989) Crim. L. R. 900 ...................................................................... 74, 76, 79
*Suleimanov* [2013] EWCA Crim 32 ......................................................................... 22
*Thornton v Crown Prosecution Service* [2010] EWCA 346 .................................. 113
*Tombling v Universal Bulb Co. Ltd* (1951) 2 TLR 289 ......................................... 172
*Woolmington v DPP* [1935] AC 462 ........................................................................ 46

# UNREPORTED UNITED KINGDOM CASES

*R v Davis* (1978) Unreported (4138/R/77) ........................................................ 74, 76-7
*R v Dossetter* (1999) Unreported (9804926/X3-98
   05271/X3-9805038/X3) ............................................................................ 74, 76, 83
*R v Essa* [2009] 5 Archbold News 2 CA, Unreported,
   14 January 2009 ............................................................................................... 177
*R v Phillips* (1976) Unreported (2459/B/75) ............................................................ 84

*R v Prasad* (1976) Unreported (362/C/76) ............................................................................. 79
*R v Quartey* Unreported (4936/A/74, 314/B/75) ................................................................. 79
*R v Ricardo* (1976) Unreported (2243/A/74) ........................................................................ 78
*R v Warring-Davies* (1978) Unreported (5854/c/77) ..................................................... 74, 76
*Williams and Williams* (1975) Unreported (5166/C/74) ..................................................... 78

# SCOTLAND CASES

*Balgowan v HM Advocate* (2011) SCCR 143 ............................................................ 201, 209
*Du Plooy and Ors v HM Advocate* (2005 JC1) ........................... 197-8, 204-206, 214
*Colin Ross v HM Advocate* [2013] HCJAC 111 ................................................................ 215
*Doherty v HM Advocate* [2012] HCJAC 106 ..................................................................... 209
*Gemmell and Ors v HM Advocate* (2011)
 HCJAC 129 ........................................................................ 197-9, 201-204, 206-207, 209
*George Gerald Doherty v HM Advocate* [2012]
 HCJAC 106 ............................................................................................................................ 209
*George Gerald Ottaway v Nisbet* [2012] HCJAC 36 ........................................................ 210
*HM Advocate v Bell* (1995) S.L.T. 350 ................................................................................. 210
*HM Advocate v Graham* [2010] HCJAC 50 197, ............................................................. 214
*HM Advocate v James East* [2013] HCJAC 124 ................................................................ 215
*HM Advocate v Lee McNamara* [2012] Scot HC
 HCJAC 54 ............................................................................................................... 198, 208-209
*HM Advocate v Lyttell (Adam)* [2012] Scot HCJAC 72 .................................................. 209
*HM Advocate v Q* [2013] HCJAC 23 .................................................................................... 210
*Harkin & Anor v Procurator Fiscal, Falkirk & Anor*
 [2012] Scot HC HCJAC 100 ........................................................................................ 201, 209
*James Tough v HM Advocate* [2012] HCJAC 119 ..................................................... 209-210
*Khaliq v HM Advocate* (1984) SSCR 212 ........................................................................... 193
*Lees v HM Advocate* [2012] HCJAC 143 ............................................................................. 209
*Luke Sinclaire v Procurator Fiscal, Stranraer* [2013]
 HCJAC 65 ............................................................................................................................... 193
*MacDonald v Procurator Fiscal Aberdeen* [2010]
 HCJAC 36 ............................................................................................................................... 190
*Reedie v HM Advocate* [2005] HCJAC 55 ........................................................................... 193
*Shawn Ernest Divin v Procurator Fiscal, Dundee* [2012]
 HCJAC 82 ............................................................................................................................... 209
*Spence v HM Advocate* 2008 JC 174 ............................... 197, 206-207, 211-12, 214
*Stephen Murray v HM Advocate* [2013] SCL 243 ...................................................... 209-12
*Steven McArthur v HM Advocate* [2013] HCJAC 121 .................................................... 215
*Strathern v Sloan* (1937) JC 76 ............................................................................................... 190
*Strawhorn v McLeod* [1987] SCCR 413 25, ............................................................... 193, 198
*Wishart v HM Advocate* [2013] HCJAC 116 ..................................................................... 215

# EUROPEAN COURT OF HUMAN RIGHTS CASES

*Barbera, Messegue and Jabardo v Spain* (1989) 11 EHRR 360 ................................ 3
*Gillan and Quinton v United Kingdom* (2010) 50
    EHRR 45 .............................................................................................. 32, 34-5
*Kaufman v Belgium* (1986) 50 DR 98 ................................................................. 170

# OTHER NATIONAL COURT CASES

### Australia

*Cameron v The Queen* (2002) 209 CLR 339; 187 ALR 65 ........................... 202-203
*Markarian v R* [2005] HCA 25 ........................................................................ 205
*R v Shannon* (1979) 21 SASR 442 ............................................................. 202-203
*Siganto v The Queen* (1998) 194 CLR 656 ....................................................... 203

### Jersey (Decided by the Privy Council)

*Michel v The Queen* [2009] UKPC 41; [2010] 1 Cr. pp. R. 24;
    [2010] 1 WLR 8 ............................................................................................ 220

# Table of legislation

## STATUTES

Bail Act 1976 ..................................... 9

Criminal Justice Act 1967 ............... 167

Criminal Justice Act
  2003 ................ 45, 47, 60-61, 89, 226

Criminal Justice and
  Immigration Act 2008 ................. 167

Criminal Justice and Public
  Order Act 1994.... 60, 89-90, 167, 220

Criminal Law Act 1977 .................... 45

Criminal Proceedings Etc.
  (Reform)(Scotland) Act 2007 ...... 213

Criminal Procedure and
  Investigations Act 1996 ....... 167, 173

Criminal Procedure (Scotland)
  Act 1995 ..... 195-7, 201-202, 204-205,
  ............................................. 207-208

Criminal Procedure (Scotland)
  Act 2004 ....................................... 196

Legal Aid, Sentencing and
  Punishment of
  Offenders Act 2012 ..................... 181

Police and Criminal Evidence
  Act 1984 ......................................... 60

Prevention of Terrorism
  Act 1989 ................................... 60-61

Protection of Freedoms
  Act 2012 ........................................ 29

Public Order Act 1936 ................ 13-15

Serious Organised Crime and
  Police Act 2005 ..................... 61, 236

Terrorism Act 2000 ..................... 29-31

Youth and Criminal Evidence
  Act 1999 ....................................... 226

## STATUTORY INSTRUMENTS

Criminal Procedure
  Rules ..... 47, 167-172, 178-9, 181, 251

## CONVENTIONS AND TREATIES

European Convention on
  Human Rights .......................... 1950

Article 5 ........................................ 33-4

Article 6 .................................. 2-3, 169

# 1. Criminal justice: system, process and legitimacy

> Alexander Hamilton, writing in the Federalist (No. 78), described the judiciary in a democracy as the weakest and least dangerous department of government. More than 200 years later I would argue that his statement accurately describes the role of the judiciary in the governance of our country.
>
> (Lord Steyn, 1997)

At a general level, the highest courts in both England and Scotland have enjoyed an authoritative status over many centuries in the sense that they have secured a substantial measure of public confidence. They have not only attained *de facto* authority but, by providing considered and reflective judgments, have secured 'normative-justificatory' authority.[1] They have, in short, offered persuasive reasons why people should respect their role as well as their individual rulings. In this process, courts have garnered public respect, deference and trust even though particular judgments have been controversial. In political science terms, this equates to having secured 'diffuse support', that is, loyalty to an institution which is not contingent upon satisfaction with the immediate outputs.[2]

Our concern in this book goes beyond the issue of public confidence and, instead, is with the question of the *legitimacy* of British courts by reference to their law-making or policy functions in the arena of criminal justice as seen through the lens of State-induced guilty pleas. State-induced guilty pleas, here, include all practices commonly referred to as 'plea bargaining' (a term we occasionally use in the same sense) to cover, for example, direct or indirect offers from State officials (police, prosecutors and judges) to reduce a sentence in return for a guilty plea, offers to reduce the number of charges or alter the charge(s) from a more serious to a less serious offence, or offers to present the 'facts' (the basis of the guilty plea) in a favourable light.

Courts seek to secure authority by anchoring their determinations in

---

[1] Less tangible considerations such as exposure to the symbols and rituals of law no doubt contribute to public confidence.
[2] Gibson (2006).

terms of *formal legal rationality* directed by internally-generated principles and values which claim independence from other arms of government and 'political' influence. Key elements of the notion of formal legal rationality include protecting the right to a fair trial, ensuring the autonomy of the legal actors, providing individual, rather than aggregate, decision-making and, through reasoned judgments, holding law-makers and prosecutors to account by requiring that they justify their actions.

*Legitimacy*, however, cannot simply be tied to the formal claims of the prevailing legal order since, for various reasons including 'interpretive' decisions of the courts, formal legal rationality may not respect the rights of individuals. Legitimacy, accordingly, must have a moral basis which respects the basic rights of its citizens, such as the right to liberty and the right to privacy. Ronald Frey (1980) defines a moral right as 'a right which is not the product of community legislation or social practice, which prescribes the boundary beyond which neither individuals nor the community may go in pursuit of their overall ends'. Accordingly, our analysis of criminal justice goes beyond formal claims and interrogates the system's intrinsic rationale and its relationship with the moral rights of citizens.

## RIGHT TO A FAIR TRIAL

A key moral basis of the adjudication of criminal disputes, the right to a fair trial, is set out in Article 6 of the European Convention on Human Rights (ECHR):

ARTICLE 6
1. In the determination of his civil rights and obligations or of any criminal charge against him, everyone is entitled to a fair and public hearing within a reasonable time by an independent and impartial tribunal established by law . . .
2. Everyone charged with a criminal offence shall be presumed innocent until proved guilty according to law.
3. Everyone charged with a criminal offence has the following minimum rights:
    (a) to be informed promptly, in a language which he understands and in detail, of the nature and cause of the accusation against him;
    (b) to have adequate time and the facilities for the preparation of his defence;
    (c) to defend himself in person or through legal assistance of his own choosing or, if he has not sufficient means to pay for legal assistance, to be given it free when the interests of justice so require;
    (d) to examine or have examined witnesses against him and to obtain the attendance and examination of witnesses on his behalf under the same conditions as witnesses against him;

(e) to have the free assistance of an interpreter if he cannot understand or speak the language used in court.

Underlying the right to trial is the understanding that infringement or curtailment of the moral rights of individual citizens (such as the right to liberty)[3] must be *justified* by State officials to an authoritative and disinterested third party (an adjudicative tribunal) and to a high standard of proof.[4] Trials, as Richard Lippke (2011) argues, produce a wide range of public and private goods, including: the promotion of accuracy; the affirmation of principles regarded as non-derogable (such as the prohibition against evidence produced by torture); the acquittal of innocent people; the exposure of incompetence, malfeasance or corruption on the part of State officials; the conviction of individuals proved to be factually and legally guilty by due process of law; the imposition of punishment at a level appropriate to the crime; the creation of a full record to provide a resource for checking for and rectifying error; and the reinforcement of basic norms of governance through their public demonstration.[5]

## ADVERSARY JUSTICE AND FORMAL LEGAL RATIONALITY

In Britain, the concept of a fair trial is said to find its ideal expression in trial by jury.[6] In *R v CCRC ex parte Pearson* [2000] at 145, Lord Bingham summarised the protection it was said to afford:

> It is essential to the health and proper functioning of a modern democracy that the citizen accused of crime should be fairly tried and adequately protected against the risk and consequences of wrongful conviction. To this end, police

---

[3] See also, Feinberg (1992).
[4] See *Barbera, Messegue and Jabardo v Spain* (1989). For a full discussion, see Lippke (2011).
[5] See also, Albert Alschuler (1981) who argues that trials encourage genuine advocacy by defence lawyers thereby potentially exposing flaws and irregularities in the State's case that otherwise would be glossed over; restrain abuse of legislative or executive power by ensuring that the criminal law and its enforcement do not depart too widely from communal moral norms; and increase people's participation in their own governance and educate them in the importance of principles and rights.
[6] The vast majority of court cases are disposed of in magistrates' courts. See, Carlen (1976) and McBarnet (1983) for a critical appraisal. Many criminal infractions are increasingly dealt with out of court as police and prosecutors seek to meet targets imposed on them (see further Chapters 5 and 8).

operations to investigate crime and interrogate suspects are closely controlled by statutes, codes and rules; the conduct of prosecutions is entrusted to an independent, professional prosecuting authority; and legal aid is made available to fund all but the very well-to-do to defend themselves in serious cases. The main protection of the citizen accused of serious crime is, however, to be found in our system of trial by judge and jury ... [T]he procedure is adversarial ... It is the function of the judge to direct the jury on the relevant law and to summarise (perhaps very briefly) the evidence, and to define the issues raised by the prosecution and the defence, including any possible defence disclosed by the evidence even if not relied on by the defendant. The judge need not, and should not, go further. Secondly, the decision on the defendant's guilt is made following a trial, continuous from day to day, by a jury assembled only for that trial, with no responsibility for the proceedings before the trial begins or after it ends.

Embedded in this is the general principle that the 'freedom of the individual must not be overridden by claims advanced on behalf of the State'.[7] The evidential and procedural rules of the adversary system flow from a particular conception of social organisation in which many of the interests and moral rights of the individual are separated from the interests of the State.[8] The primary interest to be protected is that of the individual. It is the defendant who is accorded fundamental rights. Each citizen has a right to personal autonomy and should be respected as an individual, not viewed as a resource; nor should the rights of any individual be subjugated to the interests of the collective in, for example, cost-effective case processing.

In this understanding, the State is not presumed to be beneficent and non-threatening but, rather, is seen as a potentially intrusive force. Nowhere is this intrusive potential more dramatised than in criminal justice where, by the very act of prosecution, the State is claiming the right to stigmatise and punish one of its citizens. One of the principal rights individuals have in this setting is the right not to be criminalised and punished for crimes they did not commit.

Because the State is claiming the right to punish one of its citizens, the State is required to *justify* its claim and every associated act of interference such as stops, search of the person and property, detention, arrest, taking intimate samples, telephone tapping, electronic surveillance and charge. Arising directly from this is the presumption of innocence. The State bears the burden of proof and must justify its every act through the

---

[7] Royal Commission on Police Powers and Procedure (1929) *Report*, p. 10, para. 25. See also, Lord Justice Aikens in *Regina v Anthony Pearce, Andrew Daniel William Galloway* [2013].

[8] Of course, it is also accepted that many of the interests of the State, such as in providing for an orderly and safe environment, are also in the interest of citizens.

introduction of legally sufficient and admissible evidence without the compelled assistance of the accused person. In other words, the State cannot convict defendants and inflict punishment on them without proving that they committed each and every element of the offence charged, no matter how inconsequential any component of that offence might at first appear. Defendants in turn, do not have to do anything by way of producing evidence, but can, if they choose, rest the defence upon the failure of the State to discharge its burden of proof.

In discharging the requirement that it justify its claim regarding punishment of a citizen the burden shouldered by the State is high: unlike civil cases in which the claimant has to prove his or her case on a balance of probabilities, in a criminal case the State must discharge its burden of proof *beyond reasonable doubt*. An accused person is entitled to be acquitted if there is, from whatever source, reasonable doubt that the prosecution has established its case.

In its ideal form, therefore, judges have made clear that the criminal justice system is deliberately designed to guard against the possibility that *factually guilty* people might be found guilty on anything other than legally sufficient evidence and according to legally correct procedures. This not only means that the system gives formal recognition to 'process values' but also that occasionally factually guilty defendants may be acquitted simply because the State is unable to discharge the burden of proof. While some may regard this possibility as providing inadequate protection of victims or other citizens who might become future victims of crime, the distinction between factual guilt and legal guilt is at the very heart of the adversary system.

There is a deeply moral dimension to this framework. As Ronald Dworkin (1985) points out, antecedent decisions taken by society may show special concern for moral harm, not only by paying a high price for accuracy but also and especially by paying a high price *in* accuracy to guard against a mistake that involves greater moral harm than a mistake in the other direction:

> This is shown, for example, by the rule that guilt must be shown beyond reasonable doubt, rather than on a balance of probabilities, and also by rules, like the rule that an accused may not be compelled to testify, whose complex justification includes weighing the scales in favor of the accused, at the cost of accuracy, as well as guarding the accused against certain kinds of mistakes and misimpressions that might compromise accuracy. (p. 89)

To use Dworkin's terminology, the framework of rules in criminal cases has been said to rest on the basis that individuals have: (i) a right that criminal procedures attach the correct importance to the risk of moral harm; and (ii) the related and practically more important right to equal treatment with respect to that evaluation. Both are strong rights: that is, they trump the balance of bare gains and losses that form a standard utilitarian calculation.[9]

In traditional expressions of formal legal rationality by courts, the principles and values underlying this model infuse every segment of the system. The basis of the adversary system[10] is party autonomy, with the trial judge (unlike his or her inquisitorial counterpart)[11] acting as an umpire who leaves the preparation and presentation of the case to the prosecution and defence. Every case is given a unique identity. Every suspect and defendant is accorded personal autonomy and granted the right to be legally represented. Trials are to be held as public events in order to require State officials (who are not disinterested parties) to demonstrate that the justice system is working, thereby giving confidence to governance values; to prevent the suppression of incompetent or wrongful behaviour by State officials; to check State power; and to open up to argument important or contentious governance issues (see Lippke, 2011).

Under the pressure of 'abnormal' conditions, however, courts may not hold to the formal legal rules that they ordinarily proclaim. In such circumstances, where fractures appear in the ideal model, judges are forced to make at least temporary adjustments to claims regarding formal legal rationality in order to justify departures. Below, we explore some examples where this has been necessitated and the implications for the ideal model ordinarily advanced by judges.

## 'ABNORMAL' SITUATIONS AND SYSTEM DEPARTURE

The legitimacy of criminal courts, as legal institutions, has to be considered within their over-arching role as an essential component of the State's

---

[9] Meaning, in this context, decisions based purely upon cost-efficient considerations. See further, Guest (2009).

[10] In successive reviews of the criminal justice system of England and Wales, official inquiries have supported the continuation of the adversary system, as for example the Royal Commission on Criminal Procedure (1981) *Report* Cmnd 8092; and Royal Commission on Criminal Justice (1993) *Report* Cm 2263.

[11] In reality, judges in civilian systems may be far from neutral arbiters in search of the truth. Hodgson (2005, 2006) shows that, for example, in the French system, much of the investigative power is delegated to the police who would not appear to be subject to any real supervision by investigating magistrates.

social control apparatus,[12] with a duty to uphold the law and without (it is claimed) any power to set it aside to avert injustice or other undesired outcomes. In this setting, their overall task has been described by Isaac Balbus (1973) as being threefold: to maintain public order; achieve formal legal rationality; and perpetuate the organisation.[13] Striking a balance between these functions – which are often in conflict – is the work of courtroom actors.[14] In this understanding, at times of social and political stability the values that should predominate are tested through adversary debate, but when there is serious political or social disruption (actual, manufactured or perceived), the discourse around values may recede, at least temporarily, and the reality of power – the repressive nature of the State – may prevail.[15]

Thus, Balbus found, in examining the response of the courts to the disorders and revolts in US black ghettos in the 1960s, that court procedures were altered, normal operating routines were changed, often contrary to procedural 'safeguards' and that whereas under more 'normal' conditions the impact of local political structure variations on policy outcomes was considerable, under crisis conditions their impact was virtually nil. Balbus saw this as explained by the self-contradictory interests of the judicial authorities: on the one hand, upholding legal-rational norms – 'formal legal rationality' in this context being 'the rule of law', 'due process of law', 'civil liberties' (equal treatment before the law), judicial decisions being made autonomously (insulated from the political sphere); on the other, their political interest in maintaining public order (ending the revolts) and the interest in organisational maintenance (in preventing the courts being overwhelmed by the inflow of cases).

Certainly, on one reading, the explanatory model proposed by Balbus appears to have similarities with the response of British courts in 'crisis' (real or manufactured) situations. We explore this question with three examples: *Operation Major* in 1982; the miners' strike in the 1980s; and the urban disorders in major cities in 2011.

---

[12] Of course, the State responds in many ways, other than through the criminal process, in addressing the issue of crime, including education, environmental design, help and support agencies and deterrence mechanisms.
[13] Balbus later explained that while the interests in formal rationality and organisational maintenance are permanent interests of the State, the interest in order (*restoring order*) does not have the same permanent status (1973; Preface to the 1977 edition).
[14] Sheskin (1981).
[15] Boyle et al. (1975).

## Operation Major

Many cities in the United Kingdom suffer from a shortage of housing accommodation[16] and this can bear heavily upon single homeless people.[17] Oxford was one such place in the 1980s. The relevant government office, the Department of Health and Social Security (DHSS), provided support to homeless people who stayed in bed and breakfast boarding houses run by landlords who received payment by the DHSS. Some boarding houses were said to be overcrowded, dirty and unhygienic such that some claimants chose to sleep in parks whilst continuing to use the property as an 'accommodation address' so that they could continue to claim benefit at a higher rate than they would otherwise be entitled to if sleeping rough. Such 'over-claiming' amounted to fraud. For their part, landlords would continue to be paid by the DHSS for all registered claimants. In some instances, the numbers of claimants allegedly using one 'accommodation address' rose towards 200 (Sandham, 1983). Claims made by landlords in respect of non-residents were clearly fraudulent and the potential fraud was alleged to be on a large-scale, far outweighing the small additional sums claimants were receiving.

In 1982, the Thames Valley Police, in conjunction with the DHSS, decided to mount a crackdown, '*Operation Major*', against claimants only, not against landlords (Franey, 1983). Claimants reporting to their normal DHSS Benefit Office were sent a notice re-directing them to a fake office set up as part of *Operation Major*. The following week, claimants signed on at the 'office' as directed and had their claims processed. The police meanwhile arranged for noisy road-works immediately adjacent to the 'office', set up video cameras, conducted a 'rehearsal' with DHSS officers and liaised with the government to free up accommodation at the local prison.

When claimants came to register they were told by 'workmen' (undercover operatives) that they had to leave by another door. On leaving they were immediately detained and arrested by police officers. Those inside the fake office who sought to alert people who had not yet entered could not because of the noisy 'road-works'.

---

[16] Because 'homelessness' is recorded differently, there is no national statistic for homelessness. However, in 2012/13, over 53,000 households were accepted as 'homeless' by the government in England; almost 6,500 in Wales; and over 34,000 in Scotland. See CRISIS at http://www.crisis.org.uk/pages/homeless-def-numbers.html. See also Rogers (2012).

[17] If a person does not have dependent children (known as 'single homelessness') and the person is not deemed to be more vulnerable than other homeless people, the individual will probably not be entitled to housing.

For some, the basis for an arrest was not the legal requirement of 'reasonable suspicion' but *mere attendance*, with arrestees including individuals who had simply accompanied those signing on. Most of those arrested were not told of their right to legal representation although some were. Social workers were not advised of what was happening although a number of those detained clearly needed such assistance. Those arrested were required to be photographed and fingerprinted.

Five Special Magistrates' Courts, depicted as 'emergency courts' (but secretly planned long in advance) were established to process those arrested. These 'daytime' courts, unusually sat from 15:00 hours to 23:00 hours, the ten magistrates themselves being previously unaware of the details of the operation. It was reported that the courts were constituted by individuals who could be relied upon to co-operate.[18]

Alongside this volume-operation, normal court procedures were set aside. Neither defence lawyers nor probation officers were given prior notice of these proceedings. As the day progressed and some solicitors became aware of what was happening, their attempts to gain access to the cells were refused by the police.

A large majority of those arrested (88%) were not provided legal representation. Most court 'hearings' (lasting about four minutes each) were described as 'shelling' exercises in which claimants were processed as quickly as possible, the court clerk reading out the charge, the prosecution applying for a remand in custody and magistrates granting the request. Defendants were not required to enter pleas to specific charges; they were remanded on 'offences of obtaining property by deception'. Although there was in law a presumption in favour of bail,[19] exceptionally, the vast majority (91%) were remanded in custody with only a few (9%) granted bail.[20]

In the weeks that followed, the courts were prepared to deal substantively with the cases of those remanded in custody. In this initial period, most were State-induced guilty pleas entered under pressure of the process to which they had been subjected, many without the benefit of legal advice and some,

---

[18] While magistrates' courts are overwhelmingly constituted by middle-aged lay personnel drawn from the middle classes with an unquestioning respect for and trust in authority (Burney, 1979; King and May, 1985; Dignan and Whynne, 1997), it is reported that they contained sufficient numbers of lower and working class members to call their reliability into question thus leading to further sieving, filtering and sifting.

[19] Under the Bail Act, 1976.

[20] A further eight had already been granted police bail.

to get it over with,[21] against the advice of their solicitors. Of the cases dealt with in the first month (158), the vast majority (88%) pleaded guilty.

Sentencing followed a privately set tariff[22] which, because it did not address the circumstances of individuals (such as differentiating between first offenders and those with a prior criminal record), amounted to *aggregate* punishment. Of those whose sentences are known, almost all (98%), received immediate custodial sentences,[23] a much higher proportion than usual for such offences. Indeed, the normal practice of the DHSS had been to not institute a prosecution at all where the overpayment involved was less than £50, which would have applied to all those convicted of a single offence.

However, and significantly, of the not guilty pleas (19), most (68%) had their cases dismissed. Those defendants were now represented by lawyers who were able to demolish the evidence of the prosecution's principal witnesses, the two landlords of the bed and breakfast dwellings. Indeed, it emerged that the pro-forma evidence of one of the landlords had been written by a police officer and sent to the landlord afterwards for signature. It became clear that, had more claimants gone to trial instead of succumbing to State-inducements, their cases would also have been dismissed.

While at first blush the proceedings might appear to fit with the theory of Balbus – that formal legal rationality may be set aside at times of social 'crisis' – Balbus held an idealised view of legal rationality and underestimated the flexible, even friable, character of the 'law'. Indeed, setting aside the accurate observation that adherence to legality has been little more than symbolic in magistrates' courts,[24] some elements of what was done under *Operation Major* fit readily into the existing legal architecture.[25] Thus, the decision to focus on the homeless[26] as opposed to landlords was within the law;[27] the decision to charge under the Theft Act rather

---

[21] See, Malcolm Feeley (1979) whose study of lower courts in America showed that the primary interest of most defendants was to get out of the system as quickly as possible, even if that meant pleading guilty.

[22] The tariff was 30 days' imprisonment for each cheque fraudulently claimed with a further 15 days for any offences taken into consideration.

[23] Two defendants were given suspended sentences. Of those remanded (47) to be dealt with later, most (68%) were remanded in custody, only 15 being granted bail.

[24] See Bridges (1975) reviewing Balbus (1973).

[25] See in this context, McBarnet (1983) and McConville et al. (1991).

[26] Press treatment of welfare claimants is usually derogatory. See, Golding and Middleton (1982) and Roche (1992).

[27] Tax fraud costs the Treasury at least 15 times as much as is lost by welfare fraud (Hyde, 2010). Official 'crackdowns' on tax evasion often target minnows

than under DHSS legislation was lawful;[28] 'special courts', though heavily criticised in many quarters, are not illegal in the UK;[29] and under the Bail Act courts retained a discretion to refuse bail because, for example, of a concern that the defendant would fail to surrender to custody, a reason that could easily be invoked in respect of homeless people.

Nevertheless, much about the whole procedure departs from the rational legal model espoused by the courts and violates basic moral precepts. The involvement of the police derived less from the character of the fraud and more from a desperate desire to restore the reputation of the Thames Valley Police whose image had been badly damaged in television documentaries earlier that year.[30] Instead of the legal requirement of 'reasonable suspicion', the basis of arrests was simply 'being there' which resulted in claimants and non-claimants alike being detained and their moral rights (the right to liberty) impugned. Even making allowance for the fact that magistrates' courts are renowned for being prosecution-oriented, legitimacy was sacrificed: claimants were not accorded individual treatment, were denied access to lawyers and to bail, detained in purposely boarded up rooms and 'shelled' before specially selected magistrates uncritically applying a pre-set sentencing tariff in proceedings that would be dignified by the appellation 'hearings'.

Courts did not, however, seek to secure legitimacy for their actions

---

rather than large corporations: see, King (2011) reporting an increase in official prosecutions for tax evasion from 107 in 2010 to 148 in 2011, with the figures revealing that 'five taxpayers arrested last week [were] all believed to be plumbers'. The figure for tax avoidance (exploiting 'loopholes' in taxation provisions to minimise or extinguish tax liability) is, of course, exponentially much higher (the HMRC official estimate of 'lost revenue' for 2011/12 of £35 billion is regarded as the 'tip of the iceberg' by the Chair of the Parliamentary Public Accounts Committee: Syal, 2013). See also, Gee and Button (2013).

[28] Franey (1983) discloses that Theft Act prosecutions were often used in other parts of the country where the defendant was a homeless person (at p. 39). Indeed, as part of a new government campaign against benefit cheats, in September 2013 the Director of Public Prosecutions issued guidelines under which prosecutors are urged to charge under the Fraud Act rather than social security laws, thereby classifying welfare cheating alongside money laundering and banking fraud and exposing individuals to up to ten-year jail terms (in 2012, 262 offenders were jailed for benefit fraud, the average sentence being six months and one week).

[29] In some jurisdictions the use of 'special courts' in this way is forbidden. Thus, for example, the Basic Law for the Federal Republic of Germany provides in Article 101(1): 'Extraordinary courts shall not be allowed. No one may be removed from the jurisdiction of his lawful judge'.

[30] The documentaries being Roger Graef's series, *The Police* (BBC 1982) and *Operation Carter* (BBC 1982).

through reliance upon formal legal rationality. Instead, the whole exercise rested on a race to the 'moral bottom': the representation that dispositive decisions were taken in respect of 'scroungers' and 'cheats', the undeserving of society.[31] The denigration of claimants in a 'massive fraud' served to discredit the welfare system and reproduced spurious police claims about the amounts involved (the actual total over-claiming being estimated at less than £50,000, the police costs alone exceeding this by more than threefold) and the character of those being 'processed'. Although lawyers, social services and probation workers had been kept in the dark, the police action was immediately preceded by a covert stage-managed police briefing of the media. An obedient press[32] characterised impending arrests as 'The Sting',[33] set up to break a massive fraud racket:

> *Daily Star*: THE STING: Police yesterday mounted a Sting-style operation to smash a massive social security racket.
> *Daily Express*: THE STING: £1.5m fiddle smashed as 286 are held in bogus social security offices.

The police were lauded for their ingenuity in deceiving claimants, variously described as 'fiddlers', 'cheats' and 'swindlers', coupled with insinuations of spurious racist connections.[34] The alliance of police, courts and a compliant press[35] thus sought legitimacy without recourse to the prevailing legal regime which was side-lined and wholly symbolic. Criminalisation and degradation of claimants was used to 'justify' 'aggregate justice', deflect attention from abnormal procedures and divert criticism from the lack of moral engagement with the problem of homelessness in society.

---

[31] In fact, while overpayments due to fraud comprised 0.7% of total welfare expenditure in 2012/13 (£1.2bn of £166.8bn), a further 0.9% (£1.5bn) was overpaid because of claimant error and an additional 0.5% (£830m) because of errors by officials: 'Welfare fraud and error: how much is the UK losing?' *Guardian*, 13 May 2013.

[32] News media were carefully selected beforehand with the less-obedient not informed.

[33] Thereby likening the police operation to the film, *The Sting*.

[34] *Sun* newspaper, for example, published a cartoon which showed 12 'scroungers' on a conveyor belt in front of magistrates, four of whom were black. In reality, of the 283 arrested, only four were people of colour, only one of whom was actually convicted.

[35] Police relationships with the media have the potential not only for distorting public perceptions but also for involving the police in corrupt activity amounting to misconduct in public office. See, for example; *BBC News*, 23 January 2013, 'Police corruption: criminals "give officers steroids"' *BBC News*, 26 April 2013, 'Former police officer admits selling stories to Sun' 26 April 2013. See further, Chibnall (1977), Howitt (1998), Leishman and Mason (2003) and Hohl (2011).

**Miners' Strike**

The miners' strike in 1984 had many of the same characteristics as displayed in *Operation Major*. The strike was triggered by threatened pit closures on a huge scale by the Conservative Government led by Margaret Thatcher[36] with the intention of closing pits and breaking the labour union, the National Mineworkers Union. With proposed massive job losses and the consequent destruction of many communities, miners sought to protect mines from closure and prevent coal from being transported by establishing picket lines and blockades at key pits.

Whatever was to happen in terms of policing or court processes, the question of 'legitimacy' in these respects was never to be settled by recourse to formal legal rationality. Long in advance of and during the strike, miners, together with their leader, Arthur Scargill, had been demonised by influential sections of the media. Incitive headlines such as 'Godfather Scargill's Mafia Mob' (*News of the World*, 7 October 1984) and 'Scargill's Real Aim is War' (*The Sun*, 5 April 1984) were accompanied by vitriolic attacks on the miners.[37] As Williams (2009, p. 38) noted: 'Readers were left with a view that the strike was precipitated by the power-crazed antics of Arthur Scargill, and that extreme measures taken by the police at the pit gates and in the courts were caused solely by picket-line violence'.

Miners from other parts of the country were prevented from joining the picket by police road blocks sometimes set up 200 miles from the intended destination. This 'intercept policy' was purportedly based in the common law power available where police reasonably believe that a breach of the peace will be committed 'in the *immediate* future by the person arrested' (emphasis added) even though that person has not yet committed any breach.[38] The police were also able to use section 5 of the Public Order

---

[36] See, Fine and Millar (1985), Scraton (1985), Smith and Thomas (1985), Christian (1985) and Green (1990).

[37] Arthur Scargill's claim, which underlay the concern of miners, that Margaret Thatcher had a 'secret hit-list' of more than seventy coal pits marked for closure, though officially denied at the time, has since gained support from newly released cabinet papers recording details of a secret meeting in 1984 (attended by a small group which included the Prime Minister and the Chairman of the National Coal Board) at which a plan to close a further 75 pits was unveiled: Higham (2014).

[38] *R v Howell* (1981). The Divisional Court dismissed an appeal against the intercept policy, ruling that: 'The situation has to be assessed by the senior police officers present. Provided they honestly and reasonably form the opinion that there is a real risk of a breach of the peace in the sense that it is in close proximity both in place and time then the conditions exist for reasonable preventative action including, if necessary, the measures taken in this case. The possibility of a breach

Act 1936 which allowed a police officer to intervene 'when a breach of the peace occurs or is *imminent*' (emphasis added). Police actions in the setting of road blocks and 'snatch squad' arrests were based on classifying the gathering of miners as involving 'public order' rather than an 'employment or industrial dispute'.[39]

Prosecuting strategies were devised to further undermine the strike. Arcane offences such as 'watching and besetting'[40] were resurrected to counteract difficulties that the prosecution would otherwise have met in producing individual proof of specific abusive words or intimidatory behaviour.[41] In Nottinghamshire, the police were allowed to by-pass the prosecuting solicitor altogether so that they could present cases directly to court and avoid questions relating to 'reasonable cause' and appropriateness of the charge. Defendants were almost all subject to a standard bail condition[42] that had been attached to the bail sheets *before* the justices announced their decision. By a synthetic interpretation of the 'law', the Divisional Court held that this practice did not vitiate the decisions: while putting into the dock together defendants who had been arrested on different occasions or at different places was to be 'discouraged' as it made it difficult to avoid the appearance of 'group justice', and while it did the magistrates 'no credit' if standard conditions were affixed to bail forms even while applications were being made for unconditional bail, the fact that 'the outcome of the bail application was correctly anticipated did not mean that the justices were not exercising their discretion properly' (*R v Mansfield Justices* [1985]). In this 'creative' way the courts 'legalised' what clearly *was* 'group justice' and 'pre-determined decisions' and thereby avoided engagement with the political strategy the government was using, as outlined by Janie Percy-Smith and Paddy Hillyard (1985):

> The aim of these practices was clearly containment, in the sense of preventing miners from taking any further part in picketing, rather than the prosecution and conviction of those committing criminal acts. There can be little doubt that

---

must be real to justify any preventative action. The imminence or immediacy of the threat to the peace determines what action is reasonable.' *Moss v McLachlan, The Times*, 29 November, 1984.

[39] See, East and Thomas (1985).
[40] Under the Conspiracy and Protection of Property Act, 1875.
[41] Christian (1985).
[42] In each case a condition was imposed in the following terms: 'Not to visit any premises or place for the purpose of picketing or demonstrating in connection with the current trade dispute between the N.U.M. and the N.C.B. other than peacefully to picket or demonstrate at his usual place of employment.'

the policy of using this wide range of coercive powers rather than the powers in the new employment legislation was part of a coordinated and deliberate strategy. It criminalized those involved and discredited the miners' case in the eyes of the public and other trade unionists by casting them in the role of criminals or violent demonstrators rather than workers engaged in a legitimate industrial dispute. (p. 354)

Police 'snatch squads' were used to effect mass arrests of individuals, many of whom were simply engaged in lawful picketing, and these individuals were charged under section 5 of the Public Order Act 1936 which provided *inter alia* that: 'Any person who in any public place . . . uses threatening, abusive or insulting words or behaviour . . . whereby a breach of the peace is likely to be occasioned, shall be guilty of an offence'. This provision enabled prosecutions to proceed based entirely upon police evidence. In these circumstances, and given that the magistrates were predisposed to view all picketing as actually involving or likely to occasion a breach of the peace (a view extraordinarily supported by the higher courts),[43] many miners succumbed to State-induced guilty pleas in order to avoid jail, often acting on legal advice.[44] As in *Operation Major*, had miners not succumbed to State inducements, the outcomes might have been very different, as the Orgreave trial showed.

The defining clash in the strike took place at Orgreave, a coking plant near Rotherham which the miners attempted to blockade. This descended into mass violence after the police on horseback charged the miners and attacked them with truncheons. A subsequent trial involved 15 miners charged with riot (the punishment for which could be up to life imprisonment); with more than eighty others awaiting trial. According to the prosecution, the miners, armed with implements such as an axe, ball

---

[43] The argument that picketing was in any sense peaceful was summarily dismissed by magistrates, who, in turn, were supported by the Divisional Court. In *R v Mansfield Justices* [1985] the Divisional Court, ruled that it must have been clear to everyone, including the justices that 'any suggestion of peaceful picketing was a colourable pretence and that it was a question of picketing by intimidation and threat. It must have been obvious to all those participating in the picketing that their presence in large numbers was part of the intimidation and threats. It must have been clear to them that their presence would, at the least, encourage others to threats and/or violence even if they themselves said nothing.' This finding, described accurately as 'devastating' (Christian, 1985, p.129), meant in consequence that any miner involved in a picket was thereby guilty of an offence under section 5.

[44] See, for example, Ian Lavery, MP: 'Solicitors were telling them that if they accepted a public order offence they would avoid going to gaol', cited in Townsend (2012). An investigation is under way by the IPCC.

bearings and metal bars charged at police lines[45] 'hurling missiles in a quite terrifying display of violence which lasted several hours . . .'. As the trial proceeded, however, it became clear that police statements were unreliable and had in many cases been dictated to them by senior officers. The signature of one officer may have been forged (the statement 'disappeared' during a lunch interval). After 48 days, the police evidence fell apart and the prosecution 'caved in'.[46] Michael Mansfield QC, who defended three of the acquitted miners, described South Yorkshire police's evidence then as 'the biggest frame-up ever', adding that, 'South Yorkshire police operated a culture of fabricating evidence with impunity, which was not reformed after Orgreave, and allowed to continue to Hillsborough five years later'.[47] Subsequently, examination of police statements by Mark George QC has revealed 'several dozen' examples of officers using exactly the same phrases, signifying 'widespread collusion'.[48] According to Mr George: 'You can't get statements in the way they have been done here – by police officers from different forces involved in different arrests – and find such a degree of similarity between those statements without there being some degree of collusion'.

**Urban Disorders, August 2011**

Between the 6th and the 10th of August 2011, England experienced some of the most extensive street disorders in its history, recalling the disturbances of three decades earlier in 1981 in Brixton, London, Moss Side in Manchester and Toxteth in Liverpool. The fatal shooting of Mark Duggan on Thursday 4 August 2011 by a police officer (code name V53)[49] in Tottenham, London precipitated public protest in the area, which later sparked massive public disorder in London and other large cities such as Manchester, Liverpool and Birmingham.[50] During this period, five people

---

[45] A BBC film transposed events and showed miners initiating the attack by throwing stones at the police rather than, as happened, the other way round. It was not until 1991 that the BBC issued an apology in which it said that the film had been 'inadvertently transposed'.
[46] Mansfield (2009).
[47] Conn (2012).
[48] *BBC News*, 22 October 2012.
[49] In the 15 years to September 2010, 55 officers have opened fire on and killed 33 members of the public in England and Wales. In only two cases have the names of the officers been released (Leake et al., 2010).
[50] It is noteworthy that fatal shootings by the police, even where the shooting was mistaken or unlawful, do not generally lead to civil disorder, which might suggest, where this occurs, a clear link with police–community relations.

died. Significant looting, burglary, arson, violence against the police and criminal damage was widely experienced, with close to 15,000 people actively involved.[51] The response of the courts was swift: by August 2012, some 2,138 people had been convicted and sentenced.[52]

Long-standing community grievance (fuelled by ambiguity over the circumstances of Mark Duggan's death)[53] was cited as a spark for the initial disorders which ignited two days after the shooting.[54] While the full extent of the disorders and the possible causes have been documented elsewhere[55] our interest here is with the legal aftermath. Nonetheless, the relationship between 'causes' and 'outcomes' remains vital to understanding the draconian attitude adopted by judges towards riot-related defendants.

Initially, the Justice Secretary, 'on-watch' during the disorders, was quick to rationalise events away from government austerity measures, deep frustration and community anger over police practices (including a massive use of stop and search powers disproportionately directed against members of the black and Asian community)[56] and more generally a loss

---

[51] Singh et al. (2012).

[52] Ibid.

[53] See Chapter 2. Ambiguities continued thereafter. Thus, at the inquest into the death of Mark Duggan, a police officer (W70) gave evidence on 23 October 2013 that he saw Duggan reach towards his waist before revealing 'the shape' of a handgun. In a written account made hours after the shooting in August 2011, W70 made no mention of a gun, although in a written statement made three days later he said that he had seen him with a gun. When asked for an explanation, he said that his solicitor had told him to leave mention of the gun out of his account.

[54] In the intervening time, there was a series of errors by the police and the IPCC without which the disorders might not have occurred: Bridges (2012).

[55] See, in particular, Bridges (2012). See also *Guardian*/LSE (2011) and Singh et al. (2012). Anger within the black and minority ethnic community (BME) has been fuelled not only by stop and search but also by deaths in police custody (some 200 since 1990) and by the lack of police accountability in any of these matters. For statistics, see INQUEST.

[56] See Bridges (2012) who, by way of example, reports statistics showing that in the three months to the end of June 2011, there were 6,894 police stop and searches in the local borough of Haringey, with only 87 (1.2%) of these resulting in an arrest and conviction. *The Guardian*/LSE survey, *Reading the Riots*, found widespread complaints of harassment and unjust targeting by the police across the country: *Guardian*/LSE (2011, Chapter 5). See also, HM Inspectorate of Constabulary (2013a) which goes a long way to confirming the concerns of communities and a substantial body of research over the last fifty years (see further, Chapter 2 *infra*); and the EHRC Report (2012), which shows (excluding stops under anti-terrorism laws) that overall black people are six times as likely as white people to be stopped but that in some areas the ratio was much higher, as in Thames Valley (10.4 times) and West Midlands (29 times). See also the careful review of evidence in relation

of legitimacy between the State and the individual in Tottenham (the scene of previous disorders in 1985 also following a police operation that led to the death of Cynthia Jarrett[57] and an area with a large ethnic minority population which has been the focus of police stop and search and other intrusive powers for many years) and other urban areas to which disorder spread,[58] by directing blame at a causeless '*hardcore* of rioters [who] came from a *feral underclass*' of whom all '. . . were in fact known criminals'.[59]

As Ball and Drury (2012) point out, the then Lord Chancellor Kenneth Clarke's term 'hardcore' conveys the notion that 'even if "known criminals" did not make up the numerical majority, they were most instrumental in what happened' (at p. 8). However, Clarke's misleading assertion about the 'hardcore' was to be adopted in spirit days later by the Court of Appeal in *R v Blackshaw* [2011], a decision which avoided any meaningful examination of the individual circumstances of each appellant, instead relying on an *aggregate* approach that effectively tarred all with the same judicial brush. In *Blackshaw*, the appeals by two men who attempted to incite a riot on *Facebook* were rejected, as were those of five people convicted of burglary, though it reduced the terms of three others for dishonest handling.

By refusing to take acts in isolation, instead preferring to couch their analysis and eventual sentence outcomes in rhetorically forceful but under-articulated terms of 'public protection' and 'interests of justice', the courts subjected defendants to the punitive repercussions of 'the speedy administration of justice'.[60] In doing so, the Court spared itself the task of coming to terms with a more considered analysis of the underlying causes and motivations, including police–community relations.

Bearing in mind that the material cost of the disorders alone was estimated at more than half a billion pounds,[61] it might be thought that determining the varying causes would be an important measure in 'public protection'. As Lea and Hallsworth (2012) have commented:

---

to stop and search under section 60, Criminal Justice and Public Order Act 1994 by Shiner (2012).

[57] Cynthia Jarrett died from a stroke after being pushed to the floor during a police search operation.

[58] After initial targeting of the police, a significant element of general looting and criminal damage took place.

[59] Clarke (2011, emphasis added). As Bridges (2012) points out, given that many defendants were identified through subsequent analysis of CCTV images, the arrested population was bound to over-represent those 'known to the police' by reason of previous offences.

[60] *R v Blackshaw* [2011] at para. 141.

[61] Singh et al. (2012).

... if previous riots had a specific target or grievance – stop and search, competition for jobs – last summer's riots were a diffuse and generalised rage of a dispossessed population angry at a system that has failed them but with no vision of an alternative. This is why they are more serious than any that have gone before. (p. 32)

Instead, what was seen through media accounts of 'frenzied sentencing' was a lack of any proper analysis of the sentencing principles that might reflect the actual level of criminality of individuals, readily abandoned in terms of the immediate management of the 'feral underclass' and manipulation of public opinion.[62] A distinct feature therefore was the rapidity with which large numbers of defendants were processed then subject to a deterrent-led 'uplift' on their sentence.

One strategy for expediting the case-load was for police and prosecutors to circumvent the obstacles of *riot* – in its legal sense. Rather than charging suspects with the substantive offence of riot, which presents the prosecution with onerous requirements of proof, including the need to evidence unlawful violence for a common purpose, the Ministry of Justice (MoJ) statistics show that the majority of offences brought to court were ones of dishonesty: burglary (38%), violent disorder (27%), theft (13%), robbery (2%) and criminal damage (2%).[63]

In order to further achieve faster processing, working hours at a number of magistrates' courts were extended until the late evening. At two magistrates' courts in central London, the unprecedented step of turning them into night courts was taken in order to deal with the backlog of cases that was forming.

Because of the extended court hours, where 'magistrates' courts sat, literally, through the night to dispose of the work',[64] defence advocates reported that 'the [prosecution] objected to bail in each and every case – suggesting in every instance that the defendant would commit further offences, fail to attend court and interfere with the course of justice'.[65] Of course, in terms of formal legal rationality, suspects should not have been refused bail on the basis of a *general* fear of the commission of further offences alone, but on the basis of their *particular* circumstances. Precise statistics are not available, but practitioners reported that defendants were

---

[62] *BBC News*, 29 August 2011.
[63] See MoJ (2011a) at p. 4. Although there were also charges for incitement to riot, notably those cases involving social networking websites.
[64] *R v Blackshaw* [2011] at para. 141.
[65] Young (2011). For severe criticism of one firm of defence solicitors, see *R v Ellis (Alexander Tyrone)* [2013] in which the Court of Appeal said that the solicitors 'deserve public censure'.

almost routinely remanded into custody.[66] In any event, the deluge of work that coursed through the courts led under-resourced defence lawyers to claim that '[i]t was effectively impossible, in the early hours of the morning, to counter such objections'.[67] It was not only the speed, however, but also the severity of the sanctions that was a distinguishing feature of the crime-control methods in place.

At one stage it was reported that a lay bench in Camberwell Green Magistrates' Court stated that it had been issued with a 'government directive' to jail all riot offenders, raising concerns about the professed independence of the judicial system. In response, the Judicial Office was forced to deny that such a directive had been given although a senior Court Clerk had circulated instructions to court clerks that they should advise magistrates to consider disregarding normal sentencing guidelines.[68] Indeed, a judge who sentenced offenders at Camberwell Green court made it clear there was an agenda at play when he stated that 'the deterrent sentences sent a very clear signal about the consequences of this sort of offending'.[69]

Flying in the face of research which demonstrated the absence of evidence that general deterrent sentences are effective,[70] the police and court response was united by the strong 'belief' that the visibility of the criminal justice system in action reduced copycat disorder and attrition rates.[71]

This was most noticeably achieved though self-serving 'transparency' from the Government. In what also appears to be an unprecedented measure, the MoJ instructed magistrates' courts nationwide to provide full details of their court outcomes of all riot-related cases. To bolster this strategy, the MoJ and the Home Office made concerted efforts to publish a statistical review of cases which reached the courts, and their progress through the criminal justice system.[72] For example, in October 2011, the MoJ published an analysis of all cases up to 12 October,[73] and then followed this up with further analysis of cases up to 1 February 2012.[74]

The research conducted by the Home Office found that there had been over

---

[66] Kalsi (2011).
[67] Young (2011).
[68] Bowcott and Bates (2011).
[69] Lakhani (2012).
[70] Von Hirsch et al. (1999) and Doob and Webster (2003).
[71] Metropolitan Police Service (2012).
[72] Other sources of non-governmental statistical information came from organisations such as the National Centre for Social Research.
[73] MoJ (2011b).
[74] MoJ (2012a).

4,000 arrests as a result of the disorders with 5,112 individual related crimes across 10 police force areas. Most were recorded by London's Metropolitan Police, with 68% (3,461) of the total, followed by Greater Manchester (11%, 581), West Midlands (10%, 495) and Merseyside (4%, 195).

Public outrage, fuelled by widespread political and media denunciations,[75] was soon exacerbated by the deaths of five people and the 200 plus police officers who sustained injuries in the course of tackling the rioters; miscreants whose totality of misbehaviour led to 1,649 burglaries, 141 incidents of disorder and 366 incidents of violence against the person and close to 2,000 incidents of criminal damage and arson.[76]

These statistics were of avail to the courts, allowing them to more easily project the impression that they were 'forced' to deal with an almost unprecedented wave of violent, theft-related and public order cases. Such was the overall scale of the disturbances, that by the time *Blackshaw* was heard, the Lord Chief Justice of England and Wales remarked that there would 'be very few decent members of our community who are unaware of and were not horrified by the rioting'.[77]

The Courts' imperative that there is an 'overwhelming obligation on sentencing courts to do what they can to ensure the protection of the public . . .'[78] was to play an important legitimating role in allowing judges to set aside official sentencing guidelines, give enhanced sentences and discharge them from the rigmarole of an individualised sentencing exercise. In response to this Mitchell (2011, p. 5) argues, '[t]he fact that, when aggregated, the total amount of harm done throughout the country was considerable is not *per se* a good reason for putting such a high priority on protecting the public when sentencing individual offenders'.

Evidently though, feeling the broad support of the public behind them, judges were able to more easily process those implicated in the urban disturbances by exercising their discretion to depart from the Sentencing Council's guidelines on the grounds that it would be contrary to the 'interests of justice' to follow them. On this point, Roberts (2012, p. 440) observed: 'If the enhancement for the riot context was modest, there would be little need to consider how courts go about augmenting sentence severity. However, if the enhancement is considerable, the consequences for principled sentencing are likely to be greater.'

---

[75] Violence, looting and destruction is to be deprecated but the terms in which politicians characterised the disorders were often ill-informed and inflammatory. See, Bridges (2012).
[76] HO (2011).
[77] *R v Blackshaw* [2011] at para. 1.
[78] Ibid., at para. 4 per Lord Judge.

In this regard, the Government's own research would indicate a greater need for principled sentencing. An appraisal of the figures produced by the MoJ (up to February 2012) shows the degree to which sentencing enhancements were imposed in response to the urban disorders.[79] By drawing a comparison between the sentences imposed in the lower courts following the disorders in 2011 with similar offences in 2010, a striking inflationary picture emerges. Taking burglary as an example, the immediate custody rate went from 23 per cent to 42 per cent. The uplift for 'riot-related' theft was more impressive, rising from 2 per cent to 41 per cent. Taking the figures overall, the rate went from 12 per cent to 37 per cent (in other words, more than triple the levels seen in 2010). The length of custody similarly ballooned by more than double (Roberts, 2012).[80]

Indeed subsequent data which looked at those found guilty at the Magistrates' Court but sentenced at the Crown Court, showed stark results. Over 1,400 people received immediate custody with average sentence lengths over four times longer than in 2010: 17.1 months following the disorders compared with 3.7 months in 2010 (Singh et al., 2012).[81] There are many illustrative cases of severe sentencing for traditionally less serious offences that according to the judges were designed to deter others from similar criminal activity. Some examples include a college student (aged 23) who was sentenced by a District Judge to six months imprisonment for stealing bottled water worth £3.50 from a looted supermarket in South London; another (aged 19) was jailed for 10 months for stealing two left-footed trainers which she left outside the shop; while one defendant (aged 24) was jailed for 20 weeks for stealing a looted bag of alcohol and sweets he found in the streets.[82]

In the absence of specific directions other than the Sentencing Guidelines, HHJ Gilbart QC, the Recorder of Manchester and vanguard tasked with the first riot case in *R v Carter & Others* (16 August 2011)[83] set out unofficial guidelines for sentencing in the context of August 2011 riots. His comments that the context of riot 'hugely aggravates the seriousness of each

---

[79] See Tables 4 and 6 from MoJ (2012a).

[80] A similar picture is seen at Crown Court level between 2010 and 2011 with a near tripling (33% to 85%) of the rate of immediate custody. As with the lower courts, custodial lengths doubled (50%) with some offences receiving a 110% increase in sentence length (e.g., criminal damage).

[81] The data also take into account the 'discounts' defendants received for guilty pleas.

[82] See also *Suleimanov* [2013], where the defendant who had not been rioting but pleaded guilty to burglary of a bottle of water and was sentenced to 15 months imprisonment.

[83] *R v Carter & Others* (Sentencing Remarks) [2011] (16 August 2011).

individual offence' and accordingly allowed departure from Sentencing Guidelines were swiftly adopted by other judges across the country.[84] Judge Gilbart's starting point (for convictions following a trial) was a high one: '*any* adult offender who took part in the events in Manchester/Salford on the evening of 9 August *must* expect to lose their liberty for a significant period'. He justified the enhanced sentence ranges by stating that 'these will send a clear and unambiguous message ... which I trust will deter others from engaging in this type of behaviour in the future'.[85]

Delivering sentence on behalf of the court in *Blackshaw*, Lord Judge crucially endorsed the observations of Judge Gilbart QC, in particular that the nature of disorders took the offences 'completely outside the usual context of criminality'. However, Lord Judge, re-asserting the primacy of the Court of Appeal, set aside the sentence ranges proposed by the Recorder, stating that it was 'inappropriate for Crown Court judges to issue, or to appear to be issuing sentencing guidelines'. While Lord Judge declined to propose any revised starting points himself, the decision reflects the judicial practice of sentencing outside the definitive sentencing guidelines in moments of 'crisis'. In considering the various sentences passed on the offenders, the Court of Appeal was also given an opportunity to comment on the relationship between the offending itself and the overall disorder.

As a preliminary point it can be noted that it is uncontroversial that, as a general principle, an offender who contributes to the harm of a mass riot might merit an enhanced sentence. This is not the same, however, as saying that the individualised nature of sentencing becomes redundant, despite the Courts' efforts to the contrary. As Roberts (2012) has observed, 'the decision to depart should be taken on an individual level, and not because all offending committed during a period of public disorder necessarily and always falls outside the ambit of the existing guidelines' (p. 440). With these disorders, there was a patent need for individualised sentencing because, as the research touched on above amply demonstrates, the crowds involved were heterogeneous and had different incentives and motivations.

Ashworth (2012) cogently argues that the judgment in *Blackshaw* is significantly flawed by its failure to justify its conclusions on these appeals by reference to the applicable legislation, to relevant guidelines,

---

[84] See, for example, the sentencing remarks of HHJ Chapple in the first case on the riots in London (Inner London Crown Court), *R v Alagago & Ors* (25 August 2011); also *R. v Twemlow & Ors* (Sentencing Remarks) [2011].
[85] *R v Carter & Others* [2011] at 11.

or to the giving of adequate reasons. For example, Lord Judge, as indicated earlier, said nothing about the appropriate starting points in the judgment. Moreover, while three of the sentences (the handling offences) from the ten cases examined in *Blackshaw* were halved, there was no indication as to the calculation that was involved, leading Ashworth to observe: '[s]tepping outside a guideline should not mean stepping into an entirely unstructured realm where proper justifications are absent' (2012, p. 95).

Whatever the disorders represented in terms of the tension between individual culpability, socio-economic disadvantage, marginalisation and negative police–community relations, issues that the courts fastidiously avoided, the sentencing practices that sought to punish those caught up in the 'ghastliness' are thus revealed as a model example of the courts seeking to legitimate aggregate justice over individual justice, where the unashamed tendency to overlook mitigation of various kinds was eclipsed by the focus upon under-articulated, court-defined contextual seriousness of the public disorders.

## 'NORMAL' CASES: COURTS' RESPONSE

The response of the courts to what they treated as 'abnormal' situations demonstrates why issues of legitimacy must be disentangled from formal legal rationality. Although many of the provisions and procedures relied upon in these situations could be accommodated (with strained interpretation) into the prevailing legal order, routine deviations were regular features.[86] As Bridges (1975) has pointed out, sanitising such departures was easy in magistrates' courts where formal legal rationality has never been thought necessary by the justice system. Elsewhere, legal cleansing was sought to be secured, not principally through reliance on formal legal rationality (though court decisions sanitised certain police actions) but rather on disparaging characterisations of defendants processed on a group basis, often de-individualised by the media through submergence in a negative social category ('scroungers', 'mobs', 'thugs', 'bullyboys', 'feral'), assisted by a forged consensus with politicians and the media. In

---

[86] The empirical work of Balbus (1973) disclosed similar findings although Balbus himself gave these little recognition in his theoretical model. See Petra Shattuck (1974) who points out that Balbus does not give full recognition to the wholesale departure from the 'norms' that characterise so much of legal and judicial practice (and thereby inadvertently reinforces the image of blind justice and the idealised judicial system).

these situations, what was thought of as 'rights' turned out to be purely symbolic, with a value not to the individual but to the legitimating fabric of the system.

However much courts struggle to legitimise treatment of defendants at times of social 'crisis', the question arises whether such practices may be applied in 'normal', that is, 'non-crisis' situations, and, if so, how courts seek to rationalise their actions. The issue directly arises in relation to the formalisation of State-induced guilty pleas since this involves replacing in large part a system in which trial is celebrated as the ideal mode of legal rationality with a non-trial process in which State officials are no longer proclaimed to be disinterested parties.

In State-induced guilty pleas, there is no requirement on the prosecution to prove its case by the introduction of admissible and persuasive evidence; there are no restrictions on what might count as 'evidence'; no witnesses are produced to give evidence (indeed, none may be available); there is no independent tribunal of fact; there is no settled procedure under which it should operate (or none that judges and practitioners seem able to follow); and there is no public trial or other independent decision-making tribunal. As the 'fiscal crisis' of the State was invoked in some quarters to openly promote non-trial dispositions, the way in which courts, as State agencies concerned with the appearance of justice and rationality, responded is accordingly a matter of legal and sociological interest.

## STATE-INDUCED PLEAS AND THE BOOK PLAN[87]

Our principal concern in this book is with the responses of the English and Welsh courts in their struggle to preserve a sense of their own legitimacy while engaging with the demands of State-induced guilty pleas. Scotland has been chosen as a useful comparator because although its system of criminal justice is predominantly adversarial and most crimes are common law crimes,[88] it has traditionally displayed hostility to the idea of State-induced guilty pleas[89] and it has followed an independent path in the manner in which it addresses the principles and values thereby implicated.

---

[87] For a full exploration of ethical issues involved in the choice between trials and 'plea bargains', see Lippke (2011). See also Bridges (2006).

[88] See Leverick (2006) for a detailed account.

[89] Following disapproval of sentence discounts in *Strawhorn v McLeod* [1987], there was 'something of an antipathy towards the practice of sentence discounting in Scotland' (Leverick, 2006, p. 18) and it was not formally operated between the mid-1980s and mid-1990s.

Nevertheless, and for different reasons, both jurisdictions are now in the grip of State-induced guilty pleas.

In Chapter 2 we examine whether the 'rights' and 'principles' that are said to underlie criminal justice in England and Wales and guarantee the traditional adversary system prevail in non-crisis situations. In Chapter 3 we look at the forces that caused the emergence of State-induced guilty pleas into the public realm in England and Wales and how the courts responded to this in the case of *Turner*. In Chapter 4 we trace how the deep-seated message of *Turner* was brought to the surface, sanitised and rationalised by the influential Report of Lord Justice Sir Robin Auld (2001)[90] in the quest for the proclaimed cost-efficient disposal of criminal cases. Next, we examine the extent to which the State actors and their respective institutions (Chapter 5) and defence lawyers and their institutions (Chapter 6) provide assurance that concerns over State-induced guilty pleas may be properly allayed. Chapter 7 focuses upon Scotland in the practice of negotiations over pleas and the jurisprudential struggle of the courts to rationalise it. Chapter 8 draws out the legal and sociological implications of courts adopting the practice of State-induced guilty pleas and seeking to make it legitimate.

---

[90] We intend no discourtesy to Sir Robin if we refer to him from now on by his surname for convenience.

# 2. Helping the police with their inquiries

## INTRODUCTION

As seen in Chapter 1, at times of social crisis, actual or manufactured, there is a propensity for courts to disregard traditional understandings of adversarial adjudication. In this chapter we examine whether the 'rights' and 'principles' said to guarantee the adversary system prevail in non-crisis situations. Certainly, we would expect that individual rights would be prominent if only because the existence of 'formal legal rationality' (*legal formalism*) has been cultivated by judges through, for example, the 'rule of law', 'presumption of innocence', 'right to silence' and 'no detention without arrest'.

We argue that the idealised trial model and the very 'rights' once said to be the 'British tradition' going back through Dicey (1885) and Blackstone (1765) to Magna Carta have either not existed in fact or have been dismantled by judges, aided and abetted by official inquiries (in turn, drawing on prior judicial actions) and by politicians engaged in populist 'law and order' campaigns. At root, while espousing fidelity to individual rights and upholding them occasionally, there has been almost unconditional support for police practices in the face of known police illegality. This posture has set the scene for the diminution of individual rights in fact, in legal rhetoric and in law.

While 'law' has provided various legitimating canopies through a particular construction of the relationship of the individual to the State and through the promise of distributive justice for all, in reality the 'law' has proved both deceptive and friable for the citizen but legitimating and enabling for the police.[1] Moreover, in criminal justice, rather than being the outgrowth of a forensic adversary process, 'law' commonly emerges, mule-like, without pride of ancestry as a cover for illicit social control practices. Not only are police given wide discretion, and their infractions routinely winked at by judges, but both judge-made law and legislation is

---

[1] Feeley (1976); McBarnet (1983); McConville et al. (1991).

thereafter crafted to be in alignment with and a cover for actions hitherto said to have been illicit.

At the same time, official discourse constructs new forms of legitimacy to secure or restore public confidence (the basis of political legitimacy) in the system.[2] While sometimes resisting certain highly divisive proposals,[3] judicial rulings betray an ideology deeply embedded in police operational practice which has to be accounted for by a new legitimating discourse. In these circumstances, as the following sections illustrate, courts must of necessity advance contradictory positions: celebrating the 'rule of law', its values and principles, while compelled in pursuit of 'social order' to undermine these at every opportunity.

## STOP AND SEARCH

In respect of stop and search, statutorily regulated since the 19th century,[4] judges might be expected to be vigilant in guarding against unnecessary intrusions into *individual freedom*, a 'cherished tradition' according to Lord Bingham.[5] This is particularly so since research has long questioned whether police practices are 'reasonable' and non-discriminatory.

Research has demonstrated, for example, that, in place of statutory requirements, the police use 'profiles'[6] or typologies founded in criteria related to class, race, ethnicity and gender. This has engendered antagonistic relations between police and various communities[7] underpinning urban disorders, including that started in Brixton in 1981 (Scarman, 1981),

---

[2] Burton and Carlen (1979).

[3] Thus, many judges were unwilling to support the highly controversial proposals of the Criminal Law Revision Committee's *Eleventh Report, Evidence (General)* (1972) that previous convictions should be more widely admissible. See objections to this in 388 H.L. Deb., February 1973, by, among others, Lord Diplock (col. 1648), Lord Gardiner (col. 1577), Lord Salmon (col. 1669) and Lord Widgery (col. 1661). Judges have also been reluctant to openly endorse certain aspects of the ongoing legal aid reforms (detailed in Chapter 6).

[4] See the Vagrancy Act, 1824. Other statutes include: Criminal Justice and Public Order Act 1994, s. 60; Knives Act 1997; and s. 87, Serious Crimes Act 2007.

[5] Bingham, *Gillan* [2006] at para. 1.

[6] 'Reasonable suspicion', in turn, is an elastic concept used to justify almost any stop.

[7] See, for example, Demuth (1978); Brogden (1981); Kettle and Hodges (1982); Scraton (1985); Ward (1986); Institute of Race Relations (1987); Dixon et al. (1989).

following saturation policing and indiscriminate stops and searches under the provocatively named '*Operation Swamp 81*'.[8]

Accordingly, the watchfulness of judges was particularly necessary following the introduction of stop and search powers under the Terrorism Act, 2000 which did *not* require 'reasonable suspicion'.[9] In fact, the implementation of these powers is a model example whereby judges set aside the principle of individual freedom (as they did with the 'intercept policy' during the miners' strike) in favour of police powers. Though subsequently repealed, the role of the judges deserves scrutiny in light of the principles involved and the fact that similar powers exist today.[10]

Under the terrorism powers, people could be stopped by the police *without reasonable suspicion* – providing they were within a specific area in which this power had been authorised by a senior police officer who considered this 'expedient for the prevention of acts of terrorism'. This impressively loose threshold conferred a wide discretion on senior officers, with no requirement even to assess proportionality.

Once authorisation had been given, as prior research predicted, the power was prone to being exercised *intuitively* without the need for suspicion of criminal activity or intention (in other words, *arbitrarily*). While the powers contained limitations (including that the search was to be carried out for the sole purpose of ascertaining whether prohibited items were being carried), in reality no accountability mechanisms were in place, thereby rendering safeguards nugatory. Worse still, authorisations were given on a rolling basis with the result that the power was used *indiscriminately* over the whole of London from April 2002 until May 2009. Most stops were carried out by the Metropolitan Police Service (MPS) and the British Transport Police,[11] who stopped a range of unorthodox targets including 2,331 persons under the age of 15,[12] a senior retired cabinet minister and a queen's counsel.[13]

Unsurprisingly, the power was applied *excessively*. Annual reports by the statutory independent reviewer of terrorism legislation, Lord Carlile

---

[8] A thinly-coded reference to a speech of Margaret Thatcher in 1978 in which she said that there was a fear that Britain might be 'swamped by people of a different culture'.

[9] Sections 44–7, now repealed, although see Cape (2013) who gives an assessment of subsequent counter-terror legislation (Protection of Freedoms Act 2012).

[10] Section 60 CJPOA 1994; section 47A (47A) Terrorism Act 2000. See also *Miranda v SofS* [2014].

[11] Human Rights Watch (2010) at 11.

[12] Ibid. at 38–9.

[13] Carlile (2010) at 177.

QC, recorded a rise in the exercise of the s. 44 power from about 33,000 in 2004/05 to about 117,000 in 2007/08, with minimal results ('at most morsels of counter-terrorism intelligence') in terms of discovering terrorist activity.[14]

As should have been expected, the power was also used *illegally*. On 33 occasions authorisations were for 29 days and on two occasions for 30 days – the lawful maximum was 28 days. In two cases the Home Secretary did not confirm authorisations within 48 hours, as required by law. A reasonable inference is that scores of people are likely to have been stopped and searched without proper authorisation. Inferences aside, the gravity of misconduct is further apparent from anecdotal reports of stops and searches conducted (on white people) in order to achieve 'racial balance in the Section 44 statistics'.[15]

The English judges were tested in the '*Gillan* litigation' which involved the use of s. 44 against two white people, a student (Mr Gillan) and a journalist (Ms Quinton) while they were attending a demonstration in London's Docklands. Police stopped Mr Gillan for 20 minutes, Ms Quinton for approximately 5 minutes. No prohibited articles were found on either.

In challenging the police actions, the essence of their claim was twofold. First, there were inadequate legal safeguards against police misuse of power. Second, various ECHR rights had been violated, including their liberty and security of person (both relying on Articles 5 and 8 of the Convention).

In the domestic courts they argued that Parliament had not enacted sections 44–47 with authorisations with such broad geographical coverage in mind. The Divisional Court rejected this outright.[16] While the Court was more willing to engage with the challenge to the discretion exercised by the individual officer, the Judges took a paternalistic approach, simply offering up training advice to the police. The claimants further relied on Articles 8, 9, 10 and 11 of the ECHR. In this regard, the Court invoked the 'grave' threat of terror as sufficient justification for the infringement of these rights.[17]

---

[14] Carlile (2010): s. 44 searches rose almost seven-fold in just two years (from 37,000 in the year ending April 2007 to over 256,000 for the year ending April 2009). In the last 12 months for which complete data are available (January 2009 to December 2009), s. 44 was used to stop more than 148,000 people. No one has been successfully prosecuted for a terrorism-related offence as a result of a s. 44 search.
[15] Carlile (2010) at 113–14.
[16] Paras 31–5.
[17] Para. 62.

In the Court of Appeal,[18] similar justification along 'counter-terrorism' lines was pursued. The Court bypassed the self-evident truth that this was an exceptional power, pointing to a number of 'safeguards': that it was necessary for a senior police officer to make the authorisation; that the Secretary of State was then required to confirm this; that the authorisation was for a limited duration; that regular renewal was a requirement; and that the power was constrained in that it was given a 'precisely defined purpose'.[19]

As to the limited duration, the Court knew that this safeguard was hollow having seen it transmogrify into a 'rolling authorisation' almost from its commencement.[20] Equally concerning was the Court of Appeal's dismissive attitude that limiting police to search only for articles 'of a kind which could be used in connection with terrorism' was a problem in and of itself despite the decision of that court describing s. 44 as a 'random' procedure.[21] The Court was also hostile regarding challenge to the individual officer's discretion and rejected the ECHR claims on a number of bases, much of this replicated in the House of Lords (see below).

In the unanimous decision of the House of Lords, Lord Bingham's lead judgment revealed almost complete reluctance to encumber the police with meaningful checks and balances. For example, he placed undue reliance on Code A as a safeguard, which provides that the power was only to be used to search for articles of a kind which could be used in conjunction with terrorism.[22] Reliance was undue because the breadth of the power was so great that the potential for misuse existed, as was clear from the statistics available to the Court (including Lord Carlile's Report) indicating the frequency with which it was being employed inappropriately by the police.[23]

As to the legality of the authorisation process, Lord Bingham held out a handful of safeguards he deemed were in place:

---

[18] *R (Gillan) v Commissioner of Police of the Metropolis* [2004].
[19] Paras 8 and 30.
[20] Ip (2013) at p. 10 highlights the findings of Human Rights Watch (2010) at p. 21 that the repeated authorisations complained of up until 2009 would have required in excess of ninety continual authorisations and confirmations.
[21] Para. 51.
[22] PACE Code of Practice 'A' does emphasise that powers 'must be used fairly, responsibly, with respect and without unlawful discrimination' but also states such suspicion 'can sometimes exist without specific information or intelligence and on the basis of a person's behaviour . . . [S]uspicion that a person is a terrorist may arise from the person's behaviour at or near a location which has been identified as a potential target for terrorists' (para. 2.3).
[23] Also Anderson (2011) at para. 8.15.

> It is true that [the constable] need have no suspicion before stopping and searching a member of the public. This cannot, realistically, be interpreted as a warrant to stop and search people who are obviously not terrorist suspects, which would be futile and time-wasting. It is to ensure that a constable is not deterred from stopping and searching a person whom he does suspect as a potential terrorist by the fear that he could not show reasonable grounds for his suspicion. (para. 35)

While the rhetorical force of 'public safety' is undoubted, as Sanders and Young (2010, p. 89) point out, if the safeguard is that an officer must suspect someone of being a potential terrorist, this is self-evidently not a demanding test and 'opens the door to the highly problematic practice of ethnic profiling'. It is difficult to believe the House of Lords failed to appreciate the flawed reasoning, particularly considering the 'public sensitivity' that surrounds an issue as prone to bigotry as profiling 'terrorists'.[24]

In an acute demonstration of this, while Lord Hope's view was that 'the mere fact that the person appears to be of Asian origin is not a legitimate reason for its exercise' he worryingly expanded on what had seemed an irrefutable point:

> *An appearance which suggests that the person is of Asian origin may attract the constable's attention in the first place.* But a *further selection process* will have to be undertaken, perhaps on the *spur of the moment* otherwise the opportunity will be lost, before the power is exercised. It is this *further selection process* that makes the difference between what is inherently discriminatory and what is not. (emphasis added)[25]

This appears to suggest that it *is* legitimate to target individuals on the basis of their so-called 'Asian appearance' providing there is a subsequent rationalisation. The partial reliance here on race is troublesome because the inference is that there is a sufficient connection between racial origins and terrorist suspects (Walker, 2006, p. 754). In this sense, Lord Hope effectively endorses racial ethnic profiling in the context of a regime that is grounded in intuitive decision making.

By contrast, the ECtHR in *Gillan and Quinton* (2010) grounded its view in the context and realities of policing under permissive legislation:

---

[24] Walker (2006 at 753) cites the example of the House of Commons Home Affairs Select Committee which found 'a clear perception among all our Muslim witnesses that Muslims are being stigmatized by the operation of the Terrorism Act: this is extremely harmful to community relations' (House of Commons, 2005, para. 153).

[25] *R (on the application of Gillan) v Commissioner of the Police of the Metropolis* [2006], at para. 46.

In the Court's view, there is a clear risk of arbitrariness in the grant of such a broad discretion to the police officer. While the present cases do not concern black applicants or those of Asian origin, the risks of the discriminatory use of the powers against such persons is a very real consideration.... The available statistics show that black and Asian persons are disproportionately affected by the powers, although the independent reviewer has also noted, in his most recent report, that *there has also been a practice of stopping and searching white people purely to produce greater racial balance in the statistics.* There is, furthermore, a risk that such a widely framed power could be misused against demonstrators and protestors in breach of art.10 and/or 11 of the Convention. (para. 85)

In relation to Article 5 (the right to liberty and security of the person), Lord Bingham equated a stop and search to 'a temporary restriction of movement' and as being 'kept from proceeding or kept waiting'. Walker has already pointed out this is far from convincing on any analysis.[26] The assumption that Article 8 (right to privacy) was infringed raised the observation from Lord Bingham that it was 'doubtful whether an ordinary superficial search of the person can be said to show a lack of respect for private life' since as the power was 'an ordinary superficial search of the person and an opening of bags, of the kind to which passengers uncomplainingly submit at airports, for example, [it] can scarcely be said to reach that level'.[27] The ECtHR gave the puncturing reply that:

An air traveller may be seen as consenting to such a search by choosing to travel. He knows that he and his bags are liable to be searched before boarding the aeroplane and has a freedom of choice, since he can leave personal items behind and walk away without being subjected to a search. The search powers under s.44 are qualitatively different. The individual can be stopped anywhere and at any time, without notice and without any choice as to whether or not to submit to a search. (para. 64)

In response to rolling authorisations and confirmations Lord Bingham gave the perfunctory response that they still complied with the statutory requirements and had not become a 'routine bureaucratic exercise'.[28] By contrast, the ECtHR found, as any cursory familiarity with the facts would have shown, that the procedures relevant to authorisation/confirmation had become a 'rubber stamping' exercise, in part evidenced by the fact the Secretary of State had *never* modified or refused an application[29] and the

---

[26] See Walker (2006) at 755.
[27] As with Article 5, the hypothetical justification under 8(2) was invoked and affirmed. Doubt was raised over the applicability of Articles 10 and 11 which were dealt with similarly.
[28] Para. 18.
[29] Paras 84–5.

28-day limitation on authorisation was undermined by its 'rolling' approvals. As such, the blanket-type coverage of the power was deemed problematic[30] in that the safeguard it was intended to provide was rendered ineffective by the 'failure of temporal and geographical restrictions'.[31]

The ECtHR's censorious reaction should not have come as any surprise to Lord Bingham, who, extra-judicially, had lectured others on the significance of the rule of law in assessing the arbitrariness of a measure: 'The broader and more loosely textured a discretion is, whether conferred on an official or judge, the greater the scope for subjectivity and hence for arbitrariness, which is the antithesis of the rule of law'.[32]

The *Gillan* litigation exemplifies an almost total unwillingness by the English courts to uphold the principle of individual freedom. It took the Strasbourg Court to rule that the 'safeguards' proclaimed domestically 'have not been demonstrated to constitute a real curb on the wide powers afforded to the executive so as to offer the individual adequate protection against arbitrary interference'.[33]

Indeed the English judiciary only had to take a cursory glance at the stop and search figures[34] (or the numerous reports which flagged up worrying trends) to recognise why they needed to apply caution rather than condone police behaviour in this area.[35]

The report by the Equality and Human Rights Commission puts it

---

[30] Paras 84–5.
[31] Para. 81.
[32] Lord Bingham, 'The Rule of Law' (2006).
[33] *Gillan* (2010) at para. 79.
[34] Stop and search has increased steadily since 2001/02, from less than 750,000 to a peak of almost 1.3 million in 2010/11, more than 1.2 million of which were carried out under PACE and associated legislation. Despite a slight decline, there were still more than one million stop and searches carried out in 2011/12: Home Office (2012).
[35] This applies as powerfully in Scotland where stop and search figures have catapulted to become the highest in the UK. Research by the Scottish Centre for Crime & Justice Research at Edinburgh University (Murray, 2014) found that people are four times more likely to be stopped and searched in Scotland than those in England, and twice as likely as those in London. Although issues of race and ethnicity perhaps have less pertinence in the Scottish context, there is compelling evidence that stop and search procedures (similar to those in England and Wales) are unfair and disproportionately targeted towards younger citizens: children under 14 were searched 26,000 times in 2010 without statutory authority, including 500 searches of children aged 10 or under, and 72 searches of children aged seven or younger. Police further made 145,600 stop-searches without legal cause against 15- to 20-year-olds across Scotland. The success rate for finding alcohol, drugs, stolen goods or weapons on teenagers was below 10 per cent which is lower than the average for adults (Carrell, 2014).

bluntly:[36] a black person is *at least* six times as likely to be stopped and searched by the police in England and Wales as a white person. An Asian person is around twice as likely to be stopped and searched as a white person.[37] In each instance, the ratios are far higher in some areas.[38]

The figures are highly suggestive that some forces are exercising their powers not on the basis of intelligence or reasonable suspicion but on stereotypical assumptions, thereby contributing to fractured community relations (and public disorder). The heightened rates of stop and search of ethnic minorities was effectively discounted by the UK judges in *Gillan*, despite the reality that these powers had long been a key concern for police legitimacy and public trust. As Shiner summarised the position in his Report on the cognate power under section 60 Criminal Justice and Public Order Act, 1994 (CJPOA):[39]

> Neither the massive growth in section 60 searches nor the disproportionate focus on people from black and minority groups can be justified as an objective response to violent crime. Nor can the likely costs of damaged relationships and lowered confidence be justified in terms of operational benefits. Arrest rates are low and the evidence indicates that section 60 searches have no measurable impact on violent crime. (Shiner, 2012, p. 2)

This is an ongoing concern officially highlighted by HM Inspectorate of Constabulary (2013a).[40] The report from such a source, confirming earlier research, is effectively an indictment of the role of English judges in protecting individual liberty. To quote its opening remarks:

---

[36] EHRC (2010). Another report echoes its findings: 'Since 1995, per head of population in England and Wales, recorded stops and searches of Asian people have remained between 1.5 and 2.5 times the rate for white people, and for black people always between 4 and 8 times the rate for white people' (Eastwood et al., 2013).

[37] The biggest impact in terms of numbers of 'excess' stops and searches is seen in London where the stop and search rate is highest at 60 per 1,000 in 2007/08 and where a high percentage of the UK black and Asian population lives.

[38] For subsequent supporting research by Dr Ben Bradford at Oxford University (marking the 20th anniversary of Stephen Lawrence's murder) which echoes the 'racial penalty' found within stop and search procedures, see Dodd (2013a).

[39] Shiner (2012).

[40] The Report also noted: stop and search practices were accorded little priority by senior officers; an 'alarming' 27% of stop and search records examined did not contain reasonable grounds to search people; there was great variance in what constituted reasonable grounds for suspicion; and a majority of officers had not received training in the exercise of stop and search powers.

> The public expect the police to protect them from harm by using the powers granted to them by Parliament in an effective and fair manner. *Arguably, some of the most intrusive and contentious powers are those of stop and search. For decades the inappropriate use of these powers, both real and perceived, has tarnished the relationship between constables and the communities they serve, and in doing so has brought into question the very legitimacy of the police service.* Thirty years after the riots in Brixton, concerns about how the police use stop and search powers were again raised following the riots in England in August 2011.
> 
> Over a million stop and search encounters have been recorded every year since 2006; but only 9% of these led to an arrest in 2011/12. Statistics also showed that members of black and minority ethnic groups were stopped and searched more than white people (compared to the resident population). Whilst there is strong public debate about the disproportionate use of the powers on certain groups, there is surprisingly little attention paid by either the police service or the public to how effective stop and search powers are in reducing or detecting crime. (p. 3, emphasis added)

It is clear that in the shadow of such powerful evidence lurks a judiciary unwilling to protect individual freedom or to guard against these potential harms.

We need not go as far as this damning indictment on stop and search practices to be aware of the negative impact on public confidence in the police among ethnic minority communities. The civil disturbances in Brixton and other cities in the 1980s and nationwide in August 2011 speak volumes as to the true cost and untold damage caused by policing methods deemed illegitimate by those segments of the public disproportionately exposed to their application.[41]

Despite the now incontrovertible truth which renders police practices as anything but exemplary, this judicially-endorsed image of 'integrity', as will be shown, has been an enduring pillar to the manufacture of State-induced guilty pleas; the removal of which would see its structure disintegrate.

## JUDGES' RULES

Historically in England, two related constructs formed the axis of formal legal rationality, both arising out of fear of a police state. The first was the liberty of the citizen. As the Royal Commission on Police Powers and Procedure (RCPPP, 1929) put it, it was 'a principle inherent in English law that no person shall be deprived of his liberty except by a magistrate

---

[41] For example, the use of stop and search powers was identified as one of the factors that had contributed to the cause(s) of the August 2011 disturbances (Singh et al., 2012).

or Court', (p. 57, para. 153). Under the second, while actually engaged in social control (Storch, 1976; Brogden, 1982) officially, the police, absent specific statutory authority, had no special powers: they were constructed in official discourse as mere 'citizens in uniform'.

As part of this legitimating architecture, the police could investigate crime with the consent of citizens. However, they were given few statutory powers and no interrogation powers because arrest was in legal theory merely a power to bring suspects before a magistrate:

> Neither judge, magistrate nor juryman, can interrogate an accused person unless he tenders himself as a witness, or require him to answer questions tending to incriminate himself. Much less, then, ought a Constable to do so, whose duty as regards that person is simply to arrest and detain him in safe custody . . . (Lord Brampton's address to the police, 1882)

In line with this, 19th-century case law was expressed to protect prisoners from extorted confessions. In the face of admonishments from courts (see, e.g., *R v Mick*, 1863; *R v Gavin*, 1885; and *R v Knight and Thayre*, 1905), however, the police continued to breach these rules and some courts admitted evidence thereby obtained (e.g., *R v Brackenbury*, 1893), generally on the assertion that this was needed to solve crime (as in *R v Booth and Jones*, 1910).[42]

Following a request for clarification from the Chief Constable of Birmingham to the Chief Justice in 1906, the judges issued the *Judges' Rules* (1912) which were expanded in 1918, re-issued with further guidance in 1930 and revised in 1964. Although these *Rules* – which were never placed before Parliament – were explicitly created 'for the guidance' of police officers, they formed the basis of investigative 'regulation' until the Police and Criminal Evidence Act (PACE) 1984.

Importantly, the *Judges' Rules* were *not* rules of law: they were *judicial* guides in how to deal with suspects so as to obtain admissible evidence.[43] In this regime, suspects had few rights and the police were accorded significant latitude. For example, the police were now permitted to interrogate prisoners; there was no right of access to legal advice before or during interrogation; and police questioning of suspects was not contemporaneously recorded. In the absence of regulation, the police could and did use coercive methods to extract confessions.

Nevertheless, the *Rules* had more important objectives: to confer

---

[42] See Choongh (1997) and Bryan (1997).
[43] Lord Devlin: 'It must never be forgotten that the Judges' Rules were made for the guidance of the police and not for the circumscription of judicial power', cited in Devlin (1960).

legitimacy upon a new policing regime and to impose on judges a central corporate governance and disciplinary structure. On the one hand, the *Rules* sought to confer legitimacy on the police under the pretext that their interactions with citizens were being closely regulated. On the other, centralisation was designed both to restore respect for the unity of 'law' which had been shaken by divergent court rulings and to provide a framework by which errant judges could be admonished.

Key to the *Rules* were provisions which required the police to administer a caution once the officer had 'made up his mind to charge a person with a crime' and the 'rule' that 'persons in custody should not be questioned without the usual caution being first administered'. These were manifestly elastic and gave a licence to custodial questioning, the only sanction being the exercise of the trial judge's discretion to exclude unfairly obtained evidence.

The police need not have feared because judges were ideologically disposed to support them. The judges decided that their function was not to discipline the police for breach of the *Rules*. Accordingly, non-compliance with the *Rules* did not, of itself, amount to an offence, civil or criminal. In other words, given the discretion accorded to judges, they were not 'rules' at all and the (few) 'rights' of citizens lived only in legal rhetoric.[44]

## JUDGES' RULES: ARREST AND CUSTODIAL INTERROGATION

Originally, the power of arrest was based upon 'reasonable suspicion' and the police were not permitted to question suspects under detention: they could release the suspect with or without bail or charge the suspect and produce the individual to court as 'soon as practicable' which was interpreted to mean within 24 hours (RCPPP, 1929, paras 143–4). In fact, the Metropolitan Police did arrest without reasonable suspicion precisely in order to obtain evidence which would then 'justify' the arrest, openly admitting this to the RCPPP. Further, they confirmed that they sometimes engaged in sweeps, arresting 'the usual suspects' for questioning (paras 153–4).

While the RCPPP declared these practices illegal (a declaration of no legal effect), the police continued to use various devices to continue 'interrogation' of persons in custody without serious overview. Glanville Williams reported that whereas between the two World Wars confessions

---

[44] As was said in *R v Prager* (1972) a voluntary confession made in breach of the rules could not be made inadmissible because that would 'exalt the Judges' Rules into rules of law'.

obtained through custodial questioning were often excluded, from about 1950 they were almost uniformly admitted. He continued:

> Detention for questioning, and questioning after arrest, are still practised by some police forces, without serious check. To add to the anomaly, it seems from reported cases that the judges have given up enforcing their own rules, for it is no longer the practice to exclude evidence obtained by questioning in custody.[45]

Although guidance issued in 1930 asserted that the *Rules* were never intended to encourage or authorise the questioning or cross-examination of a person in custody after being cautioned, Williams (1961) said that: '... this interpretation may now be said to be a dead letter. Notwithstanding the circular, the police still interrogate persons in custody, and the judges admit the resulting confessions in evidence.'[46] The practice continued thereafter.[47]

Indeed, the 1964 revision legitimated detaining individuals in order to question them *prior* to administering a caution. As Michael Zander (1978) remarked, the courts took the position that a suspect should be advised of his 'right to silence only when the police have the case against him virtually wrapped up'. Nonetheless, the police continued to push the boundaries.

Giving evidence at trial, senior officers openly told the court that individuals had been detained (i.e., arrested) 'for further inquiries' (*R v Houghton and Franciosy*, 1979). Although the Court of Appeal said that the police could only arrest for offences, their sympathy for the police was an invitation to carry on as normal despite the mandatory language in which the *Rules* were couched ('he *shall* caution'; 'a record *shall* be kept'; 'the offence *must* be contemporaneously recorded', etc.).

## JUDGES' RULES: ACCESS TO LEGAL ADVICE/ RIGHT TO SILENCE

Until 1964, the *Rules* were silent regarding access to legal advice and most suspects were left to face the police alone.[48] They fared little better

---

[45] Williams (1960) at p. 331.
[46] Ibid. at p. 50.
[47] See, *R v Chandler* [1976]. As McBarnet (1983) explained, Judges by-passed contradictions within the *Rules* through 'gradual refinements and vacillating metaphors of legal reasoning by which [they] ... established a limbo, sitting uneasily between the law of arrest and the law of interrogation' (p. 43).
[48] Indeed, the emphasis of early socio-legal research was upon the unrepresented defendant. See, for example, the pioneering studies of Borrie and Varcoe (1970) and Zander (1971, 1972a). See also JUSTICE (1971).

under the 1964 formulation which contained no reference to defence lawyers. Indeed, the 'facilities for the defence' set out in the accompanying 'Administrative Directions' (the status of which was lower than the *Rules* but otherwise obscure) were both heavily qualified and based upon the police having unmediated access to the suspect, Direction 7(a) stating: 'A person in custody should be allowed to speak on the telephone to his solicitor or to his friends provided that no hindrance is reasonably likely to be caused to the processes of investigation, or the administration of justice by his doing so'. Whereas the police openly disregarded this provision,[49] courts treated it with contempt. In *Stephen King* [1978], the court perversely 'interpreted' it to mean that in the absence of the suspect raising the matter, 7(a) 'places no obligation on the police to inform the suspect that he may, before answering questions, speak with a solicitor'. In practice, as the pioneering work of Zander (1969, 1972b) showed,[50] not only were suspects left without legal advice, the majority of defendants in magistrates' courts were left undefended.

Growing public concern over access to legal representation fed directly into concern over the plight of suspects in police stations and suspicion over 'confessions' produced therein. The first reported response of the courts came in *R v Allen* [1977]. The defendant, an almost illiterate man, was arrested and questioned at a police station by two officers. During questioning, he was told that while he could remain silent, he could not have access to a solicitor. The trial judge, Justice MacKenna, ruled that the interrogation evidence after that denial was inadmissible because: (i) it was unfair for the Crown to take advantage of an official's wrong; and (ii) the police should not be allowed to use in court evidence of suspects whom they hope will incriminate themselves by being denied the advice of a solicitor.

The Court of Appeal swiftly corrected these liberal tendencies, *R v Lemsatef* (1977) (see below) making it clear that the judges were sympathetic to the 'problems' faced by investigators. *Allen* is the *only* reported case in which the 'right' to legal advice was given any substance by the courts. This is illustrative of the general point that the *Rules* were simply a fig-leaf covering police and judicial practice. Indeed, the Fisher Inquiry into the *Confait* case (Fisher, 1977) unsurprisingly found that 'some of the

---

[49] Thus, Ronald Milhench, friend of then Prime Minister Harold Wilson, was held in detention on the basis that he was 'helping the police with their inquiries', was denied access to his solicitor for 27 hours and when access was granted, they were allowed to speak together 'only in the presence and hearing of a police officer': *New Law Journal*, 13 February, 1975, p. 145.

[50] See also, Dell (1971); King (1971); JUSTICE (1971).

[Judges'] Rules and Directions do not seem to be known to police officers and members of the legal profession' (Fisher, 1977, para. 2.17).

## NO SEARCH AND SEIZURE WITHOUT A WARRANT

In line with the liberty of the citizen, the common law 'rule' was that the police had no power to search the home of an individual unless under a court warrant. The police, however, often breached the rule. Their actions were challenged in *Ghani v Jones* [1970], where, inquiring into the alleged disappearance of a woman, they entered the house of her father-in-law *without a warrant of any kind*. The police seized documents including the passports of the father-in-law, his wife and daughter. No arrest or charge was made. When later requested, they refused to return the documents. Lord Denning overturned the long-standing rule by denigrating citizens and making clear that the courts would endorse police action:

> The police have to get the consent of the householder to enter if they can: or, if not, do it by stealth or by force. Somehow they seem to manage. *No decent person refuses them permission. If he does, he is probably implicated in some way or other.* So the police risk an action for trespass. It is not much risk. (p. 705, emphasis added)

Thereafter judges admitted evidence obtained from unlawful searches: *Jeffrey v Black* (1978).[51]

## NO SEIZURE BEYOND THAT AUTHORISED BY THE WARRANT

At common law, the police were bound by the terms of any search warrant and could not engage in a fishing expedition. As Lord Denning put it:

> Our English law has always had great regard for the integrity of a man's home. In 1604 Lord Coke declared that 'every man's house is his castle' (see Semayne's Case and 3 Inst., cap. 73), and his aphorism has come down the centuries. (*Chic Fashions v Jones* [1968], p. 307)

In the same case, however, where the police seized goods *not* mentioned in the warrant and which were, in fact, the lawful property of the owners

---

[51] The police and former DPP continued to criticise the rules surrounding investigation: *The Times*, 15 June, 1978; *The Guardian*, 8 January, 1979.

of the searched premises, Denning effectively nullified that rule, conferred wide-ranging powers on the police and again denigrated the 'rights' of citizens:

> *In these present times, with the ever-increasing wickedness there is about, honest citizens must help the police and not hinder them in their efforts to track down criminals* ... In my opinion, when a constable enters a house by virtue of a search warrant for stolen goods, he may seize not only the goods which he reasonably believes to be covered by the warrant, but also any other goods which he believes on reasonable grounds to have been stolen and to be material evidence on a charge of stealing or receiving against the person in possession or anyone associated with him. (*Chic Fashions v Jones* [1968], p. 313, emphasis added)

As Doreen McBarnet observed: 'Common law thus managed to justify invading personal liberty to recover property by the principle that reversed its own justification, making the right to recover *possibly* stolen property outweigh the right to individual freedom from interference from the police'.[52]

## CROSS-EXAMINATION

Criminal trials in common law systems are lauded as 'adversarial'. This follows from a jurisprudential position that the truth of a proposition is best accessed through cross-examination of witnesses by skilled advocates. This theory rests on the premise that the witnesses have not colluded in preparing their accounts. Discrepancies between witnesses provide a basis for raising doubts as to their credibility or reliability. Cross-examination, it is said, is the 'greatest legal engine ever invented for the discovery of the truth'.[53]

To minimise, if not eliminate, the effects of cross-examination, police adopted the unlawful practice of collaborating.[54] Where the only explanation for identical evidence was prior collaboration, police witnesses routinely denied this, thereby committing perjury.[55] As Morton (1993) put it:

---

[52] McBarnet (1983) at p. 40.
[53] Wigmore (1940), para. 1367.
[54] Brogden (1991, p. 121) describes how one officer admitted this in evidence to the discomfort of the Judge who said: 'I have often heard it suggested that policemen do these things but I have never heard a policeman on oath say that he did them'.
[55] See, Williams (1960) who says that such denials could 'almost be said to be standard police practice' (at p. 227).

> [Police officers] went through the farce of producing notebooks made up identically down to the last comma and, in the teeth of the evidence, stood their ground denying there had been any collaboration with other officers. And however much they were made to look at best foolish and at worst liars, time and time again they were backed up by the magistrates and judges. (p. 263)

The issue arose in *R v Bass* (1953) in which the incriminating evidence consisted entirely of a 'confession' allegedly made in the presence of two officers. The records made by the officers at different times were almost identical but they denied that they had collaborated. The Court of Criminal Appeal remarked:

> This court has observed that police officers nearly always deny that they have collaborated in the making of notes and we cannot help wondering why they are the only class of society who do not collaborate in such a matter. *It seems to us that nothing could be more natural or proper when two persons have been present at an interview with a third person than that they should afterwards make sure that they have a correct version of what was said. Collaboration would appear to be a better explanation of almost identical notes than the possession of a super-human memory.* (p. 59, emphasis added)

The Court, in short, changed the rules to legalise police perjury, discarding a core principle of the adversary system and rendering the most potent weapon in the defence armoury nugatory. Police officers were now able to, and did, collaborate in preparing their accounts, thereby rendering their version virtually bulletproof.[56]

One illustration of the continuing effect of the devious rule in *Bass* can be seen in an incident in which Mark Duggan, a 29-year-old black man, was shot and killed by a Metropolitan Police officer (code name V53) in August 2011, an action which provoked street disorders nationwide. As mentioned in Chapter 1, the trigger for these events was pulled in Tottenham, the site of long-term conflict between the police and local black community, the locus of the street 'riots' of 1985 which also were sparked by the death of a member of the black community, Cynthia Jarrett, during a police operation. At this latest shooting were 11 other police officers.[57]

---

[56] It has been reported that the practice of police conferring before the writing up of their notes is to be abandoned where 'serious incidents' are involved in order to restore public confidence (BBC, 5th March, 2014).

[57] See, Bridges (2012) for a full account. The verdict in the Mark Duggan Inquest has proved controversial and perplexing. Despite officer V53 informing the jury that he was '100% sure [Duggan] was in possession of a gun', using precise detail to recount events, they concluded both that 'Duggan did not have a gun by

Initial reports were contradictory: an Independent Police Commission (IPCC) spokesperson stated that there had been a shoot-out during which a police officer was first hit by a bullet that lodged in his radio, after which he returned fire and killed Duggan. In fact, it was another officer's radio that was struck by a ricochet from the police gun. A witness (Miss J) stated (and later testified) that she saw an officer emerge from the mini-cab, a gun in the palm of his hand and that officers dragged the body away from the cab. The officer who fired (V53) was later to testify that he had no doubt that Duggan was preparing to raise a handgun he was clutching and open fire on the officers around him (*The Guardian*, 26 September 2012).

In the course of the IPCC investigation, the firearms officers provided written statements but refused to be interviewed.[58] In September 2012, Kevin Hutchinson-Foster was put on trial accused of giving Duggan a gun said to have been recovered from near the scene. It emerged at the trial that, before making their first notes, the 11 officers had a meeting with legal representatives and members of the Police Federation and were read guidance on statements prepared by the Association of Chief Police Officers. These guidance notes allow officers to confer on issues other than their 'honestly held belief' of the situation. Following the briefing, the officers are reported to have sat in a room together and to have spent eight hours writing an account of events.

The problem with such a scenario (which needs no comment) is seen in the first trial of Kevin Hutchinson-Foster in which the defence counsel cross-examining the Superintendent who was called in after the shooting of Mark Duggan asked the following question (*Mail Online*, 28 September 2012):

> *Counsel*: These police officers are friends and colleagues. Did it occur to you that in those circumstances if you put all eleven in a room they might not seek to ensure they protected their friend and colleague who had used the gun?
> *Superintendent*: I did not see that then or now as a potential problem.

---

the time he stood on the pavement before officers,' but also decided that the killing by officer V53 was lawful: Ryder (2014).

[58] Historically, police officers often refused to attend interviews called for by the IPCC or, if attending, to answer questions put to them during interview. Anne Owers, Chair of the IPCC, informed the public of the posture of officers to changes in the law in the following terms: 'The law has now changed and we can compel officers to come in for interview. However, they can and still do refuse to answer questions verbally at interview' (Owers, 2014).

## COURT OF TRIAL: JURY OR MAGISTRATES

The adversarial system is strongly identified with jury trial which leading judges have held up as 'the lamp that shows that freedom lives'.[59] Despite this encomium, judges themselves have been instrumental in undermining the jury, already under constant attack from politicians and prosecutors,[60] and laying the foundation for a shift in case load to magistrates' courts and the introduction of judge-only trials.

Thus, an inquiry headed by Lord Justice James (1975), recommended the removal of a range of offences from the Crown Court to magistrates' courts, with those relating to public order implemented by the Criminal Law Act 1977. Another attempt to move more offences to magistrates' courts was made by the Royal Commission on Criminal Justice (RCCJ, 1993), despite government research showing that a majority of defendants and solicitors believed that 'magistrates are on the side of the police'[61] and Vennard (1982) – the Research Director of the RCCJ – finding substantial bias in favour of police evidence by magistrates.

In the same tradition, the Criminal Law Revision Committee, led by Lord Justice Edmund Davies, in its *Eleventh Report (Evidence)* (1972) recommended abrogation of the right to silence on pain of adverse inferences, a proposal that was based upon the bare assertion, unsupported by *any* evidence, that too many professional criminals were avoiding conviction.[62]

Similarly, a Fraud Trials Committee chaired by Lord Justice Roskill (1986) proposed the removal of complex fraud trials from the jury system. No evidence was ever produced in support of its suspicion that juries could not understand such cases.[63] Without empirical evidence, the Auld Report's support of the Roskill proposal led to the Criminal Justice Act, 2003, which enables the prosecution in cases of serious or complex fraud to apply to a Crown Court Judge for a trial before a judge without a jury and additionally provides for judge-only trials in cases in which there have

---

[59] Devlin (1956) at p. 164.
[60] In addition, the right of the defence to peremptorily challenge prospective jurors was reduced from 7 to 3 before being abolished by the Criminal Justice Act, 1988, section 118(1); with juries secretly 'vetted' to exclude any individual thought to be, so far as the State was concerned, unreliable.
[61] Hedderman and Moxon (1992), p. 15; see Gregory (1976) to the same effect.
[62] This recommendation in essence eventually found its way into law under the Criminal Justice and Public Order Act, 1994. The Home Secretary advocated its adoption in Parliament because the right was being abused allegedly not only by 'professional criminals' but also by '*hardened criminals and terrorists*'.
[63] For contrary evidence, see Honess et al. (1998); Lloyd-Bostock (2007); Jackson and Doran (1995).

been alleged attempts at jury 'nobbling'. Further changes were presaged in a speech by Lord Thomas, CJ in which he raised the spectre of moving some cases currently dealt with by juries into a new judge-led, non-jury, intermediate court as well as further changes to fraud trials (Rozenberg, 2014).

## BURDEN OF PROOF

Whatever the mode of trial, it has been a cardinal principle of the adversary rhetoric that the accused is presumed innocent and the prosecution bears the burden of proof beyond reasonable doubt.[64] A corollary was the rule that a suspect's silence could not be used against them and that it was no part of the defendant's responsibility to assist the prosecution:

> There is an inconsistency of principle in requiring the onus of proof at trial to be upon the prosecution and to be discharged without any assistance from the accused and yet in enabling the prosecution to use the accused's silence in the face of police questioning under caution as any part of their case against him at trial. (Royal Commission on Criminal Procedure, 1981, para. 4.51)

As the courts put it, 'the accused is not bound to give evidence . . . he can sit back and see if the prosecution have proved their case' (*R v Bathurst*, 1968).

Nonetheless, the way had been paved for politicians to make inroads into the 'right' by curial and extra-curial attacks from senior judiciary. In *R v Alladice* (1988) Lord Lane CJ commented upon section 58 of PACE 1984 which provided a right of access to a lawyer as soon as practicable:

> The result is that in many cases a detainee, who would otherwise have answered proper questioning by the police, will be advised to remain silent. Weeks later, at his trial, such a person not infrequently produces an explanation of, or a defence to the charge the truthfulness of which the police have had no chance to check.
> 
> Despite the fact that the explanation or defence could, if true, have been disclosed at the outset and despite the advantage which the defendant has gained by these tactics, no comment may be made to the jury to that effect. The jury may in some cases put two and two together, but it seems to us that the effect of section 58 is such that the balance of fairness between prosecution and defence cannot be maintained unless proper comment is permitted on the defendant's silence in such circumstances. It is high time that such comment should be

---

[64] The 'golden thread': *Woolmington v DPP* [1935].

permitted together with the necessary alteration to the words of the caution. (p. 385)

In the result, the right to silence was attenuated by the Criminal Justice and Public Order Act, 1994 enabling a court or jury to draw such inferences as appear 'proper' from the failure to mention any fact relied upon in defence. In addition, the Criminal and Procedure Investigation Act, 1996 introduced the principle that the defence should disclose an outline of its case in advance of trial. Whilst this latter provision proved wholly ineffectual, the defence being able to satisfy its obligations by means of a generalised indication, the ground was laid for the idea to be strengthened. That was to come with the report of Auld (2001).

Auld (2001) further undermined the right to silence by asserting that neither the prosecution's obligation to make the court sure of guilt nor the defendant's right to silence were threatened 'by requiring a defendant to identify with some precision the matters of fact and/or of law that he intends to put in issue' (Report, Chapter 10, para. 5) because those fundamental principles, he asserted, 'are there to protect the innocent defendant from wrongful conviction, not to enable the guilty defendant to engage in tactical manoeuvres designed to frustrate a fair hearing and just outcome on the issues he intends to take' (Report, Chapter 10, para. 5). In saying this, Auld ignored the conventional understanding that required the prosecution to discharge its burden *without the compelled assistance of the accused*.

Additionally, Auld set aside the burden of proof itself by the crude division of defendants into 'guilty' and 'innocent' categories whereas the heart of the adversary system has been the distinction between *factual* and *legal* guilt with its procedures designed to ensure that factual guilt does not displace legal guilt as the test to determine whether someone should be convicted of the offence charged. Politicians were quick to take up the invitation.

The Criminal Justice Act 2003 imposed strict disclosure requirements on the defence on pain of adverse inferences being drawn. This was followed by the further requirement under the Criminal Procedure Rules (CPR) for the defence to assist the court in the 'management' of the case. One example exemplifies the way in which the burden of proof has been turned on its head. If there is a deficiency in the prosecution case on which the defendant wishes to rely, the CPR require that the defence *must* identify the issue, even if the technical defence is thereby lost, or the deficiency is rectified because the prosecution is put on notice (see, Chapter 6 *infra*).

## JUDICIAL IDEOLOGY

Underpinning a police and judicial process designed to generate confessions, non-trial dispositions and system bias against putting the state to proof, is the undercutting of 'rights' by judges for reasons which are, at best, prejudicial, at worst, bigoted and unworthy. For fully one hundred years, judges have systematically stripped the last vestiges of formal legal rationality in criminal cases whilst holding fast to a permissive attitude to police demands and violations of the 'rights' of suspects and accused persons.

A classic statement of judicial rhetoric about the adversarial system is found in the statement of Lord Bingham CJ in quashing (forty years too late) the wrongful conviction of Derek Bentley which had been obtained in no small part by a shamefully biased 'summing up' by Lord Goddard CJ. Bingham stated:

> The guilt of a defendant is to be judged by the jury as the tribunal of fact on all the evidence in the case. That tribunal should make its collective judgment on the evidence in an open-minded and fair-minded way. There is an obvious risk of injustice if a jury is invited to approach the evidence on the assumption that police officers, because they are police officers, are likely to be accurate and reliable witnesses and defendants, because they are defendants, likely to be inaccurate and unreliable. (*R v Bentley*, 1998, para. 59)

The fact, however, is that Goddard's animus towards the defence is simply one example of a judicial prejudice that has stained English criminal jurisprudence the origins of which are to be found in hostility to the rights of individuals and a blind, bordering on complicit, commitment to police evidence.

Writing in 1964 on the new *Judges' Rules*, Hoffman (later to be a judge), demonstrated faith in police investigations and scepticism of the need for cautioning suspects despite acknowledging police perjury. Commenting upon the old rule which caused a doubt about custodial questioning, Hoffman said: 'The rule produced a great deal of learning on the exact moment at which persons were regarded as having been taken into custody, *and frequent improbable denials by the police that they had put any questions at all*' (p. 25, emphasis added).

In a similar vein, Lord Parker CJ (Berlins, 1971a) favoured abolition of the caution and of the rule preventing comment to the jury on an accused's failure to give evidence. The next Chief Justice, Lord Widgery, said that the administration of a caution was a rule 'we could no longer afford' and that any rule requiring the presence of the suspect's lawyer during police interrogation was 'quite unacceptable'. In a blatant attempt to influence the Royal Commission on Criminal Justice (then deliberating) Lord Taylor CJ attacked the right of silence and other rules of evidence on the ground that they tilted the system in favour of criminals and thus encouraged police fabrication (Young, 1992). Such extra-curial statements have been more than matched by in-court pronouncements.

## STATEMENTS IN THE COURT OF APPEAL

In *R v Wattam* (1952), for example, the Court of Appeal made it clear that the judges did not wish to enforce the 'rule' that a person in custody should be cautioned: 'The police must investigate matters of this kind, or there would be no protection for anybody'. Similarly in *R v Northam* (1968), in an open attempt to influence the Criminal Law Revision Committee (1971) then deliberating, the Court of Appeal stated:

> In these days it really does seem that the undoubtedly well-established doctrine of our law that persons who are minded to make a confession or admission to the police or other authorities must be very strictly safeguarded against any persuasion or inducement to make any such confession or admission is in some respects somewhat out of date. In these days the criminal classes are only too well aware of their position of virtual immunity in the hands of the police. *It does seem that some of the present doctrines and principles have come down in our law from [an] earlier time when the police of this country were not to be trusted, as they are now to be trusted in almost every single case, to behave with complete fairness towards those who come into their hands or from whom they are seeking information.* (p. 102, emphasis added)

Again, in *R v Gilbert* (1978), the Court of Appeal said that the rule regarding the right to silence had to be applied 'even though in some cases its application seems inconsistent with the exercise of common sense' and that it was acceptable for a trial judge to tell the jury that there are those 'who think that the law should be altered in that it operates to protect the guilty'. In *R v Houghton and Franciosy* (1979) the Court of Appeal, in condoning the admission of a 'confession' obtained after an unlawful arrest and detention in police custody for five days without a caution being administered, stated that they were of the view that the *Judges' Rules* 'can hinder the police in bringing criminals to justice'.

The judicial attitude which developed is heavily at odds with the declamation of Lord Hewart:[65]

---

[65] *Ludlow v Shelton* (1938).

> One of our most priceless possessions is the liberty of the subject. If once we show any signs of giving way to the abominable doctrine that because things are done by officials, some immunity must be extended to them, what is to become of our country?

But it must be obvious why trust (blind or otherwise) in the police is misguided. There is no other agent in the criminal process so intimately connected to each stage of attaining conviction. The police are both gateway and gatekeeper to the initial incrimination mechanism (requiring their observation to satisfy grounds of arrest). The prosecution often depend on police testimony to assemble a case, the persuasiveness of which is ordinarily bolstered by the guise of authority which officers carry into court ready-made (McBarnet, 1983). Structurally then, the police have an in-built dominance, which heightens the risk that more vulnerable agents (defendants and jurors) might succumb to the impression that police evidence is shrouded in infallibility.

## SUMMING UP AT TRIAL

The implicit faith in the police extended to jury trial when the 'summing up' of judges often lacked any link to actuarial principles or evidential mathematics.

In the notorious *Birmingham Six* (1975) case in which the defendants had been beaten (the marks on their faces visible to the court) and 'confessions' fabricated, Justice Bridge told the jury:

> Is it entirely coincidence that [they] all showed discoloration of the chest, scratch marks, scrawls and scrapes. Are those the sort of injuries that the police are likely to inflict obviously visible but not one would have thought causing any intense pain? If a man wants to inflict injuries upon himself, what more obvious place in which to do it than by scratching his chest? . . .
> 
> If the defendants are giving you honest and substantially accurate evidence, there is no escape from the fact that the police are involved in a conspiracy to commit a variety of crimes which must be unprecedented in the annals of British criminal history.

In the appeal of March 1976, Widgery LCJ shamefully considered (referring to one of the men's black eye) that this was nothing 'beyond the ordinary'. When the Home Secretary sent the case back to the Appeal Court in 1987, forensic specialists denigrated the scientific tests used against the *Six*. Lord Chief Justice Lane, however, said the experts were either lying or mistaken and 'the longer this hearing has gone on, the more convinced this court has become that the verdict . . . was correct'. He even criticised the Home Secretary for referring the case to the court.

Even worse, perhaps, were Lord Denning's infamous words in the civil proceedings brought by the *Birmingham Six*, which were simply symptomatic of a refusal to allow the prospect that a trial might expose fabricated evidence, coerced confessions and police perjury. In refusing the men's civil claim to proceed, Denning said:

> Just consider the course of events if this action is allowed to proceed to trial. If the six men fail, it will mean that much time and money will have been expended by many people for no good purpose. If the six men win, it will mean that the police were guilty of perjury, that they were guilty of violence and threats, that the confessions were involuntary and were improperly admitted in evidence and that the convictions were erroneous. That would mean the Home Secretary would either have to recommend they be pardoned or he would have to remit the case to the Court of appeal. This is such an appalling vista that every sensible person in the land would say: 'It cannot be right that these actions should go any further.'

As Ludovic Kennedy (1990, p.199) said of this:[66]

> If this does not mean that it is better that six possibly innocent men should continue to rot in prison rather than run the risk of a number of police officers being found guilty of perjury, violence and threats, it is difficult to know what it does mean. And if it does mean that, then it seems to me that judges who refuse to entertain the idea of police corruption when it is the most likely explanation of the case, or part of the case, against the accused become no less corrupt themselves. It is moreover a vicious circle, for the police, relying on the judges' support, are encouraged to continue their malpractices.

## THE COURT OF APPEAL

Just as judges can exhibit bias at trial, so too can the Court of Appeal and official inquiries. There has been an official determination to uphold convictions in the face of abundant contrary evidence. In the *Luton Post Office Murder Case*, in which convictions were obtained by the false account of an habitual criminal (who was disbelieved in *all* other aspects of his evidence and was certainly one of the participants in the robbery that went wrong) in the pay of a corrupt senior Metropolitan Police Officer (Kenneth Drury, who was later jailed for eight years for unrelated corruption), the Court of Appeal turned down appeals on *five* occasions, the two men being released eventually by the Home Secretary, but with Lord Chief Justice Lane blocking a royal pardon so as not to embarrass the judges. Only in 2003 did a sixth appeal succeed.

---

[66] See also, Foot (1986) on the summing up in the Carl Bridgewater Case.

Prolonged waits were the fate of other defendants in miscarriage of justice cases with Court of Appeal judges setting their face against any criticism of fellow judges. For example, in the *Bridgewater* case, three of the defendants (the fourth had died in prison) wrongfully convicted in 1979 were not exonerated until 1997 after six separate police inquiries and two earlier failed appeals; the *Guildford Four*, convicted in 1975 were not exonerated until 1989, one of their number (Giuseppe Conlon) having died in prison; in the related case of the *Maguire Seven*, their appeals did not finally succeed until 1991; *Stefan Kiszco*, convicted in 1976 of a murder he could not have committed, had his appeal dismissed in 1978, with Bridge (the trial judge at the *Birmingham Six*) stating that there were 'no grounds whatever' to allow the appeal with the result that Kiszco was not cleared until 1992; the *Tottenham Three* convicted of murder in 1987 had their convictions overturned in 1991; and the *Cardiff Three* convictions for murder in 1988 were not overturned until 1992 and the defendants not exonerated until the real killer was convicted in 2003. Indeed, appeals arising out of the activities of the notorious West Midlands Serious Crime Squad, disbanded in 1991, resisted for so long, continue today with more than fifty false convictions quashed trailing clouds of police corruption around the halls of justice.

## OFFICIAL INQUIRIES

If the Court of Appeal has dragged its feet, the reputation of official inquiries (often led by judges and lawyers, acting or retired) is equally besmirched. In the *Timothy Evans* murder case (1950), following a botched inquiry by Scott Henderson QC which failed to confront police illegality, an Inquiry by Justice Brabin incredulously concluded that it was 'more probable than not' that Evans had murdered his wife but that he had not murdered his baby daughter. This not only contradicted the prosecution case at trial (that both murders had been committed at the same time by the same person) but used the civil standard of proof to reach an erroneous conclusion.

The same shoddy reasoning appealed to the Inquiry conducted by retired Justice Fisher (1977) into the *Confait* killing. In connection with the death of Maxwell Confait whose body was found in a burnt-out house, three young boys faced various charges: Ronny Leighton (aged 15, murder and arson); Colin Lattimore (aged 18, murder and arson) and Ahmet Salih (aged 14, arson). The Inquiry heard plenty of evidence of prosecution wrongdoing, including police breaches of the *Rules*, alteration of police records, unreliable 'expert' evidence and improper conduct by prosecuting counsel. However, Fisher's ingenuity in protecting the integrity of the system resulted in the bogus conclusion that all three boys had been involved 'on the balance of probabilities' (the civil standard of proof) and that Salih was actually guilty of involvement in the killing, an offence with which he had not even been charged.[67] All were subsequently proved entirely innocent, the real killer (Douglas Franklin) later committing suicide.

## THE TECHNIQUES OF LEGITIMACY

As Burton and Carlen (1979) observe, official law and order discourse has been[68] constructed 'in terms of an ideal of distributive justice which cannot admit to the material conditions which render that ideal impossible' (p. 95). If official discourse is to succeed, it has to negotiate or deny the material conditions out of which it emerged. The political purpose is to reaffirm public confidence in a fractured criminal justice system and to reconstruct new forms of legitimacy. All this is demonstrated in the techniques of legitimacy utilised by judges and official commissions and inquiries.

**Blurring the Boundaries**

A prominent masking strategy has been blurring the meaning and sources of 'law'. In a system in which the rule of law is supposedly upheld through legislation and dispositive case precedents, the regulatory 'oversight' of the acquisition of evidence, primarily through police investigation, originated in a twilight world created by judges which masked the status of the 'law'. There is no authoritative account of how the *Judges' Rules* came into being except that they arose out of no parliamentary deliberation or case law. Indeed, consideration of the *Rules* of 1964 had been earlier withdrawn from the Royal Commission on the Police (1962), itself established to address police corruption, and 'smuggled' into 'law' in what was described by (later to be) Lord Hoffman as 'an atmosphere of crisis and haste worthy of most desperate emergency legislation' (Hoffman, 1964, p. 23). If the *Rules* were not 'law' but 'guidance', the accompanying *Administrative Directions*, which set out the 'rights' of suspects, had an even more reduced status, with no one knowing even whether they had been approved by judges or, if they had, which judges.

---

[67] See McBarnet (1978).
[68] But see Chapter 8.

## Sources of 'Law': Police Practice

Even judges and commissions need, in certain instances, to find a basis for regulation and for the creation of new 'rules' or 'law' and here we find classic instances of how 'law' can come into place without consideration of principle and without democratic input.

One strategy is for police practice to be simply adopted as 'law'. Thus, the Royal Commission of 1929 endorsed police practice, for which 'there [was] no express power', of search of persons on arrest at police stations and that of searching the dwellings of arrested people for which there was no power absent consent and that 'in the opinion of the Home Office, it has become part of the common law'.

Similarly, the 1964 *Judges' Rules* altered the legal position of suspects by giving the police new powers. As Hoffman (1964, p. 26) wrote of the relevant provision: 'The effect of the new rule is to give *implied recognition* to *the well-established practice* of "detaining for questioning" by means of an arrest on suspicion followed by a period of investigation before charge' (emphasis added). Another insight into the masking process is provided by *Mohammed-Holgate v Duke* (1983) where it was explicitly recognised that the police practice of detaining and interrogating persons in order to obtain confessions, though 'surprisingly, and perhaps significantly, bare of direct authority', was not deemed wrong because the power 'has for a long period been so exercised without apparently any question or challenge until the instant case' (pp. 533–4).

## Justification for New 'Law'

Judges are, of course, aware that police practice cannot simply be invoked as a source of 'law' without some rationalisation. This has come in several guises. On the negative side, Judges avoided having to look too closely at police practices by deciding that it was not part of their function to discipline police:[69] 'It is no part of a judge's function to exercise discipli-

---

[69] As McBarnet (1983) observes: 'The underlying cause of this situation interestingly enough is the democratic ideology of the separation of powers, whereby judges shall not be lackeys of the government, in order to prevent political manipulation and protect the civil liberties of the citizen against the state – interestingly, because it is precisely protection of civil liberties that the Judges' Rules might claim to be providing. So a state structure geared to the dominant ideology of democratic rights prevents specific rulings to preserve those democratic rights from being enforced. The structure behind democratic ideology thus ironically legitimises the failure to enforce it' (p. 67).

nary powers over the police or prosecution as respects the way in which evidence to be used at the trial is obtained by them' (Lord Diplock in *R v Sang*, 1979, p. 290).

In taking this position, the judges knew that civil remedies were of little avail to any whose 'rights' were infringed and that there was no other meaningful institutional oversight of police practices, the Police Complaints Board (formed in 1977) and its successors (Police Complaints Authority, 1985; and IPCC, 2004) being devoid of real powers or credibility.[70]

On a more assertive note, judges simply stated that police practice must be permitted on the grounds of 'necessity' or of 'crime control', as we have seen in *Chic Fashions v Jones* [1968] and *R v Houghton and Franciosy* (1979). Thus, in *R v Booth and Jones* (1910) police questioning was considered acceptable because: 'If this sort of investigation were not allowed very few crimes would ever be discovered'; and in *R v Voisin* (1918) the Court of Appeal said that: 'It is desirable in the interests of the community that investigation into crimes should not be cramped . . .'.

A superficially more jurisprudential argument occurs when judges and commissions purport to weigh the arguments and come down on one side or another: the 'balance' strategy. This has a long history. For example, the 1929 Royal Commission stated: 'We do not suggest that any system could be devised which would ensure that in all cases the balance should be evenly held between the interests of justice on the one hand and the rights and liberties of the subject on the other' (RCPPP, 1929, p. 10). To similar effect, as we have seen, was Lord Denning in *Ghani v Jones* [1970]. This artifice is favoured by politicians, as when the terms of reference of royal commissions are set (RCCP, 1981) and by royal commissions themselves in seeking to justify their approach (RCCJ, 1993, p. 8). The core defect in this approach is that the reasoning, as Ashworth and Redmayne (2010) have persuasively argued, is fundamentally flawed in the absence of stipulating 'exactly what is being balanced, what factors and interests are to be included or excluded, what weight is being assigned to particular values and interests, and so on' (pp. 41–5).

---

[70] The IPCC's 18-month investigation into the death in police custody of Sean Rigg in 2008 is demonstrative of its weaknesses. The subsequent independent external review contradicted the IPCC's initial findings that there was no evidence of neglect or wrongdoing and that the police had acted 'reasonably and proportionately'. Aside from the problem with officers being allowed to confer with each other before making initial statements to investigators, the independent external review criticised the IPCC for accepting accounts from officers that were 'improbable' and 'implausible' (Casale, 2013, pp. 5–6).

## Displacing and Individuating Malpractice

Another problem for State actors is that very often there *is* clear malpractice, particularly on the part of the police but also sometimes by prosecutors and trial judges. Three strategies for dealing with such malpractice have been routinely adopted: *legitimation*; *displacement*; and *individuation*.

On occasions, where police malpractice has occurred, courts have sought to *legitimise* the behaviour and provide for its continuance in judicially disinfected form. An example referred to earlier (*Bass*), was the decision to cleanse police perjury and to provide a mechanism by which police could tailor their evidence. Another example is *R v Lemsatef* (1977) in which investigating officers (customs officials) detained the defendant for questioning, denied him access to a lawyer and then relied upon oral and written statements he allegedly made while in custody. The answers of investigating officers under cross-examination violated the *Judges' Rules* because: (i) the detention was based upon 'helping with inquiries' rather than upon arresting for an offence; and (ii) denial of access to a lawyer was based upon the concern that 'his solicitor could be asked by him to contact someone else and possibly something of evidential value might be lost'.[71] Depicting the answers as 'inept' rather than 'unlawful', the Court provided recipe answers that would allow the practice to continue *within the law*. Since there was no such ground for arrest as 'helping the police with their inquiries', the Court of Appeal provided a model cross-examination answer:

> *What [the customs officer] should have said, when he was asked these questions by counsel*, was that he had detained the defendant because he reasonably suspected him of having committed an offence against the Customs and Excise Act 1952, and that, as he was entitled to do, whilst the accused was in detention he had asked him some questions for the purposes of helping his inquiries. (*R v Lemsatef* (1977), p. 246, emphasis added)

So far as denial of access to a solicitor, the Court was equally helpful:

> We do not consider that the answer which [the custom's officer] gave was a sufficiently good reason for refusing to allow the defendant to consult his solicitor. *The answer should have been* that solicitors could not reasonably be expected to turn up until ordinary business hours and that delaying interrogation till then might have caused unreasonable delay. (p. 246, emphasis added)

---

[71] The Court sought to depict the problem as one of *balancing* the interests of investigating officers with the rights of suspects when it was nothing of the kind.

These template answers were subsequently taken up with relish by police.

*Displacement* occurs where the focus is shifted away from State wrongdoing and onto defendants and/or their lawyers, either individually or collectively. Denning's insistence that 'no decent person' would stand on their rights in the face of police power unless they were 'implicated' in some way (*Ghani v Jones*) is more than matched by Auld's comment that:

> There is the problem to which I have referred, of the *uncooperative or feckless defendant and/or his defence advocate* who considers that the burden of proof and his client's right to silence justifies frustration of the orderly preparation of both sides' case for trial. (2001, Chapter 10, para. 8, emphasis added)

Despite discreditable police malpractice in cases like the *Birmingham Six*, the *Guildford Four* and the *Tottenham Three*, strenuous efforts were made to denigrate the defendants, not simply through a whispering campaign, but also by assertions that the only impropriety was that the convictions had been secured by the wrong means (Bennet, 1993; Hillyard, 1994).

The very method of case determination makes it possible for judges to treat each case as unique and unrelated to other cases or contexts: *individuation*. In this way, any wrongdoing (for example, by a police unit) such as fabrication of 'confessions', torture, suppression of evidence or erroneous 'expert' evidence, if acknowledged at all, can be isolated as failings in *that case*. The possibility of systemic malpractice (in that unit) is thereby ruled out. Yet evidence to the contrary is often staring judges in the face. For example, individual appeals arising out of cases handled by the West Midlands Serious Crime Squad were routinely dismissed by the Court of Appeal in the 1980s without arousing in the Court's mind the suspicion that there was something rotten with the whole Squad. It was the tide of wrongdoing exposed by others that caused the Squad to be disbanded in 1991 (with many members simply re-assigned).[72]

**What Was Not Looked For or Seen**

Judges have consistently failed to open their minds to the fact that, far from problems being isolated, malpractice is often *systemic*, encouraged

---

[72] It is believed that some 97 convictions were obtained by wrongful means. A similarly tragic history can be seen in the evidence of repeat 'expert' witnesses effective in securing convictions and frustrating correction for years, as in the cases of Home Office 'scientists' eventually retired on the grounds of 'limited efficiency' as happened to Dr Frank Skuse, a key witness in the trials of the *Birmingham Six* and *Judith Ward*, and Dr Alan Clift, described in the Scottish Court of Criminal Appeal as discredited not only as a scientist but as a witness.

by a conviction-at-all-costs approach and cover-up mentality on the part of the prosecution organisations. Cases such as the *Birmingham Six*, the *Guildford Four*, the *Tottenham Three*, and those caused by the West Midlands Serious Crime Squad could not have occurred without the direct involvement of numbers of officers (in several instances involving officers from different police forces) and the collusion of others, the cover-up mentality being admitted by serving officers and documented by researchers[73] (see, further, Chapter 8).

In short, if judges had looked more assiduously in a whole swathe of cases, they would have found evidence of systemic corruption and cover-up, a determination to protect other officers and/or the organisation at any cost. Nor would they have expressed surprise, as they did in *R v Maxwell* (2010) that the officers in question had not been disciplined or prosecuted because, in fact, this is standard practice.

**Integrity and Public Confidence: Official Discourse**

Instead, judges and commissions alike have turned a blind eye to systemic malpractice. An illustration of the approach of judges is that of the Court of Appeal in the *Bridgewater Four* case, where Roch LJ observed:

> This Court is not concerned with the guilt or innocence of the appellants' but only with the safety of their convictions. This may, at first sight, appear an unsatisfactory state of affairs, until it is remembered that *the integrity of the criminal process is the most important consideration for courts* which have to hear against appeals against conviction. (emphasis added)[74]

The elevation of 'system integrity' as the gold standard slants appeals in one direction; as Denning (cited in Whitton, 1988) infamously put it: 'It is better that some innocent men remain in jail than that the integrity of the English judicial system be impugned'. Meanwhile, the judges express puzzlement at the police, inhabiting what is described as 'a closed world' (*R v Maxwell* (2010), para. 42) and beyond regulation: 'On the face of it, there is a strong case of conspiracy to pervert the course of justice and forgery. No explanation has been provided to the court as to why there have been no such disciplinary or criminal proceedings' (para. 37, Lord Dyson).

---

[73] See the devastating Ellison Report (2014) on the Stephen Lawrence case cover-up and McConville and Shepherd (1992) for a discussion of the literature and revelations by officers.

[74] *R v Hickey and others*, CA, unreported, transcript, 30 July 1997, quoted in Davis, Rowe and Johnson (2000) 30 EHRR 1.

## ONE STEP FORWARD, TWO STEPS BACK

Recently, judges have sought to distance themselves from the shameful past, at least in relation to their handling of wrongful convictions. *Nunn v Chief Constable of Suffolk* [2012] is an example of this rhetoric in a case involving an application for post-conviction disclosure of forensic material collected during the initial investigation. The court's self-satisfaction is easy to see:

> Not unsurprisingly, it was common ground that the mark of our system of justice was that it was the duty of the State to guard against miscarriages of justice and, when things had gone seriously wrong, to do everything possible to put them right . . . (para. 20)

It then cited Lord Steyn's *apologia* in *R v Mirza* [2004], which, after reciting some of the appalling miscarriages and the establishment of the Criminal Cases Review Commission (but not mentioning its limited terms of reference and powers), claimed that there had taken place

> . . . a more general change in legal culture. The philosophy became firmly established that there is a positive duty on judges, when things have gone seriously wrong in the criminal justice system, to do everything possible to put it right. In the world of today enlightened public opinion would accept nothing less. (p. 1130)

As we shall see later, there is simply no evidence of any 'general change in legal culture', but quite the contrary; and the claim is undermined if not discredited by *Nunn* itself which refused a man claiming to have been wrongfully convicted of murder an application for defence forensic advisers to have access to forensic material collected by the prosecution during the original investigation. As Andrew Roberts (2012, p. 970) remarked, 'The decision in [*Nunn*] will go a long way to ensuring that flaws and shortcomings in an initial investigation are unlikely to be uncovered with any greater regularity'.

## SYSTEMIC CONSEQUENCES

Although the *Judges' Rules* may be dead,[75] they still rule us from their graves. Not only have judges been aligned with the police for more than one hundred years and steadfast in their opposition to any notion of

---

[75] They were abolished by the Police and Criminal Evidence Act, 1984.

the 'rights' of suspects or defendants but, more significantly, they paved the way for 'Law and Order' politicians to drive through this embedded ideology. What the judicial construction of 'the balance' produced was a plethora of legislation, the combined effect of which has been to extend police powers and further erode the 'rights' of the defence, all of which has been fully endorsed by the judges. The approach of all political parties is most succinctly set out in the Labour Party's approach to criminal justice policy: 'We asked the police what powers they wanted and made sure they got them'.[76]

Beginning with the Police and Criminal Evidence Act, 1984 (PACE), among the changes introduced by legislation, police were accorded a general power to stop and search almost anyone by converting restrictive local powers to stop and search people 'reasonably suspected' of having in their possession stolen goods into national powers and extending these to include 'offensive weapons' which can, in law, include anything which can be used for an offensive purpose, such as keys, credit cards, pens or combs;[77] detention powers were broadened and drafted in such a way that a 'need to question' became a ground for detention which, on police authority, could last for 36 hours in respect of 'serious arrestable offences' or, with the authority of a magistrate (hardly a constraint in practice), 96 hours; and the police were additionally given powers to take intimate body samples. The Criminal Justice and Public Order Act, 1994 (CJPOA) attenuated a suspect's rights to remain silent, with penalties for failing to account for one's presence at a particular place, objects in one's possession, substances or marks on one's person, or to disclose any fact relied upon at trial, while giving police powers to stop and search in particular localities *without reasonable suspicion*[78] and providing for sentence incentives in return for guilty pleas. The Prevention of Terrorism Act, 1989 was amended in 1996 to permit stop search without reasonable suspicion. The Criminal Justice Act, 2003 amended PACE to allow custodial detention

---

[76] Labour Party (2005). The Conservative Party similarly stated its determination to 're-balance' the system which has been 'tilted too far in favour of the criminal and against the protection of the public' (Brown, 1993).

[77] These powers were extended by the Knives Act 1997 based on a 'reasonable belief' of a senior officer that there are persons carrying dangerous instruments or offensive weapons and were extended again by the Serious Crime Act 2007.

[78] The 'reasonable suspicion' requirement meant little in practice, as research with the Metropolitan Police showed. This requirement was, for the police, satisfied, for example, if someone was running, hurrying or loitering, criteria into which anyone could clearly be fitted. See, Smith (1983). Other powers not requiring reasonable suspicion were included in the Terrorism Act, 2000 and the Antiterrorism, Crime and Security Act 2001.

for up to 36 hours for all arrestable offences (now all indictable offences by the Serious Organised Crime and Police Act 2005). It further allowed judges, subject to conditions, to order non-jury trials and provided incentives to entice defendants to plead guilty and forego a trial.

While it is right to note that access to a lawyer has increased since PACE (see Phillips and Brown, 1998; Skinns, 2009, 2011), this has come when the value of the 'right' itself has been diluted by, *inter alia*, attenuation of the right to silence and strictures on legal advisors and the nature of advice available (to which we will return in later chapters). The courts have shown no appreciation of the established distinction in policing culture between the people the police serve and the 'troublemakers' they seek to control; between the people they do things *for* and those they do things *to* (Hughes, 1971; Shearing, 1981) – a distinction that starts on the streets in the inner city areas that become the focus of police interest and which predictably become the focus of mass street disorders as the style and intensity of policing reproduces the fractured social order in extreme forms (Bridges and Bunyan, 1983; McConville and Shepherd, 1992).

## CONCLUSION

As we have seen, official discourse of judges is dedicated to denying both the originating conditions underlying social disorder and their own role in imposing order on society. In so doing, legitimacy has been sought in the rhetoric of 'system integrity' and 'public confidence' variously manipulated to justify a crime control ideology and claims of a change in culture which enlightened public opinion demands. In the theatre of criminal justice, however, the 'law' has become identified with police practice which, where it continued long enough, gave them a prescriptive right endorsed by judges and then by legislation. Judicial claims concerning the 'rule of law' and the 'right to a fair trial' have proved to be rhetorical devices which mask the system in action. In fostering the idea of the fairness of the police, judges already alter the burden of proof by requiring defendants to displace this assumption. Once judges align themselves with *institutions*, that which they should be assessing, namely, *evidence*, must take second place as the terrible history of miscarriages of justice demonstrates. Judges have never exhibited real belief in trial by jury or indeed in the adversarial system and while the legislature did not get around to openly discouraging trials until 1994, the judges had, as we shall see in the next chapter, already acted in advance.

# 3. State-induced guilty pleas and legitimacy

## INTRODUCTION

In the rhetoric of the common law, the adversarial system placed the burden of proof on the State to be discharged without the compelled assistance of the accused. A guilty plea – which was deemed to be an admission of each and every element of the offence charged enabling a court to move directly to sentencing – had attached to it formal conditions which paid tribute to the trial model: it had to be unequivocal,[1] free from duress and personal to the defendant. These conditions were also necessary because an appeal against conviction in such circumstances was practically ruled out.[2] Although guilty pleas have always been allowed at common law, placing institutional pressures on defendants to plead guilty has to be reconciled with these formal conditions.

## GUILTY PLEA RATES

While many suspects commit the prohibited act and confess to the police under interrogation[3] with, as we have seen, little protection afforded by judges for defendants' 'rights', various forms of pressure have been institutionalised by the State to better secure a compliant posture. The statistics are suggestive. In the Crown Court,[4] guilty pleas as a proportion of all defendants where a plea was entered stood at 70 per cent in 2011. While

---

[1] See *P Foster (Haulage) Ltd v Roberts* [1978].
[2] An appeal may be permitted where a defendant has been given inappropriate, misleading or wrong advice: *Ali Reza Sadighpour v R* [2012]; *R v Boal* (1992); or where there has been a serious abuse of process: *R v Tougher* [2001] and *R v Bhatti* [2000].
[3] An early study by Bottoms and McClean (1976), for example, found that some two-thirds pleaded guilty because they were guilty and confessed to the police.
[4] *Judicial and Court Statistics 2010*, p. 62 and Table A3.6. In magistrates' courts in 2010, 92% of defendants entered guilty pleas.

the guilty plea rate has risen from 56 per cent in 2001 to the current rate of 70 per cent, the evidence shows that at least over the past fifty years, the guilty plea rate has been running at over 50 per cent.[5] The principal court technique for pressurising defendants to plead guilty is the State-induced guilty plea.[6] Our focus here is on the higher courts (Crown Court) where judges seek to persuade defendants to give up the right to jury trial by offering a reduced sentence for a guilty plea (direct sentence-bargaining).

While it is not possible to gauge with any certainty how many defendants who have committed the offence in question would, other things being equal, plead guilty and forego their 'right to trial', there are indications that for many years in the higher courts guilty pleas exceeded 50 per cent in England and Wales. For example, Rose (1971) reported a rate of 57 per cent for 1967 and Bottoms and McClean (1976) a rate of 65 per cent to all charges for 1971–72. There was, however, a story behind these statistics onto which empirical research threw some light.

## EARLY EMPIRICAL RESEARCH

Early research disclosed that covert pre-trial discussions involving barristers and judges were undertaken with regularity, prompting worries at various levels.[7] In her London study, Dell (1971) raised concern about defendants pleading guilty while maintaining a claim of innocence (termed 'inconsistent pleaders'), a general concern also voiced by Davies (1970). Alongside this, in Oxford, McCabe and Purves (1972) found

---

[5] Thus, for example, Zander (1974) was supplied by the Home Office with figures which showed that the not guilty plea rate nationally was 69% in 1968 and 72% in 1969. In his case sample, drawn from London courts, the guilty plea rate at the Old Bailey was 50% and 70% at the Inner London Crown Court.

[6] This includes cases where the prosecutor may offer to accept a plea to a lesser alternative charge or drop one or more charges (charge-bargaining); or agrees to present the 'facts' so that aggravating features are de-sensitised or dissolved altogether (fact-bargaining).

[7] Anecdotal evidence from judges themselves supported the thrust of this research. In evidence to the Royal Commission on Criminal Procedure (1981), Judge Pickles said that 'bargains between judges and defendants as to sentence happen every day ... Some judges send for counsel before the case starts and virtually give directions for 'carving it up' ... Some judges negotiate more subtly, by sending and receiving messages through their clerks or court-clerks.' See also, Judge David (1978): 'Magistrates will be familiar with the scene. The time is 10.29. There is a knock on the retiring-room door and the clerk announces, "Counsel to see you". Thereafter follows a swift-moving scene, more reminiscent of a cattle-auction than a court of law, and the business of the day is all but disposed of.'

that the decision to plead guilty generally followed 'certain good advice' from the defendants' lawyers who, 'drawing on their general court experience and their knowledge of the supposed idiosyncrasies of the local judiciary, play a crucial role in the plea-changing process' (p. 9). While there was no overcharging, there were grounds for believing that 'the prosecution will charge fully, sometimes in order to allow for, if not prompt, plea-bargaining' (McCabe and Purves, 1972, p. 19). In Cardiff, Phil Thomas and Geoff Mungham (1976, 1977) identified solicitors who were willing to make 'deals' on behalf of their clients, supposedly in their best interests, but found that '... pressure of time and conveyor belt operations of certain "successful" solicitors sometimes brings client-orientated values into question' (Thomas and Mungham, 1976, cited in Thomas, 1978).

In Sheffield, the study of Bottoms and McClean (1976) uncovered evidence from a small number of defendants that they had been 'forced' by the police to confess (p. 116) and that there was a small group who, if one accepted their accounts, were 'quite possibly mistaken convictions' (p. 120), the most significant influence on the plea (34 per cent) being their lawyer's advice. They uncovered evidence of last minute pressure from barristers, strong hints in three cases of plea bargaining and, in about 25% of cases, that defendants were unhappy. Expecting a trial for many weeks, when from nowhere a barrister appears on the morning of the trial suggesting a guilty plea, it was 'hardly surprising if defendants acquiesce, faced with this predicament; it is also hardly surprising if some of them subsequently resent having acquiesced to last-minute pressure' (Bottoms and McClean, 1976, p. 130).

In their study of Birmingham's Crown Court, Baldwin and McConville (1977) found that bargaining over plea was common; that virtually all defendants were exposed to a variety of pressures calculated to persuade them to plead guilty; that some defendants claimed to have been offered a specific sentence; that others pleaded guilty on the advice of counsel which was viewed as coercive; and that claims of innocence were not uncommon. In his London study, Seifman (1980) identified pressure/influence to plead guilty from police, solicitors, barristers and judges, and, while generally viewing bargaining as an essential means of dealing with case load, reported that often solicitors and barristers felt that no safeguard existed against innocent defendants being persuaded to plead guilty, stating that 'injustice resulting from practices such as plea bargaining is not a fair trade for the alleviation (or attempts to achieve this goal) of a growing backlog of cases' (p. 191).

## LEGITIMACY AND JUSTIFICATIONS

Collectively, this body of research strongly suggested that, at the very least, the common law's idealised trial model as the standard method of disposition fell short of reality and that an informal practice existed with its own argot, procedures and customs that tended towards non-trial resolution of cases in a private rather than public setting. Should this jealously-guarded world be exposed to the sunlight, courts would be forced to declare such practices inconsistent with adversarial justice or confer legitimacy upon them as a rational procedure.

State-induced guilty pleas are of critical importance in examining the role of courts because they juxtapose maintenance of order and formal rationality. The dilemma for courts historically was how to establish and approve a practice which disposes of large numbers of cases by *aggregate* means in *private* while maintaining the ideology of *open* and *individual* justice. Since State-induced guilty pleas are detached from the rhetoric of adversarial justice, judges were faced with having to construct a new set of 'rational' principles regarding the reception of guilty pleas or risk inconsistency, contradiction and irrationality. It is therefore useful to say something about what might count as 'justifications' in the new order.

As Fuller (1978) has argued, the distinguishing characteristic of adjudication traditionally lies in the fact that it confers on the affected party a peculiar form of participation in the decision, namely: 'that of presenting proofs and reasoned arguments for a decision in his favour' (p. 364). Because adjudication gives formal and institutional expression to the influence of reasoned argument it assumes a burden of rationality not borne by any other form of social ordering and accordingly a 'decision which is the product of reasoned argument must be prepared itself to meet the test of reason' (Fuller, 1978, pp. 366–7).

Securing rationality for State-induced guilty pleas, thus, requires courts to frame and articulate a coherent set of reasons, that is, as Scanlon (1999, p. 19), puts it, considerations 'that really [count] in favour' of some judgment-sensitive attitude underlying this form of decision-making. Reasons here must be embedded in principles and values that relate in a clear way to considerations of justice, fairness and equality and account for and justify the 'judgment-sensitive attitudes' of decision-makers.[8]

---

[8] As Scanlon (1999) puts it, 'judgment-sensitive attitudes' are attitudes that 'an ideally rational person would come to have whenever that person judged there to be sufficient reasons for them and that would, in an ideally rational person, "extinguish" when that person judged them not to be supported by reasons of an appropriate kind' (p. 20).

The legitimacy project, accordingly, involves courts engaging in a *deliberative process based in structured reasoning* of sufficient depth and quality to give assurance that they have considered relevant evidence in a reasoned and coherent manner, irrespective of their eventual conclusions on the practicability, desirability or fairness of the process itself. A process of State-induced pleas is problematic for courts because, as a practice, it does not readily align with conceptions of individual rights in the sense that punishment of persons whose rights have not been protected in the criminal process is generally not justified.[9] The issue directly arose in *R v Turner* (1970).[10]

## LAITY VERSUS THE PROFESSIONALS

Although there had been earlier public indications of the practice in Britain,[11] 'plea bargaining' was brought into the open in *Turner* because, following Turner's plea of guilty, the defendant's solicitor had made it, as Lord Parker CJ put it, 'extremely public throughout the country' that the conviction had been reluctantly entered as a result of private discussions over sentence between defence counsel and the trial judge. The occasion for the disclosure was the appearance of Turner's solicitor, Mr Louis Paul Laity,[12] on *Braden's Week* on BBC Television,[13] which, as anticipated on the show itself, caused a public uproar. The furore resulted both from the allegation that plea bargaining was common practice and from the detail and language used to describe it.

Mr Laity related the story of an 18-year-old boy of previous good character who was charged with stealing two packets of popcorns [sic]. Having been advised to go for trial before a jury and being told at the magistrates'

---

[9] In the British system, individual rights are sought to be protected through the law of evidence and rules of criminal procedure, both of which have been fashioned on the expectation of an adversarial trial, principally, in fact, trial by jury.

[10] Earlier cases such as *R v Hall* (1968) had only partly addressed the issue.

[11] For example, the way in which the case of the tycoon, John Bloom, had been handled caused public discussion. Bloom, having been indicted on eight counts relating to the collapse of his business and a jury panel summoned, at the last minute pleaded guilty to two counts, the other six being dropped, in a deal that resulted in a fine rather than prison. See, for example: *The Guardian*, Tuesday, October 14 1969: '"Plea bargains" on the way?'.

[12] In conformity with Law Society Rules, the solicitor's name was not disclosed.

[13] Broadcast on Saturday, 21 February 1970.

court that he need have no worry of any pressure to persuade him to make an admission of his guilt, when he got to the trial at Crown Court, the Judge sent for his barrister and told his barrister that on the documents which he had, it was clear that the boy was guilty and he thought he would be convicted. The Judge said that if he persisted in a plea of not guilty, then although he had no previous convictions, he would send him to a Detention Centre. If, however, he was 'sensible' and pleaded guilty, he would fine him:

> Mr Laity: His barrister was put in this position of having to go back and tell him of the threat that had been made. In fact, the boy held out for a whole day before he was pressurised by his mother and by the threat that was hanging over him and eventually did change his plea and was fined ten pounds.

When asked to explain why the barrister would not just say 'no' to the Judge, Mr Laity said that the barrister would know that the outcome would be very severe for his client:

> Mr Laity: You see, it's not an idle threat. I've had another case where a similar threat was made where he was offered a six-month sentence if he pleaded guilty. This man had the temerity to go on and fight and finished up with 30 months imprisonment, which was two years more than if he had pleaded guilty . . .
> Braden: Are you also suggesting that he can do the barrister harm – the judge – if the barrister turns him down?
> Mr Laity: Well, I think there is a possibility. I mean, the barristers obviously hope one day probably to be judges. If they offend judges then there's a possibility that the word may go round that they are troublemakers.

When asked was it not the case that barristers simply did what the instructing solicitor told them, he replied:

> Mr Laity: It's quite true but there is this sort of 'old boy' network between the barristers and the judges. A far, far closer relationship exists between them than exists between solicitors and barristers and this does tend to work against our views. We're also . . . if a threat has been held out to a client of ours . . . we're in this difficulty in persuading him to fly in the face of his barrister's advice. Also the barrister, at that stage of the proceedings, represents, you know, a much more potent force to the client. He's dressed in the trappings of the law with his wig and his gown and of course his advice may well supersede any advice that we might give.

But surely, it was asked, why does the barrister not report this to their professional body? Mr Laity replied:

> Mr Laity: It's very difficult to get the judges and the barristers to admit that this goes on. My impression is that they don't consider the public as adult enough

> to know that this goes on and for this reason you can't challenge this. If you tried to challenge it in say the Court of Criminal Appeal you wouldn't get very far with it. Everybody would pretend that it didn't happen and there'd be great resistance to it . . . any question of calling the barrister to give evidence of what went on in the judge's room . . . and I think you would just be stopped wherever you went.

Evidently, the impact of the solicitor's comments was ultimately heightened by the language of 'threats', the cosy relationship between barristers and judges (old-boy network), the concern that counsel's hope of elevation to the judiciary could be harmed by non-cooperation with the judge, the subordinate position of solicitors (they were, unknown to the public, subject to an exclusionary rule so far as intimate discussions in the Judge's Chambers were concerned), the secrecy of the deals and the confidence that there would be official denial that this covert practice was taking place.

Extensive publicity, most of it adverse to the legal system, quickly followed. Under the headline, 'MPs protest at "rigged" trials', an all-party group of MPs stated that they would protest to the Home Secretary about a practice 'that is being carried on to a dangerous extent'.[14] The concerned discussion that ensued in public[15] was, if anything, topped by the Law Society's evasive, snooty and irrelevant public statement:[16]

> Saturday 21 February marked the occasion of an appearance by a Solicitor on the Bernard Braden Show BBC Television.[17] His comments on the fact that Judges sometimes call Counsel to their Chambers to discuss a case in question led to newspaper headlines of 'Rigged trials' etc. . . . A transcript of this interview has been obtained and is being studied by The Law Society. Meanwhile suffice it to note that the solicitor concerned was admitted in 1963 and is not a member of The Law Society.[18]

The justified opprobrium which this attracted was more than matched by the issues of principle which were raised, including: how did this differ from being persuaded by an interrogating officer to plead guilty

---

[14] *Daily Mail*, 23 February 1970.
[15] See, for example, MacPherson (1970); see also, *The Daily Telegraph*, 2 April 1970 and Leon (1970).
[16] *Law Society Gazette*, March 1970, p. 152. See, 'Plea Bargaining – Conflicts of Interest', *New Law Journal* (1970).
[17] This is a reference to *Braden's Week*, BBC Television.
[18] In an act of fitting irony, Mr Paul Louis Laity Esquire was elevated from his rank as Law Society 'outsider' to Recorder by Royal Appointment on 16 February 1990: see *The London Gazette* (1990). He died in 2001.

to the lesser of two charges with the promise of a lighter penalty; whether plea bargaining might be pursued with greater zeal and persuasiveness because the cost to the public purse would be reduced; and whether, with congested lists, conflicting considerations of public and private interest might confuse the pursuit of 'unimpeachable standards of justice'.[19]

Other cases began to surface. Ronald Price, charged with riot, affray and possessing an offensive weapon, was told by his barrister that the Judge wanted him to change his plea to guilty to one charge, the rest would be dropped and that he would receive a lesser sentence if he did. Price fought on and was acquitted, saying: 'It doesn't matter what the cost is, we should be prepared to pay it rather than have the possibility of an innocent person plead guilty under this sort of pressure'. Price's solicitor disclosed that he (along with other solicitors) was not allowed down to the cells to talk to clients without a certificate from the court clerk and without being accompanied by the client's barrister, adding: 'Consequently, we knew nothing about it until the offer had been made'.[20]

Individual cases gave rise to broader investigative journalism in which more questions were raised. Thus, under the banner, 'Are innocent persuaded to plead guilty?' a *Newsight* investigating team looked into 'backstairs deals' which were designed to save 'overworked courts time and money'.[21] Concerns were raised that judges were asking barristers to persuade 'young clients with clean records' to plead guilty, a task which many barristers found 'unpleasant' and around which was 'a wall of silence'.

Hot on the heels of this, JUSTICE (the British section of the International Commission of Jurists) announced that it was establishing an investigation into the practice of plea bargaining.[22] The Law Society's equivocal and timorous stance continued, a comment in its *Gazette* stating that: 'It would be quite wrong to brush aside criticisms that are made of these private meetings between judge and legal advisers, but the lesson to be learned is that the dangers inherent in the practice should be recognised and kept constantly in mind . . .' (*The Daily Mail*, 1970e). The comment is remarkable not only for its failure to engage with the practice but for

---

[19] See, 'Plea Bargaining – Conflicts of Interest', *New Law Journal* (1970).
[20] *Daily Mail*, 13 April 1970. In a similar case, the case of Stephen Carver was given publicity. He too had been made an offer but went to trial and was convicted. His solicitor also complained that he should have been consulted on any deal: *Daily Mail*, 13 April 1970.
[21] *Daily Mail*, 13 April 1970.
[22] *Daily Mail*, 14 April 1970.

70   *Criminal judges*

failing to do so when solicitors, as they publicly stated, were excluded from these 'private meetings'.

## THE FIRST LEGITIMATION PROJECT

### Turner and the Three Freedoms

It was in this setting that the Court of Appeal had to deal with Mr Laity's client, Frank Reginald Turner. In *Turner*, it was alleged that Turner's plea was induced by advice which he believed had come from the judge that, if convicted after trial, he would go to prison but that he would receive a fine or other non-custodial sentence in return for a guilty plea. The plea discussions arose from counsel's concern that he was instructed to accuse the police of fabrication in conjunction with prosecution witnesses. The consequence of such a defence was that any previous convictions of the defendant would almost certainly be placed before the jury increasing the likelihood that the defence would be rejected. No other consequence was, however, permitted. As Lord Parker CJ had put it in *R v Harper* (1967):[23] 'The Court thinks it is quite improper to use language which may convey the impression that a man is being sentenced because he has pleaded not guilty and run his defence in a particular way'.

Despite this clear authority, which was not adverted to in *Turner*, Lord Parker himself now took an entirely different approach.

Although the Court in *Turner* did not say that it was shocked or disturbed by the fact that counsel had consulted the judge in chambers (Curran, 1991), its 'observations' opened the door to State-induced pleas and sought to legitimate such encounters under the cloak of outlawing them. The rhetoric in *Turner* focused on the 'Three Freedoms': the 'complete freedom' of counsel to give advice, if need be in strong terms; the 'complete freedom' of the defendant over plea; and the 'freedom' of access between counsel and judge. Although the Court said that the only matter that was permissible for a judge to discuss in private was that, whatever the plea, the sentence will or will not take a particular *form* (such as probation or a fine) and they could not say anything about quantum, the attempted rationalisation assuredly inaugurated the age of plea bargaining. This primarily flowed from two core precepts in *Turner*: the freedom

---

[23] In line with the earlier case of *R v Behman* (1967) in which Lord Parker had also delivered the Court's judgment.

of access between counsel and the judge; and the purported basis of any sentence differential dependent on plea.

The Court gave two examples of the need to maintain freedom of access to the judge, neither arising out of the facts in issue. The first was that defence counsel may by way of mitigation wish to tell the judge that the accused does not have long to live, perhaps because he is suffering from a serious health condition such as cancer, of which he is *and should remain* ignorant.[24] This melodramatic example, which demonstrated how even judicial inventiveness can run dry, is easily dismissed as risible and, so far as is known, barristers did not thereafter hold their breath waiting for such a case to arise. In any event, an extraordinary situation of this kind could not possibly provide a basis for a general rule.

The second example postulated by Lord Parker was that counsel may wish to discuss with the judge whether it would be proper, in a particular case, for the prosecution to accept a plea of guilty to a lesser offence. This was significant because criminal offences are commonly graded in law (murder/manslaughter; robbery/theft; wounding with intent/wounding; rape/indecent assault, and so on) and this, accordingly, left the judge's door open in practically every case in which counsel sought a discussion on sentence.

## Turner and the Four Deceptions

This open-door policy became of cardinal importance because of the purported basis of any sentence differential dependent on plea offered by *Turner*:

> Counsel must be completely free to do what is his/her duty, namely to give the accused the best advice he/she can and if need be advice in strong terms. This will often include advice that a plea of guilty, *showing an element of remorse*, is a

---

[24] Adams (1971) highlights a number of compelling ethical problems with the 'deliberately induced ignorance' sanctioned by Lord Parker's Third Freedom. Notably that 'Lord Parker . . . seems to give judicial blessing to what can not too fancifully be categorised as a conspiracy between the one party (the doctor) and the agent (the lawyer) to deceive the principal (the patient-client)' (at p. 258). Lord Parker's instruction not to disclose information to the client which reads 'and should remain' is particularly concerning. Contrary to the authority of professional codes and case law admonitions in place, '[i]t is a basic premise of his argument that the advocate enjoys an independent status permitting him to judge, wholly in his own right, what is best for his client' (p. 262). The Third Freedom thus establishes a 'particular and even novel form of privilege personal to the advocate and operative in his favour and at his discretion against the rights of his own client' (p. 263) despite running counter to authority denying this (see e.g. *McMenemy* [1962]).

mitigating factor which *may well* enable the court to give a lesser sentence than would otherwise be the case. Counsel of course will emphasise that the accused must not plead guilty unless he has committed the acts constituting the offence charged. (emphasis added)[25]

In this artfully drawn passage, Lord Parker sought to legitimate private plea discussions by four sleights of hand.[26]

First, without consideration of any of the authorities (in many of which he had been the central actor), Lord Parker replaced the jurisprudentially defensible principle which allows a sentence to reflect *genuine remorse* with a sophistry that allows such a reduction for a guilty plea '*showing an element of remorse*'. This judicial artifice meant that there could now be a 'sentence discount' merely for a guilty plea.

Second, it sought refuge from judicial coercion by placing on defence counsel's shoulders the responsibility for giving the defendant 'best advice'. However, counsel's responsibility could be carried out only under a system-imperative (the 'discount' that judges were commanded not to utter) which conditioned the advice that could be given. Yet that system-imperative had been specifically rejected in *Harper* (1967)[27] in a judgment delivered by Lord Parker himself where it was said that it was 'quite improper' to increase a sentence because a person has pleaded not guilty and, in defending himself, committed perjury.

Third, it purported to leave the judge entirely out of the matter on the basis that judicial involvement 'could be taken to be undue pressure on the defendant'. This, however, involved another artifice since only the judge could offer the 'discount' that counsel was mandated to communicate to the defendant.

Fourth, the assurance that the defendant had '*complete* freedom of choice whether to plead guilty or not guilty' was far from 'complete' since any who elected to plead not guilty were faced with the likelihood of an enhanced sentence should they be convicted, a threat which had hitherto been emphatically rejected by the courts.

---

[25] (1970) 54 Cr. App. R. 352 at 360.

[26] Lord Parker was no stranger to judicial deceit. See Robertson (2013) who provides a graphic account of the circumstances surrounding Stephen Ward's trial stemming from which those attending the Court of Appeal, headed by Lord Parker CJ (with Sachs J and Widgery J) were 'treated to nine minutes of pre-planned judicial cover up', Parker himself operating with a 'lack of frankness' in an 'atmosphere of furtive manipulation' (p. 98). Parker was also at the helm when the re-ordered Judges' Rules were withdrawn from the Royal Commission on the Police (1962) and smuggled into 'law' in 1964.

[27] In this regard, Harper followed *Behman* (above), another judgment of Lord Parker.

## Turner and the Five Consequences

In turn, the four deceptions had five consequences, four of them foreseeable. First, sentence 'discounts' were sought to be legitimated on an unprincipled and, crucially, unpredictable (*'may well'*) basis. Second, counsel, in an effort to resolve the uncertainty (is this a case where a discount 'may well' be given or a case where it 'may well not'?) or to obtain the best discount possible for clients, would inevitably be drawn, as moths to the flame, to seek 'guidance' by private visits to the judge's room. Third, at least some judges would make themselves available for such discussions and some might indeed initiate them. Fourth, all defendants were likely to be placed under such pressure that a guilty plea could no longer be said to be a product of a free choice. Fifth, and perhaps less foreseeable, the Bar Council rolled over and without qualification welcomed *Turner* on the largely self-serving basis that it would 'prevent any further suggestion that an accused person may be persuaded against his wishes to plead guilty'.[28]

In combination, other far-reaching consequences were now foreshadowed. The decision's sub-text *formally* altered the role of the Bar in relation to the trial judge. Any claim to 'independence' by the Defence Bar was now heavily qualified: it was the judges, not the Bar Council, who determined the content of advice that was proper, barristers now being commanded to include the 'discount' in the calculus of advice. Because of the uncertainty surrounding any 'discount', barristers were now placed in a *dependent relationship* with trial judges, underlining their reduced role. In fact, this presaged the total formal subordination of defence lawyers to judges that was to develop, as we shall document, over the next forty years.

Additionally, it was now clear that practice would drive 'law' and that 'law' would reflect a covert move away from the rhetoric of adversary justice. By formally unbolting the door of adversarial justice, judges gave a head of steam to those who operated under a presumption of guilt and who saw defendants, at least those from the lower end of the social stratum, as undeserving of trial. In the event, all of these outcomes would come to fruition, some of the interactions initiated by counsel and some by the judge.[29]

---

[28] See, 'Guilty Pleas: Counsel's Role', *New Law Journal* (1970).
[29] In many cases, it is not clear who initiated the meeting. Thus, for example, Donald Cook's solicitor could only say that both Cook's barrister and prosecution counsel met with the judge privately, Cook himself disclosing that he had been persuaded to plead guilty to a lesser offence so as not to risk a prison sentence: White (1973).

## Counsel-initiated Bargaining

Predictably, counsel spontaneously or at the instigation of the client often sought private meetings with the judge to discover the likely sentence. Such approaches also involved prosecuting counsel who was, generally, happy with the course of events. Thus, in *R v Quartey* (1975):[30] '[Defence counsel] has candidly told us that he himself requested that interview with the Judge so that he might, if possible, find out what was in the Judge's mind as to the likely sentence'; in *Smith* (1989):[31] 'In the instant case both counsel for the prosecution and for the defence thought fit to see the judge about what to this court appears to be a perfectly straightforward case with sentencing options open to the judge dependent upon his view of the facts . . .'; and in *Dossetter* (1999),[32] where counsel visited the trial judge on four separate occasions, '[w]hat took place was the most blatant attempt, particularly by counsel for Dossetter, to engage in plea bargaining with the judge, before Dossetter decided whether or not he was going to plead guilty'.

## Judge-initiated Bargaining

Equally common were cases in which sentence discussions were initiated by the trial judge.[33] Thus, in *R v Cain* [1976],[34] during the prosecution case the judge sent for counsel and said that the defendant had no defence and that if he persisted in his not guilty plea he would get a very severe sentence, but, if he changed his plea that would make a considerable difference to the sentence; in *R v Llewellyn* (1978) the Court of Appeal said: '[t]his Court feels bound to say with all the emphasis it can command, that it can see nothing which justified this learned judge in sending for counsel'; in *R v Winterflood* (1978), at the close of the prosecution case on a charge, *inter alia*, of robbery, the judge called counsel to his room and asked if the defendant would plead guilty to handling stolen goods if that

---

[30] Unreported (4936/A/74, 314/B/75).
[31] Other examples include: *Inns* (1974); *Plimmer* (1975); *Warring-Davies* (1978); *Davis* (1978); *Pitman* (1990).
[32] Unreported (9804926/X3–9805271/X3–9805038/X3).
[33] There are also many cases where it is not clear who initiated the private discussion, for example: *Brook* [1970]; *Howell* [1978].
[34] See also *Bird* [1978]; *Grice* (1977); *Eccles* [1978]; *Cullen* [1985]; *Keily* [1990]; *A-G Ref No.17 of 1998* [1999] in which the judge initiated the sentence discussion in the course of being informed by both counsel that discussions were taking place between prosecution and the defence because, *inter alia*, no prosecution witnesses had attended.

count was added to the indictment; and in *R v James* (1990), at the end of day one, the judge sent for both counsel and made it clear that he thought the prosecution case a strong one, that he had yet to hear any real defence put, and that although the defendant was entitled to have the verdict of the jury, a guilty plea even at a late stage would allow for a reduction in sentence.

**State-induced Guilty Pleas as Practice**

The sheer volume of appeals, which generally represent the tip of the iceberg,[35] must have made clear to the Court of Appeal that State-induced guilty pleas, as empirical research had shown, were embedded in day-to-day practice and, if that was not enough, other indicators abounded. Thus, practitioners and judges spoke not in terms of isolated instances but of their habitual way of dealing with cases. For example, in *Llewellyn* (1978) the Court of Appeal said:

> We have been told that the recollection of very experienced counsel is that this particular judge, at any rate until recently, made a practice of issuing this sort of summons to counsel before the beginning of each case. Indeed [defence counsel], at the outset of this appeal, went so far as to say that this practice was not limited to this judge in this court in South Wales. [Counsel for the Crown] challenged that statement. We do not propose to inquire to what extent (if at all) any such practice has hitherto prevailed in South Wales. (p. 153)

Similarly, in *Plimmer* (1975), counsel 'following a custom if not a practice' went to see the judge whose note to the CA referred to 'my general practice in this matter'.

Indeed, several judges openly stated that this was how business was conducted. Thus, in evidence to the Royal Commission on Criminal Procedure (1981), Judge Pickles said that 'bargains between judges and defendants as to sentence happen every day' and, while conceding that the practice of Crown Court Judges varied widely, added: 'Some judges send for counsel before the case starts and virtually give directions for "carving it up" . . . Some judges negotiate more subtly, by sending and receiving messages through their clerks or court-clerks.' In a similar vein, Judge David (1978) spoke of the experiences of magistrates sitting with judges in the Crown Court as follows:

---

[35] Appeals would not occur where guilty defendants received what they considered a good deal and where defendants, factually guilty or innocent, would be induced to believe that this was the best that could be achieved.

Magistrates will be familiar with the scene. The time is 10.29. There is a knock on the retiring-room door and the clerk announces, 'Counsel to see you'. Thereafter follows a swift-moving scene, more reminiscent of a cattle-auction than a court of law, and the business of the day is all but disposed of.

Rozenberg (2000) reported that a judge held discussions with defence counsel alone and, clearly furious that prosecuting counsel had refused to take part, demanded an explanation from the Chief Prosecutor for Kent, and the Court of Appeal itself acknowledged on many occasions that, as it stated in *R v Smith* (1990), such private discussions were continuing '. . . up and down the country'.

**Court of Appeal Empty Protestations**

Given the widespread nature of the practice, a necessary part of the legitimating process was feigned indignation on the part of the Court of Appeal. In case after case, the Court affected outrage as to what was happening alongside empty exhortations to barristers and judges to mend their ways, as in the following examples[36] spread over the years:

*R v Atkinson* (1978): 'Plea-bargaining has no place in English criminal law . . . Our law having no room for any bargain about sentence between court and defendant, if events arise which give the appearance of such a bargain, then one must be very careful to see that the appearance is corrected.'

*R v Davis* (1978): 'It has been said time and again in this Court that counsel should not approach the judge with the object of discovering what course the judge will take on a plea of guilty. We are surprised that, even now, that message has somehow not percolated . . .'

*Smith* (1989): 'We find it disturbing that despite frequent observations made in this Court discouraging unnecessary visits to the judge's room, they appear to continue up and down the country. In the hope – we hope it is not a vain one – that some notice will now be taken of what we are about to say, we remind those who have responsibility in these matters . . .'

*R v Dossetter* (1999): 'For the last 30 years, this Court has repeatedly said that the nature of discussions, in private, between a judge and counsel, must be limited and exceptional. Plea bargaining, in the sense of seeking to extract from a judge an indication of sentence which he will give if a particular defendant pleads guilty, forms no part of English Criminal jurisprudence.'

---

[36] See also *Warring-Davies* (1978) 'If I may adapt Polonius's advice to his son: "Keep your feet out of the Judges' room"'; *Llewellyn* (1978): 'All we desire to say, with all the emphasis that we can command, that what happened in this case was irregular and ought not to have taken place'; *Pitman* [1990] where the Court cited fully from *Harper-Taylor* (1991) and explained that they had done so 'to draw to the attention of courts up and down the country a point which we hope may at last go home . . .'.

## Individual but Excusable Deviancy

The approach of the Court, in order to preserve at least the 'appearance of justice' in a series of appeals involving judges (and counsel) who had strayed from the line, was to seek to preserve the legitimacy of courts *as institutions* by labelling individual judges and counsel engaging in bargaining practices as *deviants* who needed reminding of their duties in this regard:

> As we see it, the words [in *Turner*] are a direction to the effect that visits to the judge by counsel to discuss sentence are, in nearly all cases, to be strongly deprecated. . . . It was wrong for counsel to approach the judge as they did. It was, we have to say, unfortunate that the judge did not resolutely maintain the very proper attitude which he exhibited at the first visit. (*R v Davis*, 1978)

The Court sought to avert further concern by depicting violations as *isolated aberrations* and deviant counsel and judges were, in turn, largely absolved because they had been acting, it was said, only out of *the best motives*: 'Of course the judge was not striking any bargain with the defence. He was indicating the difference in sentence that a man can on occasions secure in his favour by a plea of guilty' (*Atkinson*); 'No doubt [the Judge] did it with the best of intentions . . .' (*R v Grice*); 'although [the Judge] no doubt had done so with the best of intentions' (*Llewellyn*); 'This was not a case, as [*Inns*] was, where the judge was deliberately putting pressure on the defendant to plead guilty. Indeed, the whole of the unfortunate circumstances which resulted in this pressure came about from the best of motives' (*R v Ryan*); 'No doubt counsel had what was, to say the least, an extremely difficult client who insisted that they made the effort to get this information out of the judge' (*Davis*); and the private discussion was done 'with the best of intentions and produced in the result a shortening of the trial' (*Winterflood*).

## Confusions Sidelined

The problems with State-induced guilty pleas were not, however, confined to individual or aggregate deviancy on the part of the courtroom actors. Whereas the idealised trial model was underpinned by values and principles proclaimed over the years, without such underpinning, confusion reigned at every stage such that the Court was often at a loss as to what to say or do to paper over the cracks. Confusion began with the procedure. For plea bargaining none existed. Accordingly, the Court had to fabricate a set of rules to govern such interactions.

A structural problem was that, in the absence of a trial transcript, the

Court could not be sure what had happened and it was often reliant on the recollections (or notes) of the respective parties, leading to embarrassment when these differed. Early signals had been raised in *R v Hall* (1968) where the Court disposed of the appeal, usually argued 'on the papers', only after the defendant had given 'evidence' to the Court and defence counsel, prosecuting counsel, junior counsel to the prosecutor and the solicitor's managing clerk had been called 'as witnesses'.

In these situations, where the content of the secret meeting was challenged, the court faced various sorts of embarrassment: no procedure existed for finding out what had occurred; it was mortifying, unedifying and unseemly if counsel and judge differed in recollection; it raised difficult questions as to counsel's duty of confidentiality. Sometimes the Court received 'evidence', sometimes it sought information:

> *Williams and Williams* (1975):[37] 'We asked [defence counsel at the original trial] through the Registrar for a statement and she gave that statement. She has also given evidence on oath in the witness box.'
> *Ricardo* (1976):[38] '[T]he Court caused inquiries to be made of counsel who represented the appellant in the court below, of counsel for the Crown and of the Judge.'

In fact, such was the secretive nature of the practice that courtroom actors, including judges, could be led into deceit. An example is given by Henry Cecil Leon (1970)[39] where a judge had made an undisclosed sentence promise to one of two co-defendants which led that defendant to falsely deny that such a promise had been made in cross-examination. The Court of Criminal Appeal (presided over by Lord Hewart CJ) denied that any such action could have happened for the 'unworthy' object of covering up for the trial judge (who had, in Henry Cecil's view, acted in order to attain justice).

This particular example is illustrative of the more general practice of the Court[40] which couched its decisions, in the event of a dispute, without having to take the unedifying step of deciding from among the courtroom actors whose recollection was to be preferred:

---

[37] Unreported (5166/C/74).
[38] Unreported (2243/A/74).
[39] Henry Cecil Leon (Henry Cecil) had been a barrister and County Court Judge before delivering the Hamlyn Lectures from which this account is derived.
[40] In *Warth* (1991) the Court found counsel's recollection plainly at fault on one point since it could compare counsel's note with the actual transcript of the sentencing homily which, it said, accordingly cast a great deal of doubt upon counsel's recollection so far as the rest of the interview with the judge is concerned.

*Llewellyn* (1978):[41] 'Wherever the precise truth may lie, and at this distance of time it is almost impossible to be certain of the accuracy of the various recollections, whether of the judge or of counsel or of the appellant himself or of his co-accused, a man named Jenkins, from whom we have got a statement . . .

We have not thought it necessary to hear oral evidence because to hear oral evidence is not going to carry the matter further.'

*Prasad* (1976):[42] '[N]o member of this Court has the slightest hesitation in unreservedly accepting the evidence of counsel and in rejecting that of [the defendant].'[43]

Greater confusion was caused by the very nature of the private meeting: was it 'confidential' and, if so, whose 'confidentiality' was it? The position seemed clear in *Quartey* (1975) where counsel made two visits to the judge in chambers and the Court of Appeal said that information derived from the judge must be passed to the defendant:

> It was regrettable and wrong that information as to the sentence was sought and received on both occasions. It was regrettable that information was given that the sentence would be reduced if there were a change of plea because such information must be passed to the defendant and might result in a wrong plea being made under pressure.

In *Cain* (1976), however, the Court of Appeal said that counsel (who was not familiar with 'the tariff') could seek confidential guidance from the judge as to sentence so that the client could be advised, but the fact that the judge had given defence counsel this guidance must not be disclosed to the defendant, *as the judge and counsel had a 'confidential relationship'*. By contrast, in *R v Bird* (1977) the Court ruled that counsel have a duty to the client to make public what ought not to have been said in the privacy of Judge's Chambers. Indeed, in *R v Harper-Taylor and Bakker* (1988) counsel for Bakker had revealed his instructions in a meeting in Chambers but thereafter his account was never given nor sought by the Court of Appeal because that 'might very well make matters worse'. Yet in

---

[41] A similar stance was adopted in *R v Inns* (1974) where recollections differed between counsel (supported by notes made shortly after the event) and the judge. See also, *Smith* (1989) in which there was an 'unseemly' dispute as to what was said between the judge's account and the affidavit evidence of defence and prosecuting counsel.

[42] Unreported (362/C/76).

[43] The Court reached this conclusion even where the evidence (of a managing clerk) regarding a visit said to be made to the defendant at the Central Criminal Court cells was not supported by any reference in the Visitors' Book.

*R v Harper-Taylor* (1991)[44] the Court of Appeal went so far as to describe the embarrassment of private meetings as involving the risk to solicitors and counsel for other parties, who, '. . . might hear something said to the judge which they would rather not hear, putting them into a state of conflict between their duties to their clients, *and their obligation to maintain the confidentiality of the private room*' (emphasis added).[45]

### Dangers Sidelined

Just as the Court cast aside the professional problems plea bargaining engendered, so it marginalised the dangers to defendants. These dangers came in two forms: innocent defendants who were pressurised into pleading guilty by loss of confidence in their own counsel and the threat of a heavy sentence if they were convicted at trial; and the ancillary problem of defence counsel acquiescing to the dictates of an overbearing judge thereby destroying the freedom of choice the defendant was supposed to enjoy. We illustrate these dangers with two cases.

In *R v Peace* (1976), the defendant pleaded guilty to arson of his own shop having first met his barrister on the day set for trial. He said that he formed the impression that his barrister was not familiar with his case, told him that he would be sent to prison for three or four years if convicted and that if he brought in his girlfriend to support his defence of alibi she might be prosecuted for perjury. Subsequent to the conviction, a private investigation showed not only that he did not commit the crime but also that he *could not have committed it* and he was granted a free pardon. Because it was uncertain whether a pardon removed the criminal record, he applied to the Court of Appeal to have the conviction formally set aside. The Court of Appeal ruled that the facts did not make the plea a nullity because a defendant who had pleaded guilty following advice of the kind given 'albeit he did so unhappily and regretfully' could not be said to have lost his power to make a voluntary and deliberate choice.

As we have seen, while defence counsel may seek a sentence indication in private, there are many occasions where the initiative comes from the judge or where, whoever called for the meeting, the judge imposes their view on counsel with consequent disastrous effects upon the defendant's decision-making. A classic example is *R v Inns* (1974). Inns, a 17-year-old boy and his co-defendant were charged with theft of copper wire. Before arraignment,

---

[44] Endorsed in *Pitman* [1991].
[45] See Curran (1991).

the judge called counsel to his room. Counsel for Inns prepared a note of what happened and this was agreed by all the other counsel present:[46]

> Judge: I understand there is some doubt as to whether your clients are pleading guilty. [Counsel for Inns]: My client will be pleading not guilty. Judge: What is his defence? [Counsel for Inns]: He says he was not dishonest; he thought the wire was abandoned. Judge: This was presumably signalling wire? [Prosecuting counsel]: Yes. Judge: If these men are asking the jury to believe that they thought they could just go and take railway property, one of them used to be an employee of the railway. If that is what they are saying, if they are convicted, they will go to detention centre. That is quite certain. [Counsel for Inns]: I was sceptical myself when I read the papers, but if you look at the wire – it is in court – it looks as though it could have been abandoned – lots of pieces just thrown together. Judge: I was virtually standing counsel to the railways for about 20 years at the Bar – I know all about signalling wire. I take a very dim view indeed of going on to railway property and stealing things. If they are convicted, they will be going away. If they plead now, I may be able to take a more lenient course – I may be able to implement recommendations in the social inquiry reports. . . .
>
> [After returning to report to Inns and his co-defendant, counsel returned to see the judge]
>
> [Counsel for Inns]: My instructions are that Inns will be pleading not guilty. [Counsel for co-defendant]: My client instructs me in the same way. Judge: Well, you know the position. They both made statements saying that they took it and were going to sell it. [Counsel for Inns]: Their statements are not inconsistent with what they are saying now. Judge: And they ran away when the police came. [Counsel for Inns]: In the circumstances I must ask for trial before another judge. Judge: No, you will have to take your chances before me. There is no question of another judge. It is now 11.15 – it's a pity we have not got on with it. I can't sit tomorrow if we do not finish, it will have to go over to Wednesday. I think it is fairer that the speeches should all come together. [Counsel for Inns]: I will have to renew my application in open court for the record. Judge: You are welcome to, but I can tell you I will not be granting it. [Counsel for co-defendant]: I should say that I support my friend's application. Judge: Well, you have heard what I have said.[47]

Although the Court of Appeal was forced to declare the conviction a nullity, the defendant having 'crumpled' on receiving this news and pleaded guilty, it showed no recognition that such encounters were very likely to happen since it knew full well that many plea discussions were at the initiative of judges who felt able to cajole or browbeat defence counsel, with an inevitable impact upon the defendant. Indeed, the danger of such

---

[46] The Judge took a different line and the Court of Appeal said that it did not intend to decide whose recollection was the most reliable.
[47] (1974) 60 Cr. App. R. 231 at 232–3.

coercion was precisely the reason why historically judges had been formally excluded from involvement in private discussions.

**Lauding Adversary Justice**

As we have seen, the basic ideological framework of the adversarial system envisaged a trial. This ideal model included public open examination of evidence through witness testimony, cross-examination under fixed procedures and rules regarding relevance and admissibility of evidence and final determination by an independent fact-finding body. Although officially-induced guilty pleas in Judge's Chambers contradicted this model in almost every way, courts were faced with a practice which, being apparently uncontrollable, had to be denied and the adversary model lauded.

Unexpectedly, soon after the *Turner* decision, the Court of Appeal attempted to endorse plea bargaining in the case of *Cain* in which Chief Justice Widgery (who had been a party to the decision in *Turner*) said:

> It was trite to say that a plea of guilty would generally attract a somewhat lighter sentence than a plea of not guilty after a full dress-contest on the issue. Everybody knew that it was so, and there was no doubt about it. Any accused person who did not know about it should know it. The sooner he knew the better.[48]

Such blunt and public endorsement of plea bargaining through a sentence differential gave voice to the Court's social control function but without any legitimating rhetoric. This crude approach proved unacceptable to the extent that the Chief Justice was himself embarrassingly forced to retract by issuing a very short Practice Direction,[49] albeit couched in terms of the withdrawal of the wounded rather than the flight of the defeated: 'The decision in Reg. v. Cain ... has been subject to further consideration by the Court of Appeal. In so far as it is inconsistent with Reg. v. Turner ... the latter decision should prevail.'

However, as the Chief Justice/Court of Appeal was made aware that the rhetoric of the adversary system could not be crassly abandoned, its skeletal figure continued to be displayed in rhetoric, made the easier, as we have seen in Chapter 2, precisely because it had never had any flesh on its bones. Symbolic homage was now paid to the trial just as it was being consigned to the wings:

---

[48] *The Times* (London), 23 February 1976, at 11.
[49] Practice Direction (Crime: Inconsistent Decisions) 1976 July 26 WLR 799.

*Harper-Taylor* (1991): 'A first principle of criminal law is that justice is done in public, for all to see and hear. By this standard, a meeting in the judge's room is anomalous: the essence, and indeed the purpose, being that neither the defendant nor the jury nor the public are there to hear what is going on.'

*Bird* [1978]: 'It has long been one of the essential requirements of our system of justice that it should not only be done but those that see what is done should respect what is done and understand that it is done as a matter of justice and for no other reason.'

*Inns* (1974): 'The whole basis of a plea on arraignment is that in open court an accused freely says what he is going to do; and the law attaches so much importance to a plea of guilty in open court that no further proof is required of the accused's guilt. When the accused is making a plea of guilty under pressure and threats, he does not make a free plea and the trial starts without there being a proper plea at all.'

*Dossetter* (1999): 'Plea bargaining, in the sense of seeking to extract from a judge an indication of sentence which he will give if a particular defendant pleads guilty, forms no part of English Criminal jurisprudence . . . Justice in this country, save in the most exceptional circumstances, identified by Lord Parker in *Turner*, must be conducted in public . . .'

## The Search for 'Legitimacy'

As the adversary model continued to be celebrated, judges faced the problem of unabated plea bargaining to which legitimating strategies had to be applied. In seeking to secure formal legitimacy a new rhetoric had to be developed which avoided the crudeness of *Cain* but permitted the practice to continue. An early signal that the expediency of plea bargaining would not be easily set aside was given in *Llewellyn* (1978):

> We do not wish to say anything in this judgment which will make the task of circuit judges, who carry the burden of so much indictable crime tried in this country, more difficult or which will result in greater and unnecessary expenditure of time or which will preclude a proper pre-trial review being held at the proper time. (p. 153)

In *Atkinson* (1978) the court made similar hints:

> Nevertheless it should not be thought that we are in any way criticising the practice of pre-trial review in criminal cases. It is well known that the Crown Court throughout the country has tremendous problems in the expedition of its cases and in organising the lists, and it may indeed be helpful, even in a simple case such as this, for the court to know whether there is going to be a plea of guilty or whether the matter will proceed to trial.[50]

---

[50] (1978) 67 Cr. App. R. 200 at 202.

Because of case load concerns, it was, therefore, inevitable that the Court of Appeal would, in one form or another, seek legitimacy through the guise of *administrative efficiency*. Hence, a sentence discount was justified if it saved 'public time and money' (*R v Phillips*, 1976); because a defendant who pleads guilty can say, 'Well, I am sorry. I am showing, by pleading guilty, I am not going to put the public to further expense" (*Atkinson*, 1978). In this understanding, trials are not the desired method of disposition and they are more than an inconvenience; they are a *nuisance*, as the Court set out in *R v Boyd* (1980):

> The policy of the courts is that where a man does plead guilty, which does give rise to public advantage and avoids the expense and *nuisance of a trial*, which may sometimes be a long one, the court encourages pleas of guilty by knocking something off the sentence which would have been imposed if there had not been a plea of guilty. (emphasis added)[51]

This approach did not square with traditional sentence justifications which gave recognition to remorse or, as *Turner* had qualified it, 'an element of remorse', and so the Court adjusted its stance. Remorse did not have to be present in fact; it could be *imputed* by the courts.

> *R v Landy* (1995): 'As a matter of general policy, courts will give credit to a defendant who pleads guilty because the court recognises thereby some remorse, the savings of time and the avoidance of witnesses having to attend court.'
> *R v Hastings* (1996): 'It is a well-established principle that courts will recognise a plea of guilty, whether on the grounds of public policy or as an indication of remorse in appropriate cases, by reducing the sentence which would otherwise have been imposed in order to reflect the plea.'

Such an approach, in which the discount becomes detached from the individual case underlines the move to aggregate justice which had always been the sub-text of State-induced guilty pleas.

Contingencies were built in to seek to avoid the conveyor-belt image of justice, to increase the discretion of the judge and to further buttress the notion of formal legitimacy. Thus, while a discount was ordinarily to be accorded to those who pleaded guilty, it could be reduced or withheld where the defendant had engaged in a 'tactical' plea or where the defendant had been caught red-handed and a conviction was deemed inevitable (*R v Costen*, 1989). Thus, the Court of Appeal upheld the sentence in *Landy* (1995)[52] where the trial judge had said:

---

[51] (1980) 2 Cr. App. R. (S.) 234 at 235.
[52] See also, *Hastings* (1996).

> You pleaded guilty and ordinarily that would attract a reduction in sentence but the circumstances in which you were arrested, namely, at the wheel of the [stolen] car, albeit a car upside down, your conviction for this offence was inevitable and therefore your plea of guilty, it seems to me has little, if any, weight to carry in determining what is a proper sentence.[53]

There were other uncertainties. Thus, in *Regina v R (a Juvenile)* the Court of Appeal, in dealing with a case of car theft and reckless driving, said that:

> [A]lthough in most cases the court would give credit for a plea of guilty, the public interest dictated that that was not to be seen as an inflexible rule. There were cases in which, despite the plea of guilty, the offences were of such seriousness, the more so when it was so prevalent in a locality as the instant offence was and potentially highly dangerous to life and limb the public interest required the imposition of the maximum sentence.

More generally, the Court set out other qualifications to the 'ordinary' discount, though in flawed reasoning:[54]

> *R v Hollington and Emmens* (1986): 'The Court had long said that discounts on sentences were appropriate in guilty plea cases, but everything depended on the circumstances. If a man was arrested and at once admitted guilt and cooperated with the police, he could expect a substantial discount: but if a man was arrested in circumstances in which he cannot hope to put forward much of a defence, he cannot hope for much by way of discount. In between came the sort of case where the court had been put to considerable trouble as a result of a tactical plea.'

Ironically, such contingencies reinforced the dependency of defence counsel on the judge and intensified the very thing it was purporting to limit.

## CONCLUSION

While the process of establishing the foundations of plea bargaining compromised the integrity of courts and laid bare superficial and disingenuous reasoning, assembling its infrastructure simply marked the start of senior judges' efforts to rationalise a non-individuated assembly-line production

---

[53] [1995] 16 Cr. App. R. (S.) 908 at 909–10.
[54] The fact that a person is caught red-handed does not exclude genuine remorse nor does it lessen the savings that might be made (in time, cost and witness inconvenience) by a guilty plea.

process. Once, however, practice became detached from the formal principles which were earlier claimed to have animated the system, courtroom actors were thrown back on the personal, anecdotal and the pragmatic; the values represented became detached not only from the vaunted adversarial principles but from principles of rationality, consistency and morality.

Underpinning this movement, at both the formal and substantive levels, was a change in the relational position of judges and counsel which left a more significant legacy. Whatever the actualities of daily practice in the past, *Turner* and its progenies marked the formal subordination of the Bar, a position accepted with little resistance from the Bar Council. From now on, defence counsel would be in a dependent relationship, seeking the favour of trial judges or placing their clients in peril. The humiliation of the Defence Bar had not yet been achieved; that, as we shall see in the next chapter, was a task that would soon be assimilated by other judges and the legislative change, which they impelled.

# 4. Lowering the Bar

## INTRODUCTION

The formal re-ordering of power relations within the criminal justice system which *Turner* had instituted was only the start of a transformation which would continue for the next forty years. Over this period, the often-claimed 'neutrality' of the trial judge would be openly discarded, the professed 'independence' of the Bar further attenuated and 'the interests of the client' sidelined on the altar of State-defined 'efficiency'. In this chapter, we trace how the deep-seated message of *Turner* was brought to the surface and sanitised in the quest for the proclaimed 'cost-efficient' disposal of criminal cases.

## ROYAL COMMISSION ON CRIMINAL JUSTICE

As courts were putting in place the building blocks of State-induced guilty pleas and characterising trials as a 'nuisance', formal political authorisation in a 'law and order' climate was soon forthcoming. The starting point was the Report of the Royal Commission on Criminal Justice (RCCJ), 1993[1] which, ironically, was established as a damage limitation exercise[2] following exposure of the miscarriages of justice for alleged terrorist bombings of the *Guildford Four* and the *Birmingham Six* and the anticipated overturning of other similar miscarriages involving, among others, the *Maguire Seven*, *Judith Ward*, *Stefan Kiszko*, the *Taylor Sisters*, *Ivan Fergus* and, over a period of more than twenty years, an astonishing number (over fifty) of false convictions secured through torture, fabricated 'confessions' and suppressed evidence by the discredited West Midlands Serious Crime Squad and others by Metropolitan Police Officers stationed at Stoke Newington police station. It is doubly ironic that underlying many of these miscarriages of justice was false and perjured police evidence, the challenging of which, as in the *Turner* line of cases processed over the same time

---

[1] Cm 2263 at p.113.
[2] This is the general role of such Commissions: Thomas (1982).

period, had been of such concern to some defence lawyers and judges that they preferred instead to persuade defendants to enter guilty pleas.

Under its terms of reference the RCCJ was asked to 'examine the effectiveness of the criminal justice system in England and Wales in securing the conviction of those guilty of criminal offences and the acquittal of those who are innocent, having regard to the efficient use of resources . . .'. For present purposes we can note that its proposals were based upon a misreading of its own terms of reference so that the background resource context became a systemic *objective* of the way criminal justice was to be understood.[3]

The RCCJ [4] ultimately recommended that:

> . . . at the request of defence counsel on instructions from the defendant, judges should be able to indicate the highest sentence that they would impose at that point on the basis of the facts as put to them. . . . We envisage that the procedure which we recommend would be initiated solely by, and for the benefit of, defendants who wish to exercise a right to be told the consequence of a decision which is theirs alone.

While the idea that the proposed procedure would be initiated by defendants disguised the process,[5] the assertion that defendants had a 'right' to know the 'highest sentence' was either an example of unexpected creativity on the part of the Commission or it was a further example of the malleability of language. Its merit appears to be only that it was broadly in accord with the responses of barristers[6] and judges[7] to a question which asked them whether *Turner* should be reformed to allow 'full and realistic discussion between counsel and the judge about plea and especially sentence'.[8] However, the recommendation gave short shrift to the dangers of the *sentence discount*, the RCCJ merely noting that 'it would be naive to suppose that innocent people never plead guilty because of the prospect

---

[3] See, McConville and Mirsky (1993a).

[4] Cm 2263 at p.113. The Royal Commission on Criminal Procedure (1981) considered that the issue of discretion in sentencing was outside its terms of reference and accordingly they refrained from making any recommendations on this subject.

[5] The *Crown Court Study* (Zander and Henderson, 1993) shows that the 'sentence discount' influenced over half of those pleading guilty (p. 146) but was unable to answer how defendants as a whole got to know of the discount in the first place, though obviously the legal profession must have played a significant role.

[6] Eighty-six per cent of prosecution barristers and 88% of defence barristers agreed with that question.

[7] Sixty-seven per cent of judges agreed the need for reform.

[8] Zander and Henderson (1993), p.145.

of a *sentence discount*;[9] nor did it sit easily with its own research findings that some '1,400 possibly innocent persons [pleaded] guilty every year'.[10]

If protection of the innocent and conformity with commonly understood adversarial principles were not at the forefront of the Commission's proposals, the animating force was readily located in its concern over 'the efficient use of resources'. The RCCJ was particularly exercised over so-called 'cracked trials', cases listed for trial by jury but where, often on the day of the trial itself, the defendant pleads guilty:[11]

> 'Cracked' trials create serious problems, principally for all the thousands of witnesses each year – police officers, experts and ordinary citizens – who come to court expecting a trial only to find that there is no trial because the defendant has decided to plead guilty at the last minute. This causes in particular unnecessary anxiety for victims whose evidence has up to that point been disputed.[12]

Although not adopted wholesale, the RCCJ's proposals in regard to sentence discounts were a foundation stone for a series of changes which ultimately impacted upon the question of court and judicial legitimacy.

In the light of the critical reception of the RCCJ's Report on this and other topics, the first legislative intervention was a tentative but important step towards formalising plea bargaining. It came with the Criminal Justice and Public Order Act, 1994 (CJPOA, 1994) section 48, now replaced by the Criminal Justice Act, 2003, section 144(1) of which provides:

> In determining what sentence to pass on an offender who has pleaded guilty to an offence before that or another court a court must take into account:
> (a) the stage in the proceedings for the offence at which the offender indicated his intention to plead guilty,[13] and
> (b) the circumstances in which this indication was given.

Section 174(2)(d) of the same Act added that where as a result of taking into account any matter mentioned in section 144(1), the court imposes a punishment on the offender which is less severe than the punishment it

---

[9] RCCJ (1993), p. 110 (emphasis added).
[10] Ibid., p. 111.
[11] Ibid.
[12] Ibid.
[13] The meaning of the stage at which a defendant 'indicated his intention to plead guilty' (which is relevant to the amount of sentence discount, if any, which can be expected) was considered in *Caley & Ors v R* [2012]: 'The first reasonable opportunity is normally either at the Magistrates' Court or immediately on arrival in the Crown Court – whether at a preliminary hearing or by way of a locally-approved system for indicating plea through his solicitors' (p. 18).

would otherwise have imposed it must state that fact in open court. Since neither of these provisions *required* that judges offer a discount let alone state the extent of any discount actually given, practices in this regard would remain a matter for individual judges unless and until the recommendations were accorded judicial and political authority. 'Authority' was to come from the Auld Report (2001), an official one-man inquiry into the criminal justice system. Even as it demonstrated the limits of self-education, the Auld Report was set to shape the future of criminal justice in England and Wales.

## AULD REPORT

As with the RCCJ, 'effectiveness' and 'efficiency' were the core criteria moving the Auld inquiry,[14] with the terms of reference being to inquire into:

> the practices and procedures of, and the rules of evidence applied by, the criminal courts at every level, with a view to ensuring that they deliver justice fairly, by streamlining all their processes, increasing their *efficiency* and strengthening the *effectiveness* of their relationships with others across the whole of the criminal justice system, and having regard to the interests of all parties including victims and witnesses, thereby promoting public confidence in the rule of law. (emphasis added)

Although the Review was said to be concerned with how the criminal justice system works in so far as it involves the courts but not with criminal justice policy or philosophy or principles of sentencing,[15] it undertook no systematic research. Its recommendations went to the heart of sentencing and its link to the process by which pleas of guilty are, to use a neutral word, secured, and to the general obligations and role performance of defence lawyers. The basic recommendations of Auld were:

- there should be . . . a system of sentencing discounts graduated so that the earlier the tender of plea of guilty the higher the discount

---

[14] This was confirmed by the Lord Chancellor announcing the appointment: 'The Government's aim is to provide criminal courts which are, and are seen to be: modern and in touch with the communities they serve; efficient; fair and responsive to the needs of all their users; co-operative in their relations with other criminal justice agencies; and with modern and effective case management to remove unnecessary delays from the system' (Auld, 1991, Foreword, para. 2).

[15] Auld (2001), Foreword, para. 4.

for it, coupled with a system of advance indication of sentence for a defendant considering pleading guilty;
- on the request of a defendant, through his advocate, the judge should be entitled, formally to indicate the maximum sentence in the event of a plea of guilty at that stage and the possible sentence on conviction following a trial;
- the request to the judge and all related subsequent proceedings should be in court, in the presence of the prosecution, the defendant and his advisers and a court reporter, but otherwise in private, and should be fully recorded;
- the judge should enquire, by canvassing the matter with both advocates, as to the mental competence and emotional state of the defendant and as to whether he might be under any pressure falsely to admit guilt;
- the prosecution and defence should be equipped to put before the judge all relevant information about the offence(s) and the defendant, including any pre-sentence or other reports and any victim impact statement, to enable the judge to give an indication;
- the judge should only give an indication if and when he is satisfied that he has sufficient information and if he considers it appropriate to do so.

## AULD'S UNDERLYING PHILOSOPHY

> It should be recollected, too, that the object of penal laws is the protection and security of the innocent; that the punishment of the guilty is resorted to only as the means of attaining that object. When, therefore, the guilty escape, the law has merely failed of its intended effect; it has done no good indeed, but it has done no harm. But when the innocent become the victims of the law, the law is not merely inefficient, – it does not merely fail of accomplishing its intended object – it injures the persons it was meant to protect; it creates the very evil it was to cure, and destroys the security it was made to preserve. (Romily, 1810, p.74)

Under conventional formulations,[16] the criminal justice system posits that the State and the defendant are adversaries and that the defendant not the State is to obtain the benefit of the doubt. The State is presumed to be an intrusive force which, because it is claiming the right to punish one of its citizens, is required to justify its claim through reliance upon

---

[16] See, for example, McConville and Mirsky (1993b).

legally sufficient and admissible evidence proving beyond reasonable doubt that the defendant has committed each and every element of the offence charged, no matter how minor or inconsequential any component part of the offence might at first sight appear. The defendant in turn may rest without offering a scintilla of evidence by showing that the State has failed to discharge its burden. The system is weighted in this way to guard against the possibility that a factually innocent individual might be found guilty. It consciously means that on occasion, factually guilty persons may be acquitted because the State is unable to discharge its burden. The distinction between legal and factual guilt has traditionally been at the core of the adversarial system and its rules and procedures have been designed to ensure that factual guilt does not displace legal guilt as the test to determine whether the defendant should be convicted of the offence charged.

The keystone of Auld's recommendations was his embedded re-characterisation of the basis of the criminal justice system in opposition to this conventional understanding, as set out below:[17]

> ... regard must be had to the prosecution's obligation to make the court sure of guilt and the defendant's right of silence. But neither is threatened by requiring a defendant to identify with some precision the matters of fact and/or of law that he intends to put in issue. If his intention is to put the prosecution to proof of everything, or only to take issue on certain matters, he is, of course, entitled to do so when the matter reaches trial. But to delay telling the court and the prosecution what he challenges as a matter of tactics, has nothing to do with the burden and standard of proof or his right of silence. Those fundamental principles are there to protect *the innocent defendant* from wrongful conviction, not to enable *the guilty defendant* to engage in tactical manoeuvres designed to frustrate a fair hearing and just outcome on the issues he intends to take. (emphasis added)

Within this re-configured habitus, populated only by 'the innocent defendant' and 'the guilty defendant', Auld sought to remove the obstacles to his proposals. In particular, the burden of proof, the standard of proof and the presumption of innocence of the defendant would not be compromised because there was no longer a requirement that the State, of and by itself, would have to discharge the burden of proof. By this sophistry, Auld sought to remove the traditional distinction between factual and legal guilt, and all his recommendations are to be understood in this light.

Yet it is manifestly the case that the distinction *does* underlie the criminal justice system, so that, for example, English courts will not convict (or uphold convictions already entered into) on the basis of an uncorroborated

---

[17] Auld (1991), Chapter 10, para. 5.

'confession' which has been or may have been extorted by torture; where the prosecution has completely failed in its duties of disclosure (*R v Barkshire & Ors* [2011]); where they are not satisfied with the integrity of the prosecution (*R v Wilson* [2011]); where prosecution evidence amounts to a serious perversion of the course of justice (*Joof & Ors v R* [2012]); where the basis of the conviction obtained by a plea of guilty is not made out in law (*Nolan and Howard v R* [2012]); or where the prosecution is an abuse of process.

But the guilty/innocent matrix set up by Auld had a much more important ideological function. As we shall see, this contrived dichotomy laid the foundation for an enhancement of the courts' social control function sheltered under a re-ordered canopy of legitimacy with twin elements. First, the State-induced guilty plea process was premised on the basis that defendants were, with few exceptions, guilty and undeserving, ready, if not actively deterred, to work the weak spots of the system under the protection of a 'sporting theory of justice'. This characterisation paved the way for systematic denigration of defendants as the pathologically dishonest and undeserving in society. Second, since the only realistic way in which suspects/defendants could exploit the weak spots would be through their lawyers, they too would need to be denigrated and their capacity for disturbing the orderly and efficient progress of dispositions attenuated. The precursor of this re-arrangement is captured in Auld's formulation of a core 'problem' of the system, with its artful employment of 'and/or', namely: 'the uncooperative or feckless defendant and/or his defence advocate who considers that the burden of proof and his client's right to silence justifies frustration of the orderly preparation of both sides' case for trial'.[18]

## AULD AND THE POLITICIANS

The Auld Report fed into the law and order agenda of the government, spelled out in the White Paper *Justice for All* (Home Office, 2002),[19] the basic premise of which was that while 'the fundamental principle' that the prosecution must prove its case remains, it does not follow that the system should enable a defendant 'to obstruct justice by inaction or by abuse of process'.[20] A criminal trial, it was said, was 'not a game under which a guilty defendant should be provided with a sporting chance'. Its concern with 'cracked trials', was founded on the view that '*many in the system*

---

[18] Auld (1991), Chapter 10, para.8.
[19] Cm. 5563.
[20] Home Office (2002), at para. 1.8.

*believe* that defendants' delayed guilty pleas are a tactic employed in the hope that witnesses will lose patience and decide not to testify' (emphasis added).[21] In a policy statement that tracked the proposals of Auld, *Justice for All* reassuringly stated: 'We do not take lightly the danger of putting innocent defendants under pressure to plead guilty'.[22]

One significant outcome of this policy set was the creation of a Criminal Procedure Rules Committee (Chaired by the Lord Chief Justice), provision for which had been made by the Courts Act, 2003 and which came into force on 4 April 2004 (see Chapter 6). We can note briefly here that it sought to emulate the Woolf reforms of civil justice requiring judges to '*manage*' litigation through such things as setting timetables, encouraging the parties to exchange information as early as possible, all in the context of requiring courts and all parties to deal with cases '*justly*', a concept which includes dealing with cases '*efficiently and expeditiously*' and '*acquitting the innocent and convicting the guilty*'. Courts were also required to 'have regard' to 'definitive guidelines' published by the Sentencing Guidelines Council (now the Sentencing Council) on the Reduction of Sentences for Guilty Pleas, which included the responsibility of the judge to find out whether defendants had been advised about credit to be obtained for a guilty plea. Nevertheless, so far as judges were concerned, no formal guidance had been issued post-*Turner*, a task which now confronted the Court of Appeal in *R v Goodyear*.[23]

## GOODYEAR

Given the contradictory (often, disobedient) responses by individual judges to *Turner*, the unusual step was taken to convene a Full Court of five judges (instead of the normal three judges) in the case of *Goodyear*. Some departure, it was said, from the principles in *Turner* was required by statute and there was no longer any absolute prohibition against an advance indication of sentence given the changes introduced at magistrates' courts by the 'plea before venue' procedure in which the defendant was entitled to request an indication of sentence, that is, whether a custodial or non-custodial sentence would be more likely to be imposed if he/she were to be tried summarily and to plead guilty.[24]

---

[21] Ibid., at para. 4.41.
[22] Ibid., at para. 4.43.
[23] (2005) EWCA Crim 888.
[24] Schedule 3, Criminal Justice Act 2003.

For the *Goodyear* judges, however, statutory intervention represented a step-change in criminal justice: 'These matters sufficiently demonstrate a very different culture to that which obtained when *Turner* was decided. In all these circumstances the time has therefore come for this Court to reconsider it.'[25] This is at best disingenuous since the 'very different culture' had been initiated by *judges* long in advance of statutory intervention which itself arose out of the Report of one of its own, Auld.[26]

## THE *GOODYEAR* GUIDELINES

A summary of the main guidelines in *Goodyear* is as follows:

**The judge**
55  The judge should not give an advance indication of sentence unless one has been sought by the defendant.
56  He is also entitled in an appropriate case to remind the defence advocate that the defendant is entitled to seek an advance indication of sentence.
62  ...Where appropriate, there must be an agreed, written basis of plea. Unless there is, the judge should refuse to give an indication . . .

**The defence**
63  Subject to the judge's power to give an appropriate reminder to the advocate for the defendant . . . the process of seeking a sentence indication should normally be started by the defendant.
64  ... the defendant's advocate should not seek an indication without written authority, signed by his client, that he, the client wishes to seek an indication.
65  The advocate is personally responsible for ensuring that his client fully appreciates that:
    (a) he should not plead guilty unless he is guilty;
    (b) any sentence indication given by the judge remains subject to the entitlement of the Attorney-General (where it arises) to refer an unduly lenient sentence to the Court of Appeal;
    (c) any indication given by the judge reflects the situation at the time when it is given. . . .

---

[25] *R v Goodyear* (2005), para. 45.
[26] Indeed the legitimating trick of invoking nebulous 'culture change' played a pivotal role in justifying a further (major) transfer of power from the defence lawyer to the judge with the case law immediately preceding the introduction of the Criminal Procedure Rules in 2005. See, for example, Judge LJ in *R v Chaaban* [2003] who felt inclined to take the opportunity to 'highlight a significant recent change' which he excused as 'less heralded than it might have been' (para. 37). See further, Chapter 6, *infra*.

66 An indication should not be sought while there is any uncertainty between the prosecution and the defence about an acceptable plea or pleas to the indictment, or any factual basis relating to the plea. Any agreed basis should be reduced into writing before an indication is sought . . .

67 The judge should never be invited to give an indication on the basis of what would be, or what would appear to be a 'plea bargain' . . .

68 In the unusual event that the defendant is unrepresented, he would be entitled to seek a sentence indication of his own initiative. There would be difficulties in either the judge or prosecuting counsel taking any initiative, and informing an unrepresented defendant of this right. That might too readily be interpreted as or subsequently argued to have been improper pressure.

**The prosecution**

70 . . .
   (a) If there is no final agreement about the plea to the indictment, or the basis of plea, and the defence nevertheless proceeds to seek an indication, which the judge appears minded to give, prosecuting counsel should remind him of this guidance, that normally speaking an indication of sentence should not be given until the basis of the plea has been agreed, or the judge has concluded that he can properly deal with the case without the need for a *Newton* . . . hearing.
   (b) If an indication is sought, the prosecution should normally enquire whether the judge is in possession of or has had access to all the evidence relied on by the prosecution . . .
   (c) . . . before the judge gives any indication . . . [prosecution counsel should] . . . first, draw the judge's attention to any minimum or mandatory statutory sentencing requirements . . . and second, where it applies, to remind the judge that the position of the Attorney-General to refer any eventual sentencing decision as unduly lenient is not affected.
   (d) In any event, counsel should not say anything which may create the impression that the sentence indication has the support or approval of the Crown.

**Process**

75 The hearing should normally take place in open court, with a full recording of the entire proceedings, and both sides represented, in the defendant's presence . . .

77 If the process we envisage is properly followed, there should be very little need for the judge to involve himself in the discussions with the advocates, although obviously he may wish to seek better information on any aspect of the case which is troubling him . . .[27]

---

[27] The new arrangements apply to the Crown Court only, although later consideration will be given, the Court stated, to extending them to magistrates' courts. Magistrates frequently reduce the sentence as a reward for pleading guilty.

These Guidelines manifestly fail to rationalise an irrational practice. For example, as we have seen, clandestine meetings with counsel took place in the Judge's Chambers notwithstanding formal rulings not to do so and certainly not protected by the thin pretext in *Turner*; yet *Goodyear* continues to leave the door ajar since discussions seeking an indication should '*normally*' only take place in open court. Given that judges and counsel did not respect the guidelines in *Turner*, what confidence could there have been that *Goodyear* would not suffer the same treatment?[28]

Although the *Goodyear* Guidelines purportedly privileged resource savings, it is hard to see this as anything other than a fabricated afterthought, Lord Woolf himself (a member of the Full Court in *Goodyear*), having earlier explicitly rejected such a justification. Referring to the view of the Sentencing Advisory Panel ('the Panel'), Lord Woolf CJ stated in *Millberry v R* [2002] that although many participants in the Panel's research found a sentence reduction unacceptable primarily because it was seen as about saving court time and costs and allowing defendants to manipulate the system in their favour, this was 'not, however, the reason why the courts are prepared to and should reduce sentences in a case in which the offender pleads guilty'. In the light of this, the *volte-face* in *Goodyear* looks at best incompatible with earlier reasoning: critics might say that it looks unprincipled.

However, our primary purpose is not to interrogate the Guidelines themselves[29] but to address the more fundamental question: how could a Full Court present the conclusion that plea bargaining was a legitimate response in the light of widespread concerns since its emergence in the late 1960s and in the light of a catalogue of miscarriages of justice, many caused by discredited police evidence (the Court eschewed any mention of the police), including coerced confessions and suppression of evidence favourable to the defence?[30] More central is the question of how the Court was able to manage facial commitment to formal legality while implement-

---

[28] The guidelines were, in fact, breached immediately: *A-G Ref (No. 80 of 2005)* [2005].

[29] See further, Ashworth and Redmayne (2010), at pp. 311–20. Ashworth and Redmayne deal in detail with the impact that plea bargaining has on four rights recognised under the European Convention on Human Rights, namely: the presumption of innocence; the privilege against self-incrimination; the right not to be discriminated against in the exercise of Article 6 rights; and the right to a fair and public hearing. See also Sanders and Young (2010).

[30] As Ashworth and Redmayne (2010) persuasively argue, sentence inducements compromise the right to a fair and public trial, the presumption of innocence and the privilege against self-incrimination and the right not to be discriminated against in the exercise of the right to a fair and public hearing.

ing its social control function. Key to this was the Court's acceptance of the mischief of the system in 'cracked trials'; its simultaneous 'co-optation' and denigration of defendants; its purported removal of the trial judge from the fray; and its further reduction of defence lawyers to a subaltern status.

## 'CRACKED' TRIALS

Lacking judicial precedent, the need for these Guidelines, as stated in *Goodyear*, derived primarily from the intellectual history of various committees, commissions and inquiries – the Seabrook Committee (Seabrook 1992);[31] the RCCJ (1993); the Auld Report (2001); and the White Paper, *Justice for All* (Home Office, 2002) – each of which concluded that considerable resources, court time and public money, are wasted because defendants delay pleading guilty until the day set for trial, thereby causing the scheduled trial to 'crack'. A *'cracked trial'* is officially defined as *a trial that does not go ahead on the day and does not need to be re-scheduled because the case has reached an outcome*. This occurs when an acceptable plea is offered by the defendant or the prosecution offers no evidence against the defendant.

The collective concern of the various inquiries is encapsulated in the following statement of Auld in support of a formal system of advanced sentence indication:[32]

> . . . it would reduce the number of 'cracked trials', that is, of guilty defendants only pleading guilty at the last minute, and of guilty defendants taking their chance with a trial hoping that something may just save them from conviction.

The bare statistics might appear to lend credence to court and government policies designed to address 'abuse' of the right of defendants to elect, and curb resort to, trial. Thus, Ministry of Justice (2012b) *Judicial and Court Statistics 2011* for England and Wales show that, of cases scheduled for trial in 2011 in magistrates' courts, some 39 per cent 'cracked', the equivalent figure in the Crown Court being 40 per cent.

An initial point to make in analysing these statistics, not noted in *Goodyear*, is that in both magistrates' courts and the Crown Court, a significant proportion of cases 'crack' because of decisions directly attributable to *the prosecution* rather than to decision-making by defendants. Thus, in magistrates'

---

[31] This was a Report of a Working Party set up by the Bar Committee of the Bar Council.
[32] Auld (1991), Chapter 10, para. 97.

courts in 2011, 47 per cent of 'cracked' trials cracked because of decisions taken by the prosecution: the prosecution terminated the case (37 per cent); accepted a plea to an alternative charge (8 per cent); or was content with a bind over (2 per cent).[33] Similarly, in the Crown Court in 2011, of 'cracked' trials no fewer than 35 per cent cracked because the prosecution terminated the case, accepted a plea to an alternative charge, or were content with a bind over. Although the prosecution should proceed only where there is, on the evidence, 'a realistic prospect of conviction' of the charges presented,[34] in practice many cases proceed because of 'case momentum' once the prosecution has been initiated,[35] and the Crown Prosecution Service (CPS) count as 'successful' cases where there is a conviction on a lesser plea or a bind over. Accordingly, it is entirely rational for a defendant to wait until counsel for the prosecution has considered whether this test has in fact been met, a decision often taken on or immediately before the scheduled trial date. As we can see, prosecuting counsel was clearly in agreement with defendants in a significant proportion of cases in both lower and higher courts.[36]

A further matter to take into account in interpreting these statistics, again not noted in *Goodyear*, is that there are significant unexplained *regional variations* in the rate of 'cracked' trials. Thus, for example, in magistrates' courts in 2010, whereas 33 per cent of cases 'cracked' in Avon and Somerset, Devon and Cornwall and Gloucester, the figure rose to 46 per cent in Cheshire and to 49 per cent in South Wales. There is a similar picture in the Crown Court where equivalent variations can be seen: 32 per cent in North Wales; 34 per cent in London; 58 per cent in the North East; and 61 per cent in Humber and South Yorkshire. A comparable

---

[33] A prosecutor may invite the court to consider exercising its power to bind a defendant over as an alternative to prosecution for a criminal offence. The prosecutor should only invite the court to exercise this power once a firm and settled decision has been made to offer no evidence in the criminal proceedings.

[34] The Crown Prosecution Service subjects potential prosecutions to two tests: that there must be a realistic prospect of conviction on the evidence; and, if so, is a prosecution required in the public interest: Code for Crown Prosecutors available at: http://www.cps.gov.uk/publications/code_for_crown_prosecutors/codetest.html

[35] See McConville et al. (1991); Block et al. (1993a, 1993b).

[36] See further, Genders (1999) and Henham (2002). See also Bridges, Choongh and McConville (2000), who demonstrate, in relation to ethnic minority defendants, that their election to go to Crown Court is entirely consistent with 'late' decisions by the prosecution to reduce charges, substitute other charges, accept not guilty pleas to some counts or to reduce the seriousness of the factual allegations against the defendants. Cf. Hedderman and Moxon (1992) who found a lower rate of election and a higher overall guilty plea rate than the national statistics and which did not include London in the sample.

pattern is obtained year on year in regard to guilty pleas themselves. Thus, the last report of the Lord Chancellor's Department showed that whereas the guilty plea rate was lowest in London at approximately 49 per cent, it stood at 58 per cent in the South East and in the South West, and at 68 per cent in the Midlands and the North East.[37] It seems much more likely that these variations are a result of *local legal culture*[38] than a product of defendant decision-making[39] but this too went unnoticed in *Goodyear*.

**Defendant Decision-making**

This, of course, still means that a majority of trials 'crack' because of the late entry of a guilty plea and it is important to discover why this occurs. The court in *Goodyear* proceeded on the basis that the locus of the problem lay in defendants delaying their plea for *tactical* reasons relating to sentence and prayed in aid gobbets from the various Reports cited above without, however, paying *any* attention to the basis of these extracts.

Thus, without examining the *Report* of the RCCJ (1993), the Court[40] instead relied upon the following dispositive statement taken from the *Report*:

> A significant number of those who now plead guilty at the last minute would be more ready to declare their hand at an earlier stage if they were given a reliable early indication of the maximum sentence that they would face if found guilty. (RCCJ, 1993, p.112)

However, the *evidence* before the RCCJ paints a different picture. The evidence comes from the *Crown Court Study* undertaken on behalf of the

---

[37] Department for Constitutional Affairs (2006b), Table 6.8.

[38] It is also of significance that these regional variations have persisted ever since *Judicial Statistics* were first collected in 1972, and that these variations can be seen, notwithstanding changes made in the way in which guilty pleas are counted from 2006 onwards. For example, for cases committed for trial to the Crown Court over the ten year period 1974–1983, the average percentage of guilty pleas by Circuit was: London 40%; South Eastern (Provinces) 55%; Western 57%; Northern 58%; Wales & Chester 59%; Midland & Oxford 66%; and Northeastern 72%.

[39] So far as London is concerned, it is possible that the higher proportion of black defendants there has some impact on the statistics since black defendants are less likely to plead guilty, more likely to go for trial and, indeed, more likely to be acquitted (Bowling and Phillips, 2002; Tonry, 2004); but this alone cannot explain the persistent variations in the different regions.

[40] *Goodyear* (2005), at para. 37.

Table 4.1  Reasons for late notification of plea

|  | % |
|---|---|
| Earlier consultation with client impossible/did not take place | 31 |
| Change in prosecution's approach | 28 |
| Late consultation with counsel | 19 |
| Client changed mind | 6 |
| Plea bargaining | 4 |
| Miscellaneous | 12 |
| Total | 100 |

Source:  Zander and Henderson (1993, Table 5.1).

RCCJ by one of its own members (Michael Zander) together with Paul Henderson of the Home Office.[41]

In their survey of 'cracked trials', Zander and Henderson (1993) sought to discover from defence lawyers why an earlier guilty plea notification had not been given. The answers in order of frequency are set out in Table 4.1.

It is clear from these data that the facts repudiate the dispositive statement of the RCCJ and the image of the cynical defendant promoted in official circles and swallowed whole in *Goodyear*. *In only 6 per cent of cases was the late guilty plea attributed to a last minute change of mind by defendants.* Far from being cynical, calculating and manipulative, it is clear that defendants have not been given full and appropriate legal advice prior to the crucial appearance in court[42] or face a prosecution case which changes in substance as the date for trial approaches.[43] It is precisely this picture

---

[41]  Other elements of the Study have key technical deficiencies which render some other key findings of questionable value (McConville and Bridges, 1993a, 1993b). A survey was also undertaken by the Seabrook Committee on behalf of the Bar Council which showed that the vast majority of 'cracked' trials in the sample (between 70% and 75%) resulted from factors other than the defendant 'seeing the light' (i.e. accepting that a trial is useless and that a conviction is inevitable) and are caused by a significant change in the prosecution case, judicial intervention or the case being dropped altogether.

[42]  There is a wealth of research evidence which demonstrates that defence lawyers may give priority to interests other than those of the defendant, including their own work and remuneration arrangements; that many operate on a presumption of guilt; and are trial-averse. See, for example, Baldwin (1985); Baldwin and Feeney (1986); McConville et al. (1994); Newman (2013).

[43]  Research conducted by Dawes et al. (2011) calls into further question the incentivisation of discounts at an early stage in the criminal process. Despite a

which a long line of research has established as the incontrovertible experience of the overwhelming mass of defendants.[44]

In short, there is often disorganisation in the preparation of cases which is not the fault of defendants and, indeed, of which they may be victims. Take as an example the following extract from *R v Lopez* [2013], a drugs case where the defendant was improperly tried in his absence (see Chapter 5) and which more neatly captures ordinary experience than anything to which the Auld Report alludes:[45]

> In due course, on 20th December 2012 at the plea and case management hearing ('PCMH'), the applicant was arraigned in the Crown Court and he entered a not guilty plea. He submitted a defence statement in which he retracted the admissions [under police interrogation without a solicitor present] we have just set out. He denied knowing about the drugs in the house or that he had been in possession of them and he indicated that he had never touched them or any of the paraphernalia. He said that he had slept in the lounge and he had only been in the bedroom to use a PlayStation. He said that he had lied in interview to protect the true owner of the drugs, which he regretted, and he made various requests for disclosure.
>
> During the PCMH the defence requested that PC Sturridge, the officer in the case, attend to give evidence at the trial. Although the history is sketchy, it appears that the applicant had had some medical problems in the past because there was reference during the PCMH for the need for a letter from a medical practitioner if there was to be an adjournment of the case for medical reasons.
>
> The case was transferred from Isleworth Crown Court to Kingston Crown Court. It was placed in a warned list at Kingston for a two week period that had been identified, as we understand the position, at the PCMH and at 10.00 or 10.30 on 26th March 2013, the day when the case was put in the list for trial (we assume this latter step was taken on the previous afternoon), prosecuting counsel and the officer in the case failed to attend. The reason for counsel's absence was that the clerk in the set of chambers that had been sent the brief had not been notified by the Crown Prosecution Service of the new trial venue and therefore he missed the listing because the court number allocated

---

low sample size mainly consisting of offenders in custody, their empirical findings indicate that a sentence discount only becomes a driving factor for a defendant to enter a guilty plea at the 'tipping point' when they consider a conviction to be the likely outcome. The research showed advice from their legal representative is pivotal to this assessment underlining the reliance placed upon defence lawyers by defendants.

[44] See, for example, Baldwin and McConville (1977); Bankowski and Mungham (1976); Bottoms and McClean (1976); McConville et al. (1994); Bridges, Choongh and McConville (2000).

[45] See also *R v Applied Language Solutions Ltd* [2013] in which the Court of Appeal noted: 'We notified the Ministry of Justice and HMCTS of the issues and invited them to attend. We regret to record that no-one attended to assist the court.'

to the case changed when the case was transferred. Later in the morning, Mr Stevenson, who appears before us today, attended on behalf of the prosecution. He had been briefed at the last moment. PC Sturridge, the officer in the case, did not attend court, notwithstanding the defence indication at the PCMH that he was to be called to give evidence. He had not been warned to attend, but he was contacted and fortunately was able to give evidence on 27th March. Finally on the subject of non-appearance, the appellant also did not attend court. When questioned about his absence, counsel then instructed ('trial counsel') told the court that his instructing solicitors had been contacting the appellant via his girlfriend's mobile telephone, because the applicant's own mobile had been seized when he was arrested. Contact with the girlfriend had ceased about a week before the hearing, in that the telephone was no longer answered, although messages could still be left on the answering service. Trial counsel told the court that a message had been left to the effect that the case had been transferred to Isleworth and the applicant was reminded that it was in the current warned list but no acknowledgement of that message had been received. Attempts to contact the girlfriend on this telephone number on 25th and 26th March 2013 had been unsuccessful. As the Recorder stated during exchanges with counsel, this was an inefficient and precarious method of keeping in contact with a defendant awaiting trial. (paras 6–8)

Moreover, some of the dislocations exhibited in *Lopez* (returned briefs, failures in communication, non-appearance of a witness, discontinuity of representation, disorganisation in law firms/CPS, last-minute briefings)[46] are intrinsic to the criminal justice system and will continue whatever 'reforms' are introduced. What is unacceptable is ignorance of these facts of life or wilful failure to confront them and, in either event, characterising these as iniquitous delicts on the part of the defendant.

**Prosecution Case Preparation**

Apart from the issue of late defence advice, the fact that so much of the late plea changing is related to decisions by the Crown Prosecution Service (CPS) strongly suggests that there may be weaknesses in charging procedures and in case preparation such as would not justify an early guilty plea. That, indeed, emerges clearly from the evaluation of the CPS by Her Majesty's Crown Prosecution Service Inspectorate (HMCPSI Report, 2012d) which concluded:

> There has been an overall decline in the performance of in-house advocates dealing with non-contested hearings, primarily plea and case management hearing (PCMH) courts; this is explained by the increase in the number of cases

---

[46] The *Crown Court Study* showed that almost half of briefs were returned by barristers; and many barristers appearing in contested cases receive the brief the day before or the day of the hearing (Zander and Henderson, 1993, at Section 2).

a crown advocate is required to present, late instructions to prosecute and a reduction in the amount of available preparation time. Preparation is key to effective advocacy. (HMCPSI Report, 2012d, para. 3.3)

**Cracked Trials and 'Waste'**

Even if it were the case that justice revolves around convenience and expedition, a view that judges did not previously espouse,[47] it is an *assumption* that 'cracked' trials 'waste' enormous sums of public resources and the time of witnesses. Many practitioners and law reformers have united in advancing savings of resources as justifying plea bargaining in the public interest, as the Seabrook Committee exemplifies:[48]

> The resource implications of early indications of guilty pleas are enormous. Listing becomes far more efficient. Subject to availability of counsel, cases could be listed as soon as the necessary case papers are received ... Not only would the whole process be quicker, but also the need for adjournments for [pre-sentence] reports would be greatly reduced and, in most cases, eliminated. All of this, particularly the reduction in the number of cracked trials, will save a lot of money. (Seabrook, 1992, p. 36, para. 507)

Of course, it is true that the average hearing time for a trial is greater than that expended for a guilty plea and there is a saving on public expense.[49] The facts, however, do not justify the court in *Goodyear* accepting this simple consequentialist argument at face value.

When, for example, Crown Court judges were asked in the *Crown Court Study* whether any of their time had been 'wasted' as a result of cases listed for trial turning into last-minute guilty pleas, the vast majority (81 per cent) said that *no* judicial time had been wasted and in a further group of cases (9 per cent) the judges stated that less than two hours of their time had been wasted.[50] Similarly, according to those responsible for organising and managing court cases (court clerks), cracked trials caused *no* waste of time at all

---

[47] See, for example, *R v Coe* (1969), Lord Parker: 'There is something more than convenience and expedition. Above all there is the proper administration of the criminal justice to be considered' (at p. 67).

[48] See also Mack and Anleu (1997), at pp. 125ff.

[49] The Home Office estimated in 1992 that the average cost of a contested case in the Crown Court was approximately £12,000 compared with about £1,400 for a guilty plea (Home Office, 1992).

[50] Zander and Henderson (1993), p. 151, para. 5.5. Actually, judges most often saw a cracked trial as a way of using court resources economically. As one judge put it: 'I do not regard cracked trials as wasting time. They save time' (loc. cit.). See further, Feeley (1979) and Nardulli (1979).

in the substantial majority of cases (69 per cent) and less than two hours in a further group of cases (20 per cent).[51] The other claimed wasted resources are also far less than expected: in a substantial majority of cases (61 per cent) *no* police witnesses turn up at court for trials that do not go ahead;[52] and *no* civilian witnesses' time is wasted in almost one-third of cases.[53]

Additionally, as we have seen, the overwhelming majority of Crown Court cases do not involve any question of a 'cracked' trial. Indeed, over the long term, it is arguable that systematic reliance on guilty pleas far from saving court time and public expense actually wastes time and increases the cost to the public purse. The bargained guilty plea system becomes part of a vertical process: what will happen later in the court where the guilty plea is extracted has a profound influence upon what happens at the police and prosecution stages of the process. Routine case processing in court through guilty pleas reinforces the actions and expectations of the police, who, because of the lack of court scrutiny, are encouraged to engage in ill-considered arrests and to charge suspects without close attention to the sufficiency of evidence and without careful regard to whether any social objective might be achieved by the prosecution.[54] The predictable result is a less than thoughtful, often unreflective arrest process built around police – rather than justice – priorities, the hallmarks of which, in large urban conurbations, include non-individuated stops, searches and arrests in neighbourhoods felt deserving of social discipline by the police.[55]

As research has demonstrated, this also means that prosecutors may commence or continue with prosecutions that have no realistic prospect of conviction or are otherwise not appropriate to criminal prosecution. This occurs, for example, because prosecutors, even where they initially approve the charge, may become too closely allied to police values and priorities and thereafter are carried forward by 'case momentum'. Weak cases are commenced and continued in the hope, sometimes fulfilled,

---

[51] Zander and Henderson (1993), pp. 151–2, para. 5.6.

[52] Ibid., p.152, para. 5.7. Not all of this is wasted, of course, since officers might be required to give evidence in some guilty plea cases or might need to be consulted as to the acceptability of a charge reduction which turns the case into a guilty plea.

[53] Ibid., pp. 152–3, para. 5.8.

[54] Research points to the fact that many arrests are currently undertaken in circumstances where arresting officers do not consider the evidence on arrest to be sufficient to found a charge (Phillips and Brown, 1998). In this study, even though some officers felt that they could not risk saying that there was insufficient evidence, some 30 per cent of arresting officers stated that there was insufficient evidence to charge suspects at the time of the arrest (Phillips and Brown, 1998, p. 44).

[55] McConville and Mirsky (1995).

of a guilty plea.[56] We need look no further for evidence of this than in the *Crown Court Study* and the *Judicial and Court Statistics 2011* (MoJ, 2012b). In the *Crown Court Study* (Zander and Henderson, 1993) (see Table 4.1 above), in at least 28 per cent of all cases the prosecution alters its position (usually reducing or dropping charges) at the last moment before which no proper or adequate review has taken place. This is amply confirmed by the *Judicial and Court Statistics 2011* (MoJ, 2012b) which show that, of 'cracked trials' in 2011, 37 per cent 'cracked' in magistrates' courts and 35 per cent in the Crown Court because *the prosecution dropped the case* (18 per cent) or accepted a plea to an alternative (i.e. lesser) charge (17 per cent).

There is yet additional evidence bearing on prosecutorial decision-making. In the *Crown Court Study* prosecutors were asked how they viewed 'cracked' trials. The response was overwhelmingly *positive*: almost two-thirds (64 per cent) judged the outcome (a late guilty plea) to be 'good', with virtually all the residue (34 per cent) believing the outcome to be 'satisfactory'.[57] This in itself is ample demonstration that the prosecution case that is finalised, to coin a phrase, 'at the door of the court', more accurately reflects the realities of the prosecution case file than the charges originally preferred.[58] In addition, and importantly, prosecutors judged the outcome 'good' because in *one in every seven cases* they conceded that it would have been difficult to have obtained a conviction had the case gone to trial. Indeed, when directly asked what would have been the chances of the defendant being acquitted if the case had gone to trial, prosecutors said the chances would have been 'good' in 8 per cent of cases, and 'fairly good' in a further 18 per cent of cases; these figures, on an aggregate basis, represent some 2,600 serious (Crown Court) cases each year.[59]

This problem of 'weak' prosecution cases has been noted by judges in the past and the recent evaluations of the CPS by the Inspectorate confirm these concerns. Thus, for example, the HMCPSI (2012b) Report, *CPS Gwent and CPS South Wales* concluded in relation to magistrates' court CPS files (one-third of which were found to be 'poor' in terms of case progression and case management) as follows:

---

[56] See further, McConville et al. (1991).
[57] Zander and Henderson (1993), at p. 156, para. 5.17.
[58] See also Bridges, Choongh and McConville (2000).
[59] Zander and Henderson (1993), pp. 156–7, para. 5.18. The introduction of the statutory charging procedure under which prosecutors (attached to police stations) rather than the police decide on the charge, at least in serious cases, is unlikely to affect this situation and, indeed, official reports on the CPS continue to show persistence in bringing inappropriate or weak cases or both.

Of the files examined *only 16.7% of cases* complied with magistrates' court directions in a timely way. Many first hearings of anticipated not guilty pleas are not proactively handled, resulting in many trials entering the system without the real issues being identified. Ultimately cases frequently crack on the day of trial with no more evidence than that which was available at the first hearing. (para. 3.10, emphasis added)

The evidence of prosecutorial inefficiency and incompetence is compelling: in only five out of every six cases was the CPS even able to comply with magistrates' court directions. In a recent Report on London[60] (which accounts for over 17 per cent of the CPS national magistrates' court case load and almost 21 per cent of its Crown Court case load), HMCPSI reported, among other things, that:

> Compliance with the Code for Crown Prosecutors has declined since the March 2010 Review but was comparable with that found in recent inspections in other Areas (reflecting a national drop in performance) and there is a need to drive up quality across a number of casework aspects. The standard of charging advice needs to improve, which is aligned to the need to improve feedback structures to charging units. (para. 2.18)
>
> Prosecutors need to assume greater accountability at the initial review stage to weed out weak cases at that point instead of letting them proceed on a contested basis and enter the [case progression units]. (para. 3.4)

In another Report[61] the Inspectorate expressed similar concerns:

> CPS lawyers are making errors of analysis and judgement, which lead to 7% of cases being wrongly prosecuted or discontinued, and this has significant consequences for victims, witnesses, defendants, criminal justice partners and public confidence. More worryingly, CQSM[62] reviewers are perpetuating these errors by failing to identify the majority of the Code test failures and ensure that lessons are learned; this urgently needs addressing. (HMCPSI, 2012c, Executive Summary para.1.4)

According to the HMCPSI, reviewers in the CPS were poor at identifying cases which did not comply with the CPS Code test failures, noting only 25 per cent of the cases where one or more featured. They identified only six of the 32 charging decision failures (19 per cent) and only nine of the 27 failures at later stages in the case (33 per cent). CPS reviewers (*especially Unit Heads*) were worst at identifying a failure properly to analyse the case

---

[60] HMCPSI (2012a).
[61] HMCPSI (2012c).
[62] Core Quality Standards Monitoring Scheme is a monitoring procedure introduced in 2010 to ensure compliance with the Core Quality Standards set out by the CPS to improve the quality of its work.

and whether each element could be proved. This was said to be a *'fundamental flaw'* in the way that the process is being applied and from it flow missed opportunities to learn lessons; wasted effort by the CPS and other agencies; unnecessary cost; anxiety, inconvenience and distress to victims and witnesses; adverse impact upon those defendants who should not have been charged; and reputational damage (HMCPSI, 2012c, para. 4.61).

The 'follow up' Report that HMCPSI[63] conducted showed little improvement: indeed, there were areas where standards had declined. The drive for financial savings mandated by the government (as part of the Comprehensive Spending Review 2007, the CPS was required to deliver £69 million efficiency savings by March 2011)[64] resulted in increased reliance on internal staff, whose abilities were inferior to those of external barristers, poor case preparation (beginning in 2004, the CPS had, as part of its cost-savings drive, started to recruit non-qualified staff to review cases and, later, to present non-contentious or 'straightforward' guilty plea cases at magistrates' courts) and discontinuous representation. The continued focus on financial savings resulted in late instruction of crown advocates who do not for the most part have the tools to prepare cases out of the office, and late instructions to self-employed counsel who do not have time to remedy poor preparation.

In the result, the attrition rate of cases prosecuted by the CPS in Crown Court alone is astonishingly high. Indeed, the statistics for 2010[65] show that *no fewer than 64 per cent of defendants (20,921) who pleaded not guilty in cases dealt with in 2010 were acquitted.*[66] More revealing still is the fact that of those acquitted, 62 per cent (13,037) were ordered to be acquitted by the Judge without a jury having even been convened, the CPS conceding that they would be unable to discharge the burden of proof before the case even started. Moreover, in a further 8.3 per cent (1,749) of cases, without the defence having to start its case, the Judge directed the jury to acquit, the prosecution having failed to establish a *prima facie* case against the defendant.[67] In other words, over 70 per cent of acquittals result from

---

[63] HMCPSI (2012d).
[64] CPS *Annual Performance Report* (CPS, 2009).
[65] MoJ (2011b) *Judicial and Court Statistics 2010*.
[66] This entirely supports the study of ethnic minority defendants by Bridges, Choongh and McConville (2000) who found that the overwhelming majority of their sample who had elected Crown Court trial and pleaded not guilty had the case against them discontinued or were acquitted on the order or direction of the trial judge or by the verdict of a jury.
[67] Only 28.4% of acquitted defendants were acquitted by verdict of the jury. A small number of other acquittals (204) were recorded where, for example, no plea was recorded or the defendant successfully pleaded *autrefois acquit* or *autrefois*

fatal weaknesses in the prosecution case. This also renders of little value the often-quoted statistic that Crown Court trials are seven times as costly as guilty pleas (see below).

The *Crown Court Study* and other research throw further light on these bare statistics. In the *Crown Court Study*, respondents (prosecuting barristers, CPS solicitors and advocates, police and judges) were asked why ordered and directed acquittals happened. In 20 per cent of cases, key prosecution witnesses did not appear; in 24 per cent prosecution witnesses did not come up to proof (did not say what the prosecution had relied upon them saying) or changed their evidence; in 8 per cent prosecution evidence was held inadmissible, tainted or there was another submission of law by the defence. The remaining 48 per cent was an 'other' category including such things as 'very weak' cases, poor police work and lost prosecution exhibits.[68] Other researchers have disclosed similar findings. For example, John Baldwin (1997) found that prosecuting counsel were unwilling to drop weak cases until the intervention of the judge. Prosecutors were found to share the same view as the police: that the defendant deserved to be prosecuted, especially in serious cases *notwithstanding weak evidence*.[69] Similarly, Bridges, Choongh and McConville (2000) concluded:

> In a substantial majority of cases defendants who elect for Crown Court are obtaining not a jury trial but a more thorough review of the evidence against them than has previously been undertaken, in many instances at the instigation of the Crown Court judge and/or prosecuting counsel. (p. 15)

As the *Crown Court Study* makes clear, while a large proportion of 'failures' are caused by unavoidable 'prosecution hazards' (such as non-appearance of witnesses), judges, prosecutors and defence counsel were of the view that in a number of instances the case was too trivial, the evidence

---

*convict*. Jury acquittals are also, in part at least, directly related to failures in the CPS (see, for example, The Daily Telegraph, 2010).

[68] *Crown Court Study* (Zander and Henderson, 1993, Table 6.17). Her Majesty's Inspectorate found, for example, that some domestic violence cases with weak evidence were proceeded with by the CPS because it judged that it was in the public interest to do so even though this is contrary to its own Code which requires in all cases that that there must be a realistic prospect of conviction. See HMCPSI, *Violence at Home: A Joint Thematic Inspection of the Investigation and Prosecution of Cases Involving Domestic Violence* (2004). One local study found that charge reduction became minimal following specific policy initiatives (Cretney and Davis, 1997).

[69] See also Block, Corbett and Peay (1993a), Table 5 (out of 100 ordered and directed acquittals, over one-third resulted from crucial witnesses not appearing, the victim not appearing or the victim being unwilling to testify).

too thin[70] or otherwise it was not in the public interest to have brought the case in the first place.[71] If further confirmation was needed, HMCPSI Reports repeatedly draw attention to failures of the CPS and police in the preparation of cases, in the early notification of prosecution witnesses to attend court, in communicating with victims, in the lack of proper record keeping, in discontinuous representation and in sub-standard advocacy.

## 'INEFFECTIVE' TRIALS

Apart from the fact that judges and counsel are able to make good use of available time and that court managers are able to list court cases in intelligent ways, among the reasons why cracked trials cause much less waste than propounded by officials is that the case *does terminate on the day*. In other words, *no further costs are incurred for the court or the parties*, any further hearing needed for sentencing purposes being a cost that is necessarily incurred in any event. However, this is not so in respect of trials deemed in official circles to be '*ineffective*'.

An 'ineffective' trial is defined in the official statistics as follows: 'A trial that does not go ahead on the scheduled trial date due to action or inaction by one or more of the prosecution, the defence or the court and a further listing for trial is required.'[72]

It is surprising that the issue of 'ineffective' trials has not been raised by any of the official commissions or indeed by the court itself in *Goodyear*: they are far more costly in every way because, unlike 'cracked' trials, they do not terminate there and then; they have to be *re-listed for trial* on a subsequent date; and on that re-fixed hearing it may not go ahead (be 'ineffective') for a second or third time, or indeed 'crack'. Examination of these in the context of 'costs' and 'waste' is, accordingly, essential.

The *Judicial and Court Statistics 2011* (MoJ, 2012b), reveal that, in magistrates' courts, some 18 per cent of trials were recorded as *ineffective*, a percentage which has remained broadly consistent over recent years.[73] Caution needs to be exercised because there are considerable unexplained regional variations each year. Thus, the *Judicial and Court Statistics 2011* show that in magistrates' courts, whereas 12 per cent of trials were

---

[70] One local study found that charge reduction became minimal following specific policy initiatives (Cretney and Davis, 1997).
[71] *Crown Court Study* (Zander and Henderson, 1993), Table 6.23, p. 187.
[72] MoJ (2011b), p. 65.
[73] MoJ (2013a) statistics for October–December 2012 show that 17% of cases listed for trial in magistrates' courts were 'ineffective' (MoJ, 2013e).

recorded as 'ineffective' in North Wales, the figure rose to 22 per cent in the East Midlands and Kent, Surrey and Sussex.[74] Similarly, in the Crown Court, where the 'ineffective' trial rate overall is 14 per cent, only 3 per cent of trials were 'ineffective' in Mid- and West-Wales, and 18 per cent were 'ineffective' in Avon and Somerset, Devon and Cornwall, Gloucestershire, Bedfordshire and Hertfordshire.[75]

Setting aside the issue of regional variations, the overall national figures demonstrate that almost 62 per cent of 'ineffective' trials in Magistrates' Courts have nothing to do with actions by the defendant but are the result of the prosecution not being ready or a prosecution witness being absent, or 'other' unexplained (probably 'administrative') causes.[76] Similarly, in the Crown Court, the *Judicial and Court Statistics 2011* show that 61 per cent of ineffective trials are not attributable to the defence in any way, the biggest single cause here being 'administrative problems' (23 per cent) with other major causes being the absence of a prosecution witness (21 per cent) or the prosecution not being ready (17 per cent).[77]

While a full account of these 'administrative problems' is not available,[78] one revealing piece of the story emerged in a report by the National Audit Office (NAO) (2012) on the contracting out to a private company of language services, including interpreters, to courts. The NAO found that in the first quarter of 2012, 182 trials in magistrates' courts were recorded as 'ineffective' because of interpreter availability issues, double the figure (95) for the same quarter in 2011 (at p. 24, para. 3.6).[79]

If 'cost-effectiveness' were considered of such importance, even being

---

[74] *Judicial and Court Statistics 2010* (MoJ, 2011b), Table 3.5.

[75] Ibid., Table 4.13.

[76] MoJ (2013a) statistics for October–December 2012 do not give a complete picture but disclose that 26% were ineffective because of court administrative problems, 16% because of the absence of a prosecution witness and 21% because of the absence of the defendant.

[77] MoJ (2013a) statistics for October–December 2012 confirm the overall picture: absence of prosecution witnesses accounted for 22% of ineffective trials; court administrative problems for 20%; the prosecution not being ready for 17%; and the defendant being absent or unfit for 18%.

[78] MoJ (2013a) statistics for October–December 2012 state that in magistrates' courts, 'court administrative problems' cover: 'Another case over-ran', 'Judge/magistrate availability', 'overlisting (insufficient cases drop out/floater/backer not reached)' and 'equipment/accommodation failure'.

[79] The NAO point out that this figure excludes delays that were not severe enough to cause an ineffective trial and delays and cancellations of non-trial hearings 'which were numerous, according to complaints' data, the Senior Presiding Judge, and staff that we interviewed in four courts' (NAO, 2012, p. 24). See further, Baksi (2012a, 2012b).

elevated to a goal of the system, ineffective trials illustrate once again that inefficiencies are *system-led* and cannot be laid at the door of and used to stigmatise defendants.

## 'WASTE' AND COST SAVINGS

As an addendum, it should be noted that the idea of 'cost savings' is *an assumption* not the result of any actuarial calculation.[80] A comparison between the cost of trials in the Crown Court and guilty pleas, the former said to cost almost seven times as much (Harries, 1999), is far from dispositive for a number of reasons.

In the first place, a primary reason for the greater expense of existing trials is that they comprise in large measure the most complex and contestable cases, thus distorting any comparison with the residue (many of which will be straightforward and relatively simple). And, indeed, it should be recalled that, of these contestable cases, so weak is the prosecution that, in the Crown Court, 64 per cent of defendants sent for trial are acquitted.

Second, there is no empirical support for the assumption that sentence discounts offered by judges are needed in order to produce a high guilty plea rate, even if that was desirable. Thus, an early analysis in Canada suggested that most (approximately 71 per cent) of guilty pleas in Toronto had *not* been produced through plea bargaining (Ferguson and Roberts, 1974). Elsewhere, more aggressive screening by prosecutors eliminated weak or pointless prosecutions with a concomitant increase in open guilty pleas to the stronger cases that remained in the system.[81]

Third, with a State-induced guilty plea process, further costs are incurred by: the need to introduce new court procedures designed to elicit an early guilty plea (through what are now termed preliminary hearings and Plea and Case Management Hearings (PCMH),[82] numbers

---

[80] See, for example, Thomson (2004) who assumes it is 'manifest' that guilty pleas save considerable sums of public money.

[81] See Wright and Miller (2002); Berger (1976); and Parnas and Atkins (1978). Wright and Miller report on policy changes introduced by the new District Attorney in New Orleans which sought to divert cases not worthy of being on the docket and prohibited plea bargaining, with the result that, although the plea bargaining rate fell from 60–70% to 7–8%, the guilty plea rate remained high with 65% of defendants pleading guilty as charged. See also, Verdun-Jones and Hatch (1988) for qualifications to early appraisals.

[82] The latter introduced by the Criminal Procedure Rules (MoJ, 2005). See Zander and Henderson's *Crown Court Study* (1993) which reported in regard to these pre-trial hearings that in as many as two-thirds of cases (66%), the judges

of which have to occur on multiple occasions);[83] new procedures;[84] new forums to ascertain the factual basis for the plea where there are conflicting versions of the facts underlying the charge (e.g., *Newton* hearings),[85] themselves requiring repeated litigation in the Court of Appeal itself; new official bodies to establish the procedural framework (Sentencing Guidelines Council and the Sentencing Advisory Panel now replaced by the Sentencing Council); the proliferation of appeals by defendants (against conviction, against alleged inadequate discount, against alleged failure to honour sentence, or, in multiple-defendant cases, against lack of comparative justice)[86] and 'references' to the Court of Appeal by the Attorney-General against what is viewed as an 'unduly lenient' sentence[87]

---

said they did not think the pre-trial hearing had saved much time and money. In another quarter of the cases (24%), they said that a little time and money had been saved. In 29% of cases they said that 'a fair amount of time and money' had been saved and in 2% that it had amounted to 'a great deal'. To the same effect see Levi (1993) in his study of serious fraud cases. A fully argued position can be found in Zander's Dissent in the RCCJ Report.

[83] See the detailed response from Zander (2001) to the Auld Report. No official statistics are available on this but repeated hearings can be seen in appellate reports relating to sentence. Thus, for example, in *A-G Ref Nos. 80 and 81 of 1999 (Thompson and Rodgers)* [2000] the two defendants (and one other) appeared at the Crown Court at Nottingham in December 1998. They were thereafter arraigned and appeared at a preliminary hearing on 26 February 1999; the case was re-listed for hearing on 31 March 1999 at which one defendant was again arraigned and pleaded guilty. The case was re-listed for a further preliminary hearing on 12 April 1999; the case was listed for a further directions hearing on 4 October 1999 when, on an amended indictment, the second defendant pleaded guilty. Finally, there was a further hearing and sentencing of both defendants on 8 October 1999. See also: *A-G Ref No. 19 of 2004 (Brett Charlton)* [2005] where there were at least five separate hearings following arraignment.

[84] See, for example, *R v Tolera* (1999); *R v Myers* (1996); *R v Beswick* (1996); *A-G Ref No. 81 of 2000 (R v Jacobs)* (2001); *A-G Ref No. 58 of 2000 (R v Wynne)* (2001).

[85] *R v Newton* (1983). This case has spawned a tranche of Court of Appeal cases of which the following are but examples: *R v Smith (PA)* (1986); *R v Myers* (1996); *R v Kerrigan* (1993), CA; *R v Underwood* (2005). See also: *R v Dudley (Stephen Paul)* [2012].

[86] See, for example, *R v Kulah* [2007]; *R v Seddon* [2007]; *Thornton v CPS* [2010]; *R v Newman* [2010]; *A-G Ref Nos. 11 and 12 of 2012* [2012].

[87] For a recent example, see *A-G Ref No. 6 of 2011* [2012] in which the defendant initially pleaded guilty to possessing a prohibited weapon and prohibited ammunition charges and, after a *Goodyear* sentence indication that the judge would not impose a sentence of more than five years' imprisonment, pleaded guilty on the morning of the trial to a count of possessing a firearm with intent to endanger life. On a reference, the Court of Appeal (Criminal Division) said that the defendant was entitled to credit of 10% for his late guilty plea but substituted a sentence of 10 years' imprisonment.

that an inchoate procedure involving 'sweeteners' necessarily gives rise to from time to time; not to speak of the various statutory provisions, court procedures, Practice Directions and Attorney-General's Guidelines that have had to be created to impose some semblance of order on proceedings that, to put it generously, continue to cause confusion in the ranks of the judiciary[88] and the Bar.[89] It is no answer to say that some or all of these expensive appurtenances[90] can be scrapped to save resources because they have proved indispensable (though inadequate) precisely because judges cannot contrive 'guidelines' which are clear and dispositive (let alone principled) and because neither judges nor counsel can be trusted to keep to such guidelines and procedures as are instituted for this purpose.

## CO-OPTATION AND DENIGRATION OF THE DEFENDANT

Administrative systems gain greater acceptability where they are able to 'co-opt' the subject individuals into the processing procedures, and, indeed, it is regarded as essential to do this both in terms of so-called

---

[88] See, for example, the question whether the discount should be reduced or withheld where, notwithstanding an early guilty plea, the judge decides that the case against the defendant was overwhelming. The original judicial position was that in such circumstances, little or no credit should be given for the guilty plea: *Costen* (1989). The Sentencing Guidelines Council took a different view: that the discount should not be withheld in such cases, a practice followed by the courts: *A-G Ref Nos. 14 and 15 of 2006 (French and Webster)*. This is at least consistent with the proclaimed rationale relating to the saving of resources. However, the Sentencing Guidelines Council revised its stance in 2007 to state that (Guideline 5.3): 'Where the prosecution case is overwhelming, it may not be appropriate to give the full reduction that would otherwise be given. Whilst there is a presumption in favour of the full reduction being given where a plea has been indicated at the first reasonable opportunity, the fact that the prosecution case is overwhelming without relying on admissions from the defendant may be a reason justifying departure from the guideline.' This, too, has led to a lack of clarity and further appeals. See, for example, *R v Simpson (Dean)* [2009]; *R v Wilson (Paul Anthony)* [2012].

[89] See, for example, *A-G Ref No. 48 of 2006 (R v Farrow)* [2007] in which, notwithstanding *Goodyear*, prosecuting counsel failed to remind the judge of the reference power where 'it should have at least passed prosecuting counsel's mind that a question as to whether or not a suspended sentence was appropriate might well arise' (at para. 22).

[90] Interestingly, in the *Crown Court Study*, Judges said that pre-trial hearings (reviews) did not save time and money in 66% of cases, saved only a little in another 24% of cases, saved a fair amount in 8% of cases and saved a 'great deal' of time and money in only 2% of cases (Zander and Henderson, 1993, p. 72).

'efficiency' (i.e., cost-effectiveness) and to avoid accusations of being affectless. Integral to this is the personal autonomy and integrity of the human subject thereby affected; possessed of 'rights' and 'entitlements', the individual is portrayed as being able to make *free choices* within the system and even to disengage from it (at least in some measure) altogether. As such, 'voluntary' participation – which, it is implied, rational choice would dictate – lends it authority and legitimacy and further encourages its refinement and perpetuation. This cannot happen, however, without resort to the manipulation of principles and values and, in the case of State-induced guilty pleas, the language of the law itself.

The starting point is the system captured in guidelines laid down by the Sentencing Guidelines Council (2007):[91]

> The level of reduction should reflect the stage at which the offender indicated a <u>willingness to admit guilt</u> to the offence for which he is eventually sentenced:
> (i) the largest recommended reduction will not normally be given unless the offender indicated willingness to admit guilt at the **first reasonable opportunity**;[92] when this occurs will vary from case to case . . .;
> (ii) where the admission of guilt comes later than the first reasonable opportunity, the reduction for [a] guilty plea will normally be less than one third;
> (iii) where the plea of guilty comes very late, it is still appropriate to give some reduction;
> (iv) if after pleading guilty there is a *Newton* hearing and the offender's version of the circumstances of the offence is rejected, this should be taken into account in determining the level of reduction;
> (v) if the not guilty plea was entered and maintained for tactical reasons (such as to retain privileges whilst on remand), a late guilty plea should attract very little, if any, discount. (original emphasis)

The administrative system here follows a particularised template determined by the defendant's 'willingness' to comply through a timely admission of guilt displaced only in exceptional circumstances, such as by the defendant seeking 'tactical' advantage.

A foundational step in the process of legitimating this mode is the payment of symbolic homage to the defendant's rights. Courts construct the defendant in a criminal case as an individual with fundamental rights in control of and hence responsible for any and all decisions that are required to be made.

---

[91] At para. 4.3.
[92] The meaning of 'first reasonable opportunity' is not without difficulty and has been the subject of consideration by the Court of Appeal in *Caley & Ors v R* [2012]. See also, *R v Rawson* [2013]. For earlier consideration, see *R v Chaytors* [2012].

As the court in *Goodyear* put it: 'The starting point is fundamental. The defendant is personally and exclusively responsible for his plea. When he enters it, it must be entered voluntarily, without improper pressure' (at 30).

To enable cost-effective processing, however, defendants cannot be given their *actual* personality as this would require individual consideration, sorting and grading; instead, the individual needs to be endowed with an *imputed* personality, which not only allows for standardisation but rather *demands* it.

While coercive systems find it necessary to present the subjects as being 'willingly co-opted' into their project, it is also essential to impugn those subjects through public degradation ceremonies,[93] eliminating so far as possible any residual claims they might make. For a coercive bureaucracy to work effectively, the subjects need to be characterised as belonging to the under-classes, the indigent, the unworthy or the undeserving, a challenge that is made easy with 'criminal defendants'. In line with this, courts, commissions and official committees have been adept at stigmatising defendants as manipulative, scheming and inevitably guilty. We see this throughout the Auld Report, the authority of which was not thereby diminished in the squinted eyes of the court in *Goodyear*. Thus, Auld sets out the issue in this way:[94]

> Many of the judiciary and most criminal practitioners would like to see a return to the pre-*Turner* regime, albeit conducted in a more formal manner. They regard the matter pragmatically – given the existence of a system of sentence discounts for pleas of guilty – as a means of encouraging defendants to face up to their guilt at an early stage and before putting the public, victims and others involved to the expense and trouble of an unnecessary trial. *Put another way, it would reduce the number of 'cracked trials', that is, of guilty defendants only pleading guilty at the last minute, and of guilty defendants taking their chance with a trial hoping that something may just save them from conviction* . . . (emphasis added)

In plain English, those who go to trial are guilty and are playing the system in a disreputable way; it is a prime example of *petitio principii*, assuming the very thing it sets out to prove.

The same thinking is seen in the Home Office White Paper, *Justice for All*:[95]

> All too often defendants will elect trial, then after some time plead guilty in the Crown Court and receive a sentence which magistrates could have passed.

---

[93] See Garfinkle (1955).
[94] Auld (2001), Chapter 10, at para. 97.
[95] Home Office (2002), para. 4.21.

Alternatively they will hope to avoid a trial altogether, or perceive a better chance of being acquitted although guilty. The motive will often be to prolong the process in the hope of reducing the chance of either victim or necessary witnesses giving evidence.

This generalised attribution of base motives naturally has its source in a pre-supposition of guilt, a systemic feature set out succinctly in *Justice for All*:[96] 'And many in the system believe that defendants' delayed pleas are a tactic employed in the hope that witnesses will lose patience and decide not to testify.'

Although the reliance on unsubstantiated attributions is little more than prejudice dressed up as empirical data,[97] this neatly captures the approach of the State to the processing imperative. The coercive ideal cannot be seen to be founded in naked prejudice; it must be sanitised and legitimated through 'social data' relating to 'guilty' but ill-motivated and 'tactical' defendants.

For Auld, 'cracked' trials resulted from defendants being unwilling to face up to their guilt until the door of the court, and pre-trial indications of sentence were needed in order to compel better forensic discipline from feckless defendants/defence lawyers. Tellingly, in an effort to justify enhanced sentences being given to defendants who have simply exercised their right to trial, Auld's prejudice bubbled to the surface:[98]

> In my view, once guilt has been established, there is no logical reason why a dishonest plea of not guilty should not be openly treated as an aggravating factor just as an honest plea of guilty is treated and rewarded as a mitigating factor.

As Lee Bridges (2006) notes:

> Auld LJ here engages in a sleight of language, associating the word 'honest' solely with a guilty plea and 'dishonest' only with a not guilty plea (whereas a guilty plea can be equally dishonest). In this way he is able to circumvent the contradictions in his position, since he accepts that *'no system can guarantee that individual defendants, however innocent, will not regard the likelihood of a lesser sentence as an incentive to trade it for the risk of conviction and a more serious sentence, or that lawyers will not sometimes advise their clients badly.'*[99]

---

[96] Ibid., para. 4.41.
[97] Equally reliant on the emotive 'science' of public opinion as opposed to empirical data was the claim that '[t]he people are sick and tired of a sentencing system that does not make sense', ibid., at 86. See to similar effect, Royal Commission on Criminal Justice, *Report* (1993) at para. 48, p.112: 'It is often said too. . . .'
[98] Auld (2001), Chapter 10, para. 103.
[99] Ibid., Chapter 10, para. 105.

> Thus, Auld LJ appears to characterise the guilty plea by an innocent defendant as amounting to no more than a miscalculation or mistake based on poor advice. Otherwise, he would have to acknowledge the reality of the current sentence discount, that a guilty plea (whether honest or dishonest) is to be treated *per se* as a mitigating factor and rewarded by a lesser sentence. (p. 89, footnotes omitted)

To deal with the 'problem' of the innocent defendant, both the RCCJ and Auld adopted an identical solution: collateral damage is the price that must be paid. Thus, the RCCJ accepted that, although there was uncertainty as to precise numbers (i.e., you cannot stop the production line in order to count the casualties) it was 'naïve' to suppose that innocent people never plead guilty because of the prospect of a sentence discount. However, that concern should be subordinated to the (alleged and unspecified) 'benefits' of the process:[100]

> Against the risk that defendants may be tempted to plead guilty to charges of which they are not guilty must be weighed the benefits *to the system* and to defendants of encouraging those who are in fact guilty to plead guilty. We believe that the sentence discount should remain. (RCCJ, 1993, emphasis added)

If anything, Auld's formulation was as intellectually dishonest and even more cynical:[101]

> Of course, no system can guarantee that individual defendants, however innocent, will not regard the likelihood of a lesser sentence as an incentive to trade it for the risk of conviction and a more serious sentence, or that lawyers will not sometimes advise their clients badly. But those are not reasons for rejecting a sentencing practice if *in general* it serves a proper sentencing purpose, operates justly and assists the efficient administration of justice. (emphasis added)

The outcome for Auld is that individuals charged with crime must be treated as guilty, dishonest and unworthy; in so far as 'individual defendants' are innocent, they have to be sacrificed.[102] In this way, the ordinary goals of sentencing as repeatedly set out by courts (punishment, deterrence, retribution, reform, protection, reparation) are trumped by the '*proper sentencing purpose*' of coercing defendants, some of whom are innocent, to plead guilty. Ultimately, the defence of a coercive bureauc-

---

[100] Ibid., p. 111, para. 45.
[101] Ibid., Chapter 10, para. 105.
[102] That innocent people plead guilty is an established fact in England and Wales. Studies elsewhere show worrying numbers of wholly innocent people pleading guilty to serious crimes, including rape and murder. See, for example, Bowers (2008) and Thomas (2010).

racy is crude and untested 'utilitarianism' to which, incidentally, Bentham never subscribed (see Chapter 7, *infra*).

Cynicism is also found in the further claim that a system which *intentionally* convicts the innocent can be said to '*operate justly*' if it, *in general*, works, an astonishing formulation that underhandedly seeks to sanctify an otherwise discreditable stance. This bears comparison with Lord Denning's infamous bloody remark that:

> Hanging ought to be retained for murder most foul. We wouldn't have all these campaigns to get the Birmingham Six released if they'd been hanged. They'd have been forgotten, and the whole community would be satisfied . . . It is better that some innocent men remain in jail than that the integrity of the English judicial system be impugned.

Whereas Denning was troubled by continuing campaigns to exonerate people wrongfully convicted because he thought that exposure of mistakes would bring the whole system into disrepute, Auld regards it as *necessary* that the innocent be convicted in order to better secure the system's integrity.

Auld was also dismissive of the impact of the 'discount' upon Afro-Caribbean defendants who, through mistrust of magistrates' courts, elect trial in Crown Court more frequently than their white counterparts and also plead not guilty at a higher rate,[103] thereby 'forfeiting' the sentence reduction that otherwise would have been available.[104] The indirect discrimination effect was sneeringly dismissed by Auld:[105] 'Whether or not this nevertheless justifies the description of indirect discrimination, it is one that is self inflicted, for whatever reason.' The probity and consistency of Auld's reasoning may be seen in his final line of defence, that the discrimination issue needs to be 'thoroughly researched and monitored', when he himself offered no empirical support for his general proposals which were founded on his unsubstantiated bedrock idea that the 'discount' system worked well 'in general'.

In fact, there has been a substantial body of research, statistics and

---

[103] See Fitzgerald (1993) and Hood (1992).
[104] Research shows that when black defendants elect jury trial they do so commonly to reduced charges and that a substantial majority are acquitted or have the charges dropped (Bridges et al., 2000).
[105] Auld (2001), Chapter 10, para. 107. Complaints of race discrimination also arise from within the police where ethnic minority officers remain massively under-represented: see, for example, 'Met race claim victims "made to suffer"', says retiring officer', *BBC News*, 9 May 2012; 'Police chief Dal Babu criticizes ethnic recruitment', *BBC News*, 4 February, 2013. In London, for example, with an ethnic minority population of around 40%, there are 9% of ethnic minority officers in the Metropolitan Police.

writings which pointed to institutional racism in policing and courts (see Chapter 8, *infra*) which Auld cast aside. Moreover, official data alone are a damning verdict on his purblind approach. Statistics from the Ministry of Justice (2013c) show that black people are six times more likely to be stopped and searched than their white counterparts; three times more likely to be arrested; and more likely to be proceeded against rather than receive police cautions or Penalty Notices for Disorder (despite the fact that a higher proportion of their white counterparts have previous convictions). Their most common sentence on conviction is custody whereas for white criminals it is a community sentence, and their average custodial sentence was 23.4 months, that for whites being 15.9.[106]

## THE DISAPPEARING JUDGE

One of the problems of the 'plea bargaining' and 'sentence indication' discourse was that direct involvement of judges would constitute such pressure that it would destroy the defendant's 'freedom of choice'. Accordingly, the judge had to be taken out of the equation. The first step was a re-characterisation of the process. 'Plea bargaining' was to be distinguished from 'advanced indication of sentence'. Auld tackled the issue in this way:[107]

> I have called this section 'Advance indication of sentence' to underline its distinction from what is commonly called 'plea' or 'charge bargaining'. In this country, where the prosecutor has no responsibility for seeking or recommending a particular sentence, the bargaining mainly takes the form of his agreeing to drop certain charges or proceed on lesser ones in exchange for pleas of guilty to other or lesser charges. . . . Unlike plea or charge bargaining, [advanced indication of sentence] would not amount to a reduction of charge in exchange for a plea of guilty, but it would introduce *an element of a bargain* between the defendant and the court as to sentence in the event of a plea of guilty. (emphasis added)

Just as 'remorse' was re-branded as 'an element of remorse' so 'advanced indication of sentence' now had only 'an element' of a bargain. It is rather as if, in making a register of countries that retain the death penalty, those conducting executions in private are left out of account. *Goodyear* took this illusion a stage further:[108] 'There is to be no plea bargaining with or by the judge.'

---

[106] Similar disparities were shown in respect of different types of crime such as burglary and supply of class A drugs.
[107] Auld (2001), Chapter 10, para. 91.
[108] *Goodyear* (2005) at para. 30.

Not only is it not plea bargaining, it is *not pressure* either.[109] The way in which *Goodyear* reaches this conclusion while concurrently authorising the threat of an increased sentence of 50 per cent or more involves legal flimflam of a subtle kind. A defendant's freedom of choice over plea is not affected by 'robust advice' from defence counsel. This remains the case, contrary to earlier court rulings,[110] even where this includes communicating in 'strong terms' the court's sentencing policy: it becomes compromised only if the Judge deals *directly* with the defendant, an occurrence that would be 'unacceptable'. The 'absence of pressure' is now re-defined to mean the absence of *improper* pressure, itself characterised in terms of judge–defendant discussions.

Of course, how plea discussions can be initiated presented a further challenge to the court in *Goodyear*. The starting point, said the *Goodyear* court, begins with *Turner* where the court failed to address the circumstance in which a defendant *personally* requests a sentence indication from the judge. In so far as this remark deserves any credence it is only because up to *Turner* and indeed beyond, defendants had been excluded from plea discussions which took place in the privacy of Judges' Chambers. However, this was because, as the court in *Turner* and subsequent cases made absolutely clear, involvement of the judge, for whatever reason, was said to be prohibited as it amounted to undue pressure on the accused.[111] Yet this startling observation was to provide the *Goodyear* court with the opening for its re-definition of 'pressure' and the lawfulness of covert judicial involvement in plea bargaining.

According to the court in *Goodyear*, while freedom of access between counsel and judge was not prohibited, problems arose from any discussion between them about sentence. This created the danger of pressure, or the appearance of pressure on the defendant to plead guilty. Such pressure, *coming from the court*, was unacceptable. Having said this, the court proffered an ingenious way out:[112]

---

[109] The RCCJ, on which *Goodyear* relies, had no doubt that facing a defendant with differential sentences amounted to 'unacceptable pressure' (RCCJ, 1993, p. 113) and placed the innocent at risk. Of course, the RCCJ immediately proceeded to ignore its own warnings on the very same page of its Report.

[110] Earlier cases made clear that barristers were permitted unique access to the judge in the Judge's Chambers to enable guidance to be offered as to sentence. However, 'the whole point would be destroyed if [counsel] disclosed [to the client] what the judge had told [counsel]. The confidentiality of their relationship would be broken' (*R v Peace* [1975], per Lord Chief Justice Widgery).

[111] See, for example, *R v Nelson* [1967]; *R v Barnes* (1970); *R v Inns* (1974); and *R v Cain* [1976].

[112] *R v Goodyear* (2005) at para. 49.

> In our judgment, there is a significant distinction between a sentence indication given to a defendant who has deliberately chosen to seek it from the judge, and an unsolicited indication directed at him from the judge, and conveyed to him by his counsel. We do not see why a judicial response to a request for information from the defendant should automatically be deemed to constitute improper pressure on him. The judge is simply acceding to the defendant's wish to be fully informed before making his own decision whether to plead guilty or not guilty, by having the judge's views about sentence available to him rather than the advice counsel may give him about what counsel believes the judge's views would be likely to be.

This particular piece of judicial alchemy requires translation which we provide here:

1. The defendant cannot directly ask the judge for a sentence indication. This would be improper.
2. The defendant can ask defence counsel to ask the judge to give an indication of sentence. This is proper.
3. The judge, if asked by defence counsel on behalf of the defendant, is not required to provide such an indication but may do so. If the judge decides to give such an indication, it would be wholly proper to do so.
4. If the judge gives an indication of sentence to defence counsel (but not directly to the defendant), defence counsel can pass this to the defendant. Indeed, counsel *must* do so and can give the defendant advice on this in strong terms. This is proper.
5. If, having heard of the judge's sentence indication from defence counsel, the defendant agrees to plead guilty on the basis of this sentence indication, the defendant will inform counsel who in turn will inform the judge. This is proper.
6. If counsel is forgetful, stupid or incompetent, the judge should remind counsel of the defendant's entitlement to seek a sentence indication. This is not an unsolicited sentence indication from the judge. This is proper.
7. Once reminded by the judge, counsel should inform the defendant that he or she can request the judge through counsel for an indication of sentence so that the process can go forward as in (2) above. This is unsolicited and proper.
8. If the judge gives a sentence indication to counsel in a private discussion in chambers which counsel has sought of his or her volition and this is transmitted to the defendant, this is improper and will vitiate any resulting guilty plea.
9. If the judge gives a sentence indication to the defendant directly, this will vitiate any resulting guilty plea. This is improper.

The best that can be said of this, to adopt Orwell's comment on another subject, is: 'One has to belong to the intelligentsia to believe things like that: no ordinary man could be such a fool.'[113]

The court in *Goodyear* knew full well that the plea bargaining process they chose to legitimise would work across the board only if it was a matter of routine court policy or calibrated by the trial judge for the individual case; and, in the latter event, only if there was a duty on counsel to find out the precise policy at work. The *Goodyear* code is simply meant to disguise this reality. Once unpacked, the formulation is self-contradictory: what is being proffered *as a generality* is an unsolicited (if counsel does not advise the defendant, counsel will be instructed to do so) sentence offer *from the judge* which manifestly amounts to improper pressure, the nature of which has to be concealed. Portraying the judge as 'simply acceding to the defendant's wish to be fully informed' is a fiction masquerading as a half-truth.

Of course, the reality comes to the forefront where there is an *unrepresented* defendant who has, unknown to him or her, an 'entitlement' to a sentence indication but no counsel to act as go-between and no access to the judge who, in turn, is not allowed to convey a message to the defendant. The way out of this self-evident problem, which no amount of judicial prestidigitation could resolve, was left hanging in the air in *Goodyear*:[114]

> In the unusual event that the defendant is unrepresented, he would be entitled to seek a sentence indication of his own initiative. There would be difficulties in either the judge or prosecuting counsel taking any initiative, and informing an unrepresented defendant of this right. That might too readily be interpreted as or subsequently argued to have been improper pressure.

But the problem is real and growing in the courts. Government policy, as the Court must know, has increasingly sought to restrict eligibility for legal aid. Indeed, the government-sponsored Carter Inquiry (2006) into legal aid, using a market-based approach, was intended to save £100 million on the 2005/06 criminal legal aid budget, resulting in a 20 per cent reduction of the budget over the next four years in real terms.[115] Among

---

[113] Orwell (1945).

[114] *R v Goodyear* (2005) at para. 69.

[115] The problem will come to the surface on a daily basis if the *Goodyear* rules are extended to magistrates' courts. While most defendants (82%) in magistrates' courts appear to be legally represented, Kemp (2010) found that, apart from those failing the means test, others were discouraged by court staff regarding the seriousness of the offence and hence by-passed the 'interests of justice' test. Government fiscal restrictions led to the introduction of standard fees in 1993 and, following

its proposals, discussed by Bridges and Cape (2008), was the following recommendation:

> The duty solicitor call centre and CDS Direct should be monitored closely by the Legal Services Commission. The monitoring should be on a monthly basis and at a local scheme level, and should look at the volume of cases, and review their effectiveness and quality of service. *If this fails to control any increase in volume of work being undertaken in the police station then DCA [Department of Constitutional Affairs] and the Commission should consider options for restricting defendant eligibility. This should happen alongside the introduction of the new police station fees in October 2007.* (p. 38, emphasis added)

Ongoing cuts imposed by the Government will result in a growth of unrepresented defendants and, at some point, the court will be forced to acknowledge that it cannot simply apply the *Nelson*'s touch to the problems thereby created within its own scheme. Practitioners are increasingly raising the concern that an unrepresented defendant may 'naturally . . . want to know and will ask of the judge the question which [under *Goodyear*] should be for his lawyer' leading to 'an inappropriate narrowing of the defendant's free choice' (Rhodes, 2013).[116] What is more, leading counsel are already refusing briefs in complex fraud cases because of cuts in legal aid. Owen Bowcott (2013a), for example, reported on an alleged 'land bank' fraud case involving eight defendants at Southwark Crown Court in which 17 sets of chambers had declined to act because of the 30 per cent reduction in legal aid rates for 'Very High Cost Cases'. The judge warned the defendants that the trial would proceed and that they may have to represent themselves.

---

the Carter Report, their replacement in 2008 by fixed fees for legally-aided police station advice work. Means testing was introduced for magistrates' court work in 2008 and Crown Court work in 2010. The Legal Aid, Sentencing and Punishment of Offenders Act, 2012 came into force on 1 April 2013 abolishing the Legal Services Commission and replacing it with the Legal Aid Agency.

[116] The concern was triggered by discussion of a court martial case, *Nightingale* (13 March, 2013, CA No 1206575 D5) in which the Court of Appeal recognised that there are circumstances in which a judge's 'uninvited indication' of the likely sentence can amount to inappropriate pressure on a defendant which can 'narrow his freedom of choice' such as to induce a guilty plea. In *Nightingale*, the judge advocate indicated (without invitation) that if the defendant fought the charges (which had a minimum statutory term attached) he would be facing a sentence close to five years in a *civilian* prison. A plea of guilty, however, would result in no more than two years in a *military* prison with the added inducement of potentially having the option of a military career on serving his sentence. A guilty plea was thereafter entered which he then appealed (appeal allowed).

## THE DEFENCE LAWYER

As we have seen in Chapter 3, *Turner* altered the formal position of the defence lawyer from 'independent' counsel to the subordinate status of a supplicant waiting, like Oliver Twist, for any 'discount' that the Judge might ladle out. Auld and *Goodyear* took the story one scene further. Under this formulation, defence counsel become judicial emissaries with no choice but to convey to the defendant either the general discount policy of the court (if this is settled) or the precise sentence indication communicated by the judge. In this setting, professional judgment, knowledge, experience and skill are not requisite attributes of a defence lawyer (as commonly understood); indeed, they are obstacles.

As a *Goodyear*-type defence lawyer, it is not necessary to know anything about things that might deflect you from your court-mandated duty: the burden of proof; admissibility of evidence; the law; or, indeed, the facts. These would be unwelcome complications and divert you from your responsibilities. The procedure established by the judges in *Goodyear* demands only a warm body; the ability to grasp the rudiments of an elementary procedure; the aptitude to transmit the judge's simple message; and, of course, the possession of a digestive system that is able to break down great dollops of pride. While it might become increasingly difficult to find individuals possessing such attributes, for defence lawyers (and, of course, defendants), there is worse to come, as we will see in the next two chapters.

## CONCLUSION

With the sidelining of *Turner*, the Court in *Goodyear* sought to achieve formal rationality while in pursuit of its social order maintenance function. Process became valued primarily in so far as it could guarantee the State's interest in outcome measured in terms of cost-efficient throughput and the rate of conviction. Masking strategies, inherited from Auld and earlier Commissions, depicted defendants, exercising 'freedom of choice', 'voluntarily, without improper pressure', 'deliberately' starting the discount conveyor to activate an otherwise passive judge who could remain inert in the face of a 'try on' by defendants engaged in 'tactical manoeuvrings'. The social imperative of this stereotypical policy was the 'uncooperative or feckless' defendant whose delayed guilty plea caused scheduled trials to 'crack', resulting in public expense, private disturbance and anxiety. At the same time, the direct involvement of the judge in this process, once outlawed by courts as unquestionably constituting improper pressure, was deemed to be beneficent, giving defendants information to which they were now entitled; and the ancillary threat to increase the sentence on conviction at trial by 50 per cent was now ruled perfectly proper. After all, those subject to order maintenance were both guilty and undeserving; and any who were not but succumbed to the threat, were considered necessary, if collateral, damage.

As commodification of defendants was continued by *Goodyear* so as to 'ensure common process', its (unstated) parallel and necessary purpose was to reinforce the formal disciplinary framework on defence lawyers initiated by *Turner*. *Goodyear* attempted to conceal the assertion of judicial power by giving defence lawyers a role in the process while ensuring their impotence as mere conduits through which the system's detritus passed. In the result, by putting a premium on convictions above the risk of miscarriages of justice and their subsequent exposure, the courts found another mechanism by which Lord Denning's 'integrity of the system' might be achieved.

# 5. Institutional distress: the State

## INTRODUCTION

The guilty plea process established by judges, while placing a premium on cost-effectiveness, remains embedded in a legal framework, which, it is claimed, serves to secure correct outcomes and protect against error. This, indeed, is a necessary requirement both to deliver justice on the ground but also to project the appearance of formal legality. The certainty and celerity of punishment which State-induced guilty pleas claims to achieve must be accompanied by the assurance that expedition does not imply less vigilance, so that, to use for pedagogic purposes the categories made fashionable by Auld (2001), 'the innocent' are protected from wrongful conviction and 'the guilty' receive punishment. In the absence of an independent tribunal of fact and conventional procedures to secure compliance with rules regarding admissibility of evidence and the burden and standard of proof, the guarantee is primarily to be found in the personnel of the law: prosecutors, judges and defence lawyers. In this chapter we examine the extent to which prosecutors and judges provide such assurance that concerns over State-induced pleas may be properly allayed, before turning to defence lawyers in Chapter 6.

## THE PROSECUTOR

The frontline of prosecutions is the Crown Prosecution Service (CPS) established by the Prosecution of Offences Act 1985 and headed by the Director of Public Prosecutions (DPP). The CPS is divided into 13 geographical Areas across England and Wales each of which is led by a Chief Crown Prosecutor.[1] At the end of March 2013, of the 6,841 people

---

[1] A 'virtual' 14th Area, CPS Direct, provides out-of-hours charging decisions to the police. Two specialist casework groups – the Central Fraud Group and Serious Crime Group – deal with the prosecution of all cases investigated by the Serious & Organised Crime Agency, UK Borders Agency and Her Majesty's Revenue & Customs as well as serious crime, terrorism, fraud and other challenging cases that require specialist experience.

employed by the CPS, some 34 per cent were qualified prosecutors. The structure itself does not guarantee formal legality in terms of independence and rationality because the DPP is under the superintendence of the Attorney-General (A-G), a government law officer who is, in turn, accountable to Parliament for the CPS.

When Auld proposed 'advance indication of sentence', he did so to distinguish it from 'plea' or 'charge' bargaining on the ground that these were matters for the prosecutor:[2]

> In this country, where the prosecutor has no responsibility for seeking or recommending a particular sentence, the bargaining mainly takes the form of his agreeing to drop certain charges or proceed on lesser ones in exchange for pleas of guilty to other or lesser charges. The advantage to the prosecutor, as representing the public, is that it avoids the need for a trial and consequent ordeal for victims and witnesses; and the benefit to the defendant is that he can expect a discount on sentence for his plea of guilty. The court is not a party to the agreement.

In setting this issue out, Auld referred to *R v Jenkins* (1986) in which the Court cited guidance to prosecutors offered by the Bar Committee of the Senate of the Four Inns of Court and the Bar:

> (1) Counsel for the prosecution is in court personally responsible for the conduct of the case. In discharging this responsibility counsel must decide in each case whether to offer evidence against the defendant and whether to accept or refuse to accept any pleas tendered by him. Although counsel should notify the prosecuting authority of his views on these questions and should take account of any reasons advanced to justify a contrary view before reaching his final decision, [and here are the very important words] the ultimate responsibility for the decision remains with him. (2) Counsel may in his discretion invite the trial judge to assist him in his decision but he is never under a duty to do so nor should he do so as a means of avoiding his personal responsibility. (3) Counsel should in any case be ready to explain his decision to the trial judge in open court and to reconsider it in the light of any observations made by the trial judge.[3]

As is clear from these quotations, the Auld Report and the courts have taken the view that the CPS has primary responsibility for prosecutorial decisions (now formalised by the Criminal Justice Act, 2003),[4] including 'charge' and 'plea' bargaining, with limited oversight by judges.[5] Implicit

---

[2] Auld (2001), Chapter 10, para. 91 (footnote omitted).
[3] Bar Committee of the Senate of the Four Inns of Court and the Bar, headed *Guidance to Prosecution Counsel*, dated May 24, 1984.
[4] This transfers the power to charge suspects, except in minor cases, from the police to the CPS.
[5] For earlier statements on the role of the prosecutor, see, *R v Berens & Others* (1865); *R v Holchester & Others* (1868).

in this is general satisfaction with the discharge of these responsibilities. Accordingly, the role-performance of the CPS is a key factor in the framework of legality within which guilty pleas occur. Any meaningful assessment must, however, begin with some account of the organisational, political and evidential context within which the CPS is situated.[6]

## CPS Organisational and Political Context

Since its inception, the CPS has been beset with organisational problems which have resulted in limited efficiency in terms of decision-making and the capacity to respond to reform initiatives. In part this is a function of its relational position to the police, in part of its organisational culture and in part of the fiscal pressures under which it operates. Although responsible for charging decisions in non-minor cases, the CPS is police-dependent, largely captive to the file of evidence compiled by the police and objectives underlying the file.[7] This may induce it to continue with cases which should have been discontinued altogether or prosecuted at a less serious level resulting in a high level of ordered and directed acquittals. At the same time, the CPS operates under government-imposed targets which, among other things, requires it to 'narrow the justice gap', defined as the difference between the number of crimes recorded by the police and the number of crimes for which an offender is brought to justice.[8] On top of this, the CPS is under pressure to save money. For example, under government financial targets, it reported that over the period 2007/08 to 2010/11, £66 million of savings were to be achieved by, *inter alia*, improving the efficiency and effectiveness of the prosecution process and expanding the CPS Advocacy Strategy Programme under which greater use is to be made of in-house lawyers.

The CPS exhibits levels of organisational dysfunction which impact on its decision-making. This is evidenced in reports by HM Crown Prosecution Service Inspectorate (HMCPSI). In a recent report,[9] inspectors found that:[10]

> ... effective implementation of the advocacy strategy is being hindered by two factors, namely: the oversupply of crown advocates ...; and *the local approaches to allocating work which appear to be based on the pursuit of the*

---

[6] For a more comprehensive discussion of the CPS see, Ashworth and Redmayne (2010) and Sanders and Young (2007).
[7] McConville et al. (1991); Clarkson et al. (1994).
[8] See, Jeremy (2008).
[9] HMCPSI (2012d).
[10] Ibid., 'Chief Inspector's Foreword'.

*maximum amount of savings in counsel fees, rather than achieving and developing good quality advocacy.* (emphasis added)

While the inspectors found a commitment to focusing on quality at the highest strategic level, this was not reflected at local level,[11] where Area managers largely continued to focus, in the allocation of work to in-house crown advocates, on fee savings in Crown Court cases.[12] Over the review period (2009–2011), inspectors found a decline in the quality of in-house advocates and an improvement in that of self-employed counsel, particularly at the higher level. Among the deficiencies of CPS advocates,[13] inspectors pointed to: lack of preparation; discontinuity of representation; returned briefs; and late allocation of work. The inadequate responsiveness of the CPS as an organisation is shown in the fact that only two of the 22 issues identified in the 2009 review had been fully achieved. In advocating new institutional arrangements, HMCPSI (2012d) reported that the CPS must seek to overcome some of the previous difficulties experienced in working with the self-employed Bar, 'including late return of briefs, lack of continuity of advocate, and an absence of preparation time, *which are now mirrored by in-house practices*' (emphasis added).[14]

The combination of failed prosecutions (principally ordered and directed acquittals) and the imposed 'narrowing the justice gap' target produces institutional tendencies well documented in the socio-legal literature: that changing the rules leads to changes in behaviour but not necessarily in the desired direction.[15] As a result, both police and the CPS have disposed of

---

[11] A similar example was unearthed in the Metropolitan Police Area by the Independent Police Complaints Commission (IPCC, February 2013). The IPCC found that an 'under-performing and over-stretched' police unit in an effort to improve performance and meet targets subverted the formal rules of the organisation by encouraging police officers and victims to retract allegations where they thought the allegation might be withdrawn or the standard for prosecution might not be met (resulting in 'no crime' being recorded). Authorised by senior officers, this practice increased the number of incidents that were classified as 'no crime' and therefore 'increased' the sanction-detection rates for the police unit.

[12] HMCPSI (2012d), paras 1.2–1.3.

[13] The Report found that a larger proportion of associate prosecutors in magistrates' courts were competent and performed well.

[14] The DPP said that it was time to 'consolidate' so that criminal trials were being handled by the best advocates. The CPS was creating a network of 13 sets of 'chambers' so that CPS advocates would be hived off to operate more like an independent Bar.

[15] For a recent parallel example, staff at a cancer unit in the NHS have said that they were pressurised into falsifying data relating to patients in order to meet waiting time targets at the Colchester Hospital University NHS Foundation

cases through non-prosecution procedures (such as warnings, cautions and conditional cautions applied inappropriately),[16] downgraded initial charges or reduced charges already proceeded with because a conviction of *any* charge will be counted as 'successfully' meeting the target.[17] This tendency is intensified by the fiscal pressures to which the CPS is subject and its dysfunctional character which, despite repeated re-organisations, continues to replicate the problems for which it has historically been criticised. While withering criticism by courts of CPS advocacy failings[18] and

---

Trust. The *Care Quality Commission* found 'inaccuracies' in waiting time data and police are reviewing whether a criminal investigation is necessary: *BBC News*, 5 November, 2013.

[16] Prosecution decision-making (by the police or approved by the CPS) in these instances may have little to do with 'public interest' or concern for victims. Conditional cautions have, for example, been used in respect of non-trivial offences including dishonesty, theft, serious assault and even serious sexual assault (Edwards, 2010). Indeed, the Justice Secretary misleadingly told the House of Commons in 2013 that, while a caution for rape would be 'completely unacceptable' in some cases 'where the victim is absolutely unwilling to give evidence it may be the only way to get something on the record about an offender' (Hansard HC Deb Col 116, 5 February, 2013). For a caution to be administered there needs to be sufficient evidence to charge and the person accused must accept guilt. See, Criminal Justice Joint Commission Inspection: *Exercising Discretion: The Gateway to Justice* (June, 2011); *BBC News*, 18 May, 2012, 'Sex offenders in Yorkshire given police cautions' (reporting that between 2008 and 2011, *inter alia*, 125 sex offenders in South Yorkshire were given cautions or warnings, seven kidnappers were cautioned in West Yorkshire and 156 burglars were dealt with out of court in North Yorkshire; other offences dealt with out of court included arson with intent to endanger life, abduction of a child, violent disorder and racially or religiously aggravated assault. A Criminal Justice Joint Inspection Report by HM Inspectorate of Constabulary and HM Crown Prosecution Service in 2011, *A New Approach to Tackling Offending in Communities Needed*, pointed to the fact that the number of crimes dealt with outside the formal criminal justice system (excluding restorative justice outcomes) had 'risen dramatically in a five year period by 135 %' with significant variations in the use of out-of-court disposals around the country. Moreover, in a sample of 190 cases reviewed, the inspection found that about *one third were administered inappropriately* as the offending was too frequent (prolific offenders) or serious and a brief rationale for the decision 'was only recorded very rarely' (2.34). On cautions, see also, Leigh (2013). Ellis and Biggs (2013) highlight the issue with a reference to cautioning: 'Radio 4 Today listeners were no doubt spluttering on their cereal on April 3, 2013 as they listened to John Fassenfelt, Chairman of the Magistrates' Association, tell Evan Davis that a caution for a priest who sexually assaulted a 13-year-old girl was "typical" of the way cautions are currently being used by the police' (p. 6).

[17] Her Majesty's Crown Prosecution Service Inspectorate (2003).

[18] See, for example, Baksi (2013b). The CPS has been criticised by two separate Crown Court judges after sending an 'incompetent' advocate to prosecute a

a plethora of institutional apologies[19] catch the headlines, we concentrate here on structural problems which relate to State-induced guilty pleas and their impact upon the quality of justice.[20]

**Technical Incompetence**

A foundational prerequisite for any prosecution system to be considered fit to engage in discussions directed towards persuading individuals to plead guilty might be thought to be technical competence. Technical competence here would at a minimum include: the ability to identify and select the appropriate criminal offence; proficiency in drafting indictments in terms which accurately reflect that offence;[21] the ability to identify relevant authorities; and the competence to draw to the attention of the judge relevant rules of sentencing and procedure. The CPS has been unable to satisfy these basic standards on numerous occasions.

The following are recent examples in which the CPS failed to charge an offence known to the law or failed to draft the indictment so as to establish an offence on which the defendant could be convicted:[22]

---

murder trial and for 'lamentable failures' that delayed a rape trial. 'Insurance Fraud Bureau and City of London case collapses' reported on a trial involving 14 defendants which collapsed after the CPS failed to present any evidence of wrong-doing in what was described as 'normal business practice'. The trial judge described the prosecution as 'scandalous'. Reports on administrative incompetence are frequent: e.g., failing to arrange for witnesses to appear in court.

[19] See, for example, 'CPS apology over woman's murder' (*BBC News*, 5 March, 2009) regarding a woman murdered by her husband. She had reported him to police for threatening to kill her; he was ordered to stay away from her but repeatedly breached his bail, the CPS stating: '[W]e accept that the wrong decision was made not to charge Mr Mannan at an earlier stage'; 'DPP apologises to woman failed by courts after sexual assault' (*The Guardian*, 20 September, 2010); 'CPS apologises to woman over assault case collapse' (*BBC News*, 7 October, 2010); 'CPS issues apology after collapse of assault trial' (*Wales Online*, 12 April, 2012); 'Rochdale child sex ring: Crown Prosecution Service apologises to teenage sex victim for "not taking her seriously"' (*Mancunian Matters*, May 9, 2012).

[20] The CPS, together with the police, has a long history of non-disclosure of evidence. Where this fails to come to light, defendants may be significantly disadvantaged. Where it comes to light, cases often collapse to the disadvantage of victims.

[21] The Courts will not quash a conviction where an error can be described as a 'pure technicality' causing 'no prejudice' to the defendant: *R v Stocker* [2013] which, of course, leaves open to argument whether an error is or is not a 'pure technicality'..

[22] Other failures will not emerge unless there is an appeal. For an egregious example, see, *R v Banfield & Banfield* [2013] where, on appeal, *defence counsel* conceded that the victim was murdered either by both Appellants together or by one

- *R v Shields* [2011]: The offence with which the appellant was in fact indicted, namely breach of a Sexual Offences Order 'contrary to section 2(8) of the Crime and Disorder Act 1998' was *unknown to law*, for it had been repealed, albeit replaced by an offence under section 113(1)(d) of the 2003 Act. The Court of Appeal said: 'The defect in the indictment was not noticed before or during the appellant's trial. Mr ['X'], who represents the Crown on this appeal, but did not appear at trial, frankly accepts that it should have been noticed by the prosecution advocate' (para. 7).
- *R v Cornelius* [2012]: The defendant was *not guilty of the offence charged in the indictment*. The Court of Appeal stated: 'The Crown was in error in failing to identify the correct basis for charging' (para. 41); the appellant 'had in fact no case to answer on the charges as framed in the indictment, though the point had not been taken by those who appeared at the trial' (para. 1).
- *R v Chaney* [2009]: Convictions on three of the counts (including rape and living on prostitution) had to be quashed because of defects in the indictment,[23] some of which were spotted only after counsel for the Crown was instructed to deal with one illegal sentence that the Crown Court had no power to rectify by reason of the lapse of time.
- *Nolan & Howard v R* [2012]: Each defendant pleaded guilty of fraud contrary to s. 35 Tax Credits Act 2003. In fact, as the Court of Appeal found in quashing the conviction, the offences were '*not made out in law*'. 'Counsel for the Crown and for the Appellants all apologise that s/he failed to analyse the law properly'.
- *R v Pelletier* [2012]: The defendant pleaded guilty to a breach of a Sexual Offences Prevention Order on agreed facts; but *he was not in fact in breach* of the relevant Order. The Court of Appeal stated: 'It follows that this is a case in which on the agreed facts the defendant, despite his plea of guilty, was not guilty of the offence which he admitted and for that short and simple reason his appeal against conviction must be allowed' (para. 6).

---

of them. However, as the Court of Appeal stated: 'The indictment did not plead, though it could have done, conspiracy to murder. Rather the Crown led a simple joint enterprise choate offence'. Had the conspiracy been pleaded, the appeals would not have been successful. As it was, both convictions for murder were quashed. See also, *R v Jonathan Dodd* [2013] in which the indictment was inappropriately drafted and the case disclosed 'an appalling catalogue of errors' and in which 'the judge did not receive the level of assistance from the trial advocates to which he was entitled'.

[23] See also, *R v C* [2005]; *CF v R* [2008].

- *R v Lawrence* [2013]: The appellant pleaded guilty, as part of a 'streamlined' process after very limited disclosure, to an offence of possessing a prohibited weapon she had not in fact committed because the firearm in question was not a prohibited weapon. To compound this, the Crown urged the Court of Appeal to substitute a conviction for possessing a firearm without a certificate contrary to section 1(1)(a) of the Firearms Act, 1968 pursuant to the Court's powers under section 3A of the Criminal Appeals Act, 1968 which, the Court ruled, could not validly be done under that provision.

It hardly needs underlining but in *Lawrence* [2013] itself, the Court of Appeal said: 'This case serves to highlight that in relation to "streamlined" procedures directed at encouraging early guilty pleas it is important that all involved are alert to check that the necessary elements of what will sometimes be relatively specific offences are in fact provable' (para. 10).

Where the indictment is properly drafted, the CPS is under a duty to remind the judge at any pre-trial hearing considering a guilty plea of the power of the Attorney-General to refer an unduly lenient sentence to the Court of Appeal and has a wider responsibility to draw to the judge's attention relevant sentencing guidelines and/or authorities.[24] It is far from uncommon for the CPS to fail in these basic responsibilities, as the following cases illustrate:

- *A-G Ref No. 48 of 2006 (Andrew Farrow)* [2006]: The Court of Appeal, reviewing the course of the case said: 'Unfortunately, in the present case, it is apparent that the prosecuting counsel did not remind the judge of that power in the Attorney-General. It may well be that that would have had no effect on the way in which these proceedings progressed. But nonetheless it seems to us that this was a case in which it should at least have passed prosecuting counsel's mind that a question as to whether or not a suspended sentence was appropriate might well arise' (para. 22).
- *A-G Ref No. 6 of 2009* [2009]: The trial judge's attention was not drawn (in a case involving guilty pleas to wounding with intent and possession of an offensive weapon) to relevant authority, as the Court of Appeal made clear: 'It is clear in our judgment that this was a case to

---

[24] The proper approach of the prosecution to bases of plea was set out in *R v Tolera* [1999] and *Attorney-General's Guidelines on the Acceptance of Pleas and the Prosecutor's Role in the Sentencing Exercise* (issued with effect from 1 December, 2009).

which there could be no "if", no "but", no "perhaps". Custody was inevitable. It is a great misfortune that the Recorder apparently did not know of the Lord Chief Justice's decision (although it has been given very significant publicity) and did not have the case referred to him. If the authority in *Attorney General's Reference No. 49 of 2008* were not sufficient, the Sentencing Guidelines Council guidelines in relation to the offence of section 18 also makes clear in respect of adults that a custodial sentence with a starting point of four years and a range of three to five years is the appropriate sentence for an adult on a not guilty plea' (para. 11).

- *A-G Ref No. 44 of 2012* [2012]: The judge at trial intimated that 3 years or longer detention in a young offenders' institution might be appropriate but he was 'then interrupted by counsel for the Crown, who pointed out, wrongly, that the judge was restricted to a 2 year detention and training order. The judge said "Really?" Another member of the Bar said "Your Honour, yes"'. Other misleading comments were made. The Court of Appeal said that the judge 'was entitled to better from the Bar' (para. 18).

These are simply examples of basic failings by the CPS in the prosecution of criminal cases.[25]

Nor is the Attorney-General free of such errors as the following example shows:

- *A-G Ref Nos. 26, 27 & 28 of 2012* [2012]: Here, in rejecting the Attorney-General's reference in cases of robbery, the Court of Appeal said: 'It is disappointing that that authority was not included in the Attorney's bundle, and even more disappointing that it was not considered before this application was made. In our judgment it is a complete answer to the Attorney's submissions' (para. 37).

Such a dismal record[26] has not been placed into the scales by those who advocate State-induced guilty pleas despite the obvious impact upon victims, the public interest and the integrity of law. The record shows that,

---

[25] For other illustrations, see: *A-G Ref No. 44 of 2007* [2007]; *A-G Ref Nos. 25–26 of 2008* [2008]; *R v Anouar Bouhaddou* [2012]; *A-G Ref No. 44 of 2012* [2012]; and *R v Court and Gu* [2012]. In the last-mentioned case the Court of Appeal said: 'We have reached the unhesitating conclusion that the circumstances described here, taken at their highest, were not capable of falling within the scope of the common law offence'.

[26] See also, *A-G Ref No. 50 of 2010* [2010].

setting aside questions concerning the risk to the innocent, the CPS cannot be considered a reliable guardian of the public interest at the most basic level. Ignorance of the law is no excuse and it ought not to be a condition of employment at the CPS.

**Prosecuting at Too Low a Level**

Relatively little attention has been paid to the consequences of plea bargaining in respect of those who *do* commit the forbidden act(s) but who are excessively 'rewarded' for pleading guilty by means of a sentence discount. This can occur through being offered: a guilty plea at a 'knock-down' sentence; a guilty plea to a lesser-included offence; a guilty plea to an alternative and less serious charge;[27] or through a 'fact bargain'.[28] In such cases, where the initial charge actually reflects the facts and the evidence to support the charge, the guilty defendant receives a sentence less than that deserved. The rapist is instead offered a guilty plea to indecent assault; the robber pleads guilty instead to theft; the predatory sex offender is offered a guilty plea to only some charges and on the basis that the offender's involvement is rendered almost benign;[29] the burglar is offered and accepts a guilty plea to theft; and the violent attacker agrees to plead guilty to simple wounding or common assault instead of wounding with intent.[30]

---

[27] There is strong empirical evidence that so-called 'charge-bargaining' is rife in magistrates' courts: Hedderman and Moxon (1992); Henham (2002). There is also clear evidence in practice of the reverse problem – 'over-charging'. See, Blake and Ashworth (1998); McConville et al. (1991); Phillips and Brown (1998).

[28] See, for example, *R v Beswick* (1996) in which the prosecutor sought to downgrade a charge of 'wounding with intent' to simple 'wounding' and to massage the 'facts' so that the nature of the injury caused to the victim was minimised in one respect and buried in another. The 'deal' foundered because the trial judge refused to accept it and called for a *Newton* hearing at which the factual basis of the plea could be interrogated. Cases involving reports of domestic violence have a notoriously high attrition rate and inspectors have found that in many cases where a prosecution has been discontinued the CPS has failed to follow guidelines or failed to make a record of its consideration, if any, of the relevant guidelines (HMCPSI, 2004).

[29] See the notorious case of *A-G Ref No. 44 of 2000* [2001]. In this case, indecent assaults by a headmaster on his young girl pupils (and a male) were minimised both in terms of the number of guilty pleas accepted and the accounts of the acts he had performed. Because a 'devil's bargain' had been made, the Attorney-General was not allowed to challenge the sentence on the basis that it was unduly lenient (Dyer, 2000). The case triggered further Guidelines by the Attorney-General in December 2001.

[30] The motive of the CPS in some cases is to avoid jury trial by preferring a charge which can be dealt with only in the magistrates' court.

The Auld Report (2001) discussed this issue and attributed the problem to 'over-charging' by the police and failure by the CPS to remedy it at an early stage because all too often the prosecutor does not review the case thoroughly or with a sufficiently realistic eye until late in the day:

> This pattern encourages defendants who believe, rightly or wrongly, that they have been overcharged to maintain tactical pleas of not guilty until the last minute. It can also give rise to hasty, ill-considered and inappropriate acceptances by the prosecution of pleas of guilty, which bewilder and distress victims, distort sentencing decisions, engender appeals against sentence and, sometimes, artificially prevent the Court of Appeal, from doing justice in the case. (Auld, 2001, Chapter 10, para. 36)

Auld's remedy (implemented since 2004) was to give decisions on charging (other than in minor cases) to the prosecutor. This recommendation was always likely to fail because it gave insufficient consideration to the reasons for late changes of charge and the context within which the CPS works. Notwithstanding evidential difficulties that the prosecution may sometimes face,[31] such cases are a predictable outcome of a system of evaluation in which 'performance indicators' include lowering the number of 'unsuccessful' outcomes and increasing the number of crimes (of any level of seriousness) for which an offender is (successfully) 'brought to justice'. And, ironically, a timely plea to the lesser charge will itself attract a sentence reduction so that the defendant gets a 'double discount'!

A graphic example of the way things go awry is provided in *R v March* (2002) in which the Judge observed that he had never dealt with a more disgusting case. The victims had been subject to bullying and wickedness; the parent victims had to be separated from their children as they were still suffering from trauma and there was nowhere for them to go as a family. The Judge criticised the CPS for having accepted not guilty pleas to two counts of indecent assault (the accused pleading guilty to certain other counts involving assaults, threats to kill; and incitement to steal). Because of the plea bargain, the Judge's sentencing powers were restricted. As the Judge put it:

> So the totality for a particularly wicked crime, and the public must think the criminal justice system is failing them when that is the position, is only two years. . . . In this case, the defendants are in an enviable position which they did not deserve by the acceptance by the Crown of lesser pleas to the same events

---

[31] Studies demonstrate that choice of charge may present difficulties such that the prosecution may be advised to proceed on a lesser charge than that initially contemplated. See, for example, Genders (1999) and Henham (2002).

and it seems to me that they have had all the discount they could possibly hope for, indeed far more because if they had been found guilty of indecent assault, two years would not have been the length of the sentence I would have imposed. (para. 15)

If the Crown had not agreed to such a plea arrangement, the Judge would have exercised his power to make a detention order and passed a sentence commensurate with the very grave crimes the defendants had in fact committed. However, the irony was even greater because the Court of Appeal said that the judge was bound by the plea agreement and had to sentence on that basis and accordingly ruled that one of the defendants was entitled to a 25 per cent reduction in sentence:

> For the Judge, the starting point should have been the offences which remained 'live' in the light of the agreement between the Appellant and the Crown. He was only entitled to sentence the Appellant in respect of those offences. What he could not do was go behind the compromise between Appellant and the Crown and sentence on the basis of offences which the Crown might have pursued but had chosen not to pursue.

Again, in *Hughes v DPP* [2012] the Divisional Court held that where a man had been assaulted from behind in an unprovoked attack and knocked unconscious, there was no evidence on which the District Judge could properly have concluded that the defendant was guilty of an offence under Public Order Act 1986 s. 4(1) because this requires the prosecution to prove that the defendant had intended that the victim would be caused to believe that immediate unlawful violence would be used against him. Being taken completely by surprise and rendered unconscious was a bar to that offence. The Divisional Court observed:

> Why it was that the appellant was not charged with an assault, or even a more serious offence given the effect of striking this man unconscious with one blow, has never become apparent and could not be explained to us by counsel for the prosecution. . . . Where the prosecution have failed to charge the obvious offence, it is quite wrong to seek to strain a view of the facts so as by some unjustifiable Procrustean method to drag it within the embrace of an offence miles away from that simple charge of assault, which is what this appellant ought to have faced. (para. 9)

The answer to the Court's question seems straightforward: the appropriate charge of either s. 47 actual bodily harm or s. 20 malicious wounding would have entailed a possible election of jury trial, which the CPS evidently wished to avoid.

Regrettably, there are many such examples where the CPS decision-making is (and has been)[32] manifestly at variance with the clear circumstances of the crime. Thus, in *R v Goodings* [2012], the CPS was given leave to amend the original indictment, charging him with an offence of possession of a false identity document with improper intention, to include a lesser charge of possession of another's identity document, to which the defendant pleaded guilty. The Judge, however, sentenced on the basis of the higher charge. On appeal against sentence by the defendant, the Court of Appeal said:

> *There was in this case ample evidence to support the original charge . . ., but for reasons which this court is unable to fathom, the prosecution accepted the appellant's plea of not guilty to that offence.* They therefore chose not to maintain the allegation that he had the document in his possession with the intention of impersonating someone else. Rather they accepted a plea of guilty to an offence of simple possession without reasonable excuse. (para. 10, emphasis added)

The CPS's approach meant that the Judge erred in sentencing the defendant on the basis that he was guilty of the greater offence. Allowing the appeal and reducing the sentence, the Court of Appeal stated that the message which followed from this was that the prosecution ought not to accept a plea of guilty to a charge which does not properly reflect the evidence or enable them properly to place before the court the facts which go to show the true gravity of the conduct.

This message is, however, not likely to hit home. The CPS is both captive to the 'narrowing the justice gap' target and fiscal pressures and subject to organisational dysfunction such that the real 'justice' objective will often be lost in its decision-making, as can be seen in *A-G Ref Nos. 50–53 of 2012* [2012]. In this case, four defendants pleaded guilty to conspiracy to commit burglaries and, in the case of one defendant, conspiracy to steal. The defence argued that the sentences were appropriate in the context of the prosecutorial lack of efficiency, the uncertainty and to some extent the disorganisation. In increasing the sentences, the Court of Appeal underlined the seriousness of the crimes and the failure of the indictment to reflect this in appropriate charges:

---

[32] See, for example, Tony Halpin (1994), discussing a case in which the trial judge said that he was 'horrified' at the CPS 'fouling up' a case by striking a plea bargain which resulted in two defendants involved in a huge forgery racket being exposed to a maximum of two years' imprisonment instead of ten years', as he considered more appropriate; and Tom Rawstorne (2003) discussing the case of a fraudster who stole £1.7 million pleading guilty after the judge assured him that in return he would not be jailed.

[T]his was a gang of professional burglars. The burglaries were committed mob-handed. Apart from the wearing of helmets and balaclavas, the very fact that so many went into the targeted premises was part of the design to intimidate and frighten if anybody happened to be inside. Doors were smashed to gain entry. On some occasions weapons were taken inside. On other occasions homes were ransacked. The burglars were after high value property. More than all this, the gang was prepared, whenever it seemed to be necessary, to use serious violence in the homes they burgled – serious, and in two cases with which we are directly concerned, terrifying violence. *Two of the offences could have been charged as robbery and section 18 grievous bodily harm against the householders or those who were present in the homes with them. The victim impact statements tell an unsurprising story of long-lasting, if not lifelong-lasting, consequences of having been the victims of these offences.* (para. 66, emphasis added)

Here, as indeed in the previously mentioned case, the conduct of the case by the CPS introduced a degree of uncertainty as to whether the Judge thought that the offenders were entitled to full credit for their pleas even though three of them had put forward a false basis of plea. The Court of Appeal initially had great reservations whether full credit in such circumstances for any of the three would have been appropriate. Nonetheless, in view of the apparent misconception that occurred throughout the entire hearings before the Judge, that each offender was to receive the maximum discount, they concluded that a discount of one-third in the case of the defendant who had not pleaded on a false basis and in the other three of around 20 per cent should be made.

Whether displayed in individual cases such as those discussed[33] or in wider prosecution policies[34] CPS decision-making is often found to be incomprehensible by any measure. Some of the consequences of this 'half loaf' philosophy, located within a financial structure that privileges cost reduction over substantive justice, become, after the court proceed-

---

[33] See also *R v Dowty* [2011] in which the CPS, having undertaken to drop two charges in return for guilty pleas on two others, was forced to back-track when counsel gave advice that the original decision was 'manifestly wrong'.

[34] As disclosed, for example, in *R v Brereton* [2012] where, 'at least in Yorkshire', in relation to disguised firearms the CPS policy was to charge a lesser rather than greater offence so that 'prisoners are serving sentences for the possession of disguised stun guns far below the minimum level which would arise if the greater offence had been charged and the minimum sentence provisions applied'. In *Brereton* itself, the Court of Appeal said: 'Firstly, it is clear that there has been an inconsistent and potentially arbitrary prosecuting policy as to whether to prosecute for the "greater" or "lesser" offence, or at the very least to accept a plea to the lesser offence as disposing of such a case. Secondly, in this case there was a lamentable series of switches of decision from one position to the other, raising and then dashing the expectations of the Appellant on more than one occasion' (para. 16).

ings, all too apparent to the victims of crime who are thereby victimised again. In such cases, the power of the Attorney-General to seek a review of an 'unduly lenient' sentence[35] may likewise be rendered nugatory, the sentence itself often being the maximum that the trial judge can impose in respect of the lesser charge.[36] It is left to the Judge, victims or media to vent anger or frustration over a course of events, as in the following:

- Barry Smith, a career criminal and prolific burglar with 34 prior burglary convictions, was arrested after burgling a house, stealing two mobile phones and the keys to a BMW car which he used to try and escape police by driving dangerously including the wrong way down a one-way system before setting fire to the car. He made a plea bargain as a result of which the CPS accepted a plea of guilty to (i) handling one stolen mobile phone; and (ii) driving the BMW car without authority. In sentencing the offender to 12 months in prison, the Judge said: 'I regard the sentence as verging on the absurd but my hands have been tied by decisions taken by the CPS with which I totally disagree. . . . If you had been convicted [of the proper charges] I would have imposed a sentence of at least four years' imprisonment'.[37]
- When a judge, unable to impose a term of imprisonment of more than six months on a wife-beater because of a decision to charge him only with common assault, asked the prosecutor why the defendant was not facing the more serious charge of causing actual bodily harm (on conviction for which the Judge said that he would have sentenced him to up to five years' imprisonment), the CPS lawyer replied that there was really no explanation. The Judge responded: 'It's a little book called the CPS Charging Guidelines. . . . Unless a victim ends up on life support, it's charged as common assault'.[38]
- A man who inflicted serious injuries on his mother, including knocking her unconscious on two occasions, had his plea of guilty to assault occasioning actual bodily harm accepted by the CPS who decided not to charge him with wounding with intent. The Judge said that this was the third such under-charging case with which he had had to deal in a month: 'The charging of this defendant was seriously flawed, in haste and without due consideration. . . . Crimes

---

[35] The power is not available in cases where the sentence is merely lenient nor where the prosecutor prompts the sentence or otherwise endorses at trial.
[36] See, for example, *A-G Ref No.44 of 2000 (Peverett)* [2001].
[37] Narain (2011).
[38] *Wales Online*, 13 June 2011.

of violence in Cumbria are not being appropriately charged. . . . [D]ecisions are being taken on grounds of expediency and cost-cutting rather than in the interests of justice . . . [thereby frustrating] the ability of the court to impose proper sentences to protect the victims.'[39]

- A man, acting as a baby-sitter, was charged only with assault occasioning actual bodily harm rather than with grievous bodily harm, after inflicting 28 separate injuries on a 19-month-old little girl. Recorder John Hardy said: 'How anyone with an iota of intelligence reading that catalogue of injuries, which is indicative of a sustained and savage assault committed on a little girl aged 19 months, can fail to spot that it amounts to GBH indicates to me that something is very, very wrong with the system . . . if it results in grotesque blunders such as this. . . . I'm concerned this case may have in part resulted from the policy which has been dressed up with the gimmicky title "Stop Delaying Justice" which is inevitably going to lead to poor and hurried decision making in cases such as these'.[40] Imprisoning the defendant for three years, Judge Hardy said: 'Had you been properly charged in this matter at the very least an extended sentence if not an indeterminate sentence for public protection would have been passed'. The CPS later apologised to the judge.
- Judge Brown criticised the CPS for 'undercharging' an offender who smashed a pint glass over a drinker's head. Telling the defendant that he was 'extremely fortunate' to be charged with common assault after a 'cowardly' attack, Judge Brown added: 'I certainly wish the prosecution advocate to take the matter back to the Crown Prosecution Service. There has been a good measure of undercharging on this particular matter. . . . I have no doubt that the general public would be astonished.'[41]
- To the same effect,[42] Judge Heywood said that his hands were tied as the basis of plea (to possessing ecstasy with intent to supply but only on the basis that the defendant was a heavy user and, apart from giving someone else a few, would have consumed all the tablets himself) had been 'negotiated and accepted' by both the CPS and Haverfordwest magistrates. 'It would be wrong for me now to interfere but I would not have accepted that it was non-commercial dealing. I would not

---

[39] *News & Star*, 5 May 2012.
[40] Airs (2012). The reference is to a system, CPS Direct, set up in 2003 under which the CPS offered charging advice to the police over the telephone.
[41] *Liverpool Echo*, 22 August 2012.
[42] *Western Telegraph*, 26 May 2010.

have entertained it.' Because of the basis of the plea, Judge Heywood could not order confiscation of the cash seized which was accordingly returned to the defendant. 'It is staggering. The whole thing is a shambles.' The Crown Court had received two letters from the CPS both dated the same day, one stated that they accepted the basis of the defendant's plea, the other said that they didn't.

These are simply illustrative of a wider practice by prosecutors in which cost-effectiveness is allowed to override considerations of justice, leaving judges unable to impose a sentence which fits the acts committed.[43]

The assumption that prosecutors are the custodians of the public interest both in the sense of knowing where that interest lies and in the sense that they can be relied upon to found their decisions upon it cannot be sustained. There is abundant evidence to question whether they know what is in the public interest and much evidence that reasons other than public interest animate their routines and decision-making. Equally diminishing in visibility is the much-vaunted CPS concern for victims. In drawing attention to areas of improvement in the CPS, a recent Report of the Inspectorate[44] adverted to earlier concern relating to 'the acceptance of inappropriate pleas' which had resulted in the compulsory training for all prosecutors scheduled for completion at the time of the inspection, and remarked: '[t]he improvement anticipated was not readily apparent[45] . . . '.

**Factual Basis of Bargain**

If the CPS cannot be trusted to understand and apply the law or charge individuals at the appropriate level, it might be thought that it would have greater success in determining the facts underlying the charge. Certainly, we would expect that, in negotiating a guilty plea, it would not agree to a factual account which was at variance with the circumstances of the crime. Clear guidance on this was given to the CPS by the Court of Appeal in *Beswick* (1996):

---

[43] For other examples, see, 'Attorney general "cannot review" GBH sentence', *BBC News*, 20 January 2012; 'Judge criticizes knife case charge', *Hexham Courant*, 28 July 2008; 'Judge hits out over handling of raid case', *Express & Star*, May 8 2009; 'Prosecutors criticized for not levelling a more serious charge in racism case', 24 March 2011; 'Carlisle judge criticizes CPS over danger driver charge', *News & Star*, 9 July 2011; 'Judge blasts CPS over savage gang attack case', *This is Cornwall*, 24 July 2009.
[44] HMCPSI (2012d).
[45] Ibid., para. 3.8.

> The prosecution should not lend itself to any agreement whereby a case is presented to the sentencing judge to be dealt with so far as that basis is concerned on an unreal and untrue set of facts concerning the offence to which a plea of guilty is to be tendered. (per Jowitt J at (i))

It appears, however, that prosecutors have experienced difficulty in complying with this straightforward injunction. Indeed, soon after *Beswick*, the former head of Dulwich College Preparatory School, Robin Peverett, was the beneficiary of a notorious fact- and charge-bargain.[46] Of the 16 charges he faced for indecent assault on 11 of his young pupils committed over a period of eight years in an appalling abuse of a position of trust, seven charges were dropped (leaving four of the complainants/victims out of the picture altogether), the nature of his conduct transformed from 'spanking' to 'tapping' and 'fondling' and the motivation (about which the CPS could have no determinative knowledge) was agreed to be a desire to express his position of power over the children rather than sexual gratification. In accordance with this agreement, the trial judge agreed to impose a suspended sentence of imprisonment. The public outrage was matched by the distress of the victims included in the deal and excluded from it.[47]

This case is far from unique. There are many instances in which the CPS has misrepresented the facts, failed to check the factual basis of the plea, failed to assess intelligently the defendant's factual claims, or engaged in extensive bargaining over facts of which it had no clear knowledge. Misrepresentation occurs in cases in which, for example, the CPS considers these not to be worthy of high priority. Examples here are cases of domestic violence where research has shown that both police and the CPS have not treated such crimes with the seriousness that they deserve. Thus, research has shown that where domestic assault cases were downgraded, prosecutors diluted the seriousness of the incidents when presenting the cases in court so that, for example, 'threatening with a knife' becomes 'showing a knife to someone'.[48] In other cases, the facts may not be checked at all. Thus, in *A-G Ref No. 50 of 2010* [2010] the defendant tendered a written basis of plea to burglary and an attempt to inflict grievous bodily harm. As the Court of Appeal pointed out, the prosecution advocate then told the judge that the basis was acceptable, when she knew, but the judge did not, that nobody had compared it to the account that was given by the victim with which it conflicted in material respects. The result

---

[46] *A-G Ref No. 44 of 2000 (Peverett)* [2001].
[47] See Dyer (2000); Ahmed (2000).
[48] Cretney and Davis (1995).

was that when the case came back for sentence the judge was presented with a different prosecution advocate telling him that the pleas should not have been accepted in the first place.[49]

Equally, 'accuracy' of fact-finding which trials aim for can easily be sidelined in the desire to conclude the matter expeditiously. *A-G Ref Nos. 21 and 22 of 2012* (*Benjamin Pugh; Jordan Naaif*) [2012] involved serious robberies in which the defendants advanced, on a guilty plea, a basis of fact wholly at variance with the evidence. As emerges from Court of Appeal discussion, not only was the behaviour of the CPS improper but it had further consequences:

> Somewhat surprisingly that basis of plea was accepted by counsel for the Crown. . . . It is a matter, in our view, of deep regret that once both offenders had ceased to say there had been no use of the knife and ceased to deny that what had been alleged, namely the sexual degradation and sexual terror that had been inflicted on the first occasion and those two issues had been abandoned, a proper assessment of both was not made again. (para. 23)

Again, in *A-G Ref Nos. 11 and 12* [2012] the Court of Appeal had to impose a substantial increase in sentence (more than double) for rape of a child, both offenders having pleaded guilty on a written basis, namely that the complainant was 'a willing participant', which the CPS had without justification accepted, the Court of Appeal stressing that: 'the prosecutor bears a burden of responsibility to ensure that factual concessions to a basis of plea or mitigation of the offence are made only when justified and that, if made, the precise import of the concession is understood by the offender and the court . . . ' (para. 34).

Lack of care over establishing the facts can have other consequences for victims. Thus, in *A-G Ref Nos. 119 and 120 of 2005* [2006] on guilty pleas for wounding with intent, one of two defendants alleged that his attack was preceded by actions on the part of the victim. The Court of Appeal judgment demonstrates the unsatisfactory nature of this for all parties:[50]

> Shusing Jim pleaded guilty on the basis that there had been a heated argument between the victim and the defendant and that, during the course of the argument, the victim had made a number of threats to the defendant and his wife. It was alleged that the victim had had connections to a gang in Birmingham who would be able to 'take care' of the defendant and his family. In the basis

---

[49] The judge ruled that the clock could not be turned back and the sentence was undisturbed on a reference by the Attorney-General.

[50] At paras 8–9.

of plea Shusing Jim also stated that, much to his regret, he had lost his temper and struck the complainant. That basis of plea appears to have been accepted by the prosecution. Subsequently, the victim of the attack made a complaint to the office of the Attorney General about those allegations, saying that it was not true that he had made any such threats. He was also concerned because, apparently, that had been reported in local newspapers.

There is little that this court can do about this, the prosecution having accepted the basis of plea. However, we make it quite clear that the existence of those threats has not been proved and that it would be unfair, from the point of view of the victim to suggest that what was said in the basis of plea was accurate.

Finally, as these cases make clear, plea negotiations provide an opportunity for defendants who have committed the forbidden act to minimise their culpability and to capitalise on CPS incompetence or on its desire to avoid a trial at any cost. A revealing insight is provided by *Caley* [2012] in which not only was the sheer scale of the 'negotiations' in respect of fraudulent activity by a mortgage broker staggering but also, as the Court of Appeal stated,[51] it enabled the defendant to secure the prosecution's agreement to a number of mitigating features at an early stage, and to avoid any risk there may have been that further investigations might have revealed a different degree of culpability or a larger number of mortgage frauds. In addition, the defendant was able to reach agreement which limited any confiscation proceedings. Similarly, in *Cairns & Others v R* [2013] the CPS accepted, in the basis of plea, that the defendant's possession of drugs was 'not a commercial supply, in the usual sense of the word, but rather to support a habit'. This, as the Court of Appeal pointed out, did not answer the real question, namely whether he was a 'street dealer' supplying to whomsoever wanted to purchase drugs or whether he was 'supplying friends and associates on a social basis'. Had the CPS addressed the factual basis with care, a different picture might have emerged, as the Court of Appeal indicated:

> It was perfectly plausible for the prosecution (or, indeed, the judge) to reject the basis of plea that he had supplied MDMA to friends and associates on a social basis in order to support his own drug habit and not for financial gain. He was not in employment (and had no history of long term employment) and a combination of the eleven wraps, the money and the mobile phone messages could have led to the inference that he was supplying drugs on a commercial basis: whether in the street or otherwise, he was, in reality, street dealing for gain. (para. 15)

---

[51] At para. 80.

**Independence**

Given the appalling record of the CPS, it would be of little comfort that the prosecutor was 'independent', free from political and other influence. That, of course, is far from true in theoretical terms, the CPS being ultimately accountable to Parliament, which means, in practice, the party in government. But at a more practical level, the CPS is unable to exert independence from the trial judge. While Auld (2001), *Goodyear* and *Caley & Ors v R* project the courtroom actors as independent entities, in the real world, the judge is not an umpireal figure but very much the dominant force.

Thus, in *A-G Ref Nos. 80 and 81 of 1999* [2000], the trial judge indicated that the offences could be dealt with on a non-custodial basis – an indication which received the '*unreserved acquiescence*' of the CPS. It followed that the Court of Appeal felt unable to increase sentences, even if these were unduly lenient:

> We have to remember that prosecuting counsel was instructed by the Crown Prosecution Service who are responsible to the Attorney General, who is now making this application. Having regard to the unfortunate history of this case, we would consider it almost, if not actually, abusive now to re-open these sentences to the potential detriment of the offenders. (per Lord Bingham, CJ)

Even more striking is *A-G Ref No. 19 of 2004* [2004]. This case demonstrates only too well how counsel may be intimidated by a forceful judge (as in earlier cases such as *Inns*), as the following extract from the Court of Appeal's judgment makes clear:[52]

> *On the facts that we have related as to what happened in this case, it seems to us that the prosecution did not act in a way in which it could properly be said that it had played a part in giving the offender the relevant expectation as to sentence.* . . . The position was this: in the first instance counsel for the offender was seeking an indication on the basis of simple wounding and the indication

---

[52] Other illustrations are where the trial judge orders or directs an acquittal or makes a terminatory ruling against the wishes of the prosecutor. See, for example, *R v H* [2010] where at the outset of the trial, the Judge made clear his view that the allegations were not worthy of trial in the Crown Court in asking 'are we really going to waste the Judge and jury's time on this?' The Judge expressed concern that the case was a waste of already strained resources and remarked that the case was a 'scandalous waste of money'. He was unimpressed that the CPS had reviewed the case several times and had decided to proceed with the case, which he described as 'rubbish'. It was held that it had not been open to the Judge to acquit the defendant and the jury's acceptance of his direction had no effect.

was given. When the prosecution returned to court on the second occasion, its stance clearly indicated that it was not prepared for the matter to be dealt with on the basis proposed by the offender's counsel and upon which the judge's indication had been given. What occurred in chambers makes it abundantly plain that the judge, without any reference to counsel at all, made it clear, and indeed crystal clear, what his view was. *Prosecuting counsel in those circumstances, whilst there is no doubt that as a counsel of perfection he should have indicated to the judge the problems of approaching the case as the judge intended to, by reason of the authorities to which we will refer later as to the appropriateness of sentencing for racially aggravated offences, was in the unenviable position of being confronted with a 'fait accompli' by the judge.* What happened thereafter does not seem to us to have changed that situation. *Prosecuting counsel was simply accepting what was clearly inevitable.* He could not properly resile from the indication he had given as to the acceptability of the plea. (para. 21, emphasis added)

## JUDGES

Criminal cases show that the claim that judges represent a protection against mistakes in the State-induced guilty plea process is not one that should be seriously entertained. There can be no guarantee at a plea hearing that defence counsel will encounter a judge who is impartial, fair-minded and open to argument. Instead, judges may be biased, bigoted and closed to alternative viewpoints. Nor do the cases give comfort that the judge will have a real grasp of the law; ignorance of which may lie undiscovered unless there is a trial transcript to examine. The cases demonstrate that the dangers in all these respects are real.

The carefully cultivated idea that judges are disinterested parties was advanced by the Lord Chief Justice in the John Harris Memorial Lecture in 2011:[53]

> Dealing with it superficially, the judge or magistrates are referees. But until recently the role of this particular type of referee has been to wait on the pitch until the teams turn up. Wait for as long as they wished. That is no good. We need referees who will go into the changing rooms beforehand, tell each side how the game will be played, warn the players who may go offside that they are being watched, and as for those who foul, that they will be sent off. And having prepared the teams for the kind of refereeing they will expect, to lead the teams out on to the pitch and put the ball down in the middle of the centre circle at the time when the kick-off is supposed to take place. And the proceedings played once.

---

[53] Available at: http://www.police-foundation.org.uk/uploads/holdingjohn harris/jhml2011.pdf

While this neatly contradicts the assertion of judges that a criminal case is not a 'game', it is an idea that is falsified in the real world of practice.

All too often judges initiate sentence discussions or conduct 'hearings' contrary to the rules. This has taken many forms, including where judges override the views of counsel and/or treat counsel disparagingly.[54] Thus, in *R v Smith* (2011), when counsel for the appellant raised with the judge her concern that the judge's (misdirection) had come without any prior warning to counsel, the judge's discourteous and dismissive response was: 'I cannot imagine that anything that you could have said could have dissuaded me from giving it, not least because if I did not give such a direction they might have used it for a wholly improper purpose'.

Of equal mention is the notorious case *R v Cole* [2008]. Here, the trial judge intervened inappropriately and discourteously during cross-examination of police officers in a manner which, effectively, came to their aid when evidence appeared inconsistent with prior statements. The judge's hostility to the defence is evident in a note sent to defence counsel and described by the Court of Appeal in quashing the conviction as follows:

> His attitude to Miss ['X'] is however more unhappily exemplified by a note which he provided to her, it should be said not in the presence of the jury, but in the presence of her client, on the morning of the second day. It is headed '**6 P's**' and then there is a list of six words, in heavy letters: '**Prior Planning Prevents Piss Poor Performance.**' We have no indication from the judge as to whether he thought that it was a humorous attempt to indicate to [Miss 'X'] what he felt or whether it was pure rudeness. It certainly appears to us to be a wholly inappropriate note to have sent to counsel. Even if he did feel that there were aspects of Miss ['X's] approach to the case which perhaps, as a young barrister, he felt might have resulted in her not helping her client as much perhaps as he thought that she should or helping the court as much as he thought she should, that was not the way to express himself. It can have had nothing but a detrimental effect on the confidence of Miss ['X']; and since it seems to us to be a touchstone of his attitude to Miss ['X'] and the way that the trial was conducted, it seems to us that it is a matter which helps us to understand whether or not this appellant can have felt that he was getting a fair trial in front of this judge. . . . The note persuades us that the complaints about which Miss ['X'] makes go beyond complaints which we can say have not affected the safety of the conviction. (para. 22)

Furthermore, advance sentence indications out of line with relevant authorities or guidelines are not uncommon. In *A-G Ref Nos. 8, 9 and 10 of 2002 (R v Mohammed, R v Habib, R v Hussain)* [2003] non-custodial sentences proposed by the trial judge triggered guilty pleas on kidnapping charges for which, the Court of Appeal said, the authorities clearly

---

[54] See also *R v Cordingley* (2007).

indicated that a custodial sentence was appropriate. The outcome is that, unless prosecuting counsel objects, offenders get less than deserved. In *R v Rollings* [2012] the guilty plea consideration by the judge was shown to be wholly insufficient. A promise (advanced indication) of 5 years' imprisonment (for possession of a loaded firearm with intent to endanger life) was honoured but woefully inadequate and increased to 10 years on a reference.

Alarmingly, judges have been known to display a lack of understanding of the fundamental issue of the burden of proof. For example, the judge in *R v Anne McGee* [2012] misdirected the jury on critical issues relating to the elements that needed to be proved in respect of an offence under the Misuse of Drugs Act, 1971, as was accepted in the Court of Appeal: 'It is unfortunate that the error was not picked up at the time . . .'. Indeed, the error in question, which had been the subject of an earlier court ruling,[55] was not picked up at trial by either defence or prosecution counsel, it being conceded before the Court of Appeal that no evidence had been adduced by the prosecution on the relevant issue.

A similar example is provided by *R v Lopez* [2013]. In this case, the Recorder failed to consider any of the relevant issues which have to be taken into account before deciding that the defendant could be tried in his absence, a decision which, the courts have said, 'should be exercised with the utmost care and caution'.[56] In addition, other aspects of the Recorder's summing up were to cause the Court of Appeal grave concern and are highly relevant to questions relating to the safety of judicial oversight of guilty pleas:[57]

> First, although the Recorder informed the jury that the prosecution had brought the case, he never explained that the burden of proof rested on the Crown and that in consequence the defendant did not have to prove his innocence. It is arguable that in a case in which the defendant was not present, even greater importance attached to that direction than in other trials.
>
> Second, although on more than one occasion the judge told the jury they should only convict the defendant if they were sure of guilt, this was fatally confused at the end of the summing-up when the judge directed the jury:

---

[55] *R v Auguste* [2003].

[56] *R v Jones* [2003], per Lord Bingham, at para. 13. In this regard, he was not assisted by counsel for the prosecution or defence who should have alerted him to the steps that needed to be followed.

[57] The Court of Appeal put to one side 'the wholesale lack of structure in the judge's remarks and the appearance that the summing-up was delivered without any real preparation . . .' (at para. 20). The Court also adverted in passing to 'many other faults with this summing-up'.

'... and the verdict which I require of you, or the verdicts, are ones where you are all unanimously satisfied that you are sure either the defendant is guilty or not guilty as charged.'

This clearly left the choices as twofold. The jury had to decide whether they were sure of his guilt or sure of his innocence. This direction undermined one of the central tenets of our system of criminal justice, namely that the accused is entitled to the benefit of a reasonable doubt. In order to be acquitted, he does not have to establish – to make the jury sure of – his innocence.

Third, the judge gave the jury little, if any, meaningful direction as to the ingredients of the two offences of possessing a controlled drug with intent to supply and the elements that needed to be proved. (paras 21–3)

It is obvious here, as the Court recognised, that the conviction had to be quashed, the Crown not seeking a retrial. More significantly, for present purposes, is the question how there can be any confidence in guilty pleas overseen or induced by a judge culpable, not of 'slips' or minor 'lapses', but of catastrophic errors on absolutely basic legal issues? Ominously, these would not come to light except in the event of a trial.

Such grave errors are not discrete. Further instances abound where judges fall into error in regard to the admissibility of evidence or the calling of witnesses. A recent and damning illustration can be found in *C v R* [2012]. There, on serious charges of rape, buggery and indecency, the Court of Appeal accepted that the trial judge fell into 'serious misdirection' in regard to 'expert witness' evidence: 'No direction as to expert evidence should have been given. It cloaked the evidence of those to whom complaints had been made with a significance which in law it did not have.' Further, referring to a relevant part of the original statement of one witness, the Court of Appeal said: 'It is unfortunate that neither counsel saw to it that that evidence was not given at trial' (para. 7). It is patent, accordingly, that misunderstandings and misperceptions in the minds of judges at trial are very likely to be replicated in 'plea hearings' or in the course of informal exchanges with counsel at the pre-trial stage prejudicing the defence and the safety of guilty pleas induced thereby.

But judicial failings stretch beyond this such as to destroy another prop of the plea bargaining illusion. While it should be evident from the foregoing compendium of procedural ineptitude that the CPS is subject to serious technical shortcomings, it should also be clear that judges are deficient in the same respect. Thus, while the CPS was wholly wrong in charging individuals with 'offences' not known to the law or with incorrectly drafted indictments, trial judges are equally at fault in allowing such cases to proceed at all; and, regrettably, there are many other such examples. In *R v Unah* [2011], for instance, in quashing the conviction, the Court of Appeal observed that the *only* reason the defendant pleaded guilty was because of an incorrect ruling in law by the trial judge which affected the question whether she had a possible defence. Similarly, in *Asmeron v R* [2013] the defendant's conviction was quashed after he had pleaded guilty to entering into the United Kingdom without a passport following an incorrect ruling by the trial judge at the outset of the trial that he had no defence to the charge.

As learned commentators have pointed out to devastating effect, the Court of Appeal itself is subject to similar failings. A striking illustration is *R v White* CLW/12/20/17, a case involving alleged mortgage fraud. The CPS produced a draft indictment containing six counts under the Fraud Act 2006 and the Theft Act 1968 and was given leave by a circuit judge to prefer the indictment.[58] As James Richardson (2013) points out, none of the charges held water, the indictment in each case being fatally flawed because, *inter alia*, (i) one offence was alleged to have been committed before the Fraud Act had come into force; and (ii) because the actions of the defendant were not ones caught by the Theft Act. The indictment was then amended by replacing two counts with another defective count. White eventually pleaded guilty to two counts of fraud under the Fraud Act, 2006 and two counts of obtaining a pecuniary advantage under the Theft Act, 1968. Thus, as Richardson (2013) points out: '[A] second circuit judge . . . plus prosecution counsel, plus the solicitor advocate acting for the defendant, had disposed of a case without anyone noticing that three counts were nullities and one count alleged non-compliance with a non-existent legal duty'. Worse was to follow. The Court of Appeal not only failed to notice the flaws but, additionally, disposed of the case on the basis of the original (flawed) indictment, not upon the (flawed) amended indictment, confirming that two wrongs don't make a right.

In like manner, in *R v Talbot* (2013) David Thomas commented that the case 'exhibits characteristic muddle' where the appellant, though not convicted of having an intent to cause grievous bodily harm, was dealt with by the Court of Appeal as if he had such an intent. Additionally, the Court wrongly relied upon a prior authority and twice referred to the intent to escape as being an aggravating factor when it was an ingredient of the offence to which the appellant pleaded guilty. 'The unpalatable truth' Thomas remarks, 'is that the court has treated it as a case of causing grievous bodily harm with intent to do so, which was aggravated by the fact that it was committed in the course of trying to escape. Such an approach is unprincipled and indefensible'.

Occasionally, it is possible to trace errors in the sentencing exercise

---

[58] Leave was needed, it seems, because the CPS failed to comply with the 28-day time limit.

to the air of expedition that so often pervades. For example, in *A-G Ref No. 71 of 2012* [2012], the Court of Appeal referred to the fact that only one authority was drawn to the attention of the judge; it added that it had read other cases and stated: 'We cannot help but think that a reading of these authorities might have informed the judge's sentencing approach' and, in the absence of consideration of those cases, 'We wonder how thorough was the attention of parties to the sentencing exercise'. Similarly, *A-G Ref Nos. 61 and 62 of 2012* [2012] in which the judge was reminded of a once-leading but now outdated authority with only a fleeting reference to the modern authority, the significance of which can be seen in the Court's comment: 'The relevance of the case, *hardly developed in front of the learned judge*, was that it reflected that change in approach. Altered sentencing starting points and ranges in homicides had had an inevitable effect on offences falling below them on the scale of seriousness' (para, 35, emphasis added).

In like manner, sentencing may be given insufficient priority precisely because the guilty plea is seen to put it low in the order of precedence. An exemplary illustration is supplied by *A-G Ref Nos. 82 to 96 and 104 to 111 of 2011* [2012] evident in the following extract from the Court of Appeal:

> It is not our function to make any attempt to allocate responsibility for what happened and it may be that some of the difficulties were not easy to avoid. But the sentencing was spread over no less than seven different hearings, separated by several weeks. Those hearings seem to have been squeezed into spaces between other cases, including other trials. In an effort to accommodate the commitments of the advocates and perhaps others involved the defendants were not always presented to the judge in a rational order, nor were they always presented like with like. In the meantime there were persistent difficulties convening the court because it was not big enough, because the prisoners were produced late or there were not enough staff in the cells to manage the numbers that needed to be there. The judge was also frequently showered with loose papers, late and unmanageably presented, when the case absolutely demanded indexed and paginated documents on all sides. There were frequent and often insufficiently identified disputes as to the proper factual basis for sentencing and as to the timing of pleas of guilty. The judge made repeated efforts to resolve them and we pay tribute to the care which he brought to a difficult case. (para. 2)

Pressure of time sometimes emerges in the assignment of cases by Listing Offices to inexperienced judges as in *A-G Ref Nos. 21 and 22 of 2012 (Benjamin Pugh; Jordan Naaif)* [2012], as can be seen in the following extract from the Court of Appeal in quashing the sentences of the two offenders (terms of 3 years and 9 months; and 3 years respectively) and imposing significantly longer terms (of 14 years and 13 years respectively):

The learned Recorder to whom the case was assigned was given a case of immense difficulty. We enquired why it was that a case of this kind was placed before a Recorder and not an experienced full-time judge. It appears it was assigned to a Recorder by the listing office, without any reference to the resident judge at the court and under the mistaken belief that the case had to be dealt with that day. It is most unfortunate that that decision was made. We shall ask the Presiding Judges of the circuit to look into the matter to ensure it does not happen again. We say that because in very great fairness to the Recorder, this was not the kind of case that the Recorder ought to have been asked to deal with and if, as is inevitable from the conclusion that we have reached, which is to say that we consider the sentences were unduly lenient and deficient in a number of respects, it would not be fair to attribute what has happened to this Recorder as he should not have been placed in that position. (para. 20)

## CONCLUSION

While reliance is sometimes placed on the remarks of Lord Hailsham in support of plea bargaining[59] that a trial may prejudice the defendant not because courts consciously want to penalise but because 'the production of evidence in detail during the course of a contested case often actually aggravates the case against the accused when it comes to sentencing him', the record of State-induced guilty pleas surely shows the exact opposite: the virtue of a properly-conducted trial in providing a more accurate account of the defendant's culpability and the flaws of a coercive guilty plea process which might mask it.

As sanctioned by Auld (2001), the CPS has been given free rein over both charging decisions and plea negotiation. Setting aside technical incompetence, predictably, in a dysfunctional organisation beset with cultural and fiscal strains everyday practice is marked by case-shedding and charge-degradation. Analysis of the CPS shows the impact of this 'half a loaf' policy in which narrow organisational interests predominate rendering it meaningless and, indeed, insulting to talk about the 'interests of victims' except as a shibboleth behind which hides an incoherent understanding of public interest. Handing over the process of State-induced guilty pleas to the CPS was unreflective and damaging to the interests of justice.

For its part, the judiciary has contributed more than its fair share to this abysmal tale. Unable to restrain the rush to judgment prompted by a presupposition of guilt, rules and procedures, sloppily drafted and repeatedly re-stated, are set aside by unctuous judges, counsel browbeaten

---

[59] See, for example, McCabe and Purves (1972).

and basic standards of courtesy side-stepped, Court of Appeal precedents and guidelines cast aside. Basic legal errors are readily found even, it is sad to say, within the Court of Appeal itself. The view that judges are an adequate safeguard against abuse of the State-induced guilty plea process can therefore be laid to rest and, as the next chapter demonstrates, the Court of Appeal is increasingly arrogating to itself the power to determine, delimit and circumscribe the role that can be played by the defendant and defence lawyer in any criminal case.

# 6. Institutional distress: the defence

## INTRODUCTION

In this chapter we review the capacities and practices of defence lawyers against the rhetorical claims made about them and consider the likely impact of government cuts to legal aid in criminal cases. From *Turner*, through *Goodyear* and *Caley*, defence lawyers have been lauded in formal rhetoric as the ultimate protector or 'gladiator of the accused'[1] providing a 'fearless, vigorous and effective defence to secure the best outcome for the client' (Lord Chancellor's Department, 2001). This accords with the argument of Fuller (1961) who said that the purpose of the principle of 'equality of arms', which requires that those accused of criminal offences should be legally represented at the expense of the State,[2] is not merely to protect the innocent person against the possibility of an unjust conviction: 'The purpose of the rule is to preserve the integrity of society itself. It aims at keeping sound and wholesome the procedures by which society visits its condemnation on an erring member'.[3] As Fuller went on to point out, if the defendant is plainly guilty this representation may become in a sense symbolic, but the symbolism is important because 'it marks society's determination to keep unsoiled and beyond suspicion the procedures by which men are condemned for violation of its laws'.[4]

Following *Turner*, defence counsel was required to ensure that defendants would plead guilty *only if they were guilty*. However, research has shown that some solicitors' firms, the frontline of criminal defence work,

---

[1] Du Cann (1964) at p. 46.
[2] The presumption of 'equality of arms' has led Young and Wall (1996) to conclude that 'access to justice seems, therefore, to imply access to legal aid and lawyers' (p. 6). See also, McConville et al. (1994) at p. 2.
[3] Fuller (1961) at p. 35.
[4] Fuller went on to cite John Stuart Mill (1861) *On Representative Government*: 'We need not suppose that when power resides in an exclusive class, that class will knowingly and deliberately sacrifice the other classes to themselves: it suffices that, in the absence of its natural defenders, the interest of the excluded is always in danger of being overlooked: and, when looked at, is seen with very different eyes from those of the persons whom it directly concerns'.

may develop cultures and organizational practices which give priority to interests other than the protection of the rights of suspects and defendants[5] and they, along with barristers, may operate with a presumption of guilt.[6] In both professions, those who do strive to offer a professional and empathetic service are, together with their differently motivated colleagues, at risk of being channelled into the guilty plea processing machine or being forced out of the profession altogether by judicially inspired policies and by governmental cuts to legal aid.

We begin our account by reviewing evidence which bears upon whether the judiciary are, in a technical sense, justified in reposing trust in the legal profession to be the guarantors of the rights of suspects and defendants. We then discuss how, irrespective of the competences of defence lawyers, judges have re-deployed defence lawyers away from the traditional role they were said to occupy in order to make them part of the prosecution. Following this, we outline the climate of fear and 'reform' under which defence lawyers operate and the way in which the storm of discontent that this has brought affects the daunting commitment of lawyers and new entrants to the profession to be involved in State-funded legal services.

## SOLICITORS

### Technical Competence

In reflecting upon the formal rhetoric surrounding defence lawyers, it is important to recognise that the accolades stand against a body of socio-legal research which – collectively – raises serious questions about whether the criminal defence profession has been and continues to be deficient

---

[5] This is a conclusion that has traditionally met with resistance by the judiciary: Lord Steyn (1997), 'I am not willing to countenance the thought that the legal profession might be too absorbed with self-interest to care about the integrity and well-being of our constitution' (p. 95). Newman (2013) (see discussion below) provides a wealth of empirical data which exemplify legal practices where the 'bottom-line' takes precedence. One senior partner told him: 'You should go through the unused material, chase witnesses up, go the extra mile for the client. But you don't. You realize that you can't do that. At the end of the day, every case has to be about trying to make a profit'. A junior solicitor from a different firm echoed: 'It's got to be run now like a business to survive' (p. 86). Similarly, Blackstock et al. (2013) draw attention to the risk that some police station advisers, 'in striving to maintain cordial relationships with the police may, perhaps unconsciously, substitute the client's interests with considerations of their own interests' (p. 408).

[6] See also Mulcahy (1994).

and its representation inadequate. This is something the 'reformists' have chosen to ignore, recognition of which would place their project at great divergence with the (artificial) construct of an 'active' defence profession. This construct, as we have argued, allows the legitimation of State-induced guilty pleas to continue. Indeed, the premise upon which *Turner* and subsequent cases rested and the theory advanced by Auld operated on the basis of competition within a robust and independent defence service. The contradiction is two-fold.

First, empirically, the evidence shows that notwithstanding excellent individuals within the legal profession (and there *are* many), a growing number of firms seem unable to fulfil a committed defence function. It is not clear whether there is a single reason for this but a sizeable number operate under a presumption of guilt (often inadvertently), all have been debilitated (financially or otherwise) by legal aid strictures, and all have been unassailably demoralised by Government policies.[7]

Second, there is a contradiction because the Criminal Procedure Rules or CPR (see below) puts these lawyers into a position where the traditional role has been jettisoned and takes them further towards (if they were not there already) the image portrayed in various damning accounts, which draw their conclusions from empirical studies.

Research conducted by Mike McConville, Jackie Hodgson, Lee Bridges, and Anita Pavlovic (1994) (hereinafter, '*Standing Accused*') found, following detailed observational research into the working practices of nearly fifty criminal law firms, that legal advisers often had a deficient overall grasp of clients' cases, that they tended to assume that their clients were guilty and that police and prosecution versions of events were true, and that clients' allegations of police malpractice were almost invariably ignored or met with a bland response.

*Standing Accused* argued that these assumptions and practices derived from the closeness of defence and prosecution lawyers' and the police's

---

[7] Strike action by legal aid lawyers has been a continuing threat. The Criminal Law Solicitors Association (CLSA) and the London Criminal Courts Solicitors Association (LCCSA) in solidarity with the Criminal Bar Association (CBA) declared a 'mass non-attendance' day in protest at reductions in legal aid, the CBA Chairman warning that the profession was being 'dismantled into non-existence' (Bowcott, 2013b, 2013c). The legal aid protests are the first time barristers have taken such action in legal history (records go back as far as 1466). Criminal courts have seen temporary closures as a consequence (Bowcott et al., 2014). In a letter from the CPS dated 27th February 2014, barristers were warned that their participation in strike action would lead to loss of future work. Barristers were given 'until the following day' to confirm their strike position via their Head of Chambers (Baksi, 2014).

working circumstances, attitudes, culture and ideologies, compared with the lack of empathy between defence lawyers and their clients, with the result that poor defence work resulted. Defence lawyers were often said to be inadequately funded to prepare cases for legally aided clients.[8] The research also raised concerns that defendants were frequently incompetent to know what case preparation should be done, were unable to persuade their solicitors to carry out adequate preparation and powerless to persuade counsel that their cases should be conducted as they, rather than counsel, wished.

*Standing Accused* stood for almost two decades with nothing in the way of equivalent follow-up ethnographic studies.[9] Since then, changes to the provision of legal advice at police stations,[10] the legal aid landscape and fundamental alterations made to criminal procedure, much of which we refer to in passing throughout this book, raised questions as to whether the study could be said to provide a current reflection of the law firms and the legal profession in England and Wales.[11] Daniel Newman's (2013) recent ethnographic fieldwork, which offers the latest 'health-check' of defence lawyers in legal aid firms is, therefore, a timely contribution.

Over a 12-month period, Newman undertook his study in the belief that more current data would 'contradict' the 'prevailing understanding' originally put forward in *Standing Accused*. Newman's belief stemmed in part from the 'various steps' that had been taken to 'improve the quality of legal aided criminal defence in the intervening period' since the publication of *Standing Accused* (p. 39).[12]

---

[8] Such was the state of affairs that some defence solicitors were asking clients to carry out investigations for themselves.

[9] A recent study by Alge (2013), supporting *Standing Accused*, argues that some barristers deliberately 'crack' trials as it serves their financial interests. Alge accepts, however, that these conclusions are not necessarily generalisable owing to the small sample involved.

[10] Thus, those sent to give advice to suspects must now be accredited, having undergone training directed to this purpose. Bridges and Choongh (1998) found evidence of improvement in this area in their study. See also, Blackstock et al. (2013), a comparative study of police station advice in four jurisdictions. This found, among other things, a more active intervention in interrogations by accredited advisers than previous research had shown. Partly this might be explained by the fact that the study focused on specialist defence firms (p. 408).

[11] See, for example, Bridges and Cape (2008).

[12] The changes included the introduction of a scheme to ensure that representatives of firms sent to police stations to see clients under arrest were 'accredited', cognisant of the prevailing legal regime and their role within it.

Newman conducted a two-stage survey: formal interviews and participant observation.[13] When collecting data, Newman attempted to structure his findings in a way that would ward off criticism that criminal lawyers would receive a 'raw deal' in adopting the type of 'structuralist' research favoured by *Standing Accused*.[14] He reported, however, that '[i]t did not matter how much room I gave the lawyers, this became merely rope on which they would hang themselves' (pp. 38–9). Newman's findings are of significance because of their empirical foundation:[15]

> This research *purposively targeted firms that it was supposed would show lawyers in a good light*, and this inevitably affected my pre-suppositions. Initially if anything I was inclined to put a positive spin on all I saw and heard as that was what I had wanted to believe. Over time, though, the flood of negative data made it necessary to take a far more skeptical approach. (p. 39, emphasis added)

Newman first looked at perceptions lawyers held towards their clients ('attitudes'). He further examined whether those attitudes were reflected in their actions ('behaviour'). Newman then proceeded to 'follow lawyers' attitudes and behaviour to their logical end-point' (classified as 'outcomes'). Newman categorised the firms into two groups: *'radicals'* who represent a 'dying breed' of lawyers devoted to their client-base, and *'sausage factories'* which represent self-interested working practices that put profitability before clients (p. 30). His research pointed to a continued 'malaise' at the heart of significant sections of the defence profession.

Far from Newman's original ambition of 'draw[ing] out the positive elements of legally aided criminal defence [work]', the evidence produced a 'dispiriting picture' which 'suggested conclusions more in line with the negative image portrayed by McConville *et al* (1994)' (p. 143). According to Newman, this blight manifests itself in a number of ways:

---

[13] Newman conducted his research at three law firms in a large city in England. However, he spent a longer and more consistent duration at each (4 months) in order to immerse himself and 'see significant progression in cases' and to provide 'the chances of generalizing to some level on the routine work undertaken and the results this produced' (p. 29) as well as 'offer[ing] an indicator of some reality which may or may not be replicated elsewhere' (p. 164).

[14] One critic of the *Standing Accused* study felt the methodology adopted resulted in '... an idealized, negative version of criminal lawyers' (Travers, 1997a, p. 370). Newman (2013) notes in reply that '[while] McConville *et al* (1994) at least proceed with their values open and acknowledged, Travers (1997b) fails to note his own epistemological, or professional, biases' (p. 28).

[15] Newman's ethnographic study builds upon the sampling, methods and methodology informed by both McConville et al. (1994) and Travers (1997b).

- A 'striking divergence' in attitude saw lawyers in interview 'emerge as holding a strong public service orientation' claiming positive lawyer–client relations, while under participant observation the data gathered 'showed the lawyers in a very poor light' (p. 39);
- In this sense, Newman characterises the interview 'performance' of the lawyers under examination as 'an attempt at deception, [or] subterfuge' (p. 50);
- A 'pervading cynicism' amongst lawyers who routinely assumed the factual guilt of their clients 'whether or not they had talked to them or read their file'. Despite frequent instances where clients claimed innocence, lawyers were 'unsympathetic' and 'refused to believe them' and were 'openly derogatory' (pp. 47–48);
- Newman found repeated instances of clients who were not only treated in a '*disrespectful* manner' by lawyers 'engaging in rude conduct with a lack of courtesy' (p. 71), they were 'dehumanised' (p. 83) and left 'in a continual state of ignorant dependence' (p. 98) via 'conduct that worked to degrade them' (p. 101), including 'contact and access to suit the pursuit of volume and maximisation of profit rather than to benefit their clients' (p. 101). Behaviour went beyond '*speaking over*' (p. 107) clients, with 'most lawyers' demonstrating a 'presumption of guilt' towards clients (p. 112) in that they 'assumed that clients would plead guilty, and thus helped ensure that they did just that' (p. 112), despite protestations to the contrary (pp.114–15);
- Lawyers who 'regardless of firm, seemed to share the opinion that the fundamental character trait of their client was that they were mentally lacking' (p. 45);
- Lawyers who questioned the moral fortitude of their client's perceived class (pp. 46–7);
- Lawyers who misinterpreted providing advice *in strong terms* as meaning something far stronger.[16] A client's choice was often removed by lawyers who 'sought to fool their clients into the choice of action favoured by the lawyer'. Where this form of 'client abuse' did not succeed, 'confidence tricks' were employed to 'take advantage of their client's vulnerability' (p. 119);
- Lawyers who held themselves out as radicals '. . . spoke as if they stood for active defence, while they appeared to practise something far more passive' (p. 148).

---

[16] See also Blackstock et al. (2013) who found some evidence that suspects might be encouraged towards a particular disposal (e.g. a caution) 'without any proper evaluation of the evidence having taken place' (p. 320).

Despite the various changes since *Standing Accused*, Newman provides an equally scathing judgment of the lawyer–client relationship under legal aid which should be of comparable concern today. In particular, the stark disjuncture that Newman identified between what lawyers 'said' and 'did' in regard to their clients reminds us that it would be foolish to accept an account which plainly differs from that which it seeks to describe (Bridges et al., 1997). Newman explains: 'The impression many lawyers sought to convey – that they stood up for the clients and gave them the respect others denied them – amounted to positioning themselves as akin to heroes. . . . They seemed little short of martyrs' (p. 85). Newman states this was 'a fiction'; instead lawyers appeared to treat clients 'no differently from the stance they so criticised in the general public and government'. He added that '[c]lients were pushed from pillar to post, rushed through the system as criminals who no one should or did care about' (p. 85).

A more general appraisal of his study therefore reveals 'negative attitudes, disrespectful behaviour and lawyers speaking over their clients', from which it was evident to Newman that 'the nature of the lawyer–client relationship was such as to place clients' access to justice in jeopardy' (p. 143).[17]

In the sense that Newman's research is disturbing confirmation of *Standing Accused*[18] it also highlights the reality that these courtroom actors may be far from willing (let alone able) to provide the assurance that may properly allay concerns over State-induced pleas.

If it was already known that some lawyers are prone to herd their clients through the criminal process with such control that the client's decision, in effect, is really the lawyers' (Baldwin and McConville, 1977; Worrall, 1990), the conclusion that can be drawn from Newman's affirmation of the 'fundamental contradiction' (p. 143) at the epicentre of the lawyer–client relationship, is that it is injudicious to construct a system which is dependent on the defence as it *currently* stands to offer any semblance of formal legitimacy. As we have seen, however, that is the basis of Auld's understanding and it has been taken further in the years since his report.

---

[17] Newman accepts there are 'systematic reasons' why 'a healthy relationship was difficult to achieve in practice' – the 'most obvious' being 'reduced legal aid remuneration' (p. 147).

[18] Evidently shocked by his own findings, Newman confesses he is 'aware that [his] research may further harm the reputation of this branch of the legal profession' (p. 150). He apologetically concludes that his research was not intended to be 'anti-lawyer', emphasising that it was 'undertaken to support those who practised active defence and the cause they claimed to work for' (p. 147).

# THE BAR

**Technical Competence**

As is apparent from the cases cited in Chapter 5, the traditional encomia directed toward defence counsel are at best a gospel of perfection rather than a statement of reality. In those cases in which a defendant was convicted of an offence unknown to the law or on an indictment which was drafted in such a way that no conviction should have been obtained, defence counsel was as much at fault as Crown counsel in allowing a guilty plea. Indeed, the Court of Appeal has frequently drawn attention to the failings of defence counsel, as in the following examples:

- *A-G Ref No. 50 of 2010*: '[Crown counsel], who has presented the application on behalf of the Attorney and for whose help we are very grateful, cannot avoid accepting and we cannot avoid making passing reference to the fact that the court was not well served by the advocates appearing on behalf of the Crown and indeed in due course *we have to say he seems not all that well to have been served by the advocate appearing on behalf of the defence either*' (at para. 3, emphasis added).
- *R v Shields* [2011]: '"Ms. X," who represented the appellant at his trial and appeared on his behalf again on this appeal, to her embarrassment, also overlooked the defective indictment [which charged an offence unknown to the law].'

Additionally, there are cases in which the defence lawyer has precipitated a guilty plea by wrongly advising that there is no available defence to the charge brought or failing to advise that a defence is available.[19] In *R v Boal* (1992), for example, the appellant was employed by a company as an 'assistant general manager' of its bookshop over the period that the general manager was away on holiday. During this period, serious breaches of the premises' fire certificate occurred. The appellant had been given no managerial training, least of all in matters of health and safety at work or fire precautions. Along with the company, he was charged with offences against the Fire Precautions Act, 1971 on the basis that he was a 'manager' within the terms of the Act. He was given legal advice on the

---

[19] See also Leigh (2013) discussing *Caetano v Commissioner of Police for the Metropolis* [2013] and describing the legal advice by the duty solicitor to accept a caution (the decision to caution being overturned on judicial review) as 'indefensible'.

assumption that he was incontestably a 'manager' within the meaning of the Act. Quashing the convictions, the Court of Appeal (Criminal Division) said:

> [T]his appellant could well have been regarded as responsible only for the day-to-day running of the bookshop rather than enjoying any sort of governing role in respect of the affairs of the company itself. Whether or not such a defence, had it been advanced at the trial, must inevitably have prospered, it is frankly not possible to say. . . . But we do conclude not merely that such defence would have had a realistic prospect of success but that in all likelihood it would have prevailed. (p. 277)

Similarly, in *Abdalla Mohammed v R et al.* [2010] the appellant, *MV*, was charged with an offence under the Identity Cards Act, 2006. At no time did the duty solicitor who represented *MV* at the magistrates' court, where *MV* entered a guilty plea, advise him of the statutory defence under section 31 of the Act, nor did counsel who represented him at the Crown Court give any such advice. Quashing the conviction, the Court of Appeal was satisfied that the appellant would have had 'a good prospect of a successful defence under section 31' (para. 39).[20]

By way of final example is *R v Mateta et al.* [2013]. The five appellants, when entering or leaving the United Kingdom, attempted to rely on a false passport or a false travel document issued under the 1951 Convention Relating to the Status of Refugees ('a Geneva passport'), in that the passport or travel document was a forgery or it related to a different person. None placed reliance on the statutory defence under section 31, all pleading guilty to an offence of possession of an identity document with improper intention. In relation to Koshi Mateta, the Court stated:

> It is sufficiently clear from the attendance notes compiled by the applicant's solicitors, along with their response to the Grounds of Appeal and the contents of the brief to counsel, that the availability of the defence under s. 31 was never raised with the applicant, on the basis of the incorrect assumption that there was no potential defence to the charge. (para. 30)

---

[20] In the same consolidated appeal, the Court quashed the conviction of Rahma Abukar Mohammed who, the Crown accepted, had not been advised of the potential defence open to her and accepted that she had a good prospect of success in that regard; and that of Mohsen Nofallah whose counsel candidly informed the Court of Appeal that there was a potentially good defence and that she accepted full responsibility for failing to advise him of it. See also *R v Sina Jaddi* [2012] in which the conviction on a guilty plea was quashed and a re-trial ordered after the defence lawyer advised that there was no defence.

Similarly, in respect of another appellant, Simon Anduka:

> There are no indications from the relevant attendance notes compiled by the solicitors or in the brief to counsel that the appellant received any advice on the availability of a defence under s. 31; indeed the solicitors have suggested to the CCRC that, in their estimation, the defence did not apply. (para. 36)

A third appellant, Yasin Bashir, received 'erroneous advice' that he had no defence and the remaining appellants, Amir Ghavani and Saedeh Afshar, were given no advice on the available defence, the Court of Appeal stating, in quashing all five convictions:

> Given the decision of this court in *MA* (to say nothing of the other decisions to which we have referred), it is both surprising and disturbing that neither solicitors nor counsel appear to have been aware of the position in law and we repeat that this situation should not recur in the future. (para. 56)

# JUDICIAL RE-STRUCTURING OF THE LEGAL PROFESSION

## Partners in Crime: Co-optation of a Profession

Whatever the individual failings of defence lawyers and legal-aid lawyers, these pale into insignificance by comparison with the position of structural weakness into which they have been shoe-horned by judges. The formal disempowerment of the defence, initiated by *Turner* and extended by *Goodyear*, has been intensified as a result of the Auld Review (2001). An essential platform of this was the maintenance of the formal legitimacy of the system which required the characterisation of defence lawyers as obstacles to the mass disposition of cases, by conflating them with devious and manipulative defendants and depicting them as exploiting the system's weak spots through a respect-less pursuit of a 'Sporting Theory' of justice. Such a characterisation had limits, however, and a new strategy had to be developed to maintain formal legitimacy.

Auld's answer was to propose restructuring the role-performance of defence lawyers so that they would become partners to the prosecution and judge in the 'cost-efficient' administration of justice. In other words, he intended to align the worst features of criminal lawyers identified by researchers with a new construct of formal role performance. With the theory laid down by Auld, all that remained was implementation by the politicians and the judges (by good luck including Auld among their number).

### Defence counsel's obligations: the historical position

Historically, the duty of defence counsel was 'to get an acquittal if he can, whatever the merits of the case may be'.[21] As Lord Reid famously observed:[22] 'Every counsel has a duty to his client fearlessly to raise every issue, advance every argument, and ask every question, however distasteful, which he thinks will help his client's case'. Lord Reid qualified his 'fearless advocate' through the advocate's position as an officer of the court: 'Counsel must not mislead the court, he must not lend himself to casting aspersions on the other party or witnesses for which there is no sufficient basis in the information in his possession . . .'.

His further elaboration of the duty did little to undercut the legal rhetoric which surrounded the duty of defence counsel even if, in so acting, this might well incur the displeasure of the client:[23] '. . . he must not withhold authorities or documents which may tell against his clients but which *the law or the standards of his profession require him to produce* . . .' (emphasis added).

Turning to the 'standards of the profession' it is instructive to recall Sir William Boulton's authoritative *Conduct and Etiquette at the Bar* which described the role thus:[24] 'According to the best traditions of the Bar of England and Wales, a barrister should . . . fearlessly uphold the interests of his client without regard to any unpleasant consequences either to himself or to any other person'. The Guide explained:

> Counsel has the same privilege as his client, of asserting and defending the client's rights and protecting his liberty or life by the free and unfettered statement of every fact and the use of every argument and observation that can legitimately, according to the principles and practice of law conduce to this end, and any attempt to restrict this privilege should be jealously watched.

In the past then, the lawyer's duty to the court was expressed in *negative* terms: primarily that counsel must not actively mislead the court or permit the client to give perjured evidence. In this sense alone, the duty to the court was an overriding one. But this duty did not displace the old adage, underpinning the rhetoric of the adversarial system that 'the Crown

---

[21] Poland (1898) at p. xxi.
[22] *Rondel v Worsley* [1969].
[23] Ibid. at p. 228.
[24] Boulton's Guide (1953) was subsequently reprinted on five more occasions (1957, 1961, 1965, 1971 and 1975). For the purposes of this book, its contents, by and large, remained identical throughout until 1975 when the *Turner* guidelines were adopted. It was eventually superseded in 1980 by what has become common parlance amongst members of the Bar, the 'Code of Conduct'.

asserts and the Crown must prove'. The 'standards of the profession' were emphatic on this:[25]

> In considering the duty of an advocate retained to defend a person charged with an offence . . . it is essential to bear the following points clearly in mind: – (1) That every punishable crime is a breach of the common or statute law committed by a person of sound mind and understanding; (2) that the issue in a criminal trial is always whether the accused is guilty of the offence charged, *never whether he is innocent*; (3) that the burden of proof rests on the prosecution. (emphasis added)

Modern interventions by statute introduced some qualifications to these responsibilities. Thus, the Criminal Justice Act, 1967 required defendants to give an alibi notice. The same year, the Road Safety Act introduced a reverse burden of proof in relation to samples for analysing alcohol levels in the body. Some thirty years passed before greater inroads occurred with 'proper' inferences that could be drawn from an accused's silence under the Criminal Justice and Public Order Act, 1994. Hot on its heels, the Criminal Procedure and Investigations Act, 1996 introduced a requirement for an accused to serve a defence statement when tried on indictment, the statement to include such things as the general nature and particulars of the defence, the matters on which the defendant took issue with the prosecution and why, as well as points of law and legal authority upon which the defendant proposed to rely. The generality of the requirement was expanded by the Criminal Justice and Immigration Act, 2008[26] to require the defence statement to include 'particulars of the matters of fact' the defendant proposed to rely upon in the defence.

**Defence counsel and the 'sea-change'**
Arising out of the Auld Report (2001), since April 2005 the Criminal Bar has been made to act in conformity with the 'sea-change' swept in by the Criminal Procedure Rules (CPR).[27] The CPR, in essence, represents a tool for bringing the defence Bar into line; one that is determined by judges, the perimeter of which is still being drawn. Despite vaunted aspirations for 'greater integration in the criminal justice system' (Baroness Scotland),[28] the Code has been a vestigial structure. The 'autonomy' of the Bar is now

---

[25] Boulton (1953) p. 56.
[26] The Youth Justice and Criminal Evidence Act, 1999, also limited defence cross-examination by imposing significant restrictions on the questioning of prosecution witnesses about previous sexual behaviour in sexual offence trials.
[27] Thomas LJ in *R (on the application of the DPP) v Chorley Justices* [2006].
[28] Hansard HL Deb, vol. 644, col. 645, 1 February 2003.

heavily qualified through the CPR, Statute and judicial interpretations so that the limited 'obligation' as 'officer of the court' has, as we discuss below, now become little more than 'court functionary'.

In essence, the CPR assign the Defence a *cooperative* role to work alongside the Prosecution towards the active 'management' and 'progression' of a case to ensure that all the contested issues can be 'properly' dealt with at trial.[29] This is bolstered, *inter alia*, by a nebulous obligation on defence lawyers to deal with a case 'efficiently and expeditiously' (Rule 1.1.2.(e)), to identify the 'real issues' in the case (Rule 3.2.2.(a)), to appoint (as does the Prosecution) a 'case progression officer' to liaise with the other side and the court (Rule 3.4(1)(a)) and to furnish the Prosecution/Court with information about witnesses, written evidence and procedural rules and points of law.

The CPR places the Defence Bar within a punitive society: the disciplinary weapons wielded by judges include requiring counsel to swear loyalty to 'efficiency-driven' (i.e., cost-effective) procedures, advising the court and all parties of any significant failure to take any of the procedural steps required by the Rules, any Practice Direction or Order of the Court (Part 1, Rule 1.2(1)(c)), to advise defendants regarding advanced indications of sentence, ensure that defence statements are drafted to be informative and curtail prolix cross-examination with sanctions imposed by way of 'wasted costs' orders.

This disciplinary society is founded on the premise that the parties are bound by loyalty to a reformulation of justice drawn from the civil law concept of an 'overriding objective'.[30] In charting these developments, the question as to whether the 'sea-change' is down to the Rules themselves or whether they are simply a manifestation of a pre-existing tide is revealed as largely a diversion. In fact developments have proved remarkable in the extent to which the 'standards of the profession' have been sacrificed on the altar of 'establishing truth and justice above arid, legal technicality'.[31] However, as we will see, the intensification to subordinate the Bar reached a watershed prior to the introduction of the CPR, when the Code could only hope to legitimate what was already abundantly obvious – a depleted

---

[29] *R (on the application of Lawson) v Stafford Magistrates' Court* [2007].

[30] This has resulted in a departure from the traditional stance in criminal law that '[d]isciplinary functions in regard to the Bar are exclusively vested in the Senate of the Inns of Court and the Bar and are exercised by the Bar Council. A judge who considers that he has cause to complain of the professional conduct of a barrister may make his complaint to the Bar Council but he has no power himself to take disciplinary action in that regard' (*McFadden*, 1975, per James LJ).

[31] Fields (2008).

defence workforce with formal duties diametrically opposed to its clients' interests.

Appropriating two-handedly from the civil justice reforms, Auld recommended the establishment of a single corpus of rules: 'That instrument should begin with a clear statement of purpose and general rules of application and interpretation, as successfully pioneered in the Civil Justice Rules flowing from Lord Woolf's reforms of the civil law' (Chapter 10, para. 277).[32] Politicians pounced on Auld's recommendations. A judge-heavy Rules Committee was set up under section 69 of the Courts Act 2003, and engaged in a consolidation exercise to make the Rules of Procedure (CPR) in criminal courts '... with a view to securing that – (a) the criminal justice system is accessible fair and efficient and (b) the rules are both simple and simply expressed'. This, ostensibly, became the narrow pursuit of the Rules Committee. Two parts of the CPR give particular effect to these intentions: Part 1 (the Overriding Objective); and Part 3 (Case Management), which we deal with in turn.

**The overriding objective**
The overriding objective is that 'cases be dealt with justly' (Rule 1.1(1)). Under the CPR, however, 'justice' is redefined to include:

(a)   acquitting the innocent and convicting the guilty;
(b)   dealing with the prosecution and the defence fairly;
(c)   recognising the rights of a defendant, particularly those under Article 6 of the European Convention on Human Rights; and
(d)   respecting the interests of witnesses, victims and jurors and keeping them informed of the progress of the case.

While judges had come to talk of criminal cases involving interests of the victim and the public as well as that of the defendant,[33] even before the CPR the Auld Report (2001) had introduced a new breed of 'justice' secured by judicial 'case management' as reflected in *Chaaban* [2003]:

> A trial judge has always been responsible for managing the trial. That is one of his most important functions. To perform it he has to be alert to the needs of everyone involved in the case. That obviously includes, but is not limited to, the interests of the defendant. It extends to the prosecution, the complainant, to every witness (whichever side is to call the witness), to the jury, or if the jury has

---

[32] The reference to the so-called 'success' of the Woolf Reforms in civil cases is at best misinformed. See the devastating critique of Zander (2009).
[33] For example, Lord Steyn in *A-G Ref No. 3 of 1999* [2001].

not been sworn, to jurors in waiting. Finally the judge should not overlook the community's interest that justice should be done without unnecessary delay. A fair balance has to be struck between all these interests. (para. 35)

*Chaaban* was important in hoisting the flag of future events in regard to the level of control the judge would be expected to have over advocates. The CPR was soon after devised to assuage this desire from the courts for 'balance' between the parties but also to 'bring to an end interminable criminal trials of the kind which the Court of Appeal criticised in *Jisl* . . .'.

Alongside *Jisl* [2004], *Chaaban* was therefore one of a cluster of cases (pre-CPR), within which the shift in language sharpened its focus. In *Jisl*, Judge LJ was at pains to remind all about an 'overlooked' aspect of criminal justice, through which positive duties of the Crown (to prove its case) transformed into legitimate expectations of the prosecution that could then be held against the defence. Just as a 'defendant is entitled to a fair trial . . . the prosecution is equally entitled to a reasonable opportunity to present the evidence against the defendant' (at 114). This new-born creature was to be named 'judicial management and control', a 'principle' unimpeachably declared as 'not in doubt' and one requiring judicial figures with an 'active', 'hands on' approach in legitimating the idea that the prosecution's needs must be met.

A central delivery device of the CPR which assisted this cause came in the form of the 'overriding objective'. Its chief departure from traditional principle lies in the treatment of its constituent elements as being of equal importance and as being inextricably bound together.[34] This 'balancing' approach provides limited practical guidance for its application and does little to discount from the requirement of 'dealing with the prosecution and defence fairly',[35] which should be read in the context of jurisprudence from the ECHR with its emphasis on the principle of 'equality of arms'.[36] Indeed, after the concept of 'dealing justly' had been elaborated in Rule 1.1(2), the remaining rules in Part 1 turn to the duty of the participants in the case to prepare and conduct the case in accordance with the overriding objective, and to comply with the rules and directions that the court makes. However, as the CPR jurisprudence developed alongside the Rules, 'equality of arms' proved to be an ebbing shibboleth of the courts. Two corollaries of the CPR demonstrate this point.

Most remarkable has been the increased role of the defence in the prosecution enterprise. Since each 'participant' (and that includes the defend-

---

[34] Imported from civil cases, as for example *Holmes v SGB Services* [2001].
[35] In Rule 1.1(2)(b).
[36] See, e.g. *Kaufman v Belgium* (1986).

ant and the defendant's legal team) is required to prepare and conduct the case in accordance with the 'overriding objective', defence lawyers and their clients bear the *duty* of 'convicting the guilty' (Rule 1.2(1)(a)). This can only mean that defence lawyers representing defendants who accept that they are factually guilty but wish to put the prosecution to the proof, a right they have traditionally enjoyed (in legal rhetoric at least), now have a duty to help convict their clients.

By any defence lawyers' understanding this now engages counsel in 'truth' seeking rather than testing the Prosecution's case. The contemporary defence advocate must mute themselves to promptings of conscience, in particular, that they have 'no monopoly in truth-seeking and no certainty that [they] will arrive unaided at a just conclusion as to the law' (Rogers, 1899, at p. 264). As a 'participant' under the CPR, the advocate must usurp the role of judge and jury. This edict stands in diametric opposition to the reality that adversary advocacy is not by definition about 'truth' (rather a case), nor does it take into account the structural realities of the courtroom experience.

To suggest that the involvement of *all* parties working towards a *shared* goal militates against this ignores three particular structural constraints against 'objective' truth. First, is the need to appreciate that the barrister 'is required by his professional code to make use of the material which is contained within his instruction and nothing else' (Hilbery, 1975, p. 11). Second, the witness is a respondent, 'he is there to answer questions, that is all' (Cockburn, 1952, p. 10). Third, the lawyer who examines the witness to tease out the 'truth' is structurally very much in a position of control (Atkinson and Drew, 1979) (all three cited by McBarnet, 1983).

The CPR's re-configuration drives a stake through the heart of traditional understandings of advocacy. Adversary advocacy had always been an effective solution to the insurmountable 'philosophical problem' of courtroom actors (each with inherently distinct narratives at play) attempting to reproduce reality because it bypasses the abstract challenge in the first place (McBarnet, 1983, p. 16).[37] Untestable concepts of truth give way to the practical contest between characterisations of facts and circumstances surrounding a 'case' umpired alongside a 'much less demanding legal concept' (McBarnet, 1983, p. 12). The reverse of this philosophical premise (that truth can be attained in court) ignores the process by which a prosecutor prepares a case in *advance* of trial

---

[37] In a recent revisit to this debate, Nicholson (2013) posits that 'truth, reason or justice is not capable of neutral, value-free and acontextual assertion, but is tied up with community standards and implicated in existing power relations.' (at 44)

*constructed from facts that the prosecution allege in fact happened.* The role of the prosecutor is then to persuade the tribunal of fact that its *version of events* is the correct one. Counter to this, the CPR framework envisages an artificial form of probity, from which the concept of persuasion is sliced away.

Lord Denning himself appeared clear on the role of persuasion:[38]

> The duty of counsel to his client in a civil case – or in defending an accused person – is to make every honest endeavour to succeed. He must not, of course, knowingly mislead the court, either on the facts or on the law, but short of that, he may put such matters in evidence or omit such others as in his discretion he thinks will be most to the advantage of his client. . . . The reason is because he is not the judge of the credibility of the witnesses or of the validity of the arguments. He is only the advocate employed by the client to speak for him, and present his case, and he must do it to the best of his ability, without making himself the judge of its correctness, but only of its honesty. Cicero makes the observation that it is the duty of the judge to pursue the truth, but it is permitted to an advocate to urge what has only the semblance of it.[39]

Lord Birkett put the point with equal clarity:[40]

> [T]he plain truth is that when an advocate is pleading in any case, *he is not stating his own view, and indeed has no right whatever to do so.* . . .The function of the advocate is to present one side of the case with all the skill he possesses, so that the judge, or the judge and jury, can compare *his* presentation with that of the counsel on the other side and then decide after full investigation, where the truth lies. (p. 99, original emphasis)

With the lineage of the adversarial system promoted by the judiciary in this way, it is hardly surprising that the notion of assistance to the prosecution is perceived by some advocates and commentators as inimical to the defence role (Cape, Hodgson, McEwan et al., Richardson).[41] Theirs, however, is an attitude perceived by the Court of Appeal as hostile to the 'truth-finding' function of counsel. The *volte-face* in the psychology of judges, prosecutors and (a more demurring) defence has been extraordinary, best exemplified in *Malcolm v DPP* [2007]:

---

[38] *Tombling v Universal Bulb Co. Ltd* (1951).
[39] [1951] 2 TLR 289 at 297.
[40] Lord Birkett (1961).
[41] Richardson (2013) argues, for example, that this approach confuses outcome with procedure and is fundamentally inconsistent with the adversary system by requiring the court to abandon its position as impartial arbiter and, instead, descend into the arena and take an active role in the conduct of the case.

[Counsel's] submissions, which emphasised the obligation of the Prosecution to prove its cases in its entirety before closing its case, and certainly before the end of the final speech for the Defence, had an anachronistic and obsolete ring. Criminal trials are no longer to be treated as a game, in which each move is final and any omission by the Prosecution leads to its failure. It is the duty of the Defence to make its defence and the issues it raises clear to the Prosecution and to the Court at an early stage. That duty is implicit in Rule 3.3 of the Criminal Procedure Rules which requires the parties actively to assist the exercise by the Court of its case management powers, the exercise of which requires early identification of the real issues. (para. 31)

This duty to identify the 'real issue' in fact stems from statutory obligations to indicate prior to trial any point of law that could affect how the trial is to be conducted. Crucially, that includes the legal authorities that support it (CPIA 1996, s. 6A(1)(d)). This has since been interpreted to mean that reliance by the defence upon flaws in the prosecution case is effectively part of one's defence. Put explicitly, in advance of the trial the defence must point out any legal or procedural error their opponents have made; if they do not, they will be unable to benefit from the error (broadly labelled an 'ambush') in order to secure an acquittal (Rule 3.10).

With direct lineage to his unhealthy obsession with the 'sporting theory of justice', Auld himself elaborated upon the implications in *R v Gleeson* [2003], a case where the defence was aware that it had a technical defence to the indictment. Having waited until the end of the Prosecution's case, a submission of no case to answer was made on the basis that the 'offence' charged was impossible to commit. Despite accepting the veracity of the defence argument, the judge gave leave to the prosecution to redraft the indictment to remedy the problem. The defence appeal was swiftly shot down by Auld for the Court of Appeal:

> Just as a defendant should not be penalised for errors of his legal representatives in the conduct of his defence if he is unfairly prejudiced by this, so also should a prosecution not be frustrated by errors of the prosecutor unless such errors have irremediably rendered a fair trial for the defence impossible. For defence advocates to seek to take advantage of such errors by deliberately delaying identification of an issue of fact or law in the case until the last possible moment is, in our view, no longer acceptable, given the legislative and procedural changes to our criminal justice process in recent years. Indeed, we consider it to be contrary to the requirement on an accused in section 5(6) of the 1996 Act, in particular paragraph (b), to indicate 'the matters on which he takes issue with the prosecution', and to their professional duty to the court – and not in the legitimate interests of the defendant. (para. 35)

This approach flew in the face of the Court of Appeal's general reluctance to accept incompetence on the part of a convicted person's legal representative which 'cannot in itself form a ground of appeal or a reason why a conviction should be found unsafe'.[42] Regardless, on behalf of the Court, Auld adopted a key section from his own 2001 Report:[43]

> To the extent that the prosecution may legitimately wish to fill possible holes in its case once issues have been identified by the defence statement, it is understandable why as a matter of tactics a defendant might prefer to keep his case close to his chest. But that is not a valid reason for preventing a full and fair hearing on the issues canvassed at the trial. A criminal trial is not a game under which a guilty defendant should be provided with a sporting chance. It is a search for truth in accordance with the twin principles that the prosecution must prove its case and that a defendant is not obliged to inculpate himself, the object being to convict the guilty and acquit the innocent. Requiring a defendant to indicate in advance what he disputes about the prosecution case offends neither of those principles. (para. 36)

With the authority of his self-citation behind him, Auld gave life to what some have referred to as the 'grassing' provisions contained within Part 1 of the CPR.[44] Put simply, the obligation on 'participants' does not just relate to their own compliance with the Rules. They are expected to notify the court and all parties 'at once ... of *any* significant failure' of compliance' (Rule 1.3, emphasis added).

Auld's rather indeterminate generalisations have found form in Rule 1.3. According to Auld, the defence cannot simply sit back and do nothing. Negative duties on the defence have now become positive duties: *the defence is now under a duty to remedy flaws in the prosecution case.*

Auld's argument is, at root, that these new duties do not affect the 'twin principles that the prosecution must prove its case and that a defendant is not obliged to inculpate himself'. This is wholly self-serving. If, as surely is the case, it is the responsibility of the prosecution to advance its case for conviction, it must follow that to impose a duty on the defence to repair deficiencies in the prosecution case is inconsistent with the former principle. Equally, it must be the responsibility of the prosecution and the trial judge (*not* the defence) to identify the correct legal basis of the prosecution. If the defence is required to flag up prosecution deficiencies which would otherwise justify an acquittal, how can this be consistent with the principle of non-exculpation, itself derived from the right to silence?

Auld added to that the related assertion that, since criminal trials were not 'games', defendants should not be provided with a 'sporting chance';

---

[42] *R v Day* [2003].
[43] (2001), Chapter 10, para. 154.
[44] McEwan (2011) p. 530.

but that is precisely what he arms the prosecution with by requiring the defence to identify its weaknesses. As such, referring to the provisions as 'grassing' hides from view the consequences of being an 'informer' who surely falls victim to the rhetorical conflict with the overriding objective of dealing with the prosecution and the defence fairly (Rule 1.1(1)(2)b).

By the time *R v Rochford* [2010] was decided, the momentum of the new judicial 'ideology' was detectable from the direction in which this striking case headed. Here the lack of particulars in the defence statement led the judge to state that failure to amend would be treated as a *contempt of court* and, further, that it might be regarded as contempt not only on the part of the defendant but also on the part of counsel. Though these suggestions were withdrawn as entirely wrong, they give insight into the pressures to which counsel may be subject (in this case, indeed, the evening after the threats were first issued by the judge, counsel was forced to seek the help of his head of chambers and of the Bar Council). While the Court of Appeal stated that the judge was not entitled to require counsel to reveal his instructions, he was, it said, entitled 'to ask, and indeed to ask insistently and trenchantly' (para. 17). The upshot of *Rochford* is that a defendant can claim that he is putting the prosecution to proof but *only if* he calls no evidence at all.[45] In other words, any accused who seeks to put forward a positive case is penalised by being co-opted into participating in the construction of the case against them and promoting the wider system goal of 'efficiency'[46] – again, in some instances, with the penalty of adverse inferences for non-compliance!

The tolerance of prosecution error was made alarmingly apparent in *R (on the application of Payne) v South Lakeland Magistrates' Court* [2011] where the Prosecution was unable to prove its case but, in an act of judicial mercy, granted an adjournment to 'get its case in order' (at para. 39). In judicial smoke signals which can only give hope to the ill-versed, ill-prepared lawyers gathering on the horizon, Pitchford LJ said:

> It is not in the public interest that cases should be decided upon the vagaries of forensic mistakes made by lawyers, provided no prejudice is done by delay or for other specific reasons. Cases should be decided on their merits. (at para. 40)

---

[45] Even then, an accused must state from the outset that he does not intend to assert a positive case. Any subsequent attempt to assert a positive case at trial will likely result in sanction(s) including limits on the accused's ability to raise a positive defence.

[46] *Balogun v DPP* [2010]; *R v Penner* [2010]; *R (on the application of Crown Prosecution Service) v Norwich Magistrates' Court* [2011].

The practical effect of these decisions is that the defence is leant upon to enable the prosecution to remedy deficiencies in its case. On the one hand, an acquittal on the basis of a gap in the prosecution case which is capable of being put right might be regarded as lacking merit. On the other, defendants have to act in a way that is patently contrary to their interests, by alerting the prosecution to the gap in their evidence. Jenny McEwan (2013) puts it best: 'A suspect under interrogation could not be expected to explain to interviewing officers that they have misunderstood a relevant provision in the PACE Codes of Practice'. Those who parrot Auld's unconvincing rebuttal (that it's always in an accused's interest to be acquitted on the merits of the case) offer no genuine reassurance on this point.

The inevitable result of this uncompromisingly pro-prosecution stance is the protraction of proceedings in the interests of 'accuracy' of outcome. This begs another question: why should the prosecution be able to benefit from their transgressions with multiple bites of the cherry but the defence cannot? Quite the contrary, delay by way of adjournment during which the prosecution can reconsider its case and make good its defects is likely to entail hardship to defendants, especially if the defendant has been remanded into custody. In this sense, the parameters of the CPR's overriding objective formulated to have equal (or 'not undue') weight clearly have unequal application. When the Prosecution is at fault, the aim of reduction of cost gives way to the 'conviction of the guilty'. In contrast, all hope of 'acquitting the innocent' is abandoned where the Court expects matters adversely affecting the defence to be dealt with 'efficiently and expeditiously'.

It is further evident from the disclosure regime that the defence are disempowered by the erosion of equality of arms vis-à-vis the parties. The long-held assumption, based upon judicial rhetoric, was that it was the State which faced a number of procedural obligations in order to mitigate the disparity of resources and unique legal powers to detain and search for evidence. As the Courts stated:[47]

> A disadvantage of the adversarial system may be that the parties are not evenly matched in resources . . . But the inequality of resources is ameliorated by the obligation on the part of the prosecution to make available all material which may prove helpful to the defence. . . .
> [I]n our adversarial system in which the police and the prosecution control the investigatory process, an accused's right to disclosure is an inseparable part of his right to a fair trial.[48]

---

[47] *McIlkenny & Ors* (1991) at p. 312.
[48] *R v Brown* [1994] at 1606 per Lord Steyn.

Under Auld's system any notion of 'inseparability' arrives heavily qualified. The obligations now arising from Defence Statements and Case Management Forms has put an end to any idea of being able to evaluate the full prosecution case prior to a decision upon plea.[49] Whilst most defence counsel will instinctually seek to keep the defence statement short, terse 'defensive' statements may be insufficient to ensure there is an obligation on the prosecution to give secondary disclosure of prosecution material. To hammer home the requirement of an 'up-front' defence case, judicial remonstrations are given in the form of denouncements, as in *R v Bryant* [2005]:

> In passing we note that the defence case statement was woefully inadequate. It consisted of a general denial of the counts in the indictment, accompanied by the sentence 'The defendant takes issue with any witness purporting to give evidence contrary to his denials'. That sort of observation is not worth the paper it is written on. It is not the purpose of a defence case statement. (para. 12)

Indeed, no lawyer can now properly advise his or her client not to give a defence statement;[50] nor is it open to a lawyer to advise his or her client to disobey the statutory obligation to file a defence statement.[51] As Hughes LJ in *Rochford* [2010] reminded defence practitioners in a manner befitting of the disciplinary society: 'The lawyer's duty is *not to give the accused advice on what to do*. The lawyer's duty is to explain the statutory obligation that he has and to explain the consequences which follow from *disobedience* of it' (at para. 25, emphasis added).

This pre-requisite to furnish the prosecution with as much detail as possible brings with it further difficulties. The view from the bench would appear to be that the defence statement is akin to comments an accused may make in interview (Gross and Treacy, 2012, para. 21). On this basis, the contents of a defence statement carry with them significant consequences during trial since the judge has a power to allow the jury to have copies of defence statements.[52]

Gross and Treacy's understanding, however, completely misappropriates the concept of an analogy. Comments made in interview are made through *choice*. Although the accused's right to silence is now subject

---

[49] Clough and Jackson (2012, p. 4) remind us that the principle of equality of arms was noticed even in 1859 when John Stuart Mill wrote: 'He who knows only his side of the case knows little of that'.
[50] *R v Essa* [2009].
[51] Ibid.
[52] S.6E of the Criminal Procedure and Investigations Act 1996 as amended; and *R v Sanghera and Takhar* [2012].

in certain circumstances to adverse inferences, the 'penalty' it imposes is solely aimed at the accused as opposed to a third party. By contrast, defence statements which fail to name a witness could give rise to the drawing of adverse inferences,[53] and judges retain the power, albeit rarely used, to exclude evidence of substantial probative value where time limits have not been complied with.[54] Similarly, judges have ample case management powers in this area to use against the defence which demonstrates that failure to comply with the Code will subject them to various sanctions and enforcement mechanisms, including: wasted costs orders; refusal of an application; or professional accreditation reprisal.[55]

Where there is pressure on defence representatives to ensure all matters are complete at the case management stage, the risk that they force admissions from their own clients to comply with procedural hurdles is very real (McEwan, 2013). It further follows, in relation to sanctions employed against the accused, that the use of 'procedural disclosure failings as suggestive of guilt' is highly problematic (at p. 9). In coming to this conclusion, McEwan reinforces the point first raised by Ashworth and Redmayne (2010, p. 263) that the mere fact that a defendant fails to disclose material should not, in itself, justify 'any common-sense inference of guilt'. In other words, under this new regime defendants are at increased risk of artificial adverse inferences regardless of what proper conclusions can *actually* be drawn from the evidence.

While it may, in the abstract, be tolerable to impose some obligation of disclosure (if this increases trial accuracy and does not create unfairness), this is imposed when it is known that the defence services are underfunded, when often they may be disorganised, when, if they are organised, proper engagement with the case is often late in the day (well attested by research) and made difficult because of non-disclosure or late disclosure by the prosecution (see overleaf).

**Case management**
HHJ Roderick Denyer QC prefaces his book, *Case Management in the Crown Court* (2008) with the statement that 'it is a mistake to think that case management begins and ends with the Criminal Procedure Rules' (p. 1).[56] The learned judge was no doubt referring to the fact that every

---

[53] *R (on the application of Tinnion) v Reading Crown Court* [2009].
[54] See e.g. *R (Robinson) v Sutton Coldfield Magistrates' Court* [2006]; *R v Delay* (2006).
[55] *R v Musone* [2007]; also *R v SVS Solicitors* [2012].
[56] Perhaps sensing the lesson had been learnt, this admonition is removed from the second edition (2012) of this title: ' . . . the controversial and often mis-

case now dealt with under the CPR is a 'managed-case'.[57] The corollary of this is a management approach which only the judiciary are able to answer.[58] Where the rules are not clear in their constraints, the conceptually protean design of the CPR thus ensures sufficient room to impose constraints at a future stage on a 'case-by-case' basis.[59]

The CPR does not define 'case management', but it is clear that it has a broad meaning, Rule 3.5(1) providing as follows: 'In fulfilling its duty under r.3.2 the court may give *any* direction and take *any* step actively to manage a case unless that direction or step would be inconsistent with legislation, including these Rules' (emphasis added). Given that the *only* express limitation[60] is that the court may not give a direction or take a step which would be inconsistent with legislation, 'case management' accords judges with almost unlimited powers as, indeed, was intended by the CPR.

The outcome to date has been a set of overarching rules (56 in number to date) which are porous in nature; the Criminal Procedure Rule Committee has engaged in a process of expansion and revision, using subsequent amendments to the rules to make more substantive amendments to the procedures applicable which become 'law'. In this sense, the direction of the CPR is held hostage to future cases in which the judges will elaborate further.

It is not difficult to see, on any analysis, the direction it is heading. A host of revealing clues may be gleaned from the case law as it stands. Were a Charter for Counsel to be drawn up and *simply expressed*, it might assume the following form (see overleaf).

As can be seen from this tombstone of professional admonishments the CPR represents a platform from which the demonisation of defence lawyers has continued; a crystallisation of a move away from the rhetoric of due process protections of the public courtroom towards a process that maximises the opportunities for the prosecution to obtain knowledge

---

understood elements of case management have gradually evolved into a system which now appears to be having its intended effect'. In what must surely be a most Freudian typographical mistake, Chapter 14 (Changing a Plea of Guilty) is mistakenly (one assumes!) headed: 'Changing a Plea of *Cheating*' (p. 141, emphasis added).

[57] Moss (2013).
[58] See, for example, *R v Musone* [2007]; *R v Jarvis* [2008]; *R v Ensor* [2009]; *R (Firth) v Epping Justices* [2011].
[59] For example, the extent to which a court can limit a positive case being introduced at a late stage is unclear.
[60] There may also be implied limits. In *R (Kelly) v Warley Magistrates' Court* [2008] it was held that Rule 3.5 did not entitle the court to override legal privilege or legal professional privilege, which were fundamental rights of the defendant.

# THE
# CHARTER for COUNSEL
# Granted by Her MAJESTY
# TO
# THE HONOURABLE MEMBERS
# OF
# The English and Welsh BAR

- Until otherwise directed, you may continue to style yourself 'counsel for the defence'.
- Do not advise the defendant to exercise the so-called 'right' to silence.
- You must give 'advice' in strong terms that a guilty plea is a fair bargain if the sentence discount is at least standard in that court.
- Please remember that there will be an enhanced fee for any guilty plea that you persuade a defendant to enter.
- Whether you are knowledgeable or ignorant about the case, you must inform the defendant (formerly styled 'your' client) that he or she is entitled from the outset to an indication of sentence from the judge; and if you overlook this duty, you will be reminded of it by the trial judge in open court.
- You must advise the defendant that an indication of sentence, if honoured by the judge, may be increased if the Court of Appeal deems it too lenient.
- You must inform the defendant that a sentence may be deemed to be too lenient even in cases in which the prosecutor has invited the trial judge to sentence at that level.
- You must appoint a 'case progression officer' to liaise with your allies, the prosecution, and with the court.
- You must submit a Defence Statement setting out the nature of the defence, including any particular defences upon which the defendant proposes to rely; indicating the matters of fact on which he/she takes issue with the prosecution; setting out, in the case of each such matter, why he/she takes issue with the prosecution; setting out particulars of the matters of fact on which he/she proposes to rely for the purposes of his/her defence; and indicating any point of law (including any point as to the admissibility of evidence or an abuse of process) which he/she wishes to take and any authority on which he/she intends to rely for that purpose.
- You cannot advise the defendant not to file a Defence Statement.
- Though you may have contempt (and possibly self-loathing) for what you have to do in practice, you will not (yet) be held in contempt of court for non-compliance with court demands regarding Defence Statements.
- It is your duty to ensure that the case is dealt with 'justly' as defined by the judges.
- You must assist the State in the prosecution of those charged with criminal offences and such assistance must inure to the cost-effective and expeditious disposal of cases.
- You must inform the court of any breaches by the defendant of any of the rules or procedures that must be followed.
- You must take into account the consequences for others affected, the needs of other cases and the interests of witnesses, victims and jurors.
- You must undertake to help the prosecution even though by doing so it will encourage further institutional incompetence and unprofessionalism on their part.
- You must not seek to take advantage of the prosecution's incompetence by recourse to what would be regarded as 'sharp tactics' such as waiting for their case to be presented and then pointing out failure to produce evidence of a key element of the offence or by informing the prosecution or judge (who are prone to make errors in this regard) that the 'offence' charged is unknown to the law.
- It is your responsibility and professional duty to draw the prosecution's attention to any fatal weaknesses in its case in a timely manner so as to allow the prosecution, if it can, to repair the defect: in other words, if the prosecution case is in intensive care or is suffering from a potentially fatal heart attack, you must apply CPR (cardiopulmonary resuscitation).

helpful to its case; a dramatic reversal of the 'fearless advocate' achieved under the subterfuge of 'fairness' to both sides and Auld's bogus dichotomy of 'the innocent' and 'the guilty'; and the characterisation of any challenge to the prosecution as seeking to exploit the 'sporting theory of justice'.

## LEGAL AID

Beleaguered as defence lawyers may be by the 'quiet revolution' taking place in criminal justice[61] the plan to shackle the legal profession is further evident with the mishandling of legal aid in England and Wales. In identifying 'efficient' and 'expeditious' justice as part of the overriding objective, the coordinates of the CPR can be properly deciphered by looking to the much wider canvas of 'efficiency' savings coursing their way through a criminal justice system, once deemed 'global leader' in the provision of publicly funded legal services.[62]

Propagandist policy labels such as *'Criminal Justice: Simple, Speedy, Summary'*,[63] *'Stop Delaying Justice!'*[64] and *'Swift and Sure Justice'*[65] illustrate that the cost of the publicly funded criminal defence has been in the sight-scope of the Government for some time. Cost-cutting exercises such as the Graduated Fee Scheme for Crown Court advocates and fixed fees for police station work have become established fixtures and fittings of the system's architecture and now seem mild in comparison to the onslaught promised.

Such is the force of change demanded that the Attorney-General unapologetically explains away 'death by a thousand cuts' to the independent Bar as an 'extremely painful' but *necessary* process (Hyde, 2013). Reform is set in unswerving motion by the Legal Aid, Sentencing and Punishment of Offenders Act 2012 (LASPO). This piece of legislation affecting both civil and criminal domains[66] fundamentally changes the relationship between the government and the governed, a concern to which we turn below.

The Ministry of Justice (MoJ, 2013b) has referred to its project of legal

---

[61] Lord Woolf as quoted in Gibb (2005). 'Courts to reduce time-wasting', *The Times*, 5 April 2005.
[62] Smith (2011).
[63] Department for Constitutional Affairs (2006b).
[64] Magistrate (2011).
[65] MoJ (2012c).
[66] Sections 13–43 deal with Criminal Legal Aid; Part 2 (sections 44–62) deals with Litigation.

aid reform in stark terms: 'the Government intends to radically reform the legal aid system to scale back the involvement of the State in the provision of legal aid to individuals'. Even though some of the changes it outlined concern LASPO it is apparent that a more overarching project is being referenced, claiming insidiously that, 'legal challenges are now the main threat to the successful delivery of the programme'.[67]

## Closing the Gate

The ambition of the Government agenda on criminal legal aid can be summarised thus: defence practitioners will be forced to spend the same time or more time and money on their work for much less financial reward. The quality of representation will plummet. Without proper advice and advocacy injustice will be done. Yet by restricting access to the law, the State is fortifying itself with worrying immunity from legal scrutiny. In other words, what we are seeing is a 'green light' for the continued undermining of the 'independence' of the Bar and its ability to challenge government decisions.[68]

The intended consequence of these reforms is that truths the Government wants hidden will remain exactly that. Opportunities to bring a demonstrably untrustworthy police force organisation (e.g., Ellison, 2014) to account through the courts will be stultified. Important inquiries of the past (e.g., Rosemary Nelson, Bloody Sunday, Hillsborough)[69] will acquire a phantom status. LASPO makes it clear that the Government does not

---

[67] See the response by Doughty Street Chambers (2013).

[68] This is happening in parallel with restrictions being imposed on holding the State to account through judicial review.

[69] Allied to this, the police wield enormous political power. The '*Plebgate*' debacle, involving a police report which led to a Cabinet Minister losing his job, is illustrative here. The fact that investigation(s) and judicial review proceedings – by, among others, the IPCC, the Police Federation, the DPP, CPS and Scotland Yard – of an encounter lasting a mere 45 seconds continued unresolved for more than 15 months speaks volumes. One officer was charged with misconduct in a public office, although newly appointed DPP, Alison Saunders, decided not to launch criminal proceedings against other officers involved on the basis that the evidence was inconclusive. In this regard, it should be noted that none of the tourists alleged by the police to have been present at the incident were visible in the CCTV footage, nor have any been identified or come forward. Furthermore, PC Rowland who made the widely publicised allegation against Andrew Mitchell is reported to have never been questioned under oath (*The Guardian*, 27 November 2013). In early 2014, the officer charged, PC Keith Wallis, admitting lying about witnessing the *Plebgate* row (in the guise of a member of public) and was sentenced to 12 months in prison. Further reputational damage to the police aside, the cost to the taxpayer is reported to be in the region of hundreds of thousands of pounds (Halliday, 2014).

want to have inquiries in the same way; or where unavoidable, lawyers are to play no real part.

The new Justice Secretary (and Lord Chancellor) Chris Grayling (the first non-lawyer to occupy the post since 1673),[70] swiftly declared that 'the public has lost confidence in the system'. Unconvincingly clutching 'lots of letters and emails' from people said to be concerned about legal aid entitlement (Baksi, 2013a), Grayling was quick to learn that where 'public confidence' flounders as a justification, the 'fiscal imperative' prevails.

**The Fiscal Imperative**

The fiscal imperative employed by the Government is encapsulated thus: 'At around £2bn a year, we have one of the most expensive legal aid systems in the world'. However, the MoJ appears to have forgotten the caveat it applied to its 2009 study on the 'International Comparison of Publicly Funded Legal Services and Justice Systems'. There it observed (Bowles and Perry, 2009): 'Making comparisons of international justice systems was complex due to significant differences in the methodology and reporting of data associated with justice systems. Therefore all comparisons in this report *should be treated with care as to their interpretation*' (p. 36, emphasis added).[71]

While figures published by the MoJ (2013d, p. 93) confirm that the sums involved for legal aid (since 2007) hover around £2 billion, an amount equivalent to about 23 per cent of the MoJ's total budget of £8.6 billion,[72] leaders of the six regional circuits of the Bar Council have argued that far from 'spiralling' costs, spending has been falling for a number of years.[73] In 2009–10, the total criminal legal aid spend was £1.12bn, which fell by £146m (13%) to £975m in 2012–13.[74]

---

[70] With this in mind, one commentator held the view that Grayling's main qualification for the post is that he is right wing (Rozenberg, 2012).

[71] The same document said that its findings were 'intended to be suggestive and provocative rather than definitive' (Bowles and Perry, 2009, p. 3).

[72] MoJ, *Annual Report and Accounts 2012–13* (MoJ, 2013d, p. 93).

[73] Incredibly, the MoJ's own accounts (2013d) show an under-spend of £28.9 million in the criminal legal aid fund.

[74] Similarly, the figure for very high cost cases, the most complex criminal trials involving terrorism and serious crime, has almost halved over the same period, falling from £124m in 2007–08 to £67m in 2012–13 (*The Guardian*, 3 October 2013). Other statistics support this: criminal legal aid expenditure decreased 12% in real terms between 2003–04 and 2008–09 according to the National Audit Office (2009). See also the comprehensive study by King's College London (Cookson, 2011).

Disregarding such limitations, the Government has made clear that it wants to eradicate substantial numbers of existing legal aid providers via 'managed consolidation'.[75] Under this reductionist model, few legal agencies or individuals are left unscathed by the 'fiscal imperative'. Michael Mansfield QC's chambers, renowned for its civil liberties work, is but one victim of the ongoing austerity measures, citing its dissolution in October 2013 as a 'direct result of government policies on Legal Aid'.[76]

**Austerity Justice: The 'Reforms'**

We discuss some key Government-inspired proposals for 'reform' notwithstanding that many have been withdrawn because they symbolise the developing official culture (governmental and judicial) towards defence services, and contribute, in and of themselves, to the demoralisation of the profession, discouraging any who wish to enter it with traditional understandings of the role of the advocate in mind.

In April 2013, the MoJ's consultation paper, *Transforming Legal Aid: Delivering a More Credible and Efficient System* proposed, *inter alia*, allowing large commercial firms with little or no legal aid experience (like the Lord Chancellor) to bid for key legal aid contracts. Companies, including the 'jailers', Serco,[77] and the 'Olympians', G4S[78] were thought to be in pole position to win legal aid contracts and thereby become 'defenders' also. Sensing conflict within the 'defender/jailer' dichotomy he was about to create, Grayling dismissed these challenges as 'scare stories' (Baksi 2013a). More alarm was caused by the proposal to remove choice of lawyer for persons accused of crime or, as Grayling publicly described

---

[75] Imposing a 17.5% cut, given the threadbare finances of many criminal firms, will force a consolidation of the market. Originally the target was to reduce the number of legal aid providers from 1,600 often specialist firms to 400 large, non-specialist ones.

[76] Tooks Chambers website.

[77] Serco has been at the centre of an overcharging scandal and is currently being investigated by the Serious Fraud Office following allegations that it overcharged the government 'tens of millions of pounds' in connection with overseeing electronic tagging of criminals (*BBC News*, 25 October, 2012). Its boss resigned in October, 2013. Plans to privatise three prisons have been shelved because of ongoing investigations into Serco. See also, 'Whistle-blowers criticize privatized probation service', *BBC News*, 21 November 2013.

[78] The Ministry of Justice has rejected an offer from G4S of £24.1 million which the firm says it owes after overcharging for the tagging of offenders following an audit which suggested that it was charging to tag criminals who were either dead or in jail (*BBC News*, 19 November 2013).

them, 'criminals'. Following a 'consultation period' of only eight weeks, the majority of responses were highly critical; counter-proposals, however, were pitched against the Justice Secretary's impossible stance that unless alternatives to his proposals were 'stunning' they would not be adopted.[79]

Nicola Padfield (2013, pp. 5–6) reinforces the accusation that the Government has given a 'misleading' account, such is the 'economy' of 'serious analysis of relevant empirical or other evidence' underpinning the transformation of legal aid. She gives the example of the Government's citation of Lee Bridges et al.'s (2007) *Evaluation of the Public Defender Service* which was used to create the impression that competitive tendering can be an 'essential guarantor of quality standards, minimum costs and client choice of representative in a more "managed market" for such services'. What the Government failed to mention, as Padfield highlights, is that this excerpt is massaged of any real meaning because the final paragraph actually begins: 'In summary, it is difficult on the basis of the research evaluation of the PDS pilot to recommend that the service be developed. . .'.[80]

The consultation paper was met with a chorus of nationwide disapproval. The Law Society described the proposals as likely to cause 'catastrophic' damage to the UK's legal aid system;[81] the Bar Council claimed that the MoJ 'failed to consider hard evidence' and that the proposals are 'a breathtakingly convoluted way of finding . . . savings';[82] the CPS pointed out that proposals to limit legal aid and pay fixed fees to defence solicitors might not be 'consistent with' the UK's six fundamental principles of justice and might even put up costs;[83] and some judges expressed concern that the plans amounted to 'a rank denial of justice' for vulnerable people.[84]

A begrudging Grayling was forced to back down on plans denying defendants the right to choose their own legal representative. A further about-turn was ordered on introducing 'price competition into the criminal legal aid market'. The competition model Best Value Tendering

---

[79] It was reported in Parliament that despite Michael Turner QC, chairman of the Criminal Bar Association, putting forward a plan that could save the MoJ £2 billion when the Treasury have only asked for £220m, no response from Grayling was forthcoming (Hansard (HC) Debate, Cols. 75–77WH, 4 September 2013).

[80] More fundamentally PDS could be judged a failure in the terms that the government set out for it – it was not cost-effective, proving pricier than private practice (Bridges et al., 2007, pp. 263–4).

[81] Law Society Response (2013).

[82] Bar Council Response (2013).

[83] CPS Response (2013).

[84] Lord Neuberger, 15 October, 2013; see also, Judicial Executive Board response to the Consultation, 2013.

(BVT), which courted controversy in 2009 found itself resurrected and repackaged as the equally unedifying Price Competitive Tendering (PCT). Under PCT, criminal defence franchises were to be allocated to the lowest bidder in a 'race to the bottom' as the economic viability of criminal work bled dry.[85] Any advocate acting for a defendant in a trial was to see their daily remuneration lowered the longer it went on. This strategy accorded perfectly with the Government's ambition to merely achieve 'adequate' standards of representation (MoJ, 2013b).

Although the Lord Chancellor stated that PCT 'is not an ideological choice; it is a financial necessity' it too was abandoned.[86] A second U-turn found the Government staring in the same direction in which it had begun; faced with its starting goal to deliver £220m in annual savings (by 2018/19) in whatever way it could.[87] This short-sighted trajectory produces a range of pernicious consequences, some of which we discuss here.

**The New Tax System**

First, innocence is now to be 'taxed'. The Government does not believe that it has a responsibility to fund the *accused* through legal aid. If the

---

[85] The fact the 'lowest bidder' model was even contemplated is suggestive of an indifference to a catalogue of criticism in the USA (which has relevant experience of operating price competitive systems for legal representation) including its capacity to encourage excessive guilty pleas (Lefstein, 1982; Houlden and Balkin, 1985). See Smith (2013a).

[86] Far from financial necessity, a closer inspection of crime rates in England and Wales reveals 'natural' savings will occur without need for annual reductions to the criminal legal aid budget. In reducing fees paid for police station attendance, magistrates' court representation and Crown Court litigation, the MoJ proposes to make savings of £120 million per year by 2018/19 relative to underlying expenditure levels in 2012/13. A report (Oxford Economics, 2014) commissioned by the Law Society critiques the Legal Aid Agency's (LAA) 'steady state' forecasts for criminal legal aid expenditure. The report presents an 'alternative forecast based on plausible assumptions of future trends in crime and the criminal justice system'. In highlighting 'crime has been on a steady downward trajectory for the last decade' the report provides strong evidence that the criminal legal aid expenditure savings will stem from this pattern (£84m by the year 2018–19, approximately two-thirds of the MoJ's planned savings) (Bowcott, 2014).

[87] Incredibly, the Justice Secretary subsequently announced the first ever government-backed UK Global Law Summit to be held in celebration of the 800th anniversary (2015) of the signing of Magna Carta. The Government Press Release states the country will be 'showcasing the UK's unrivalled legal expertise, based on a long history of freedom and justice' (Grayling, 2013). Such extravagance set against swingeing cuts leads one to the conclusion that the 'fiscal crisis' has nothing to do with saving money.

accused has a disposable income (or worse still, combined household income) of £37,500, no legal aid is available to cover their own legal costs. Even where the jury decides the individual is innocent, costs are incurred.[88] This leaves someone in the invidious position of self-financing the fight against a prosecution paid for by the State (which means, contradictorily, themselves!).[89]

Second, a new breed of inexperienced lawyers will be subject to financial incentives to persuade their clients to plead guilty. Such pressures arise because they will be paid the same for a trial as for a rapid guilty plea. Indeed, the London Criminal Courts Solicitors Association (LCCSA), analysing the government's latest fee proposals concluded that lawyers will be given a pattern of 'perverse financial incentives' affecting both magistrates' and Crown Court cases to encourage defendants to plead guilty early. As one lawyer put it:[90] 'The only conclusion to draw from these figures is the sad truth that the new fee structure is ideological and has nothing to do with austerity'.

The policy of the Government is to treat legal services as a commodity, priced and distributed by the market, with the barest safety net for the wrongly accused.[91] Daniele Alge (2013) has argued that there is 'little

---

[88] Clawing back 'expenses' of any sort is limited to derisory legal aid rates, an amount almost certainly less than the cost of the private legal advisor they are forced to enlist.

[89] President of the Supreme Court, Lord Neuberger, is not the first to say that the lack of access to justice could mean people taking the law into their own hands (BBC Radio, 5 March 2013). Neuberger's considered viewpoint no doubt recognises that by denying legal aid to ordinary people and therefore appearing to save money, there are hugely increasing costs within government departments who have to defend litigation brought by litigants in person. Self-representation carries with it many problems in Crown Court trials. The most important of these is the greater risk of a miscarriage of justice, either through a failure to understand the law or a failure to appreciate the forensic importance of a piece of evidence. The potential for delay in proceedings caused by self-represented defendants operating alongside law and procedure alien to them and who find themselves unable to indicate in advance what the 'real' issues are, has also been ignored or plainly disregarded.

[90] Bowcott (2013b).

[91] Such is the concern that a 'no confidence' motion in the leadership of the Law Society was tabled for an emergency meeting in December 2013 alleging that negotiations between the organisation and the MoJ over the structure of legal aid contracts have already been 'to the detriment of and against the will' of society members (Bowcott, 2013d). The Criminal Bar Association also declared a 'mass non-attendance' day in protest at reductions in legal aid, its Chairman warning that the Criminal Bar was being 'dismantled into non-existence' (Bowcott, 2013d). The Criminal Law Solicitors Association and the London Criminal Courts

in the way of effective incentives' to reduce this 'moral hazard' (p. 180) and finds 'the current fee structure is more likely to cause [the lawyer's] interests to diverge by indirectly providing incentives to "crack" a case' (p. 171).

Third, trust will evaporate from the lawyer–client relationship. In spite of the Lord Chancellor's hamstrung view of defendants (popularised as 'too thick to pick' (HC Hansard, 27 June 2013, col 523)), clients will soon learn of the dangers of the new system that their legal representative operates within. Defendants may be of the 'impression' that the lawyer has a financial incentive to betray their trust. This is not to suggest that lawyers will act against the interests of their client but the suggestion of conflict is unavoidable.

Fourth, costs will rise. Impressions count in matters of *trust*. In this new environment of financial incentives, can the client rely on the advice to plead guilty? If relied upon, a defence may be missed, necessitating the cost of an appeal. Evidently, the MoJ is purposefully blind to the way in which the innocent *and* the guilty place trust in their representative and the important role that plays in ensuring that the system runs efficiently.[92]

The Justice Secretary inadvertently demonstrated this danger when he explained that flattening fees will benefit less experienced lawyers at the bottom end of the income scale: 'We have done *careful analysis* of the case mix that the more junior lawyers have. This looks like the best way of ensuring they are *protected financially*, because they are the ones who will tend to do the simple guilty pleas' (emphasis added).[93] Disregarding the fact no analysis has surfaced, this assertion is both illogical and symptomatic of the pseudo-ideology at work. By equating almost all cases in the lower courts as 'simple' guilty pleas, in one fell swoop Grayling clutches at the same presumption of guilt that inspired the 'other' architect of modern justice, Auld.

## CONCLUSION

The overall impression of the last half century or so is one of a less than glorious history for the legal profession in which it has been taken down a peg, if not humiliated, by judges who, in turn, have had the incalculable

---

Solicitors Association both announced their solidarity in joining the action (Bowcott, 2013c). A second mass walk out was staged by lawyers on 7 March, 2014 and lawyers threatened to refuse to accept 'returned briefs' for up to a month.

[92] See Tom Smith (2013b).
[93] Baksi (2013a).

support of law and order politicians. The intermix of questionable levels of professional competence and client commitment increasingly combined with governmental antipathy towards the financing of legal aid have produced a toxic cocktail which can only serve suspects and defendants ill. The profession's cool reception towards the CPR reflects only too well the reality: one which sees a debilitation of the defence from being, historically, supplicants at the judge's table to being, in more recent times, manhandled across the courtroom floor by judges, to now becoming handmaidens of the prosecution and the left hand of the court. As it turns out, the 'rebalancing' of allegiance that occurs with the CPR stems the flow of loyalty towards the client and redirects it towards the court, making defence representatives coercively unapologetic for their various duties in conflict with the client.

# 7. Scotland: coercion and discourse

## INTRODUCTION

The experience of Scotland provides an example of a jurisdiction being forced to come to terms with State-induced guilty pleas and appearing to respond in marked contrast to the courts of England and Wales. Whereas judges in the latter jurisdiction initiated and sponsored such pleas, in the higher courts judges in Scotland were pitch-forked into the issue by statute and, having first expressed resistance, continued to show discomfort (and disagreement) after their realisation that compliance with statute was unavoidable. While the English influence can still be detected, Scottish judges confront State-induced guilty pleas both individually and institutionally in a manner which symbolises Scotland's unique engagement with the independence of its judicial system. Nevertheless, outside the higher courts, the Scottish system is showing signs of significant departure from traditional practices and ideologies.

## INFORMAL PRACTICE IN THE LOWER COURTS

Although the procurator fiscal (prosecutor) is under no obligation to accept the tendering of a guilty plea even to a single charge in the indictment or complaint,[1] substantial negotiation over plea by way of informal charge bargaining and fact bargaining appears to have been effective in securing guilty pleas especially in the lower courts,[2] but without the direct involvement of the judge[3] and without the device of an overt sentence dis-

---

[1] *Strathern v Sloan* (1937). The right of the prosecutor to refuse to accept a plea of guilty should, however, be sparingly exercised, the governing consideration in every case should be the public interest (*MacDonald v Procurator Fiscal Aberdeen* [2010]).

[2] In contrast to England and Wales, where most cases in the lower courts are heard by lay magistrates, in Scotland these cases are dealt with by 'sheriffs', who are professional lawyers.

[3] Traditionally, the judge in Scotland has had a limited role in any bargaining because, unlike the position in England, it is the Crown and not the judge who

count. The key empirical study in this regard is that of Moody and Tombs (1982) from which the following short account is primarily derived.

Moody and Tombs found that it was traditional for prosecutors to accept a 'partial plea' if this was agreed, but the practice was an 'informal, private matter' so that there was little case law on or public awareness of the prevalence of such arrangements. While the Crown Office[4] issued various circulars regarding the procedures that ought to be followed (see below) before concluding any agreement, in line with traditional resistance to the idea of 'central policy', no guidelines were issued and there was no standardisation of practice.[5]

The principal mechanism employed was 'charge bargaining' which did not require the active participation of judges. This took various forms including the use of alternative charges, removal of some charges, and amendment to the wording of charges.[6] Although Moody and Tombs found that the practice was usually initiated by the defence it was also clear that sometimes the prosecutor had inserted charges as bargaining counters,[7] including in cases where there was insufficient evidence. A key factor in the striking of plea arrangements was found to be *trust* between particular prosecutors and defence lawyers who shared a common understanding of their roles in the administration of justice. Prosecutors were motivated by the desire to cut down trials at summary level, to secure sufficient punishment and to avoid problematic outcomes at trial by jury,[8] although the acquittal rate was exceptionally low (3.5%) and cases involving alleged assaults on the police were generally not considered appropriate for negotiation. While defence lawyers saw it as their job to get the best outcome for their clients (who were not ordinarily given access to a lawyer when in police custody),[9] Moody and Tombs concluded that the idea of

---

controls the case in Scotland, so that, as Gordon (1970, p. 155) put it: 'Many Scots lawyers would regard it as unthinkable to involve the judge in plea bargaining'.

[4] The Crown Office and the Procurator Fiscal Service represent the prosecution service of Scotland.

[5] See Tata (2010).

[6] In order to reduce the seriousness of the allegation in assault cases or to remove certain items allegedly stolen.

[7] Op. cit., at p. 110.

[8] Unlike the position in England and Wales, the defendant has no right to elect trial by jury in Scotland, the prosecutor determining the trial venue.

[9] This rather startling situation was not addressed until 2010. As the Supreme Court noted in *Cadder v HM Advocate* [2010] it was 'remarkable' that nobody thought that there was anything wrong with a Scottish criminal procedure under which suspects had no right to access a lawyer during police detention and that admissions obtained in such circumstances were admissible.

the accused 'instructing' the defence lawyer had a 'rather quaint, unreal ring to it'.

Some impact upon the system occurred after 1999 when the mechanism for funding defence lawyers changed from billing for time spent and work undertaken to a 'fixed fee' system,[10] a move that was intended to make the system more cost effective by eliminating unnecessary preparatory work and putting a stop to any 'milking' of the legal aid system. Tata and Stephen (2006) found that, while these changes had mixed results in terms of fee demands on legal aid they caused a postponement of the point at which a guilty plea was entered, the exact opposite of the aim of the 'reform' proposal.[11]

The Scottish practices of charge negotiation[12] and implicit sentence reduction appear to continue and no doubt contribute to some degree to the court disposition statistics.[13] Thus, in 2010–2011, in summary proceedings, 96 per cent of District Court cases and 92.1 per cent of Sheriff Court cases were disposed of by guilty plea; in Sheriff Solemn proceedings (with a jury) the equivalent figure was 77.4 per cent and in the High Court (with a jury) it stood at 59.6 per cent. This pattern of disposals has held for many years.[14]

## OFFICIAL ENGAGEMENT WITH PLEA NEGOTIATION

In addition to what was happening in the lower court, as Moody and Tombs found, there was a level of official awareness of the practices. Thus, the Crown Office (Lord Advocate) placed notes to encourage early agreements by fiscals and defence[15] in order to avoid unnecessary

---

[10] See Tata (2007).

[11] It seems that this was caused by a reduction in the time lawyers spent with defendants with the result that they had less time to persuade them of the advantages of an early guilty plea.

[12] Moody and Tombs (1982) give an example of the informal arrangements in this way: 'It may happen that one of the police officers will mention to me that the accused is willing to plead to so and so and I will then say to the sheriff "will your Lordship take a plea of guilty to such and such?"' (p. 120).

[13] See Goriely et al. (2001) who show that, with the exception of certain categories of offence (notably, sexual offences), there was no evidence of a standard practice of sentence discounts across Scotland.

[14] The figures going back to 2006–07 are broadly the same. See also Leverick (2004) reporting on equivalent statistics for 2001–02.

[15] Crown Office Notice (1980). See also, *Scots Law Times*, February 15 1980, p. 42.

attendance by witnesses and disruption of court planning, as in the following example:

> **Procurators-fiscal and defence solicitors**
> *The Lord Advocate has instructed procurators-fiscal that it is part of their duties to meet defence solicitors for the purpose of (a) discussing the evidence available to the Crown, (b) arranging minutes of admission in respect of evidence which is not to be contested, and (c) giving to defence solicitors copies of statements of witnesses whose evidence is regarded as formal or technical.*
>
> *It is hoped that solicitors will avail themselves of the opportunity to meet the procurators-fiscal for this purpose and that as a result some witnesses may be excused attendance and that, in particular, last-minute pleas of guilty, which so disturb the planning of cost business and greatly annoy those cited needlessly as witnesses, will be considerably reduced.*
>
> *In small offices the procurators-fiscal will require to meet solicitors personally, but in larger offices a depute may be detailed to attend to this task. In either circumstance, solicitors would be advised to telephone for an appointment so that the case papers will be available at the meeting.*

Such notices, of course, did not amount to adoption of State-induced plea practices and unlike the position in England and Wales, judges in the appellate court did not establish a *policy* regarding sentence discounts or judicially condone the practice of 'rewarding' guilty pleas[16] by means of a sentence discount.[17]

When the issue of plea bargaining in the lower courts was first challenged on appeal, it immediately attracted condemnation from the highest criminal court, the High Court of Justiciary (hereinafter 'High Court'). The question arose in *Strawhorn v McLeod* [1987] in which the appellant had entered a plea of guilty at an intermediate stage in the procedure which allowed the court to advise three civilian prosecution witnesses that they would no longer have to attend the hearing. However, this plea had not been made at the earliest stage in the procedure, having come at too late a stage to avoid two police officer witnesses attending. Accordingly the lower court (Sheriff) refused to award a sentence discount. The Sheriff was quite open as to the normal sentencing practice informing the High Court that the pre-trial hearing was a procedure 'much used in this court

---

[16] In Scotland, a guilty plea constitutes a full admission of the charge in all its particulars and it can be withdrawn only in exceptional circumstances (*Reedie v HM Advocate* [2005] and *Luke Sinclaire v Procurator Fiscal, Stranraer* [2013]).

[17] In the lower courts, some reduction in sentence in recognition of an early guilty plea and one saving stress to victims was identified by researchers (Bennet and Miller, 1990), and this was given recognition in a few cases. See, for example, *Khaliq v HM Advocate* (1984).

in an attempt to obviate so far as possible the waste of time and expense caused by pleas of guilty at the trial' itself (p. 414).

Explaining that it was a procedure which had had considerable success, the Sheriff set out the rationale for the practice as follows:

> The sheriffs in this court are of opinion that an early plea of guilty, which obviates the waste of time and expense involved in the unnecessary attendance of witnesses, and in the disruption of their other arrangements, merits in appropriate cases a discount from what would otherwise be the appropriate sentence. In this case the arrangements made for the trial had to be unmade. As far as police witnesses were concerned their countermanding came too late. (p. 414)

The 'sentencing discount' principle described by the lower court was criticised by the High Court, which reduced the fine the Sheriff had imposed on the appellant. In the High Court's opinion, delivered by the Lord Justice Clerk, the practice was deprecated because it limited the judge's discretion, but more significantly because, as has been argued in relation to English jurisprudence, it contradicted basic principles including the presumption of innocence:[18]

> In our opinion the practice which the sheriff refers to in his report is not one which ought to be followed and is indeed an objectionable practice. What it involves is a form of plea bargaining. In one sense an accused person is being offered an inducement to plead guilty early and in our opinion no such inducement should be offered to accused persons. In this country there is a presumption of innocence and an accused person is entitled to go to trial and leave the Crown to establish his guilt if the Crown can. It is wrong therefore that an accused person should be put in the position of realising that if he pleads guilty early enough he will receive a lower sentence than he would otherwise receive for the offence. (p. 415)

The Lord Justice Clerk also referred to the impact of a plea bargaining practice on the sentencing powers of the judge:

> [I]t is important that a sheriff, in selecting the appropriate sentence, should be exercising a discretion, and if a practice such as the sheriff describes is in operation the result must necessarily be to disable the sheriff from exercising his discretion fully and freely in a particular case. We can quite understand why the practice to which the sheriff refers is regarded by the sheriffs as administratively convenient but, for the reasons which I have given, we are satisfied that it is an objectionable practice which should now be stopped. (p. 415)

---

[18] *Strawhorn v McLeod* [1987], at p. 415.

This judgment has to be read in the Scottish context. The practice of sheriffs inducing guilty pleas by means of a 'sentencing discount' was not outlawed: the High Court's ruling was to uphold the principle of *judicial discretion* in sentencing and to refuse to approve or lay down a *policy* in regard to State-induced guilty pleas. The offer of any inducement, accordingly, must be fact-specific.

However, statute was to intervene in the same way as it had done in England and Wales. The relevant government department (the Scottish Office) started the ball rolling when it issued a consultation paper[19] and then a White Paper, *Firm and Fair*,[20] which accepted the principle of a reduction in sentence for a guilty plea in appropriate cases but not as a matter of routine.[21] Legislation quickly followed.

By virtue of section 196 of the Criminal Procedure (Scotland) Act, 1995 it was provided that:

(1) In determining what sentence to pass on, or what other disposal or order to make in relation to, an offender who has pled guilty to an offence, a court may take into account —
   (a) the stage in the proceedings for the offence at which the offender indicated his intention to plead guilty, and
   (b) the circumstances in which that indication was given.

The statute remained permissive with subsection (1) telling judges that they 'may' take into account those factors, otherwise leaving the Scottish courts freedom to interpret it.

However, there then followed a review of court practice by Lord Bonomy (2002) in which he recommended, *inter alia*, the substitution of 'must' for 'may' in the statute. This recommendation was not based in systematic inquiry but upon *ad hoc* discussions he had with various parties, as the following extracts illustrate:

> My discussions *with practitioners* and with *some former prisoners* indicated that, given a realistic prospect of acquittal, an accused person is likely to go to trial, but, if faced with little or no prospect of acquittal, what he wants to know above all is the sentence that is likely to be imposed, and hopes that it will be less than anticipated. His decision on whether to plead guilty and when will inevitably

---

[19] Scottish Office (1993).
[20] Scottish Office (1994): 'The Government intends to introduce a statutory provision to make it clear that the courts *may* take into account a guilty plea, and the circumstances in which it was made, as a mitigating factor in considering the appropriate sentence' (para. 4.13).
[21] For a detailed discussion, see Leverick (2004).

be informed by his understanding of the likely sentence. (para. 7.8, footnote omitted, emphasis added)
There was also *wide support* for some discount in the sentence whenever an accused pleads guilty. Should the plea be tendered at a fairly late stage . . . there is *a view* that the contribution that that makes to the efficiency of the criminal justice system, and the very avoidance of the need for those affected to give evidence, merit some credit. (para. 7.17, emphasis added)

Neither the partial and unsystematic review by Lord Bonomy nor the White Paper arising out of his review, *Modernising Justice in Scotland*,[22] sought to advance any serious justification for offering sentence discounts; they simply assumed that discounts were part of the system.

Subsequently, the operation of section 196 was made mandatory and required the sentencer to specify whether having taken into account the plea the sentence in respect of the offence is different from that which the court would otherwise have imposed and, if it is not, state reasons why it is not:[23]

196 Sentence following guilty plea.
[(1)] In determining what sentence to pass on, or what other disposal or order to make in relation to, an offender who has pled guilty to an offence, a court [shall] take into account—
 (a) the stage in the proceedings for the offence at which the offender indicated his intention to plead guilty, and
 (b) the circumstances in which that indication was given.
[(1A)] In passing sentence on an offender referred to in subsection (1) above, the court shall—
 (a) state whether, having taken account of the matters mentioned in paragraphs (a) and (b) of that subsection, the sentence imposed in respect of the offence is different from that which the court would otherwise have imposed; and
 (b) if it is not, state reasons why it is not.
[(2) omitted[24]]

Whatever the theory of judicial independence in interpreting statutes and whatever leeway remained for Scottish courts to 'read down' the statute, the subordinate status of judges was sharply underlined by the Lord Justice General's[25] *Practice Note* of 2008 which 'reminded' judges, sheriffs

---

[22] Scottish Executive (2003).
[23] Criminal Procedure (Scotland) Act, 2004, section 20. The amendments are placed in brackets as [. . .]. The Scottish legislation differs also from that in England in that, by virtue of section 196 1A(a) and (b), the court is required to provide reasons whenever a discount is withheld.
[24] The omitted provision deals with defendants sentenced for a third conviction related to drug trafficking offences.
[25] The Lord Justice General is head of the Scottish judiciary.

and justices of their obligations under section 196, requiring every sentencing court to record the sentence imposed upon an accused, to specify any discount applied and to specify the greater sentence that would have been imposed but for the plea of guilty:[26]

**Recording of Sentencing Discount**
1. Judges, sheriffs and justices of the peace are reminded that, in all cases, where a discount is applied to a sentence under reference to the provisions of section 196 of the Criminal Procedure (Scotland) Act 1995, the fact that the sentence was discounted and the sentence that would otherwise have been imposed, but for the operation of section 196 of the 1995 Act, should be recorded in the court minutes.
2. The sentencing judge should take steps to ensure that the clerk of court makes an appropriate entry in the court minutes. All that the court minutes need record is that the sentence imposed was discounted in terms of section 196 of the 1995 Act and what the sentence would otherwise have been. An entry along the following lines would be sufficient: 'The sentence imposed was discounted in terms of section 196 of the Criminal Procedure (Scotland) Act 1995 and would otherwise have been X'.
3. While it is not necessary that the reasons for applying a particular level of discount are recorded in the court minutes, such reasons require to be provided by the sentencing judge in the event of any appeal.

The legislation was not accompanied by the paraphernalia of Sentencing Councils, Sentencing Guidelines[27] and the like, as was the lot of English and Welsh judges. Much accordingly lay in the hands of Scottish courts. Their response, unlike their English counterparts, was not to seek to dress State-induced guilty pleas in new clothes but instead, in the leading cases of *Du Plooy and Ors v HM Advocate* (2005)[28] and *Gemmell and Ors v HM Advocate* (2012),[29] to recognise it as an administrative procedure with explicit recognition of some of its dangers.

The Scottish courts made clear that the introduction of State-induced guilty pleas in the form of offers of a sentence discount was the result of *statutory imposition* and not caused by a change in stance on the part of the judges. Indeed, following the enactment of section 196, for a number

---

[26] Practice Note (No. 1 of 2008), *Recording of Sentencing Discount*.
[27] There are Guidelines in specific areas such as in offences involving child pornography. See *HM Advocate v Graham* [2010], in which the Court reviewed sentencing guidelines from England and Wales as well as decisions of Scottish courts but cautioned against 'too rigid adherence to guidelines'.
[28] *Du Plooy and Ors v HM Advocate* (2005 JC1).
[29] *Gemmell and Ors v HM Advocate* (2011). Prior to *Gemmell*, in *Spence v HM Advocate* (2008) the court had set levels of discount that it thought appropriately reflected the stage at which the plea was entered.

of years there was almost no discussion in Scotland as to the basis of, or the scope for, any allowance to be given for a guilty plea, nor was there any development of a clear practice as to the form of an allowance, in contrast to the position in England where the practice of judges actually *preceded* the enactment of the provision corresponding to section 196. This led the court in *Du Plooy* to observe that it could even be argued that, up to then, in Scotland section 196 had not realised the purposes which it was designed to achieve.[30]

Eventually, however, the courts accepted that, as Lord Eassie in *Gemmell* stated,[31] it was not possible to construe section 196 otherwise than reversing *Strawhorn v McLeod*. Even in that regard, Lord Eassie was at pains to point out what a reduction of sentence meant in dealing with criminals from whom the public deserved protection:

> To the extent that the discounting of the sentence to take account of the timing of the plea of guilty may impinge upon the protection of the public inherent in virtually all sentences, it seems to me that such is a consequence of the legislature's decision to reverse *Strawhorn v McLeod*. (para. 137)

Having accepted the consequences of the statute,[32] Scottish courts also recognised the true rationale behind the political intervention.[33] Attempts to imbue the new policy with an ethical content of the kind which marked the early efforts of English judges (linking the discount to signs of genuine remorse) were rejected out of hand. The explanation of the new policy rationale was introduced by Lord Gill in *Gemmell* in these terms:[34]

> The euphemism 'utilitarian value' may be thought to give the principle of discounting some ethical content; but sentence discounting is not an exercise in Benthamite philosophy. It is not based on any high moral principle relating to the offence, the offender or the victim. On the contrary, it involves the court's passing a sentence that, in its considered judgment, is less than the offence truly

---

[30] Lord Justice General (Cullen) at para. 6.
[31] Op. cit., at para. 137.
[32] There is empirical evidence that some Scottish judges expressed discomfort with the discount principle, particularly in that it might represent a windfall for the guilty defendant. Two judges interviewed in one study placed their concern on the fact that, as a result of the interaction between formal sentence discounting and fact and charge bargaining, the extent of the discount could be enormous (Leverick, 2006, p. 16).
[33] There was a glancing reference in *Du Plooy* to a justification based in remorse but that was not regarded as plausible.
[34] Op. cit., at para. 34. See also *HM Advocate v Lee McNamara* [2012] to the same effect.

warrants. It is a statutory encouragement of early pleas. In some cases, there is a saving of inconvenience to complainers and witnesses. In a small minority of cases there is a saving in jury costs. There is also a benefit to the criminal justice system in the avoidance of undue delay between arrest and sentencing. But the primary benefit that is realised in every case is the saving of administrative costs and the reduction of the court's workload.

## THE 'UTILITARIAN' JUSTIFICATION: A BRIEF INTERLUDE

The reference to Bentham and 'utilitarian' philosophy requires comment because it is just in the area of State-induced guilty pleas that crude utilitarian or consequentialist arguments are not only advanced but also falsely linked to the philosophy of Jeremy Bentham.

Bentham thought that his philosophy could supply a method of calculating the punishment *deserved* – that is, why punishment was good for society through general deterrence – and it offers no support whatsoever for State-induced guilty pleas.[35] On the contrary, Bentham's ideas about the reliability of various methods of fact-finding and the insistence on accuracy therein, when and how severely we should punish, and his argument that we should not punish persons for what they have done when it would be too expensive to do so, are based in the *correct determination of guilt or innocence* as an indispensable part of the process; and his whole idea of measuring punishment by reference to the culpability of the defendant would break down if he accepted the philosophy of State-induced guilty pleas.

Indeed, having analysed problems affecting the accuracy of extra-judicial confessions (such as in a police station), in his examination of spontaneous confessions delivered in the 'theatre of justice'[36] Bentham (1840) presciently anticipated the key circumstances of State-induced guilty pleas. Proceeding from the bedrock of his philosophy, that evidence should be accurate, reliable or true, Bentham sought to warn those involved in eliciting confessions from defendants on the ground that various forces might tend to the production of untrue confessions:[37] 'A judge, in examining an accused or suspected person, should be upon his

---

[35] While it might be possible, in theory, to argue that utilitarianism can justify the bargain *if* it could be shown to produce (overall aggregate) utility, Bentham, as we shall see, provided no support for such an argument.

[36] Bentham (1840), *The Rationale of Judicial Evidence*, at p. 36.

[37] Ibid., at p. 37.

guard against the sinister inducements, to the action of which a man in such a situation is exposed'.

Enumerating the causes which might bring about untrue confessions, *which included guilty persons confessing to lesser crimes in order to avoid the severer punishment*, Bentham addressed one of the central questions that today has assumed relevance in relation to State-induced guilty pleas, namely the innocent person who confesses. Bentham formulated his theoretical arguments in these terms:

> Not guilty of the crime charged, nor consequently, being justly subjectable to the punishment annexed to it, – but exposed, or conceiving himself exposed, to undergo some severer suffering (whether on the score of criminality or any other) at the hands of the prosecutor, or some other man in power, to whom it would be acceptable that he should suffer as for the offence in question, – he makes confession of it accordingly, in the hope of thereby escaping such severer suffering. (p. 37)

And who, reflected Bentham, might so act as to trigger such a false confession?

> Various is the description of the person by whose power (i.e. by the hopes and fears that point to it) a man may be drawn into a false confession. It will depend in a considerable degree upon the nature of the offence: an ordinary offence, or a political offence. It may accordingly, be a private individual; it may be, in a monarchy, the monarch, or one or more of his ministers; in a commonwealth, some officer or some individual invested by law or influence with appropriate power; *it may be (though without atrocious abuse of judicial power it cannot be) even the judge*. (p. 37, emphasis added)

As we see, therefore, not only was Bentham concerned with accurately establishing the facts and basis of guilt,[38] he cautioned against 'sinister inducements' which could distort the fact-finding process, including the

---

[38] This is also the underlying rationale of Bentham's theory of punishment which rested entirely on the correct identification of the guilty offender. Indeed, Bentham, acknowledging that no trial system was perfect and that mistakes would be made, was concerned that his proposals in this regard remitted, so far as possible, any punishment wrongfully inflicted, including upon the innocent. As Bentham (1781) put it: 'The general presumption is, that when punishment is applied, punishment is needful: that it ought to be applied, and therefore cannot want to be *remitted*. But in very particular, and those always very deplorable cases, it may by accident happen otherwise. It may happen that punishment shall have been inflicted, where, according to the intention of the law itself, it ought not to have been inflicted: that is, where the sufferer is innocent of the offense. At the time of the sentence passed he appeared guilty: but since then, accident has brought his innocence to light. This being the case, so much of the destined punishment as he

defendant being exposed or believing himself/herself exposed to some more severe sanction and, importantly, that the 'sinister' force at work could come not only from prosecutors but also (an abuse of power) directly from the judge, the precise concerns that opponents of plea bargaining have voiced.

## GEMMELL

Returning to Lord Gill in *Gemmell*, it followed from his analysis that section 196 applied regardless of whether the accused had shown remorse. Moreover, remorse was not a proper basis for any sentence discount unless, as an aspect of mitigation, it was demonstrated by convincing evidence. As Lord Reed put the matter in *Balgowan v HM Advocate* (2011), the statutory provisions were introduced for resource reasons and it was accordingly inappropriate to seek to explain them in other terms:

> It is, we think, reasonably well settled that the objective of the statutory provisions ... was no more nor less than utilitarian in the sense that by encouraging pleas of guilty *it was hoped* that considerable amounts of public time and expense would be saved as well as sparing witnesses the trouble, expense and, on occasion, distress of attending court and giving evidence. Although reference has also been made, in this context, to the possible importance of contrition, that has always been a relevant consideration for a sentencing judge and was plainly not the reason for the legislation. Insofar, therefore, as the provisions in question are founded in expediency it is hardly surprising if they do not lend themselves easily to legal analysis[39] or, for that matter, comparative justice. Nonetheless, the working out of these provisions has been left to the judiciary rather than the legislature. (para. 3, emphasis added)

Although, accordingly, the policy was founded in hope rather than in actuarial calculation of the kind that consequentialist utilitarianism implies[40] ('... a pragmatic way of dealing with an administrative

---

has suffered already, there is no help for. The business is then to free him from as much as is yet to come' (Chapter XIV, at XXV).

[39] It is not exactly clear what is being argued here because it must be the responsibility of judges to place legislation within an interpretive framework that makes sense in *legal* terms.

[40] The court contented itself with a simple contrast between the court (£348) and prosecution (£4,419) cost of an early guilty plea with average jury trial court (£17,492) and prosecution (£19,269) cost; and additionally a savings in defence costs supported by criminal legal aid. Scottish courts do not intend to engage in 'complex calculations' regarding supposed benefits: *Gemmell* (above); *Harkin & Anor v Procurator Fiscal, Falkirk & Anor* [2012].

problem and of avoiding public expense' as Lord Justice Clerk put it),[41] a Full Bench of the High Court[42] in *Gemmell* felt that it was safe in adopting the rationale advanced by Kirby J of the High Court of Australia in the case of *Cameron v The Queen*,[43] that the proper foundation for an advanced sentence discount is not as reward for remorse or the anticipated consequences of a guilty plea but an acceptance that it is in the *'public interest'* to facilitate guilty pleas by providing a sentence discount:[44]

> It is in the public interest to facilitate pleas of guilty by those who are guilty and to conserve the trial process substantially to cases where there is a real contest about guilt. Doing this helps ease the congestion in the courts that delay the hearing of such trials as must be held. It also encourages the clear-up rate for crime and so vindicates public confidence in the processes established to protect the community and uphold its laws.

In consequence of accepting the rationale advanced by Kirby J, the Scottish judges recognised that, whatever their own views and whatever the history of the matter had been in Scotland, 'the legitimacy of according a discount in respect of a plea of guilty, in appropriate circumstances, cannot now be challenged'.[45]

While this did not go so far as to adopt a discount *policy*, the analysis in *Gemmell* may be faulted for having uncritically accepted the rationale advanced by Kirby J in *Cameron*. In that case, McHugh J addressed the argument that the person who pleads not guilty is not being punished and given an increased sentence despite the fact that there would be a lesser sentence for a guilty plea and conceded that the 'subtlety of this scholastic argument has not escaped criticism from those who see legal issues in terms of substance rather than form' (at p. 351) referring, *inter alia*, to the observation of Cox J in *R v Shannon*[46] that a defendant 'will need a very subtle mind, unusually sympathetic to the ways of the law' to accept this

---

[41] Op. cit., at para. 35.
[42] This was a conjoined hearing involving seven different appeals against sentence with each member of the Bench delivering a separate opinion.
[43] *Cameron v The Queen* (2002).
[44] Ibid., para. 67.
[45] Lord Osborne in *Gemmell*, op. cit., at para. 112. Lord Osborne earlier said in the same paragraph that section 196 of the statute supplied the justification for the discount: 'it is right to recognise that, following upon the enactment of section 196 at least, it is beyond argument that there exists a proper rationale for making an allowance in a sentence in respect of a plea of guilty'.
[46] (1979) 21 SASR 442, at 458–9.

argument; and Kirby J in *Cameron*, referred to other judges describing the distinctions as bordering on the 'metaphysical' and having 'a certain illogicality'.[47]

A more significant concern is that the court in *Gemmell* made no reference to the fact that in *Cameron v The Queen* the purported justifications for accepting State-induced guilty pleas were based, as the majority judgment[48] put it, on the *fictions* that it was *subjective evidence of remorse* and *a subjective willingness on the part of the accused to save judicial resources*. Having cited from *Siganto v The Queen* (1998) that 'a plea of guilty is ordinarily a matter to be taken into account in mitigation; first, because it is usually evidence of some remorse on the part of the offender, and second, on the pragmatic ground that the community is spared the expense of a contested trial',[49] the majority in *Cameron* rested their judgment explicitly on the quite different ground that a defendant pleading guilty as a result of a bargain is *subjectively* intending to save judicial time and resources:[50]

> It should at once be noted that remorse is not necessarily the only subjective matter revealed by a plea of guilty. The plea may also indicate acceptance of responsibility and a willingness to facilitate the course of justice ... Reconciliation of the requirement that a person not be penalized for pleading not guilty with the rule that a plea of guilty may be taken into account in mitigation requires that *the rationale for that rule, so far as it depends on factors other than remorse and acceptance of responsibility, be expressed in terms of willingness to facilitate the course of justice and not on the basis that the plea has saved the community the expense of a contested hearing.* (emphasis added)

In other words, the court in *Cameron* was in fact trying to do what *Gemmell* assumed it was *not* doing – namely, attempting to imbue the guilty plea with an 'ethical' content, divorced, as it necessarily had to be, from the actual thinking of defendants, just as had been unsuccessfully attempted in earlier judicial rationalisations regarding 'remorse'.

This alone demonstrates that the 'resources' argument on which judges seek to justify sentence discounts is nothing more than *a construction based upon fictions*. It is resonant of the Kaldor-Hicks economic efficiency argument that a transaction is economically efficient if the loss caused to one party *could be* compensated for by the other party, *regardless of whether compensation was actually made*. This is the ultimate consequence

---

[47] Op. cit., at pp. 358–9.
[48] Gaudron, Gummow and Callinan JJ.
[49] Op. cit., at pp. 663–4.
[50] Op. cit., at paras 11 and 14. The point is repeated elsewhere in the judgment, as at para. 22.

of making assessments in a manner detached from the individuality of the persons involved. A decision would appear to be correct if everybody is either made better off by it or, to the extent that they are made worse off, *would* be willingly compensated by the other party/parties. Similarly, in State-induced guilty pleas, it seems that the individual person of the defendant is reduced to total insignificance; and there is no consideration of what is in justice due to that person, or of whether they are in a position to resist the bargain. In contrast to Kaldor-Hicks, the 'transaction' proposed is not demonstrated to be efficient in these terms. Indeed, the majority in *Cameron* openly conceded that, to address the subtleties involved, the rationale for differentiating sentences according to plea 'may need *some refinement in expression* if the distinction *is to be seen as* non-discriminatory'[51] as between those who plead guilty and those who are convicted following trial. In other words, although the rationale is neither tenable nor credible, in order to secure the confidence of the public upon which so much depends, a form of words needs to be constructed to make it appear so!

## DISCRETION VERSUS POLICY: THE PHILOSOPHICAL DIVIDE

While the Scottish courts considered that they were forced into recognising the inevitability of the statutory sentence discount, they insisted that its application was still a matter for the judge and wrestled with the practical implications of this. This meant both that an accused was not 'entitled' to any particular discount in return for a plea of guilty and also that the level of discount, if any, is always a matter for the *discretion* of the sentencer.[52] At the same time, however, judges acknowledged there was an argument, in the interests of the public as well as that of the accused, that a *policy* should be formulated so that the extent to which sentences are discounted should be known and that counsel for the accused should know, at least in general terms, the extent to which a sentence is likely to be reduced in the event of an early plea of guilty, so that they can advise the accused accordingly.[53] At the same time, it was also accepted that the application of section 196 should be *principled*:[54]

---

[51] At p. 344, emphasis added.
[52] Lord Justice Clerk in *Gemmell*, op. cit., at para. 31.
[53] Lord Cullen in *Du Plooy*, op. cit., at para. 25.
[54] Lord Gill in *Gemmell*, at para. 32.

[T]he court's discretion is not wholly unfettered. In view of the principles on which discounting is based, and by clear inference from section 196, there will be cases of early pleas in which a refusal to allow any discount at all would be perverse. Moreover, even in a discretionary matter such as this, it is desirable that the court should exercise its discretion in accordance with some broad general principles. By means of such principles, sentence discounting will not be a haphazard exercise but will instead reflect a common understanding of sentencers and practitioners.

This meant that the sentencing judge should decide upon the appropriate sentence on the basis of an 'instinctive synthesis' of all relevant factors and then simply apply the discount, if any:[55] 'In this way the sentencer is saved the effort of making complex calculations, particularly in a busy sheriff court, and the resulting sentence represents a true exercise of judgment without a spurious appearance of arithmetical exactitude'.

Unlike the English court in *Goodyear*, the caution exercised in Scotland derives in great measure from the concern that the decision-making of defendants in general could be distorted; that innocent people might be adversely affected by a sentence discount system;[56] and that public confidence in the criminal justice system might be eroded by inappropriately lenient sentences.

As to the first concern, Lord Justice General (Lord Cullen) stated the matter clearly in *Du Plooy*. Having argued that the import of the statute, while not intended to introduce a rigid system of discounts,[57] made clear that there was no objection in principle to an accused person being offered the prospect of an allowance in sentence in return for a plea of guilty, Lord Cullen continued:[58]

> At the same time it is important to bear in mind that any practice of making an allowance has to be kept within bounds, so as to avoid discouraging, or

---

[55] Ibid., at para. 59 referring to the Australian case of *Markarian v R* [2005].

[56] As long ago as 1970, Gerald Gordon, in commenting upon *R v Turner* (1970) pointed out that 'it must be realized that in practice an innocent man may be prepared to plead guilty to a lesser offence if he thinks the Crown case against him is so strong that he might well be convicted after trial of the original charge. He may also have reasons, quixotic or otherwise, for wanting to plead guilty' (Gordon, 1970, p.154).

[57] In proposing the Act, Under-Secretary of State for Scotland (Lord James Douglas-Hamilton) said that it 'should encourage those who are considering making a plea of guilty to do so timeously. It will not introduce a formal or rigid system of what is commonly known as sentence discounting' (Hansard HC, vol. 566, col. 139).

[58] Op. cit., at para. 4.

appearing to discourage, accused persons from exercising the right to put the prosecution to the proof of the charges against them.

Scottish courts have also been seized of the risk that State-induced guilty pleas will induce innocent people to plead guilty, a risk that increases with the magnitude of the discount and of the potential damage to public confidence. As Lord Gill stated:[59]

> There are two significant risks in sentence discounting. The first is that the allowance of substantial discounts may cause accused persons who have a stateable defence to play safe and plead guilty for the sake of the discount. The greater the potential discount, the greater is the risk of that, in my view. The prospect of a substantial discount is therefore a potentially dangerous incentive that may undermine the presumption of innocence.[60]
> 
> The second risk is that the allowance of substantial discounts may cause the sentencing decisions of the criminal courts to lose credibility and in this way may erode the authority of the courts generally . . .
> 
> Perhaps the most fundamental problem, however, is the possible perception of injustice, particularly in cases where severe sentences are deserved. If in such a case there are two accused, the accused who pleads guilty at the earliest opportunity may receive a sentence that is less by a matter of years than that imposed on the accused who is found guilty after trial . . .

The court in *Gemmell* was not able, however, to resolve the problem of reconciling the need for some ordering in the discount system to guide defendants and their advisers with the need to protect innocent defendants from undue pressure. Earlier non-prescriptive guidance in *Spence v HM Advocate*[61] had been provided on the basis of 'substantial experience' in the High Court and Sheriff Court of implementation of the guidance given in *Du Plooy*, which, the court accepted, had given rise to inconsistencies:

> 14 . . . The extent of the discount will be on a sliding scale ranging at its greatest from one third, or in exceptional circumstances possibly more, to nil. The utilitarian value of an early plea will be influenced by, among other things, the extent of the public resources which will be expended in preparing a case for trial and presenting it at trial. After an accused has appeared on petition, investigation and preparation will to an increasing extent be undertaken by the Crown prior to the service of an indictment. Among other courses open to an accused person during that period is the giving of written intimation to the Crown under sec 76 of the 1995 Act of his intention to plead guilty and his desire to have his case disposed of at once. If a clear indication of an intention

---

[59] *Gemmell*, op. cit., at paras 73–4, 76.
[60] Citing Ashworth and Redmayne (2010, pp. 312–14).
[61] (2008) JC 174.

to plead guilty is given during that period (and is adhered to), we would expect that a discount in the order of one third might be afforded. Such an indication at the first calling of a case at a preliminary hearing (or in the sheriff court at a first diet) might attract a discount in the order of one quarter. Thereafter, any discount can be expected to reduce further. A plea at the trial diet should not ordinarily exceed one tenth and in some circumstances may be less than that or nil. The extent of any discount allowed should be recorded in the court minutes.

This was far from the end of the matter, a sharp divide appearing between those who favoured a discretionary approach and those who thought it more appropriate to formulate a policy by which sentencers would be offered much clearer guidance.

Thus, for Lord Justice Clerk Gill in *Gemmell*, 'the court's discretion to allow a discount should be exercised sparingly and only for convincing reasons'; that where these have been given, 'it is only in exceptional circumstances' that the court would interfere on appeal; and that further consideration would have to be given to discounts as large as one-third.[62] Lord Gill was prepared to state only that sufficient guidance would be provided by the broad principle that, 'the discount will be the greater the earlier the plea ...', without offering guidance as to the circumstances when the *Spence* scale was appropriate or, more importantly, when the discount should be withheld.

By contrast, Lord Eassie thought that practical considerations necessitated guidance of a kind which would imply an indication of the quantum of discount:[63]

> While I of course agree that the allowance of that reduction is, in its essential nature, an exercise of discretion, one is well familiar with areas of discretionary judgment in which the discretion is generally guided by established rules or principles. The utility of such rules or principles guiding or directing the exercise of the discretion enables the court not only to achieve consistency in its decisions – in essence, comparative justice – but also enables practitioners to offer advice with some reasonable degree of confidence. While one may take issue with the use of language to the effect that there is an 'entitlement' to a discount, it respectfully seems to me that if the utilitarian[64] and cost-saving

---

[62] Lord Gill in *Gemmell*, at para. 79. If the objective is to increase the number of guilty pleas, one core problem with this approach is that it is unlikely to succeed without a significant and predictable sentence discount scheme, a policy with which Lord Gill was not comfortable.

[63] At para. 145. None of the other members of the Court directly addressed the issue.

[64] Lord Eassie, in using 'utilitarian' as differentiated from 'cost-savings benefits', adopts a meaning which differs from traditional characterisations of utilitarian theory whose focus is precisely upon cost-benefit analysis.

benefits underlying the principle of discounting sanctioned by the legislature are usefully to be realised, practitioners should, in general, be able to advise the client of the amount of the likely discount with some degree of confidence. That necessarily involves the elaboration of principles, or guidance, for the exercise of the discretion upon which practitioners can have some reliance and hence the creation of a legitimate expectation, peculiar circumstances apart, that the guidance will be followed.

One core problem with Lord Eassie's plea for 'guidelines' other than crude sentence discounts, is that they are difficult if not impossible to formulate once other, by themselves less exactly measurable, considerations come into sentencing decisions. For example, how would the person pleading guilty contritely – such a thing is imaginable, at least, even in a bargained situation – compare to the person pleading guilty without any contrition? More significantly, the approach of Lord Eassie would involve Scottish judges adopting a *policy* of sentence discounting which flies in the face of the historic commitment to the sentence having *discretion* in this regard.

## THE EXIGENCIES OF PRACTICE

However, despite the jurisprudential divide, following *Gemmell* there was increasing evidence that the courts began to place less emphasis upon philosophical and ethical concerns and instead acceded more to the imperatives of practice. The issue before the Scottish courts for a time became the application and quantum of discount rather than questions as to the principle of reducing sentences in return for guilty pleas. Similarly, the foundation of the discount was simply expressed, if at all, in acceptance of an unexplicated 'utilitarian' benefit that does or might flow from the plea arrangement.

Thus, in *HM Advocate v Lee McNamara* [2012], following an altercation with the victim, the defendant reversed a car over the victim, as a result of which the victim died. The defendant's offer of a guilty plea of culpable homicide was rejected and he was convicted of murder. At the sentencing stage, the defendant was sentenced to life imprisonment with a punishment part of 13 and a half years, the trial judge stating that the punishment part would have been 15 years had the accused not tendered a guilty plea at the first preliminary hearing ('diet'). The Crown appealed against the sentence as unduly lenient both because the starting point of 15 years was too low and because a 10 per cent discount was too high as no clear utilitarian value had arisen from the accused's plea offer. The High Court of Justiciary disposed of the central arguments in this way:

[Section 196 of the Criminal Procedure (Scotland) Act, 1995] . . . applies in a situation where there has been a plea of guilty, whether accepted or not, and the court is sentencing for that offence (i.e. the one for which a plea had been tendered). It is not applicable in respect of sentences for offences to which the appellant has not pled guilty. It is, for that simple reason, not applicable to the situation which arose in this case, where the respondent tendered a plea to culpable homicide and was convicted of murder. No formal discount in terms of s.196, as such a discount is to be recorded in terms of s.196(1A), ought to have been afforded in this case. The court must disagree with the *obiter dictum* in *Balgowan v HM Advocate* in so far as it may be thought to suggest otherwise.

In any event, as is set out in *Gemmell v HM Advocate* (Lord Justice Clerk Gill at p.491 (p.398) para.37), the only relevant consideration when assessing the level of discount is the utilitarian benefit of the early plea. The plea in this case had no utilitarian benefit at all. The plea did not result in the trial being shortened nor did it avoid witnesses testifying. It is clear that the respondent entered into an agreement with the Crown in relation to the evidence to be led. Many facts were agreed in the joint minute and that did result at least in many witnesses not having to give evidence. That clear utilitarian benefit is not, however, related to the plea. That benefit can be reflected, as can remorse and many other mitigatory features, in selecting the appropriate sentence for the offence. It does not, however, translate into a formal percentage discount. For these reasons, the court considers that the trial judge erred in law in applying a discount to the sentence selected. (para. 17)

Similarly, in *HM Advocate v Lyttell (Adam)* [2012] a sentence discount of one-third was deemed excessive on appeal by the Crown because the defendant's advisers chose to negotiate with the Crown and accordingly delayed tendering the guilty plea until there had been two preliminary hearings thereby reducing its value to the administration of justice.

Accordingly, with minor exceptions,[65] it was not uncommon in these cases, taking the decision in *Gemmell* as authoritatively disposing of the principles relating to discounts in return for pleas, to deal with appeals by simple reference to the 'utilitarian' value[66] of the guilty plea or to stipulate the 'standard'[67] or appropriate 'discount'[68] that the case

---

[65] Courts have occasionally insisted that 'interpreted correctly' (*Stephen Murray v HM Advocate* [2013]) there is no sliding scale of discounts, the decision on which is a matter for the discretion of the judge. One consequence, however, is that it is only in exceptional cases that the court will interfere with a discretionary decision on discounting for which the sentencer has given cogent reasons (ibid.).

[66] *Shawn Ernest Divin v Procurator Fiscal, Dundee* [2012]; *George Gerald Doherty v HM Advocate* [2012].

[67] *Lees v HM Advocate* [2012] in which the court applied 'the standard one third discount'.

[68] *Debbie Harkin v Procurator Fiscal, Falkirk* and *Selina Sin Tung Fung v Procurator Fiscal, Aberdeen* [2012]; *James Tough v HM Advocate* [2012].

merited, although it was not always altogether clear what the 'standard' was.[69] In the case of *Leggatt* (2012),[70] for example, the defendant, who raped an 11-year-old girl and tried to rape a three-year-old girl was told by the judge that he would have been jailed for 12 years had it not been for his guilty plea. In other words, his sentence of eight years, expressed by judges as a one-third discount, represents in fact a 50 per cent reduction as standard. Indeed, the 'utilitarian' precept appears to have been internalised by the Defence Bar in addition to being the bedrock of the courts as, for example, can be seen in the court's judgment delivered by Lord Emslie in *Ottaway v Nisbet*:[71] '... as the solicitor advocate for the appellant very fairly acknowledges, it is thought to be the objective utilitarian value of a plea of guilty which merits a discount rather than subjective considerations of remorse or contrition'. This had the result that, inexorably, if initially with reluctance, it appeared that the Scottish courts were being dragged into practices which were closely aligned with those in England and Wales.

## *MURRAY*: RESOLUTION OF THE PHILOSOPHICAL DIVIDE?

Nonetheless, the important divide between *discretion* and *policy* that was at the heart of *Gemmell* was not to remain dormant for long. There developed a feeling among some members of the judiciary that discounts were becoming standardised, akin to a policy, and too generous,[72] as can be seen in *Murray v HM Advocate* [2013].[73] The appellant had pleaded guilty to charges of sexual assault including rape involving patients suffering from severe dementia at a Care Home and, in consequence, had his

---

[69] In *James Tough v Lord Advocate* [2012], for example, the court, in reducing a sentence of three years to 27 months for an early plea, applied a standard discount of 25%.

[70] See *BBC News* (2012h).

[71] [2012] HCJAC 36 at para. 13.

[72] Like their English and Welsh counterparts, Scottish courts may increase a sentence deemed to be 'unduly lenient'. See *HM Advocate v Bell* (1995); and *HM Advocate v Q* [2013] in which the Court refused the Crown leave to appeal having determined that the disposals were not unduly lenient.

[73] This case provides a salutary example of the dangers involved in last minute briefing of counsel, the Court having to adjourn the appeal 'for some time to enable him to read the social inquiry and psychological reports and other papers, and to enable those instructing him to obtain details of the preparation of the defence...'.

sentence discounted from nine to seven years' imprisonment. In settling the level of discount, the sentencing judge recognised that there was a 'utilitarian' value to the plea of guilty tendered; that accordingly it would be appropriate to allow a discount from the sentence selected; that (in the light of *Gemmell*) the appellant was not entitled to any particular level of discount; that the level of discount to allow was a matter for the judge's discretion; that the judge's discretion to allow a discount should be exercised sparingly and only for convincing reasons; and that the assessment of the level of discount depended upon how far the utilitarian benefits of an early plea had been achieved, adding:

> Looking to the circumstances of the present case it seemed to me that any trial which had been necessary would not have been lengthy and of course none of the complainers would have been able to testify. That said, there would no doubt have been enormous further distress caused to their families had a contested trial taken place. It seemed to me right to take each of these features into account and also to bear in mind that other savings in preparation for trial would no doubt have been achieved by virtue of the offer made at a very early stage. It did not, however, seem to me that the relevant features translated with ease into any particular percentage figure. Furthermore I was conscious of the disproportionate effect which a fixed percentage deduction could have on an otherwise well merited lengthy sentence. In this regard I took account of the risk to the credibility of the court's sentencing decisions which the Lord Justice Clerk (Gill) identified and addressed in . . . his opinion in the case of *Gemmell*.
>
> In attempting to strike an appropriate balance between all of the competing interests in the present case it seemed to me that I should try to identify a period which was sufficiently substantial to reflect the benefit to the administration of justice which was present but which did not dilute disproportionately the view I had arrived at as to the appropriate starting point sentence. A period of two years appeared to me to strike that balance. (para. 13)

On appeal it was argued that the discount granted was inadequate and that it should have been in the region of one-third from the nine years' starting point. The Lord Justice General (Gill) sought to summarise the elements of his earlier judgment in *Gemmell* to which his fellow judges had assented:

> I expressed the view that the determination of the starting point and the appropriate discount were separate processes governed by different considerations . . . . I considered that the circumstances of the offence and the offender determined the headline sentence; but that such matters were not relevant to the amount of the discount. The amount of the discount was governed solely by the utilitarian benefits that resulted from an early plea . . . .
>
> I also expressed my concern that Spence v HM Adv 2008 JC 174 might have created a climate of expectation amongst practitioners. I repeated that

the accused is not entitled to any particular discount in return for a plea of guilty. ... I considered that the Court's discretion was not wholly unfettered. It should be exercised in accordance with broad general principles. ... In any given case, the discount would be the greater the earlier the plea was tendered. ... I thought that, since there would always be some benefit in an early plea, if only in the administrative benefits that resulted from it, an accused should be given at least a token discount. ... The level of benefit that an early plea brought would depend on the circumstances of the given case. For example, the fact that complainers and other witnesses were spared the ordeal of a trial was, in general, a relevant consideration; but it was not relevant where the potential witnesses were police officers or experts for whom the giving of evidence would have been at most an inconvenience. ... I also expressed the view that in order to maintain public confidence in the justice system and the credibility of sentences that the court imposed, the court's discretion should be exercised sparingly and only for convincing reasons ...[74]

The principal judgment was delivered by the Lord Justice General (Gill) and the Court was unanimously of the view that the sentencing judge had not erred in his approach. While the appellant had entered an early plea this had not been done at the earliest opportunity but some two months following that during which time the defence were considering their position. Lord Gill stated that *Spence* (*supra*) did not lay down a sliding scale but left the decision to the discretion of the sentence. The appeal was founded on the idea that an early plea entitles every accused to a discount of one-third which, said Lord Gill, had been discredited in *Gemmell*.[75] In the end, discretion triumphed over policy.

## A NOTE ON HASHTAG JUSTICE: THE RISE OF FISCAL DISPOSITIONAL POWER

As we mentioned earlier, it is difficult to reconcile the practice of plea bargaining in the lower courts with the apparent ignorance of this displayed by judges in the High Court of Justiciary. Although our focus is on serious cases, for completeness sake, it is necessary to note an even more radical development, practically and theoretically, that is swallowing vast numbers of 'minor' cases without recourse to the courts. Estimates suggest

---

[74] *Murray v HM Advocate* [2013], para. 16.
[75] In light of the facts, the Court considered that the headline sentence of nine years was unduly lenient. From a more appropriate headline sentence of 12 years, the court ordered a discount of two and a half years resulting in a sentence of nine and a half years' imprisonment.

that various 'alternatives to prosecution'[76] now absorb almost three-quarters of criminal cases classed as 'cleared up' in Scotland.[77]

This extraordinary figure is primarily located in the conditional offer of a fixed penalty, known colloquially as the 'fiscal fine', under which an offer is made by the fiscal (on behalf of the Crown Office and Fiscal Service) to an alleged offender of payment in discharge of liability for prosecution of the alleged offence. Introduced in 1988,[78] subsequent legislative changes[79] provided for fiscals to offer a fine for any offence triable under summary procedure[80] (which includes certain kinds of aggravated assaults, injury, weapons and robbery),[81] acceptance of which by the alleged offender did not involve a conviction and, if refused, could be dealt with in court as it normally would have. The fiscal fine gave the prosecutor a quasi-judicial function, effectively introducing an extra-curial dispositional tier and self-regulated[82] power covering all offences triable under summary procedure with additional powers to propose work orders and compensation orders.

Extraordinarily, the Criminal Proceedings Etc. (Reform) (Scotland) Act, (2007) introduced an 'opt out' system in relation to the fiscal fine. Under this, where a fiscal fine is proposed it is deemed to have been accepted by the alleged offender unless they give notice that it is to be contested within 28 days from issue. While 'acceptance' of the fiscal fine does not constitute a conviction, it may be disclosed to the court in any proceedings for an offence committed by the alleged offender within the next two years. Since its introduction in 1998, the use of the fiscal fine has rocketed from around 9,000 cases to, in 2011/12, almost 42,000.[83]

This 'default' or 'hashtag' justice is an embellishment of the ordinary process of State-induced guilty pleas and may be a pointer to the next stage in the development of plea bargaining in England and Wales. The 'consent' of the alleged offender is, as with 'advanced indications of sentence', coercively-obtained[84] in a context in which there is an unbridgeable knowledge deficit between the prosecutor fiscal and the alleged offender,

---

[76] The system seeks to avoid the protections of the criminal justice system by the pretence that the fiscal fine or conditional order is not a 'criminal charge'.
[77] White (2008).
[78] Following recommendations in the Stewart Committee Report (1983).
[79] McInnes Report (2004).
[80] With the exception of motoring offences.
[81] See Callander (2013).
[82] See Duff (1999a).
[83] For a comprehensive and insightful account, see Callander (2013).
[84] See Richards et al. (2011).

who cannot be expected, nor indeed presumed, to understand the meaning of the fiscal fine, the prospects of successful challenge or its likely impact in any future court proceedings.[85] Nor is there evidence that the fiscal fine protects the community, since early indications, at least, are that it is ineffective in dealing with persistent offenders.[86]

## CONCLUSION

Although our interest is with cases at the more serious end of the crime continuum, it is right to remark that the High Court of Justiciary in Scotland affected a curious lack of interest (even, knowledge) of practices in the lower courts, although these were well-attested by research and formed part of official policy-making. When, accordingly, the Court was directly confronted with sentence discounts it reacted as if it were dealing with a strange animal that had suddenly been introduced into the jurisdiction whose presence was unwelcome and denunciation of which would send it back to wherever it came from. This blind-eye approach could not be sustained and a more open and intelligent discourse soon followed.

In relation to serious cases, the outcome in regard to State-induced guilty pleas in Scotland is in marked contrast to that in England and Wales. While the higher Scottish Courts have grudgingly and with a measure of evident distaste, come to accept the principle of a discount in return for a guilty plea, there is not only a division between *discretion* and *policy*[87] but also a lack of clarity as to how the discount idea is to be applied.[88]

On the one hand, the approach taken in *Spence* supports a discretionary discount with guidance given to the sentencing judge approximating to a sliding scale largely determined by the stage at which the plea is entered. The argument in favour of this, as Lord Eassie spelled out in *Gemmell*, is that it promotes comparative justice (consistency in sentencing prac-

---

[85] See Leverick (2012).
[86] Richards et al. (2011).
[87] The guidelines for child pornography cases offered in *HM Advocate v Graham* [2010] have, it is said, been favourably received by the lower courts 'where sentencers have traditionally welcomed *guidance* from the appeal court on sentencing but have generally been opposed to presumptively binding guidelines' (Brown, 2013, original emphasis).
[88] Neither *Du Plooy* nor *Spence* has been overruled and, by careful judgments, neither has been disapproved. See, Shead (2013).

tices) and, by enabling practitioners to give advice to defendants with some degree of confidence, is more likely to achieve cost-savings benefits through a higher rate of guilty pleas.

On the other hand, some judges, concerned that the discount must not be seen to be an 'entitlement', that it must not be readily given, that it should not be of a level that would bring the administration of justice into disrepute, and that discounts have become over-generous, wish to go no further than to say that any discount should be at the discretion of the sentencing judge.[89] For certain judges, the argument against this approach is that it will inevitably produce inconsistent sentences, that some judges will give little or no credit for a guilty plea and that the guilty plea rate may drop because practitioners will have no sound basis on which to advise on plea.

As a result, Scottish appellate courts have been moved by statute into an open discourse over the notion that State-induced guilty pleas should be rewarded with a sentence discount. The judges, however, unlike their English and Welsh counterparts, have shown less appetite for practices that would amount to overt coercion of defendants and greater concern for the need to retain public confidence in the administration of justice which would be jeopardised by sentences which failed to reflect the true gravity of the crime. In this setting, they have found the task of reconciling these concerns with the cost-effective outcomes that such a plea system is intended to secure as one riddled with difficulty. Scottish appellate judges have shown themselves keen to assert their own autonomy and are hesitant to interfere with the discretion that sentencing judges have historically enjoyed. Differences in approach have been played out in the public setting of the High Court of Justiciary, where, in contrast to the English and Welsh Court of Appeal, judges have sought to resolve the moral hazards individually through considered judgments rather than sacrifice personal autonomy and integrity by digging one peremptory collective heel in the ground.

---

[89] The cases display varying approaches to the sentence discount. Thus, in *Wishart v HM Advocate* [2013] and *Steven McArthur v HM Advocate* [2013] the guilty plea was recognised by a discount of 10%; in *Colin Ross v HM Advocate* [2013] a 20% discount was awarded; in *HM Advocate v James East* [2013] the discount was 28% (quashed for other reasons).

# 8. Conclusion

## INTRODUCTION

The State-induced guilty plea process threatens the legitimacy of courts *as institutions* because, in contrast to the case of strikes, public disorders and homeless claimants, its practices cannot be characterised as arising out of a 'one-off' political or social 'crisis' to be responded to, however irregularly, before returning to normalcy. Because the process of State-induced guilty pleas is *intended to replace* in whole or part the promise of adversary justice, it challenges the foundations on which the claim of legitimacy of criminal courts has traditionally rested. Legitimacy and rationality are placed at risk when courts consciously promote trial-avoidance mechanisms as fair and just when they are aware that there are good reasons for their rejection.

## THE SHADOW SYSTEM

> Formerly, although the practice of judges and courts varied, the defendant's counsel could seek and obtain an indication from the judge about this in his room. However, in 1970 the Court of Appeal, in *R v Turner*, sought to put an end to private meetings of this sort with the judge, save in exceptional cases.[1]

Prior to *Turner* (1970), criminal justice operated in two different modes: an official form represented by the doorways of justice, formal, transparent and realised in its most perfect embodiment by the fanfaronade of jury trial; and an 'unofficial' private form represented by the backdoors of the courthouse, informal, non-transparent and trial-averse. These two modes were not unrelated: the existence of the latter enabled judges to pay exaggerated obeisance to the former as its asserted actuality.

This hypocritical posture gave judges significant control over most case dispositions. Prior to trial, judges could, and did, summon counsel to their chambers; they could, and did, make precipitate decisions about the

---

[1] Auld (2001), Chapter 10, para. 94.

'proper' disposal of cases; and they could, and did, use promises of favour through 'discounts'[2] or threats of enhanced sentences.

This shadow structure had significant implications for defence lawyers. It reinforced the subordinate status of barristers who, whether responding to judicial fiat or trading on personal relationships,[3] were obliged to use the tradesman's entrance in order to learn the worst or secure the best for their clients. Once privy to the judge's views and without a Code of Conduct for guidance,[4] barristers were thrown back on their own resources to persuade clients to plead guilty or risk trial before a judge who had both the capacity and demonstrated disposition to influence the result. Solicitors, like defendants, were outside this closeted environment.

Judicial control was pervasive. The acquisition of 'evidence', central to decision-making, was in the hands of an essentially unregulated police force, gifted to them by the contra-indicative *Judges' Rules* (i.e., 'rules' which were not *rules*). This occurred despite widespread concern over police malpractice, ranging from the false attribution of 'admissions' to induced and coerced 'confessions' elicited by blandishments or torture.[5]

---

[2] But see, Henham (1999) demonstrating empirically major discrepancies between courts as regards any 'discount'.

[3] The Judicial Statistics available since 1972 suggest that the relationship of barristers to judges was close in some circuits (areas) but less so in others because the guilty plea rates, though varying from area to area, tended to remain constant within each circuit each year. Thus, whereas some circuits (such as the West Midlands) had guilty plea rates of 75% or more, London (where, because of its size and configuration, personal relationships between barristers and judges would be more distant) consistently had the lowest, with 45–55% guilty pleas being typical. While the latest statistics (covering 2010) show an average guilty plea rate for England and Wales of 71%, large regional variations remain, with, for example, Humber and South Yorkshire at 82%, Cleveland, Durham and Northumbria, East Midlands and Greater Manchester all at 79%, and, at the lower end, London (Central and South) at 56%, London (North and West) at 57% (MoJ, 2011b). For an early account, see Zander (1991).

[4] See, for example, the authoritative guide to barristers, Boulton (5th edition, 1971) at pp. 70–73, advising that, where a defendant has confessed guilt to counsel, counsel can continue the defence but 'may not assert that which he knows to be a lie. He may not connive at, much less attempt to substantiate, a fraud'. No guidance was offered in respect of guilty pleas, although the standard authority on criminal law and procedure, Archbold, *Pleading, Evidence & Practice in Criminal Cases* set out basic issues regarding such matters as equivocal pleas (see Butler and Garsia, 1969, 37th edition, Chapter 2, para. 424 ff). Following *Turner*, Boulton (1975, 6th edition) simply set out the *Turner* guidelines and Archbold (Butler and Mitchell, 1973, 38th edition) included a summary thereof.

[5] See, for example, discussion in RCPPP (1929). The Sheffield Police Appeal Inquiry (Home Office, 1963) found that a specialist crime squad used various

Meanwhile, judges, at trial and publicly, lauded the police and called for a reduction of suspects' 'rights'.

Disregarding the *Rules*, individuals were routinely detained and questioned before and after charge and routinely denied access to lawyers. As judges routinely winked at evidence of police malpractice, barristers were unnerved advancing defences which alleged police wrongdoing; and, accordingly, they sought professional solace in 'deals' that judges would privately intimate. Police perjury was condoned until judges constructed a device (through *Bass*) to render the fruits of perjury routinely admissible in evidence. If the 'right to silence' was rendered nugatory at the police station, exercising it at trial risked adverse comment.

## A CRACK IN THE DOOR

The private world of criminal judges was as effective as the underworld of the police station to which it was ideologically committed. It too operated under a veil of secrecy but was protected instead by refined, stylised etiquette, manners and decorum. It too had its own black arts – sweeteners, threats and sanctions – directed at both the defendant and the lawyer whose cases and possibly future practice were heavily contingent upon maintaining beneficial relationships with the judges. Like the police station, only the trusted few knew its customs. Barristers paid tribute to these Masonic-like traditions[6] and held dear their secrets. In *Turner*, it

---

instruments, including a 'rhino whip' to inflict prolonged assaults on suspects to extract 'confessions'. See, the revelations of the activities of the London CID Drug Squad, reflecting an ethic of detective work that went far beyond isolated incidents of police malpractice (Cox et al., 1977). See also, accounts of the notorious West Midlands Serious Crime Squad (Mullin, 1986; Burrell and Benetto, 1999; Lissaman, 2011; Peirce, 2011). Such practices were also exposed in the death of Blair Peach who is believed to have died in 1979 at the hands of a notorious group of police in London (the Special Patrol Group (SPG)); a search of SPG lockers disclosed a stockpile of weapons including a rhino whip, lead-weighted leather sticks, leather-encased truncheons and wooden staves (Foley, 2009; Lewis, 2010).

[6] The masonic influence on criminal justice in England and Wales is no far-flung aspersion. Such was the level of concern of the freemasons' influence upon the criminal justice system that, in 1998, former Home Secretary Jack Straw made the order, albeit thwarted, that police and judges declare any membership of the organisation. Links to the 'secret' society have since been confirmed in two police reports (*Operation Tiberius* in 2002 and *Project Riverside* in 2008) as endemic to the facilitation of police corruption, involving, *inter alia*, infiltration of murder investigations and sensitive intelligence regarding other organised crime. One report con-

took a solicitor – not a member of the Law Society and one excluded from the secret judicial fraternity – to shine light into this dark corner.

## COMING OUT

*Turner* sought to reconcile 'backdoor justice' with formal legal rationality in various ways. Defendants had 'complete freedom of choice' over plea; defence counsel were 'completely free' to do their duty; judges were forbidden to directly offer sentence discounts; and, approximately, justice was to be administered in open court. Inevitably, however, the 'open court' ideology was subverted in practice: counsel repeatedly sought access to judges' chambers and judges readily responded or initiated meetings themselves. More significantly, *Turner* structured its 'guidance' so that counsel's subordinate status was now formalised; in advising defendants, barristers were at the mercy of trial judges.

While on its face *Turner* affirmed party autonomy, and even appeared to some to outlaw secret deals,[7] its sub-text centralised judicial power and made clear that State-induced guilty pleas could be applied *routinely*, not only exceptionally or in times of 'crisis'. Central to *Turner*'s legitimating project was the 'virtual judge'. To choke off criticism, the Court of Appeal embarked on a 'clean hands' project: to abstract the judge from the unseemly business of 'deals' by the artifice that counsel must convey to the client the 'sentence-discount' as if drawn from the heavens.

This fiction could not survive. Robes and wigs were left trailing as barristers rushed to discover what was in the mind of judges who summoned them in hushed gestures to proffer a private deal or deliver a sentence ultimatum. As this restricted-viewing pantomime continued, growing numbers of defendants expressed dissatisfaction and increasingly appeals followed. With appeals came publicity, and with publicity came judicial embarrassment at the airing of practices in manifest contradiction to traditional claims of legitimacy. Something had to be done.

The way was prepared by legislative changes which had been invited by a judicial campaign over the previous thirty years.[8] In a law and order

---

cluded resignedly that the involvement of the 'brotherhood' was one of 'the most difficult aspects of organised crime corruption to proof against' (Harper, 2014a).

[7] For example, the *Daily Mail* (25 April 1970) headline, 'Lord Parker bans court deals', over a story which opened thus: 'Secret out-of-court deals were outlawed yesterday by the Lord Chief Justice'.

[8] For a full account of these changes, see Ashworth and Redmayne (2010) and Sanders, Young and Burton (2010).

climate that dishonourably followed the most disastrous series of miscarriages of justice in British history, the 'right to silence' that suspects and defendants purportedly enjoyed, was formally attenuated.[9] At the same time, sentence discounting gained legislative recognition by an opaquely-worded statute requiring courts, in determining sentence, to take into account the stage at which the guilty plea was indicated. Nevertheless, State-induced guilty pleas remained to be legitimated and reconciled with the claims of adversarial justice.

## THE NEED FOR LEGITIMACY

The conviction-oriented criminal justice system subsumed courts in contradictions *requiring* them to openly embrace the adversary ideal and to celebrate its attendant ideology. Under this, there was said to be a right to trial for *all*:[10] 'The right to a fair trial is one to be enjoyed by the guilty as well as the innocent, for a defendant is presumed to be innocent until proved to be otherwise in a fairly conducted trial'.

Prosecutors were 'ministers of justice' who had to exclude any notion of 'winning' or 'losing'[11] and judges were neutral arbiters.[12] The outcome of this official discourse was a symbolic celebration of fairness and integrity:[13]

> It cannot be too strongly emphasised that these are not the rules of a game. They are rules designed to safeguard the fairness of proceedings brought to determine whether a defendant is guilty of committing a crime or crimes conviction of which may expose him to serious penal consequences. In a criminal trial as in other activities the observance of certain basic rules has been shown to be the most effective safeguard against unfairness, error and abuse.

This ideological construction, however, *was* a game, and one which constantly required re-characterisation of its rules.

Although the ultimate role of the court is linked to the State's repressive role and the need for it to appear legitimate, as Bridges points out, the liberal State has never given much weight to the need for full rational-

---

[9] Criminal Justice and Public Order Act, 1994, section 34. To the previous judicial campaign, there were honourable exceptions such as Justice McKenna (1970) who wrote: 'A right not to give evidence which can be asserted only at the risk of hostile comment, is obviously imperfect'.
[10] *Randall v R* (2002), para. 28.
[11] *R v Puddick* (1865) and *R v Banks* (1917).
[12] *Michel v The Queen* [2010]; *R v Grafton* (1993).
[13] *Randall v R* (2002), para. 11.

ity in areas of law that bear upon unproductive sections of the community, precisely the staple diet of criminal courts, especially the lower criminal courts. Here, formal rationality serves little instrumental purpose although it is desirable to support the proclaimed principles for ideological purposes and accordingly, 'it is exactly because this adherence is symbolic (i.e., non-institutionalized), even at normal times, that it can so easily be dispensed with in crisis situations' (Bridges, 1975, p. 85). The ideological challenge presented itself precisely because State-induced guilty pleas were now to be *normalised*; officially imposed on defendants not only at times of 'crisis' but every day in 'serious' cases. The adversary ideal was itself set to be disfigured.

## THE LEGITIMATION PROJECT

The Auld Review (2001) took the challenge head-on offering its own jaundiced view. It told a mournful story: criminal justice had been misunderstood by outsiders (the public). As gospel-giver, Auld saw a solution: 'if public ignorance stands in the way . . . take steps adequately to demonstrate to the public that it is so'.[14] Accordingly, there was no incumbent need to mention the long ladder of judicial evasions in regard to plea bargaining (after all, if judges might be shown to be untrustworthy in this regard, heaven knows how they might be regarded in other matters!); the fault lay elsewhere: 'A wide misconception of the general public is that all or most of the criminal justice process takes place in court'.[15]

While the 'general public' doubtless entertains certain misconceptions, it is disconcerting to find that one of these is 'wide' and on such an important matter. Still, plea bargaining, it was airily said, had always been practised even prior to *Turner*, rules breached thereafter but no doubt 'motivated for the best'[16] and justifiable on a number of grounds: rewarding remorse; avoiding the public expense of long trials; saving victims and witnesses the trauma of giving evidence; and getting the best possible outcome for defendants minded to acknowledge their guilt.[17] In this setting, the risk to the innocent was openly and specifically marginalised. Like Auld, courts

---

[14] (2001) Chapter 4, para. 32. Self-servingly, Auld maintained that the public should be better informed but *only* as to their own ignorance where it affects 'public confidence'.
[15] Ibid., Chapter 10, para. 1.
[16] Ibid., para. 94.
[17] Ibid.

have offered 'justifications' for State-induced guilty pleas, the most prominent of which are examined below.

**Saving Public Expense**

The mainspring for judicial elevation of cost-effectiveness to sacred status has been the claim that it addresses the evil of waste caused by 'uncooperative and feckless' defendants engaging in tactical delaying manoeuvres. Since, as we have seen, defendant decision-making is *not* the substantial cause of 'waste', this is an irresponsible and cruel deception at odds with the available corpus of evidence.

A related point is the argument that the outcome – the justification for State-induced guilty pleas – has been achieved after an evaluation of the 'balance of interests', which means here weighing the risk that innocent people might out of fear plead guilty against the 'benefits' achieved by encouraging those who are in fact guilty to plead guilty.[18] As Dworkin (2006) has persuasively argued in a related context, the balancing metaphor is deeply misleading because it assigns no weight to any part of this juristic equation and because 'it assumes that we should decide which human rights to recognise through a kind of cost-benefit analysis, the way we might decide what speed limits to adopt'. Instead, a civilised society recognises that some injuries are so grave (such as the conviction of the innocent) that it supports the right to be protected from such harms at some cost to itself. Accordingly, even if it saved public money, it would be a base reason to do so at the expense of principles that we, as a civilised society, have hitherto thought were cherished by all, including judges.

Of course, if courts truly believed in the 'resources argument', the 'discount' would be calibrated to savings that *actually* might be achieved which would not be solely (or necessarily, dominantly) time-dependent. Thus, for example, the more complex and demanding the prosecution evidence or the more vulnerable it is to attack, the greater the discount 'deserved'. The same, of course, applies in the reverse direction. No such calculation is attempted.[19] Indeed, 'discounts' are routinely offered

---

[18] See, RCCJ (1993), *Report*, para. 7.45. On this, see Ashworth and Redmayne (2010) at p. 314.

[19] The recently introduced 'Early Guilty Plea Scheme' (operating at all Crown Court centres) merely confirms that the Government is unwilling to undergo a more principled attempt to calculate sentence discounts. In order to save itself 'unnecessary paper work' and increase 'productivity' the scheme expedites the plea process. In exchange, defendants will 'secure maximum credit'. See generally, http://www.justice.gov.uk/downloads/legal-aid/early-guilty-plea-scheme.pdf

whether the case is problematic or whether the evidence is strong.[20] In this, as in other commodification systems, the process smothers principle.

Embedded in these arguments is the *'case-load hypothesis'* – the view that coerced pleas are a result of, or necessary to cope with, workload demands.[21] Of course, if this is accepted as valid, the 'right to trial' which this hypothesis directly engages, would seem to be merely symbolic since its availability is contingent upon other similarly-situated defendants not being present in numbers on the court list.[22]

But the case-load hypothesis does not withstand scrutiny. The slightest acquaintance with criminal justice demonstrates that the process of State-induced guilty pleas is today as rife in courts which have little business as it is in courts whose lists are full; and this has been true in England and Wales at least for the past fifty years in any given court which at certain historical moments has been busy and at other times under-employed.[23]

Moreover, the *'fiscal crisis'* allegedly at the heart of the case-load 'problem' is itself a State construction which politicians and judges have relied upon for more than one hundred and fifty years[24] (now a contender for the longest 'crisis' in British legal history) and in whose manufacture they have played no small part. That construction has at its core an avowed ambition to curtail jury trial by abridging the defendant's right to elect jury trial, coercing guilty pleas and shuffling classes of offences into magistrates' courts.

A parallel aim has been to reduce the burden of proof on the State, the first major step in this direction being the abolition (in practice) in 1967 of 'full committal proceedings' at which the prosecution had to establish at least a *prima facie* case by producing live witnesses open to cross-examination. Subject to the defendant being legally represented

---

[20] Courts prevaricate as to whether any discount should be awarded if the case is overwhelming. The orthodox position is that where a court is satisfied that a lower reduction should be given for this reason, a reduction of 20% is recommended by the sentencing guidelines, providing the guilty plea was indicated at the first reasonable opportunity.

[21] This, incidentally, is the discredited argument advanced to explain the emergence of plea bargaining in America (McConville and Mirsky, 2005).

[22] See Shattuck (1974).

[23] This has been shown in American studies too – see Heumann (1975), Feeley (1982) and McConville and Mirsky (2005).

[24] See, Wilmore (1850) where almost exactly the same arguments were wheeled out in a Bill 'to save expense and delay' in the administration of criminal justice by making inroads into trial by jury. As Wilmore said: '[T]here cannot be a more dangerous delusion in politics, than to suppose an institution good because it is cheap, or bad because it is deliberate or even tedious . . .' (p. 36).

(ironically to better enable the management of defendants), cases were thereafter committed to the Crown Court 'on the papers' without the production of witnesses or magistrates reviewing the evidence.

In the event, the process blinded judges and politicians to more than principle; it blinded them to fiscal realities. Those realities were, on the one hand, ill-considered and, on the other, virtuous; but each was costly. While the CPS has been able to discontinue some weak cases,[25] once full committal proceedings were abolished, the absence of rigorous internal screening[26] meant that cases lacking evidential sufficiency or public interest (described by Judge David as 'rubbish')[27] would flood the Crown Court, swelling costs, causing unnecessary stress, and with predictable outcomes – *ordered or directed acquittals*.

The other (virtuous) effect was an inevitable but exponential increase in State costs as defence lawyers were brought into the process; and they came in droves because of a parallel increase in the availability of legal aid and the collapse of other markets, notably family law after the introduction of divorce without proof of fault[28] and modern rules regarding the division of matrimonial property.[29] The 'savings' anticipated by abolishing full committals, accordingly, proved illusory.[30]

Thus, as State-inducement has forced some additional defendants to enter guilty pleas, the process itself, while incurring much greater costs in terms of honesty and integrity, has done little to achieve its stated goal – saving money. What was intended as a guilty plea mill has become an infernal harvester generating enormous costs, displacing them from one part of the system to another and doubtless increasing overall expenditure.[31] Erected by expensively constituted courts setting out the

---

[25] See, HMCPSI, *Discontinuance (Thematic Review)* (HMCPSI, 2007) which revealed in a small sample of cases reviewed in nine regions variations in the rate of discontinuance in magistrates' courts of between 8.8% and 13.0%, a large majority of discontinuances because of insufficient evidence to provide a realistic prospect of conviction.

[26] Research has identified a variety of factors that tend to militate against discontinuance, including 'case momentum', a desire to support the initial police action and role-conflict (McConville et al., 1991; Barclay and Tavares, 1999).

[27] David (1978).

[28] The Divorce Reform Act 1969 came into effect in January 1971.

[29] The Matrimonial and Proceedings Property Act, 1970.

[30] To this may be added the nature of modern criminal justice legislation which implies or assumes that the defendant is legally represented. See Cape (2004) for a fuller review.

[31] 'Doubtless' because no exact calculation can be made as the costs involve such things as the time of parliamentary draftsmen, legislative time, the time of

coordinates of plea inducements, these, in turn, by reason of their complexity (often opaque, irrational[32] or contradictory in character), periodically require other expensively-constituted courts, inevitably awash with lawyers, re-stating and refining the co-ordinates.

By way of illustration, *Goodyear* (2005) gave rise to a plethora of appeals (which still continue) as to whether a *Goodyear* sentence indication had or had not been given (*R v Ibori* [2013]); whether the *Goodyear* procedures were or were not followed; and whether there had been a loss of credit for following the procedures (*R v JA* [2012]; *R v Hackney* [2013]). Other issues pursued included whether the guilty plea was 'inevitable' because the case was 'overwhelming' and accordingly deserving of little or no discount;[33] whether there was or was not an agreed basis for the plea; whether a '*Newton Hearing*' should have been conducted to establish the 'facts' or, if conducted, whether it had been conducted properly; whether the plea had been entered 'at the first reasonable opportunity'; and whether enough discount had been given. With ten lawyers helping it, the Court of Appeal set out rules in *Caley* [2012] only for this to trigger further appeals.

To stem the avalanche, another expensively constituted Court of Appeal (disappointingly assisted by only seven lawyers) was established in *Cairns* [2013] to re-state the principles, the judgment ending with the following *cri de coeur*:

> Too many appeals against sentence are mounted on the basis that the Judge has failed to have any, or sufficient, regard to the basis on which a plea of guilty has been entered. In this judgment, we have sought to restate what should be familiar principles and we trust that similar clarity on the part of all involved will reduce the need for appellate intervention. (para. 1)

It requires little foresight to see that these pitiful sentiments, like others previously voiced, will end up in due course with another deluge on the Court of Appeal's already 'overflowing' Wailing Wall.

Additionally, all of this has to be held (approximately) in place by expensive scaffolding (Official Reports, Practice Directions, White Papers

---

committees in the office of the Attorney-General and judicial committees, in addition to appellate court costs.

[32] For example, courts commonly say that defendants should receive no 'discount' if the case is overwhelming. But this is a standing incentive to such defendants to plead Not Guilty, and for their lawyers to so advise, since by doing so they retain the chance (however small) of an acquittal in an entirely neutral sentencing environment.

[33] Yet, as the Seabrook Report (1992) concluded, 'In truth, there is probably no such thing as "hopeless case" [*sic*]'.

and Acts of Parliament); and, because of departures by lower-level judges, in constant need of maintenance and refurbishment by other premium-priced entities (Courts of Appeal, Full Courts and the judge-heavy Sentencing Council).[34] Ironically, in terms of financial carnage, the process is the punishment for the State.

**Sparing Victims and Witnesses**

It is necessary to stress that the impact of crime on victims has been notoriously neglected by criminal justice systems and that this impact does not stop with the crime itself. Victims undergo stress waiting for a case to come to court and the longer this takes the more that has to be endured. Giving evidence can cause great anxiety, particularly where details of an unpleasant crime have to be re-lived.[35]

Victims, like other witnesses, are not, however, parties to a criminal trial and, as Hall (2010) states: 'the existence of a victim is neither necessary nor sufficient for proceedings to be brought' (p. 110). Many of the needs of victims can be addressed in other ways as, indeed, some have. Thus, in respect of both vulnerable and intimidated witnesses, special measures include: screening the witness from the accused; giving evidence by live link; video-recorded evidence in chief; video-recorded cross-examination or re-examination; and examination through an intermediary.[36] Victim Impact Statements are now common and under a revised Victims' Code, victims will be allowed to personally address offenders by reading a statement in court.[37]

Even where, as in most cases, there are victims, the victim's interests can be addressed only on a case-by-case basis; to do otherwise is to deny

---

[34] We set aside here the enormous financial costs caused by prosecution failures. Thus the drain on public resources occasioned by failure to disclose the involvement of a police undercover agent in prosecutions involving some 26 defendants in *Barkshire & Ors* [2011] (and related trials) resulted in at least *five separate official inquiries* (by the Police, CPS, DPP, HMIC, SOCA) which caused the Court of Appeal in *Barkshire* to reflect whether this amounted to 'overkill' and to reject calls for it to mount an inquiry even though it would have been the only forum in which the defendants affected would have been fully engaged as parties to the proceedings.

[35] A notorious instance in which the formal system let down a victim is the 'Glasgow Rape Case' which led to the resignation of the Solicitor General for Scotland (Harper and McWhinnie, 1983).

[36] See, for example, the Youth and Criminal Evidence Act, 1999 and the Criminal Justice Act, 2003. See Hamlyn et al. (2004) and Bull (2011).

[37] See, *BBC News*, 29 October 2013.

the *individuality* of the victim. Some victims *want to* give evidence and *do* give evidence. Equally, there are the interests of justice.[38] Some will be victims but not of *this* defendant. Some will *claim* to be victims but their claims may need to be tested. Many 'victims' are or have been offenders and equally 'offenders' will have been victims.[39] There *are* false complaints even in serious cases such as rape where historically the main failing of the system has been not treating women's accounts seriously.[40]

The fact is that the *symbolism* of 'victims' (and 'witnesses') is being exploited to give credence to State-induced guilty pleas and to other market-driven policies which infuse the criminal justice system. In reality, proper support for victims is often lacking or superficial.[41] Victims are not protected or their interests served where, in a target-driven culture, crimes (among them rapes and robberies) are recorded by the police as 'no-crimes';[42] or they are pressured into withdrawing allegations

---

[38] The CPS policy requires it to take into account the views of victims in certain matters but it has historically tended to follow the wishes of victims who withdraw allegations, as in situations of domestic abuse, where, arguably, their views should not predominate. See further Dempsey (2009).

[39] See Faulkner (2010).

[40] See Rumney (2006), Duffin (2013), Hunter (2013) and *BBC News*, 10 August 2013. See also, Joint Report by Alison Levitt and the Crown Prosecution Service Equality and Diversity Unit (2013) which analysed decisions between January 2011 and May 2012. Over this period, there were 5, 651 prosecutions for rape and 35 prosecutions for making false allegations of rape; 111,891 prosecutions for domestic violence and six prosecutions for making false allegations of domestic violence; a further three individuals were charged with making false allegations of both rape and domestic violence. See also, *R v A* [2010] where a woman was convicted on her own plea of perverting the course of justice by making and retracting a true allegation of rape.

[41] See, for example, HMIC Report (2013b) expressing serious concern about the protection given by South Yorkshire Police to victims of child sexual exploitation arising out of inconsistent practice, failure of management and lack of priority; and *BBC News*, 5 October 2013, 'Courts failing child sex abuse victims, says NSPCC'. The number of Witness Care Units has fallen from 80 in January 2012 to 45 in January 2014 and levels of Witness Care staff have fallen by 57% since 2010 (*The Independent*, 25 February 2014).

[42] A Metropolitan Police whistleblower told the Parliamentary Committee on Public Administration (November, 2013) that rape and sexual offences were under-reported by as much as a quarter. The same Committee heard police or former police detail the techniques for fixing the records by 'no-criming', downgrading offences (e.g., burglary to theft or criminal damage; thefts become 'lost property') or 'cuffing' crimes by recording that they did not believe the complainant. The police admitted that 'mental health' or other 'issues of vulnerability' were used to justify 'no-criming' and that victims were pressurised in the process. The manipulation of statistics in this way was confirmed by one of the most respected

to help police meet their targets;[43] or where those committing serious offences are not charged at all or are given inadequate punishment in an out-of-court disposal;[44] or where they are cautioned in the process of 'case shedding' by the police or CPS[45] as, for example, in response to externally imposed targets;[46] or where defendants are under-charged or charged as part of a 'deal'; or where a bargained-for sentence cannot be interfered with on appeal because, though lenient, it is not '*unduly lenient*'.[47] And, of course, the grief of victims, their families and survivors is not assuaged when an innocent person is induced to enter a guilty plea. In reality, victims are often marginalised and when the process of State-induced guilty pleas needs ideological cleansing, abstract 'victims' are shamelessly invoked.

**Getting the Best Possible Outcome for Those Pleading Guilty**

The claim that State-induced pleas may secure the 'best possible outcome' for guilty defendants can only mean the lowest possible sentence. This, as we have seen, often means a wholly inadequate sentence. At a core level,

---

Chief Constables, Mick Creedon, who told the Committee that the 'real position' was that domestic violence and sexual violence was going up. The imposition of a 20% target of crime reduction set by the Mayor of London's Office meant, according to a former Metropolitan Police officer: 'That translates into "record 20% fewer crimes" as far as . . . senior officers are concerned'. See also HMIC Report (2013c), reporting that the 'target-driven culture' had led some officers to pursue crimes that were easy to solve 'rather than on their seriousness, or their impact on victims or communities'.

[43] As revealed in the IPCC Report into Scotland Yard's specialist Southwark Branch Sapphire Unit. Police statistics are not a good indicator of crime levels but the imposition of artificial targets produces perverse effects.

[44] For a review of some of these consequences see, Robson (2012) commenting upon the White Paper, *Swift and Sure Justice: The Government's Plans for Reform of the Criminal Justice System*. See also, HMIC Report (2013c), *Crime Recording in Kent*, reporting that crimes which have a serious impact on victims (such as burglary) were being dealt with by inappropriate disposals, such as cautions.

[45] For a recent example, in October 2013 it emerged that despite a 30% increase in the number of rapes reported to the police in 2012/13 (numbering 17,000), referrals to the CPS (at 5,404) recorded a five-year low (*BBC News*, 27 October 2013). Both the RCCJ (1993) and Auld (2001) recommended, for laudable purposes, expanded use of cautions and conditional cautions without seeing that these might be applied inappropriately.

[46] The police and CPS had imposed on them a target to increase the number of out of court disposals, replaced in April 2008 by a target to increase serious crime brought to justice, itself removed in May 2010.

[47] See, for example, *A-G Ref Nos. 73 & 74 of 2012* [2013].

therefore, the claim cannot be reconciled with the parallel assertion that it serves the interests of victims.

It also subjugates the risk to the innocent or, as Auld prefers, '*however innocent*' defendant to the 'justly' operating and 'efficient' administration of justice. Disregarding the specious claim to 'efficiency' (i.e., cost-effectiveness), Auld's rationalisation has to be set against a long series of judicial statements espousing core principles of criminal justice relating to the protection of the innocent. Traditional judicial statements (encapsulated in the well-known, if dubiously calibrated, dictum: 'it is better that ten guilty people be wrongly acquitted than one innocent person wrongly convicted') represented a long-standing principled rejection of consequentialist thinking, because such statements, while not welcoming the consequence of many guilty persons going unpunished, appropriately recognise that such a result would need to be accepted because it would be intolerable knowingly and willingly to accept the possibility of punishing an innocent person. This rejection is also the only way to reconcile criminal adjudication to (human) rights.[48]

## THE 'GUILTY' AND THE 'INNOCENT': THE POLITICS OF DENIGRATION

The purported justification for coerced pleas resting on the specious dichotomy of the 'guilty' and the 'innocent' involves more than side-lining innocent defendants: its more insidious effect, indeed *purpose*, is both to remove the State's obligations from the criminal process machine and to justify discriminatory treatment of classes of suspects and defendants.

The starting point of any intelligent engagement with criminal justice should not be its end-point but its foundational principle, namely: because the State is claiming a right to punish one of its citizens we require it to *justify that claim*. It is from this principle that other core principles (the presumption of innocence, the privilege against self-incrimination, the high burden of proof on the prosecution) flow.[49] It is precisely because defendants are said to carry with them into a trial a presumption of

---

[48] For a powerful statement of the importance of rights and respect for human dignity and of the fallacy of utilitarian 'balancing' of rights, see Dworkin (2006). See more generally, Ashworth and Redmayne (2010).

[49] Cf. *R v Director of the Serious Fraud Office, ex parte Smith* [1993] where Lord Mustill, in discussing aspects of the 'right to silence' as general or specific immunities of a citizen and 'the motives' for these in English law, fails to recognise the obligation of the State to its citizens as the central motivating force.

innocence that we can speak of 'innocence' upon acquittal;[50] and we maintain this notwithstanding that what is technically at issue in a trial is not 'innocence' but whether or not the prosecution has succeeded in proving guilt.[51] The *'however innocent'* category can exist only as a misunderstanding of the principles involved or as a slur. The distinctions between the 'innocent' and the 'however innocent' may be seen as attempts to intellectualise the smears and innuendoes used to deflect attention away from the failings of the system, the protection of whose 'integrity' becomes its weatherglass.[52]

Slurs, and worse, play an integral part of the politics of denigration, a vital element of the legitimation project in which State officials aided by influential sections of the media engage. This project, in which distinctions within the objects of policing are drawn between the 'deserving' (in political slogans, the 'hardworking' majority) and 'undeserving' (in political slogans, the 'idle', 'lazy' and 'feral' criminal underclass) poor, is of long lineage and long discredited.[53] This strategy has been deployed against individuals (such as Winston Silcott; Jean Charles de Menezes; Ian Tomlinson[54] and Stephen Lawrence),[55] groups of 'suspects' (such as the

---

[50] See, for example, Mr Justice Devlin in the trial of Dr John Bodkin Adams: 'The accused, as he sits in the dock, is as innocent as anyone else in the court, and will so remain until the jury by their verdict have convicted him' (Bedford, 1958, p. 194).

[51] The position after conviction is quite different where the concern is only with the safety of the conviction. In Scotland the position is more complicated because of the availability of the (rarely used) 'not proven' verdict. For 2010–11, 5% of verdicts ended in acquittal, of which 16% were Not Proven verdicts. The 'not proven' verdict is being referred for review to the Scottish Law Commission. See, Duff (1996, 1999b).

[52] See Naughton (2010).

[53] See the excellent review by Faulkner (2010). See also Stedman Jones (1971), Rowntree (1901) and McConville and Mirsky (2005).

[54] Ian Tomlinson died after being pushed to the ground by Metropolitan Police Officer Simon Harwood. Prior to this incident, Harwood had a long record of allegedly punching, kneeing or threatening suspects, had resigned from the Force after allegedly altering notes to justify an illegal arrest but had been shortly thereafter re-employed by the police.

[55] An investigation launched into alleged police attempts to smear the Stephen Lawrence campaign and undermine the credibility of witnesses attending the Macpherson inquiry damningly concluded that: there was evidence to suggest that one of the police officers involved in the original murder investigation acted corruptly; that key documents relating to corruption in the original inquiry had been systematically shredded by Scotland Yard in 2003; that the Metropolitan Police had undertaken a spying operation on Stephen Lawrence's grieving family; that the Metropolitan Police probably still retained documents which had not been

*Birmingham Six*, *Tottenham Three* and *Guildford Four*), 'suspect communities' (such as Black people from the 1950s onwards; 'immigrants' generally; Irish people in the 1970s; and the current demonisation of the Muslim community), organised labour (as in the Grunwick Dispute 1976/1977 and the Miners' Strike), political/environmental demonstrations (as in Red Lion and Southall),[56] the unemployed and those on 'benefits',[57] as well as being used to deflect attention from the wrongdoings of State officials (as in Bloody Sunday, the Stephen Lawrence murder case, the Miners' Strike and the Hillsborough[58] disaster).[59]

This process of institutional denigration of classes of people and geographical areas of cities, in which judges play a key role, forms the

---

handed over to the inquiry; and that police operations spanning many decades may have led to scores of wrongful convictions: Ellison (2014). Ellison has been requested by the Home Secretary to investigate cases involving the undercover Metropolitan Police's Special Demonstration Squad, whose members routinely gave perjured testimony in court, to see whether any should be referred to the Attorney-General after which it is planned to hold a judge-led public inquiry. Recently, Stuart Lawrence, the brother of Stephen Lawrence who was stabbed to death in a racist attack in London in 1993, complained that he had been stopped 25 times by police 'just because I am black'. While a Metropolitan Police investigation cleared an officer of any wrongdoing, the IPCC upheld his appeal in part and concluded that the officer has a case to answer for misconduct in relation to racial discrimination (*BBC News*, 12 October 2013).

[56] See, for example, Ward (1986).

[57] As in the new campaign to charge benefit fraud under the Fraud Act, thereby increasing the maximum available sentence from two to ten years' imprisonment (*BBC News*, 16 September 2013).

[58] See Scraton (2013) describing the denigration of Liverpool Club football supporters crushed to death in the Hillsborough Stadium through official incompetence, which began with a briefing by Margaret Thatcher's Press Secretary, Sir Bernard Ingham 'explaining' that the disaster would not have occurred if 'a mob, who were clearly tanked up, had not tried to force their way into the ground'.

[59] A good part of the work of the 'Special Demonstration Squad' (some 130 in number and disbanded in 2008) of the Metropolitan Police was, according to the whistleblower, Peter Francis, to seek information which might discredit Dwayne Brooks (the principal witness who saw the stabbing of Stephen Lawrence) and other members of the family. A police prosecution of Dwayne Brooks for criminal damage was thrown out as an abuse of process. It has emerged that police meetings between Dwayne Brooks and his lawyers were secretly bugged by the Metropolitan Police (Shaw, 2013). Mark Ellison QC is currently continuing his investigation of corruption in the handling of the Stephen Lawrence case, where, to put it neutrally, opportunities to arrest suspects within 24 hours of Stephen's murder were unaccountably missed. The possibility of a wider smear campaign involving witnesses to the Leveson Inquiry is the subject of continuing investigations. See *BBC News*, 5 July 2013. Other related investigations include *Operation Herne*, strands of which are being overseen by the Independent Police Complaints Commission.

bedrock of ideological constructs based on race, class and ethnicity which underpins policing policies and better secures the political management of 'crime' and 'social problems'.[60] In turn, as we have seen, the methodologies and perspectives form a key part of a wider strategy utilised by other State agencies to justify the nature of their interventions in regard to such things as homelessness, unemployment and social security 'benefits'.[61]

Against the backcloth of these analytical grids, efforts to uncover police corruption and perjury are met by the assertion that to credit such an argument would be to allege that the police were involved (as it turns out they often were) in a widespread conspiracy. While distasteful remarks of judges such as Lord Denning have been unrefined to the point of revolting, whispering campaigns commonly accompany the quashing of convictions, even where obtained through fabricated evidence, covers-up,[62] police perjury or investigative failures. Thus, in *Hallam v R* [2012], in which Sam Hallam's wrongful convictions for murder, conspiracy to commit grievous bodily harm and violent disorder in 2005 were quashed following evidence, including, *inter alia*, post-investigation examination of Hallam's mobile phones which supported his trial alibi, the Court of Appeal expressed surprise that Sam's mobile phones had not at the time 'for reasons which escape us' been examined by either police or the defence. The Court of Appeal, instead of focusing upon police failures (reflecting the burden of proof), could not resist a snide comment: 'We now know there is the real possibility that the appellant's failed alibi was consistent with faulty recollection and *a dysfunctional lifestyle*, and that it was not a deliberate lie' (para. 78, emphasis added). Disparaging the victim of a miscarriage of justice (who had no burden of proof) might be thought, to say the least, sanctimonious.

---

[60] See further, Spector and Kitsuse (2001).

[61] The ascription of the term 'benefits' has moved away from social welfare ideals to become part of the drain on State resources by 'scroungers', 'parasites' and other 'freeloaders' in an increasingly market-driven society.

[62] Covering up for colleagues has often been a core element of police culture inhibiting the identification and prosecution of wrongdoers. See, for example, the report by Commander Cass into the killing of Blair Peach at a demonstration in Southall, London who was almost certainly killed by a member of the SPG of the Metropolitan Police. Cass concluded that the investigation was hampered by SPG officers who, he concluded, had lied to him to cover up the actions of their colleagues; available at: http://www.met.police.uk/foi/units/blair_peach.htm. Raju Bhatt, lawyer for Peach's partner, said that the Report by Cass indicated that he had tried but struggled to 'undermine' evidence suggesting one of his officers killed Peach (Lewis, 2010).

# PUBLIC CONFIDENCE

The denigration project has been integral to the system's preoccupation with retaining public confidence. Despite often overwhelming evidence, the Court of Appeal has repeatedly dismissed appeals with glib remarks. The shameful catalogue of miscarriages in England and Wales over the past sixty years had to be uncovered, instead, by activism on the part of families, support groups, investigative journalists and selfless lawyers in the face of obdurate official resistance. In the same vein (see Chapter 2), Judicial Inquiries repeatedly upheld manifestly wrongful convictions against the weight of evidence infamously using the *civil standard of proof*. Subjects were even 'convicted' of crimes with which they had never been charged[63] and of which some were subsequently proved wholly innocent.[64]

The Royal Commission on Criminal Justice (1993) set up in the wake of egregious miscarriages of justice (the *Guildford Four* and *Birmingham Six*), with others appearing with great rapidity during its sitting (including the *Maguire Seven* and *Judith Ward*), chose not to examine these, dismissively referring to them as 'terrorist cases' and instead ventured that police malpractice, where it occurs:

> ... may often be motivated by an over-zealous determination to secure the conviction of suspects believed to be guilty in the face of rules or procedures which seem to those charged with the investigation to be weighted in favour of the defence. Police officers must, however, recognise that, whatever the motive, malpractice must not and will not be tolerated. The remedy lies in a better-trained, better-equipped and better-supervised police force, not in the tacit acceptance of procedural rule-bending'. (RCCJ, 1993, para. 24, p. 7)

As Nicola Lacey (1994) points out, this quotation neatly encapsulates the techniques of official discourse. First, the problem is located in individual malpractice, the aberrant police officer; any system-wide problem is rejected.[65] Second, the officer is partly forgiven on the basis that they are

---

[63] In addition to Fisher (1977), see also Lord Denning (1963) who concluded that Dr Stephen Ward had arranged various 'sadistic' events, for which no evidence had ever been offered at his trial (for good measure, Denning found him guilty of procuring girls, a charge for which he had been found not guilty at his earlier trial).

[64] As in the *Confait* case (Fisher, 1977).

[65] Cf. the various reports of the Metropolitan Police Authority (MPA) into the police shooting of Jean Charles de Menezes (e.g., MPA *Stockwell Scrutiny* in 2008). The MPA focus was upon the progress made by the Metropolitan Police in 'learning lessons' from the IPCC recommendations rather than holding any officers (whose employment they oversee) to account (Blowe, 2011).

well motivated, bending the rules only in order to secure the conviction of those genuinely believed to be guilty. Third, the rules themselves are depicted as giving grounds for the belief that they handicap investigating officers and thereby the conviction of the guilty. Fourth, the remedial medicine proposed is yet further rules, precisely the alleged cause of the rule-breaking and rule-bending the RCCJ alleges. The prescription then offered is more internal supervision and a change in police occupational culture despite the fact that it is the internal 'supervision' which is ineffective because much of the 'departure' is driven by occupational culture. The reason emerges in the justification of the RCCJ: 'A set of safeguards which prevented the police from bringing large numbers of offenders to justice would be unacceptable'.[66]

## SYSTEMIC CORRUPTION

Yet there *is* a systemic[67] problem of police corruption which the very manner and scale of the wrongdoing makes obvious[68] and which the police 'watchdog' has proved incapable of addressing.[69] In the *Birmingham Six*

---

[66] RCCJ (1993), para. 2, p. 9.

[67] We do not include individual acts of alleged wrongdoing by police officers such as the Chief of Cleveland Police recently dismissed for gross misconduct including, a disciplinary panel found, lying to the IPCC (Walker and Dodd, 2012) – the Deputy Chief of the same force was also sacked (*BBC News*, 25 March 2013) and the Assistant Chief Officer has resigned, frustrating disciplinary hearings – and the Essex police officer who falsely told an alleged rape victim that her case had been dropped, leading the victim to attempt to take her own life (*BBC News*, 6 December 2013). Recently obtained reports show police forces across the country have arrested their own officers for offences as serious as running a brothel, possession of child abuse images and selling firearms (Payne, 2014).

[68] See Miller (2003), a Home Office report which identifies problems regarding corrupt relationships based on the leaking of information, dealing in and use of drugs as well as fraud, theft and violence. Later reports from Transparency International accuse police officers of using anabolic steroids supplied by criminals and corruptly obtaining sexual favours (*BBC News*, 23 January 2013). See also, Williams (2012) and IPCC Report (2012). More than 1,000 police officers and community support officers have criminal records for offences including burglary, robbery, supplying drugs and perverting the course of justice (*The Guardian*, 2 January 2012). Accounts of the fabrication of evidence, framing of suspects, and destruction of evidence have proved easy to acquire (Porter, 2013).

[69] The Home Affairs Committee's *Eleventh Report, 2012–2013* on the IPCC (Home Affairs Committee, 2013) concludes that the IPCC 'has neither the powers nor the resources that it needs to get to the truth when the integrity of the police is in doubt'. At the end of 2012, no fewer than 11 out of the 39 police forces in

case, for example, how could it be otherwise when officers from one police force were able to use threats and violence on suspects while in another police force area and with the assistance or wilful blindness of that other force? In the *Guildford Four* case, how could it be otherwise when violence was used on suspects by officers from one police force (Surrey) immediately prior to the visit of officers from another (Metropolitan Police)? How could it be otherwise when a cadre of 'elite' officers, the West Midlands Serious Crime Squad, was caught out fabricating 'confessions', inflicting violence and unspeakable torture on upwards of a hundred[70] innocent people including subjecting them to mock executions, putting guns into their mouths, placing plastic bags over their heads to simulate suffocation until the suspect lost or almost lost consciousness, and threatening them with police dogs in the detention cells? How could it be otherwise when bundles of police statements were exposed as false leading to the collapse of the trial of the Orgreave miners?[71] How could it be otherwise when Sir Robert Mark claimed credit (much-deserved, incidentally) for getting rid of some 400 corrupt Metropolitan police detectives (not nearly enough as other cases and the Ellison Report have subsequently demonstrated)?[72]

---

England (almost 30%) had one or more of their senior leadership under a cloud. For example, within the previous 18 months, seven had been sacked for misconduct, suspended, placed under criminal or disciplinary investigation or forced to resign (Gilligan, 2012). At least four others have since then been placed under investigation.

[70] Numbers are not yet clear as appeal cases are still being processed. At least 19 trials collapsed following exposure of police corruption. One WMSCS officer (Shaw) was, following his retirement in 1998, jailed for 12 years in 2001 for two armed robberies in Birmingham and, after his release from prison, jailed for 13 and a half years for a bungled raid on a post office in Cornwall.

[71] The IPCC is still considering whether to investigate the South Yorkshire Police (*BBC News*, 14 November 2013). The trial of eight police officers accused of fitting up *The Cardiff Three* collapsed (at a cost of £30 million) after the court was told that relevant documents in the case had been shredded. A month later they were found in the office of the senior investigating officer as he cleared out his desk on, it is alleged, his forced retirement (Peachy, 2013).

[72] A similar pattern of systemic corruption occurred with Flying Squad Officers: the former head, Commander Drury, being sent to prison for corruption; and, more recently, corruption at the Rigg Approach in London. The Complaints Investigation Bureau of the Metropolitan Police found that a number of officers attached to the Flying Squad Office based at Rigg Approach had been involved in a shocking form of corruption and perversion of the course of justice. The officers concerned would equip themselves with bags containing imitation firearms and balaclavas which they would 'plant' on suspects, either to protect the position of an officer who had shot an unarmed suspect in good faith (and so provide a justification for his action) or to strengthen a case where the evidence was not

Only when confronted with unanswerable evidence is the Court forced to admit defeat (sometimes of a limited kind)[73] in hand-wringing terms. This was the case in *Maxwell* (2010) in which two brothers were convicted of murder and robbery, the key evidence supplied by Karl Chapman, a notorious criminal, 'supergrass'[74] and a serving prisoner in the custody of the police. On appeal, the Report of the Criminal Cases Review Commission showed, *inter alia*, that Chapman and members of his family had received benefits which were deliberately concealed from the CPS and Crown counsel: that Chapman, while in police custody, was allowed to visit brothels, consume alcohol and drugs (including heroin), to socialise at police officers' homes, enjoy sexual relations with a WPC, enjoy periods of unsupervised freedom, was not proceeded against in respect of a vicious stabbing attack on a fellow prisoner or an alleged rape of another prisoner or assault on the WPC with whom he had then broken up; nor was action taken against his mother for attempting to supply heroin to Chapman and Chapman's girlfriend whilst both were serving prisoners. Lord Brown summarised the position thus:[75]

> A large number of police officers involved in the investigation and prosecution of the ... robbery and murder case, including several of very high rank, engaged in a prolonged, persistent and pervasive conspiracy to pervert the course of justice. They colluded in conferring on Chapman a variety of wholly inappropriate benefits to secure his continuing cooperation in the appellant's

---

overwhelming. About 25 officers were either charged with criminal offences or were removed from duty or they retired. See also the unrelated Sean Rigg Inquest report posted by Garden Court barristers (2 August 2012) in which the IPCC Investigators failed to examine properly CCTV evidence which showed that key evidence given by a police sergeant was untrue.

[73] Two Justices of the Supreme Court in *Maxwell* (*infra*) decided, notwithstanding police wrongdoing, that there should be no re-trial.

[74] The use of 'supergrasses' was considered discredited until the Serious Organised Crime and Police Act, 2005 (SOCPA) revived the system so that supergrasses can receive total or partial immunity from prosecution. In some cases, such evidence is of central importance (as in the case of 'Boy X' identifying the killer of the schoolboy Rhys Jones). However, supergrasses are inherently unreliable witnesses with a clear incentive to minimise their own involvement and maximise that of others. A BBC *Panorama* and Bureau of Investigative Journalism study found that in 49 cases involving supergrasses, nearly half had their jail terms cut by more than two-thirds (Slater, 2012). In 2012, 12 men were acquitted of murder following the discrediting of two supergrass witnesses whom the trial judge described as having lived 'on a daily diet of lies' and who were still 'the same men in different suits' (*BBC News*, 22 February 2012), at a cost of £11.5 million (*BBC News*, 11 October 2012). See also Greer (1995), Martin (2013) and Slater (2012).

[75] At para. 83.

prosecution and trial. They then colluded in Chapman's perjury at that trial, intending him throughout his evidence to lie as to how he had been treated and as to what promises he had received. They ensured that Chapman's police custody records and various other official documents presented a false picture of the facts, on one occasion actually forging a custody record when its enforced disclosure to the defence would otherwise have revealed the truth. They lied in their responses to enquiries made of the CPS after the appellant's conviction and, in the case of the two senior officers who gave evidence to the Court of Appeal, perjured themselves so as to ensure that the appellant's application for leave to appeal against his conviction got nowhere. To describe police misconduct on this scale merely as shocking and disgraceful is to understate the gravity of its impact upon the integrity of the prosecution process. It is hard to imagine a worse case of sustained prosecutorial dishonesty designed to secure and hold a conviction at all costs.

Another 'protected witness' case shows striking similarities: *R v Joof & Ors* [2012] involved five appellants all convicted of murder.[76] Here, in what appeared to the Court of Appeal as 'a serious perversion of the course of justice', the prosecution failed to disclose material evidence that would have supported a defence attack on key prosecution witnesses including one named Simeon Taylor, then under the control of the (inappositely-named) Staffordshire Sensitive Policing Unit. Following complaint from an exemplary officer, DI Anderson, who was in charge of the Unit, a 'Management Review' was completed well before the murder trial but not disclosed to the defence. That Review could have shown that the Unit was a 'dysfunctional organization fractured by in-fighting, containing officers whose honesty and integrity were open to question and whose documentation in respect of Simeon Taylor could not be trusted'.[77] The Review examined evidence which showed that Taylor dishonestly obtained a refund of £320 paid to permit him to stay in a hotel; and that there was good reason to believe, and DI Anderson did believe, that the officers concerned had deliberately not recorded the incident in the appropriate document, intending thereby to prevent disclosure to the defence. The Management Review also revealed that [DC 'N'], one of the officers handling Simeon Taylor, had arranged for a female officer [DC 'S'] to stay with him in a hotel room whilst he was engaged in witness protection duties involving

---

[76] The Crown did not seek to uphold the convictions. It has been reported that four senior officers, former or serving Staffordshire Police officers, are being investigated over misconduct claims in connection with this case. The four are the Chief Constable and Deputy Chief Constable of Northamptonshire, along with Assistant Chief Constable of the West Midlands and Staffordshire's Assistant Chief Constable (*BBC News*, 23 December 2011).

[77] *R v Joof & Others* [2012], para. 22.

Taylor. That second officer was the disclosure officer on this case. They denied having stayed at the same hotel as Taylor and she denied having met Taylor. Crown counsel's note to the Court stated:

> DC [N] one of the handlers of Simeon Taylor was having an affair with the disclosure officer. They met where Simeon Taylor was being housed. Its potential impact is obvious. Had it been disclosed it could have been utilised by the defence to prove that Simeon Taylor's knowledge of the circumstances of the offence had not been acquired by being present when the offence was committed but by having information passed to him by someone handling him. ... It is of note that when Simeon Taylor gave evidence he said he knew that the enquiry team had no forensic evidence. He was unable to say how he knew that ... He knew about the absence of cell-site evidence. He knew what Joof had told the police.

Furthermore, we should note, there may be egregious and difficult to detect corruption associated with *failures to act* which, by their very nature, result in cases not coming to court.[78]

## CORRUPTION, POLICE AND THE JUDGES

As far as judges and police corruption are concerned we note the following:

---

[78] Examples include: in 2012, the Ellison Report (2014) into allegations that police corruption hampered the original investigation into the murder of Stephen Lawrence in 1993 when, it is alleged, suspects were 'shielded' from arrest and were allowed to take filled black bags from their homes in the aftermath of the killing without being stopped by police surveillance officers (see also: Grice and Peachey, 2012); the review into the claims that police corruption prevented a conviction in the murder of Daniel Morgan, an investigative journalist investigating corruption in the Metropolitan Police (*BBC News*, 10 May 2013) and in relation to which a senior Metropolitan Police officer has publicly stated that 'police corruption was a debilitating factor in that investigation' (*BBC News*, 11 March 2011) which resulted in a collapsed trial after boxes of potential evidence were not disclosed to the defence and 'supergrass' witnesses were not properly handled (*BBC News*, 21 May 2012); the trial of eight South Wales police officers accused of fabricating evidence relating to the death of Lynette White (in respect of whose murder three innocent men had been convicted and later exonerated) collapsed (at a cost to the taxpayer of £30 million) after the court was told that key evidence had been deliberately destroyed although it later emerged that the relevant documents were in fact in the hands of the South Wales Police (*BBC News*, 13 August 2012; *The Observer*, 28 January 2012); and the death of Blair Peach in 1979, an investigation into which by Commander Cass in 2010 concluded that Metropolitan Police SPG officers had lied about his killing (*Mail Online*, 28 April 2010).

- Firstly, because of the way in which the police are organised, police corruption often necessarily goes beyond single officers, is systemic within groups or units[79] and (as in some key non-disclosure cases[80]) may be police policy – the very thing that judges are reluctant to accept;[81]
- Secondly, police culture and ideology is underpinned by a code of secrecy which creates a 'wall of silence',[82] a 'protective armour shielding the force from public knowledge of infractions, again, seemingly unimaginable to judges';[83]
- Thirdly, setting aside established cases, none of this should have surprised judges since police officers of the highest rank have openly said that their officers engage in 'pious perjury' and 'noble cause corruption';[84]
- Fourthly, when confronted with such evidence judges have resisted until the bitter end, telling juries, in effect, that police corruption was unthinkable and, in now-established miscarriages, turning down appeal after appeal with barely a blink;
- Fifthly, in the face of judicial antipathy, it is left to families, supporters and dedicated lawyers to navigate the long road to vindication against a wall of official intransigence and hostility;[85]

---

[79] See, for example, detectives in the South-East Regional Crime Squad who sold drugs they had seized and 'fitted-up' people for serious crimes by planting evidence and the use of 'verbals' (Mullins, 2000; McLagan, 2004).

[80] See, for example, *Barkshire & Ors* [2011] in which, at great cost to the State, the convictions of 20 activists of conspiracy to commit aggravated trespass were quashed following the Crown's failure to disclose that the group had been infiltrated by an undercover police officer, Mark Kennedy, together with information helpful to the defence or potentially undermining the prosecution.

[81] As in *Maxwell* (2010) and *Joof* (2012); and see McConville (1992) where the process of falsifying a custody record was filmed by Yorkshire TV. Other ongoing examples include the Hillsborough Disaster in which the causes of the deaths of 96 football fans have been concealed for 23 years by non-disclosure and a massive exercise in redacting police statements (Scraton, 2013).

[82] Jennings and Lashmar (1990).

[83] Reiner (1985), p. 93.

[84] Added to this is the use of 'undercover' officers, many of whom have engaged in discreditable behaviour (Lewis and Evans, 2013; *BBC News*, 3 February 2013) and whose identification has led to the collapse of many trials (*BBC News*, 19 July 2011).

[85] This, regrettably, is true in cases of police inaction. Thus, for example, the Metropolitan Police have admitted police corruption in the failure of five police inquiries and three years of legal hearings (costing over £30 million) into the murder of Daniel Morgan (above) (*BBC News*, 11 March 2011). Following the collapse of a trial because of non-disclosure of evidence by the police and CPS, the

- Sixthly, barristers, knowing the resistance of judges to the possibility of police perjury are intimidated into striking 'deals' in order to avoid trial even against protestations of innocence from defendants;
- Seventhly, when the bitter end arrives, often after many years, and trial evidence is shown to be false, crocodile tears are shed by judges at the 'shock' and 'horror' of it all (while some stick it out and continue to vilify);
- Eighthly, and most importantly, judges fail to see, let alone acknowledge, that a good part of the reason for police corruption and its linked perjury is that, by their extra-judicial comments, by their manipulation of the 'law' to legalise certain kinds of police perjury, by their antipathy to defences involving attacks on police evidence, by their zealousness in coercing barristers into accepting guilty pleas, and by their hostile summing up to juries, they, the judges, have *invited* it.

This is far from saying that all police evidence is corrupt, because that is simply not the case, and, indeed, much police corruption has been rooted out at the end of the day *by* honourable and dedicated police officers.[86] However, the pre-disposition of judges towards police evidence remains an open invitation to officers willing to engage in corruption and perjury, an invitation that history teaches us some will respond to.[87]

---

Home Office announced the appointment of an 'independent panel' to look into this terrible fiasco (Dodd, 2013b).

[86] Attempts by Metropolitan Police officers to warn Scotland Yard of alleged criminal activities of a 'crime boss' led to *their* (unsuccessful) prosecution. In a related libel action, Mr Justice Simon described the prosecutions as 'misdirected' and found that the individual of whom a warning had been given was the head of an organisation involved in 'extreme violence and fraud' (*Mail Online*, 5 July 2013). It is right to note, however, that breaking ranks within the police would be made more difficult by the recommendation in Lord Justice Leveson's Report (2013) to stop police whistleblowers going to the press by, instead, proposing that 'a series of pragmatic solutions need to be devised to maximise the chance that genuine whistle-blowers will use confidential avenues in which they may have faith, rather than feel it necessary to break confidences by bringing about much wider public dissemination through disclosures to the media'(Leveson, 2013, Chapter 4, para. 8.9).

[87] So widespread is corruption in the criminal justice system that multiple agencies and actors are reported to be infiltrated by criminal gangs, including HM Revenue & Customs, the CPS, the City of London Police and the Prison Service, not discounting involvement from juries and the legal profession also. The 2002 *Tiberius* report explained 'none of these syndicates have been seriously disrupted over the last five years provid[ing] an insight into the effectiveness of their networks' (Harper, 2014b). The Ellison Report (2014), an independent inquiry into the role of undercover policing in the Lawrence murder inquiry, has further

The judicial blind spot can be demonstrated by the Auld Report and by reference to judges' handling of trials in miscarriage of justice cases.[88] Auld rejected as 'untenable' the idea that at the pre-trial stage the defence could withhold the identification of issues in order to protect against the possibility of dishonesty of police and/or prosecutors in the conduct of the case:[89]

> It may not be 'the function of law to trust those who exercise lawful powers.' But a criminal justice process cannot sensibly be designed on a general premise that those responsible for law are likely to break it. In those cases where, unfortunately, the police or other public officers are dishonest, the criminal trial process itself is the medium for protection and exposure. (footnote omitted)

On the contrary, it is precisely because trials, as conducted, have been inadequate in exposing wrongdoing, where the police compromise their

---

revealed breathtaking and monumental corruption. The Inquiry unearthed the extraordinary secrecy shrouding the work of undercover police 'spies' who participated incognito in criminal trials. Further that 'institutional racism' plagued 'the murder investigation, the Metropolitan Police Service (MPS) and police services elsewhere, as well as other institutions and organisations'. (p. 4). It condemned the prior MPS review of the initial investigation (Barker Review) in 1993 as 'an anodyne and uncritical report' that was 'factually incorrect and inadequate' leading to a 'flawed and indefensible report that had been deliberately 'toned down''. It found the impression given that the 'investigation had been a proper and professional one' was 'wholly misleading' (p. 7). Speaking in the House of Commons on the day of its publication, the Home Secretary ordered a Judge-led public inquiry into the work of undercover police officers in light of the outstanding lines of inquiry about allegations of corruption (hindered in large part by massive volumes of evidence that have been lost or shredded, including material from anti-corruption initiative 'Operation Othona' (p. 10–11)). For example, the Report highlighted a 'real possibility' that the concurrent Daniel Morgan Independent Panel set up to investigate the role played by police corruption in protecting those responsible for the murder from being brought to justice, and the failure to confront that corruption 'may hold or acquire material of relevance' (p. 12). In response to the gravity of the Report's findings, the Home Secretary proposed a new offence: 'Police Corruption'. Former Secretary Jack Straw remarked the announcement was "one of the most shocking and serious statements" by any minister in his 35 years experience in the Commons (BBC, 6 March 2014).

[88] In some instances, where convictions have been obtained on false evidence and corruption, the Court of Appeal has quashed convictions notwithstanding that they resulted from a guilty plea. See, for example, *R v Brown* [2006].

[89] Auld (2001), Chapter 10, para. 154. What is extraordinary is that any judge could, after the abject failure of judicial inquiries to get at the truth and at least forty years of disgraceful miscarriages of justice, promote the idea that the trial, as conducted in recent years, has been a reliable medium for protection and the exposure of official wrongdoing.

'integrity' and 'adjust' evidence to nullify legitimate defences so that other strategies (such as that contemptuously referred to as 'ambush') are sought by defence lawyers; and a substantial reason for that is the disposition of judges in favour of the police. Instead of looking at the *evidence*, judges have struggled to maintain public confidence in the system and, accordingly, look only at the *institution of the police* as proof of its integrity and reliability; contrary signals that would excite suspicion are simply brushed aside.

A ready example[90] is provided by the cases of wrongful convictions obtained by the West Midlands Serious Crime Squad (WMSCS). Given the scale of miscarriages, it is appropriate to ask whether they exhibited any 'alarm signals' and, if so, at what stage did judges entertain suspicion of the integrity of the prosecution case in the trial as, to use the expression of Auld, the 'medium for protection [against] and exposure' of wrongdoing? We set out below some of the alarm signals, as we see it, present in numbers of these cases:

*Alarm 1*: Defence solicitors were unlawfully excluded from interrogations.

*Alarm 2*: Defendants were recorded as having made 'confessions', usually but not invariably unsigned.

*Alarm 3*: The 'confessions' were repudiated once access was allowed to solicitors.[91]

*Alarm 4*: No attempt was made to confirm the 'confessions' once the solicitor arrived, as, for example, by conducting a formal interview in accordance with the rules.

*Alarm 5*: Where interrogation notes had been signed by defendants, defendants were frequently noted by their solicitors to be distressed, complaining of having been intimidated into signing or bearing physical injuries.

*Alarm 6*: Alteration or re-writing of pages of 'interview notes' was never accompanied by any contemporaneous account of such incidents appearing in the officers' notebooks.

*Alarm 7*: Pages (falsely) said to have been 'restarted' or 'damaged' were not retained for evidential purposes.

---

[90] We are indebted to David Martin-Sperry QC for supplying a very helpful note of the skeleton argument in the case of Trevor Campbell. David Martin-Sperry brought successful appeals in 23 WMSCS cases.

[91] In some cases, Squad officers inserted the name of a Detective Superintendent in the Custody Book as authorising denial of access to a solicitor, a practice which could not have persisted without the acquiescence or knowledge of other officers.

*Alarm 8*: Successive interviews were normally conducted by different pairs of officers requiring defendants to challenge the integrity of numbers of officers.
*Alarm 9*: Original documents which might have revealed irregularities by Squad officers would often 'disappear'.
*Alarm 10*: Eye-witness accounts inconsistent with the appearance of the defendant would be 'lost' only to be replaced with more fitting descriptions.
*Alarm 11*: Scientific examination at the crime scene which might point away from the defendant would often be curtailed or non-existent.

While there may be dispute as to when confidence in the probity of the prosecution case would sag to the point of collapse, disintegrate it surely would, well before the final bell tolled. But judges raised no alarm at *any* stage,[92] even rejecting appeals from many of those falsely convicted.[93] Indeed, the 'law' built in restrictions which individuated cases, isolating each from the series of which it formed part, to the great advantage of corrupt police *units*:[94] the right of the prosecution to call 'similar fact' evidence was held by judges not to extend to the defence seeking to show 'an alleged course of conduct or system by the police officers to defeat the provisions' of the law, a submission to that effect being dismissed as 'misconceived' and having 'no legal basis',[95] a derisory reason given the judicial habit of converting police practice into 'law'.

---

[92] We set aside here non-disclosure by the police and prosecution of which a trial judge would be unaware but which has led to the collapse of cases costing millions of pounds, as in the major drugs case at Maidstone Crown Court caused primarily, in the words of Judge Crush, by a 'culture of non-disclosure and non-compliance' (*The Guardian*, 6 November 2000). See also *R v William* [2013], *R v Cole* [2013], *R v Austin* [2013] and *R v Kinnaird* [2013].

[93] The in-built limitation (that, in the words of Lord Justice Stephen Sedley (2011), an appellate court cannot take the suggestion that, notwithstanding adherence to its own rules, it has blundered because to do so 'would be to cast a long shadow of doubt over the system itself') of appellate courts has too often been stretched past breaking point by the Court of Appeal, as Lord Devlin (1979) eloquently demonstrates.

[94] Perturbingly, the Met's inability to tackle its 'rotten core' of corrupt officers by organised crime syndicates through bribes 'at will' is laid bare in the 2002 *Tiberius* Report identifying '80 corrupt individuals with links to the police, including 42 then-serving officers and 19 former detectives' (Harper, 2014c).

[95] *R v Edwards* (1991). The law has been modified subsequently but the circumstances under which cross-examination by the defence may be undertaken remains restricted.

## IDEOLOGY AND RULES

The development of a general theory of the criminal process has already been ably performed, from differing perspectives, in the works of Ashworth and Redmayne (2010) and Sanders and Young (2010). Ashworth and Redmayne adopt a rights-based approach under which the criminal process should have the twin goals of regulating the procedures for bringing suspected offenders to trial so as to produce accurate determinations and of ensuring that fundamental rights are protected in the process. By contrast, the emphasis in Sanders and Young is on freedom: when human rights and other interests are being compared, the approach that is likely to enhance freedom the most should be chosen, with a high value placed upon justice and fairness. While these 'top-down' perspectives often lead to similar conclusions on specific topics, each recognises the problems that general theories give rise to where priorities have to be accorded between competing interests, including interests of suspects, victims and the community at large, and each is, in our view, persuasively argued.

Our approach, by contrast, is more 'bottom up' utilising court decisions and empirical studies to throw light on the wider system through the lens of State-induced guilty pleas which has rapidly become the officially favoured method of case disposition in England and Wales and also in Scotland. Though now entrenched, this model deserves re-consideration in terms of both theory and practice.

## BUREAUCRATIC JUSTICE

When first critically discussed in America, it was argued that plea bargaining could subordinate the foundational ideals of the adversary system. As Blumberg (1967) put it in depicting courts as *bureaucracies*:

> Sociologists and others have focused their attention on the deprivations and social disabilities of such variables as race, ethnicity, and social class as being the source of an accused person's defeat in a criminal court. Largely overlooked is the variable of the court organization itself, which possesses a thrust, purpose, and direction of its own. It is grounded in pragmatic values, bureaucratic priorities, and administrative instruments. These exalt maximum production and the particularistic career designs of organizational incumbents, whose occupational and career commitments tend to generate a set of priorities. These priorities exert a higher claim than the stated ideological goals of 'due process of law,' and are often inconsistent with them. (p. 19)

For Blumberg, the apparently cooperative endeavour that was the mark of guilty plea courts was explicable by the 'co-optation' of defence lawyers who were socialised into compliance. Lawyers who were uncooperative and sought a trial were quickly 'taught' to comply with throughput demands by sticks and carrots that were at the discretion of prosecutors (such as disclosure of evidence) and judges (who could, for example, call the lawyer's case early or at the end of the day).

## COURTROOM WORKGROUPS

Blumberg's expository model is at odds with the work of Eisenstein and Jacob (1977)[96] who found no evidence of a hierarchical structure within the court. Instead, they depicted case dispositions as being handled by '*courtroom workgroups*' where the emphasis is said to be on incentives and shared goals (principally 'doing justice' and 'disposing of heavy case loads') which motivate courtroom actors to discharge their tasks in mutually acceptable ways. Interdependency of the actors is said to develop values and work patterns which enable cases to be dealt with in a cost-efficient and predictable manner.[97]

## MANAGERIALISM

In contrast, some commentators have seen recent developments in Britain as giving rise to '*managerialism*'. This is persuasively set out by Hodgson (2010) and McEwan (2011). Hodgson, in a wide-ranging survey, argues that the change is driven 'by efficiency and managerialism in the form of keeping cases out of court'[98] rather than by any move towards an inquisitorial system. Similarly, McEwan points out that at the core of managerialism is the interventionist judge with a concomitant reduction in party autonomy with 'elements of party control over the conduct of the case . . . transferred to the court'.[99] Within the criminal justice system, the motor-force for this, *cost-efficiency*, is in part said to be attributable

---

[96] See also Malcolm Feeley (1977).
[97] Heumann (1978) explained the cooperative behaviour of defence lawyers as a result of a 'learning' process. Novitiate lawyers, because of their training at Law School, started professional life expecting every, or almost every, case to go to trial. Once exposed to practice, however, they came to realise that most defendants were guilty and their cases undeserving of trial.
[98] Hodgson (2010) at p. 361. See also Young (2008) who documents the movement to non-court disposition of criminal occurrences.
[99] McEwan (2011) at p. 530.

to the historic excesses of party autonomy causing delay and expense through, for example, the failure of trial lawyers to comply with statutory disclosure requirements.

## QUASI-INQUISITORIAL JUSTICE

A related response sees State-induced pleas as a movement towards a model that more closely resembles *inquisitorial* systems.[100] Indicia include: reduction in party autonomy; attenuation of the 'right to silence'; changes in rules of evidence to allow evidence of propensity; restrictions on the right to jury trial (including the introduction of non-jury trials in specific cases); reductions in legal aid support;[101] and the Criminal Procedure Rules. Thus Hall (2010)[102] detects a subtle but significant shift to an inquisitorial approach:

> Furthermore ... policy-makers appear to see the former to be a 'game' of questionable legitimacy, in which long-established procedural rights and protections exist only to obscure the 'truth' and to help the guilty escape conviction. Within this mindset, the latter approach ... is a process specifically committed to achieve truth, free from the shackles of outmoded practices; all of the lawyers – including the judge – engage in a joint endeavour to convict the guilty and acquit the innocent. (pp. 107–8)

Whereas *managerialism* places greatest emphasis upon the changing role of the trial judge in the name of cost-effectiveness rather than in furtherance of the rights of suspects and defendants, the *inquisitorial* model places greatest emphasis upon the reduction in party autonomy and the consequent threat to the rights of defendants. For some theorists, the transition to an inquisitorial system is far from complete because the core of the British model is seen to retain its essential feature, namely a contest

---

[100] Care has to be taken in categorising systems, as Hodgson (2005) convincingly shows in her study of the French criminal justice system. As she indicates elsewhere (2010) '... inquisitorial-type systems have also developed abbreviated trial procedures and forms of charge bargaining in order to reduce the number of trials' (p. 321).

[101] In traditional legal rhetoric previously available to all but 'the very well-to-do' (Lord Bingham, in *R v CCRC ex parte Pearson* [2000]).

[102] See also, Edwards (2010) discussing the damaging effects of bureaucratically imposed 'targets' resulting in the escalation of cautions and fixed penalty notices and the consequent 'criminalization of terrifyingly high proportions of the population'.

between opposing parties,[103] with the result that, though there has been a 'considerable power loss, as far as the parties are concerned [there is] . . . a distinct lack of clarity as to where it now lies'.[104]

## DISCIPLINARY JUSTICE: THE STATE, LEGITIMACY AND THE JUDGES

Historically, as part of the State's social control apparatus, a key task for judges has been to maintain public confidence in criminal justice, and, as Burton and Carlen (1979, p. 95) observe, 'to reconstruct new forms of legitimacy and to secure strategies of incorporation, which ostensibly demonstrate a willingness to respond to public concern'. In 'serious' criminal cases,[105] the strategies adopted in the past have found expression in cultivating the notion of the neutral judge and the right to jury trial of the undifferentiated individual[106] – clothed in the presumption of innocence, the right to silence and the privilege against self-incrimination – where the prosecution, shackled by rules of evidence, had to discharge the high burden of proof.

As we have seen, this ideology was not only unrealised in practice, it was traduced by senior judges themselves promoting very publicly a 'law and order' platform. The contradictions in the discourse and practice continued because as judges sought to bury 'rights' bestowed by traditional rhetoric they found it even more necessary to continue their praise. This paradoxical ideology found clearest expression in State-induced guilty pleas, and it was these that would have to be justified and rationalised because a 'new'[107] *process* was replacing a *system*, albeit one that had been purely ideological. The task facing the courts was to explain a social disciplinary policy, of which coerced pleas are a core element, as having legitimate authority. The failure of the courts to offer plausible justifications in this regard, as we have documented, leads to the more important question – how can the current practices of criminal courts be understood?

---

[103] See McEwan (2011) at p. 544 and Langer (2005).
[104] McEwan (2011), at p. 544.
[105] Magistrates' courts have been depicted as venues for dealing with 'the facts' in trivial incidents where procedures can, commensurately, be expected to be less formal, less exacting and less exact.
[106] The ideology does not allow for the segmentation of society or the individuality of people, but only admits of an idealised characterisation. In this way, class, race and gender are removed from the equation.
[107] The process had been latent before publicity forced the hand of judges.

Originally the *Judges' Rules* were presented as a code for the police to follow so that evidence obtained thereby would be admissible at trial. Disregarding the reality that the judges gave up enforcing their own *Rules*, the *Rules* had in fact two more fundamental interlinked functions with a heritage that permeates to this day.

First, the *Rules* sought to restrict the courtroom as a site for public discourse over the limits of State power in criminal cases and the concomitant rights of citizens to challenge oppressive overreach. Advocacy, where it occurred, could now function only *within* judge-set parameters; contesting the basis of the rules (whether State powers were justified and what rights and privileges suspects and defendants should have) was now largely off-limits.[108]

Second, the *Rules* operated to *discipline trial judges* so that 'deviance' on their part could be immediately corrected by the Court of Appeal. With the rise of the police as social control agents in the 19th century, powers to detain and question suspects together with custodial 'confessions' allegedly obtained were not uncontested, some judges rejecting these practices and ruling such evidence inadmissible. The introduction of the *Rules* was aimed at ending such judicial heresy.

This disciplinary framework was made practically impervious by the practices of the Court of Appeal (Criminal Division). In this Court, the hallmark of the common law – that judges are *individuals* whose personalities can be seen in their separate (signed) judgments – has been firmly interred. Notwithstanding the paid presence of three and sometimes five judges,[109] the Court delivers a *single judgment* which does not allow for differences of emphasis or approach let alone dissent; a structure and practice that is, incidentally, replicated in the People's Republic of China.[110]

If reference to 'sporting theories' was permissible, it would be fair game to ask what are the odds against *a single judge* ever dissenting in *any* appeal? Ultimately, either all judges serving in this 'court' have identical views on every issue, a matter, if true, for serious disquiet in constitutional terms; or, in the alternative, the 'shared belief' is a conspiratorial sham, a

---

[108] Unless, that is, a 'human rights' claim could be advanced under legislative provisions, such as the Human Rights Act, 1998.

[109] Also, as Richardson (2013) accurately observes, the practice of using High Court and Circuit Court judges to supplement full-time Court of Appeal judges may involve appeals being dealt with by judges drawn from the same (or lower) 'common room' as the trial judge, creating the appearance of bias in the minds of appellants and overall of a second-rate appeal system.

[110] See further, Heydon (2013) and Richardson (2013). On China's practice, see McConville et al. (2011) and McConville and Pils (2013).

matter which, if true, displays contempt for democratic debate, supposedly another hallmark of the Constitution. In either case, by this practice discussion on issues involving the rights and liberties of citizens is officially curtailed as, incidentally, in jurisdictions which are not called democracies but something else, a situation that, in England and Wales, should be a matter for judicial shame.

The Court of Appeal's practices stand in contrast to those of the High Court of Justiciary in Scotland, although, as in England and Wales, 'justice' is being increasingly obscured there, as more cases are disposed of outside the court system than within it. In Scotland, members of the Bench although compelled by statute to recognise that sentencers must give recognition to guilty pleas, continue to openly engage with each other (at least to a degree) in *separate judgments* about the implications for the justice system and the extent to which a discount should be given. In giving pre-eminence to the discretion of the sentencer, the Scottish court has, at least, underlined the unique character and individuality of every case. Moreover, judges in Scotland remain free to air their differences on the implementation of the statute and the philosophy underlying State-induced guilty pleas, thereby keeping open the possibility of reasoned debate.

In England and Wales, the inauguration of the *Judges' Rules* witnessed the dismantling of the vestigial remains of the 'rights' of suspects and defendants. Accelerating in their brazenness, judges, both in court and extra-judicially, made clear that 'rights' of suspects and defendants were inconsistent with the 'proper' administration of justice. Behind the scenes, before the trappings of adversarial justice were themselves moved offstage, judges pressured defendants and their lawyers into accepting guilty pleas. Driven into the open, the Court in *Turner* took the initial step towards ditching the rhetoric of adversary justice and enforcing the subordination of the Bar to judicial fiat.

Thereafter, judges joined senior police in an assault on defendants' paper rights and on defence lawyers, calculatedly associated with 'criminals'. The intensification of a social control ideology, focused around unqualified allegiance to the probity and reliability of police investigations, was barely interrupted by the shocking series of miscarriages of justice that disclosed discreditable police investigatory practices and shameful judicial bias. With scarcely a genuflection to the human disasters they had brought about, judges and politicians (with the aid of cherry-picked recommendations of various royal commissions) began the task of formally pulling down the façade of individual 'rights' while concurrently magnifying police powers.

The book-burning of Auld was entirely faithful to a long tradition in which his judicial forebears had rained down clods on the coffin of 'adversarial justice'. The library to which he set fire contained by this time few pamphlets of any significance, the slim volume *Defendants' Rights* having long since been incinerated by his predecessors while the *vade mecum* on *Police Powers* and *Judicial Prerogatives*, safely deposited in vaults of immunity in the Royal Courts of Justice and Petty France,[111] awaits further volumes to its already weighty tomes.[112]

Auld's legacy lies elsewhere: he fulminated on the 'rights' of suspects and defendants as written on flimsy folios whose spines were unable to withstand the flames of re-characterisation as contemptible obstacles to justice in an age of 'cost-effective' ideology and whose prominence as surrogates for legitimacy was now relegated to the archives. Rules regulating the formal adversary system, which previous judges assured had to be faithfully followed and were 'not rules of a game'[113] were now ridiculed *as* 'rules of a game'.

The scorn that Auld poured on the 'sporting theory of justice' was avidly taken up in the Court of Appeal by himself and his (largely tongue-tied) judicial disciples (who sometimes did not get the hang of the idea, referring to the new age as one in which advocates had to put their 'cards on the table'!).[114] So seductive were his recommendations that they prepared the concrete mix for the rejection of the *pretence* of the foundations of adversary justice, the formal repudiation of the notion of the independence

---

[111] The site of the Ministry of Justice and meeting point for the Criminal Procedure Rules Committee.

[112] In a chilling echo of the abuse of stop and search powers under the old s. 44 counter terrorism regime (see Chapter 2), Schedule 7 of the Terrorism Act 2000, under which Asian people are 42 times more likely to be stopped than white people (Dodd, 2011), continues to reveal protection by the judiciary against the abuse of power by an undemocratic Security Service as seriously wanting. In the *Miranda* case, the High Court held that the Security Service's detention of a journalist's partner (not suspected of terrorism) in possession of sensitive documents under legislation designed to combat terrorism was lawful, proportionate and did not breach European human rights protections of freedom of expression (*Miranda v S of S* [2014]). The three judges unanimously supported David Miranda's detention for nine hours, without a lawyer present, the confiscation of his electronic equipment and its cloning, despite the absence of any suspicion of wrongdoing (Kennedy, 2014) on the unsettling basis that he had walked into the morass of 'national security' (at 52). The judicially-backed overreach by security services is disquieting because, grave incursions to press freedom aside, this judgment affects every person in England and Wales who face the threat of similar intimidation from State agents, without an iota of suspicion needed, subject only to the nebulous caveat of 'good faith'. As Ouseley, J bluntly stated: 'An officer must act in good faith. . . . He cannot act on a merely arbitrary basis, but he can act on, for example, no more than hunch or intuition . . .' (at para. 91).

[113] *Randall v R* (2002).

[114] See, for example, *R v Newell* [2012].

of the Bar and the inauguration of an overt social disciplinary society; a renewed foundation that would soon set in a political climate defined by de-regulation of the financial sector and a manufactured concentration on 'law and order' focused on those losing out in the market economy, which judges could now openly flaunt without recourse to traditional claims of legitimacy.[115] The over-arching shibboleth of 'cost-efficiency', it must be emphasized, is not simply a creature of government, central as it is to the Secretary of Justice's handbook, but one nurtured by the judiciary with quixotic-like support. Indeed, the Secretary of Justice has agreed with the Lord Chief Justice that Leveson LJ will undertake a review of criminal proceedings not in any disingenuously 'open' manner but instead 'to identify ways to reduce and streamline them'. The Lord Chief Justice himself has sought to resuscitate the rotten corpse of the 1975 James Committee's vilified recommendations to remove 'small acts of dishonesty' (pious perjury, perhaps, or noble cause corruption?) from the jury by suggesting that these (and no doubt others) should be dealt with by a new middle-tier judge-only court (Rozenberg, 2014).

Underpinning this overall strategy has been the politics of indeterminacy: pre-*Turner*, co-optation of defendants and their lawyers was sought through an indeterminate hidden threat that otherwise something worse *might* happen. In the aftermath of *Turner*, cooperation was secured by an open threat that something worse *would likely* happen. This was bolstered by the Criminal Procedure Rules (CPR), under which defendants (supposedly having 'complete freedom of choice') and their lawyers (supposedly having 'complete freedom' over advice) were *in fact* subjected to a coercive regime with the warning that other punitive *rules* (whose content, formulated in secret by a judge-dominated committee, has replaced the myth of 'laws') and associated penalties for non-compliance (equally unspecified) might follow.[116]

'Law,' in the chimeric sense espoused by Auld and the CPR, stands tall in opposition to the notion of individual rights and stares down in conflict with those who seek to speak up for those who are the subject of repeated police intrusions into their lives (now admitted by the police inspectorate) or those wrongly accused of crime. In this way, criminal judges fulfil the prophecy of Foucault (1978) regarding 'new methods of power' whose operation 'is not ensured by right but by technique, not by law but by normalization, not by punishment but by control . . .' (p. 84).

---

[115] Cf. McConville and Mirsky (1995) and Choongh (1997).
[116] The words of Junius are an apt comment of the judge-made CPR: 'Laws are intended not to trust to what men will do, but to guard against what they may do'.

## MODELS AND EMPIRICAL REALITY

The short history of State-induced guilty pleas in England and Wales and the even shorter history in Scotland thus has important implications for the theoretical models outlined above, which, despite attractive elements, have shortcomings as explanatory frameworks. Thus, Balbus (1973) assumed that 'formal legal rationality', which he saw as disregarded at times of social crisis, was an instrument of 'due process', when, in fact, it was mostly empty rhetoric routinely set aside (as he, incidentally, documented) in 'normal' as well as 'crisis' situations.

While the emphasis on the changing role of the trial judge in the *managerialism* explanation reflects a *style of judging* in England and Wales[117] and resonates with governmental responses to 'public services' in which performance indicators are tied to targets and markets rather than based around standards and delivery, the claimed driving engine ('cost-efficiency') is problematic because this is said to derive from a 'fiscal crisis' which has been demonstrably a construction of the State, implicating judges, over a very long period of time and which today has conveniently become parasitical to the global financial 'crisis'.

Nor can courts be understood as *bureaucracies* in the way portrayed by Blumberg (1967) because this implies that they possess an internal logic removed from the wider political and social order. On the contrary, if the recent history of State-induced guilty pleas in Britain teaches us anything it is that the courts represent the State at work, reproducing all too exactly the power structures and peremptory methodologies that are applied to a social order segmented around class, race, gender and inequalities of opportunity and wealth.

While a focus on guilty plea dispositions might appear consistent with the '*courtroom workgroup*' model, a central problem, as Sheskin (1981) points out, is that researchers (and now others) simply assumed its existence because they saw individuals interacting and work being accomplished. As Eisenstein and Jacob (1977) put it, these team members share values and norms although 'they may not realize it'. But, as Sheskin devastatingly asks: '. . . [i]f they [team members] do not realize it, how can others assume it exists?' (1981, p. 84).

In England and Wales, far from there being a 'courtroom workgroup' with common norms and values, judges have created a *forced labour camp* to unsparingly circumscribe the role of defence lawyers, already debilitated by changes to the legal aid system, denigrated as 'uncooperative or

---

[117] Some other jurisdictions are moving in this direction. See, McEwan (2011).

feckless' or indiscriminately maligned as avaricious fat cats and admitted into criminal cases only on judges' terms.[118] For 'defence' barristers in this setting, the limited 'obligation' as 'officer of the court' has become little more than that of court functionary.

The ghosts of yesterday have been re-incarnated. The methodologies applied to the 'underclasses' of the past – primarily members of ethnic minority communities, the unemployed, the homeless, striking miners and those engaged in public disorder – have been normalised. All criminal courts (with new ones soon to be invented) are now 'special courts' dispensing 'group justice' where, through 'pro-forma' exercises of 'discretion', outcomes are 'correctly anticipated' and are optimally delivered through 'shelling exercises'. Watching and besetting this scenario is a Court of Appeal, stuffed with mute judges (the description 'Full Court' being presumably an inadvertent misnomer or an ironic joke), which in place of 'no credit' now gives 'full credit' for standardisation of dispositions.

This, then, is *not* a move towards inquisitorial systems: rather, criminal judges (with the aid of implacable politicians) are seeking to construct a *unitary system* – the parties (including the defendant) forced to swear to join hands and uphold a common objective, as defined by judges, working 'cooperatively' on pain of sanction for non-compliance.

In place of the myth of adversary justice, which an endless supply chain of bench players officially disparage as a 'game' (with occasional nods of feigned obeisance), and against a background in which a denigrated 'undeserving' suspect/defendant population, served by an increasingly incapacitated, and fearful defence service, participates 'freely' and 'voluntarily' in their own conviction, is a wider process, not of 'law', but of peremptory *rule-determination*, the canons of which have been *privatised* by the judiciary (in judge-dominated committee and indivisible court judgments) now engaged in what the most senior judge in the land, the Lord Chief Justice, combatively declares as 'an age of retrenchment'.[119]

Far from being the 'weakest and least dangerous department of

---

[118] This has yet to achieve complete success, the senior Bar continuing to explore and contest the weak spots of the judicially created architecture of procedural law.

[119] The Lord Chief Justice drew firm battle-lines in the assault on criminal justice and defendants' rights when he put all on notice that 'there has been a change to the role of the State and the expenditure it is *prepared* to make' (Thomas (2014), p. 2, emphasis added) in a speech ironically delivered before the human rights and law reform organisation, JUSTICE. Lord Thomas's war-cry launched itself upon the vulnerabilities of the justice system which, he proclaimed, lies 'unprotected' and 'far from being immune' to attack, it will 'continue to be cut' (p. 3).

government', judges have grown in maligned stature. Whereas once judges 'were prepared to bend rules, to behave improperly' (Robertson, 2013, p. 99), today those directing judicial policy not only bend rules, they alchemise them; transforming cast-iron rules, outside the cauldron of advocacy, into more malleable substances wholly aligned and melded with government policy, itself an alliance between warped rationalism and executive branch cynicism. Rules which juxtapose rights under one hat are in fact a rhetorical sleight of hand and reflect a misbegotten brand of politicisation which threatens to marginalise principled and empirically-based arguments about the 'disposal' of justice.

An increasingly authoritarian process no longer seeks legitimacy in formal legal rationality but in an unprincipled and contemptible claim to be 'cheap' in dealing with the 'dirt' of society. The hallmark of this shameless production-line process is that police, prosecutors, judges and defence lawyers are *commanded* to strive in unison – four workshops in the same factory (one of the few left in Britain) – assembled and dominated by criminal judges.

# Bibliography

Adams, J. (1971), 'The second ethical problem in *R v Turner*: the limits of an advocate's discretion', *Criminal Law Review*, 252.

Alge, D. (2013), 'The effectiveness of incentives to reduce the risk of moral hazard in the defence barrister's role in plea bargaining', *Legal Ethics*, 16(1): 162.

Alschuler, A. (1975), 'The defense attorney's role in plea bargaining', *Yale Law Journal*, 84: 1179.

Alschuler, A. (1981), 'The changing plea bargaining debate', *California Law Review*, 69: 652.

Alschuler, A. (1983), 'Implementing the criminal defendant's right to trial: alternatives to the plea bargaining system', *University of Chicago Law Review*, 50: 931.

Anderson, D. (2011), *Report on the Operation in 2010 of the Terrorism Act 2000 and of Part 1 of the Terrorism Act 2006*, London: Stationery Office.

Ashworth, A. (2010), 'Coroners and Justice Act 2009: sentencing guidelines and the Sentencing Council', *Criminal Law Review*, 388.

Ashworth, A. (2012), 'Departures from the sentencing guidelines', *Criminal Law Review*, 2: 81.

Ashworth, A. and M. Redmayne (2010), *The Criminal Process*, 4th edn, Oxford: Oxford University Press.

Atkinson, J.M. and P. Drew (1979), *Order in Court*, London: Macmillan.

Auld, Sir Robin (2001), *Review of the Criminal Courts of England and Wales*, London: Lord Chancellor's Department.

Baksi, C. (2012a), 'LSC improvements fail to satisfy auditor', *Law Society Gazette*, 11 July.

Baksi, C. (2012b), 'Spending watchdog trains fire on interpreter contracting chaos', *Law Society Gazette*, 12 November.

Baksi, C. (2013a), 'Chris Grayling', *Law Society Gazette*, 20 May.

Baksi, C. (2013b), 'CPS under fire for failures in two serious cases', *Law Society Gazette*, 24 June.

Baksi, C. (2013c), '"Overwhelming" support for action as 400 barristers stay away from court', *Law Society Gazette*, 22 April.

Baksi, C. (2014), 'CPS warns barristers against taking part in legal aid protest', *Law Society Gazette*, 3 March.

Balbus, I. (1973, 1977), *The Dialectics of Legal Repression*, New York: Russell Sage.
Baldwin, J. (1985), *Pre-Trial Justice*, Oxford: Basil Blackwell.
Baldwin, J. (1997), 'Understanding judge ordered and directed acquittals in the Crown Court', *Criminal Law Review*, 536.
Baldwin, J. and F. Feeney (1986), 'Defence disclosure in the magistrates' courts', *Modern Law Review*, 44: 593.
Baldwin, J. and M. McConville (1977), *Negotiated Justice*, London: Martin Robertson.
Baldwin, J. and M. McConville (1978a), 'Legal carve-up and legal cover-up', *British Journal of Law and Society*, 5(2): 228.
Baldwin, J. and M. McConville (1978b), 'Allegations against lawyers: some evidence from criminal cases in London', *Criminal Law Review*, 741.
Ball, R. and J. Drury (2012), 'Representing the riots: the (mis)use of statistics to sustain ideological explanation', *Riotstats*, 106.
Bankowski, Z. and G. Mungham (1976), *Images of Law*, London: Routledge.
Barclay, G. and C. Tavares (1999), *Information on the Criminal Justice System in England and Wales: Digest 4*, London: Home Office.
Bar Council of England and Wales (2013), 'Response to the Ministry of Justice Transforming Legal Aid Consultation', 4 June, available at: http://www.barcouncil.org.uk/media/213867/the_bar_council_response_to_moj_transforming_legal_aid_consultation.pdf
Barry, J. (2010), 'A barrister's role in the plea decision', PhD thesis, University of London, available at: http://qmro.qmul.ac.uk/jspui/handle/123456789/394
*BBC News* (2014), 'Police to be told not to confer before writing up notes,' 5 March.
Bedford, S. (1958), *The Best We Can Do*, Harmondsworth: Penguin.
Bennet, J. and K. Miller (1990), *Delay in Summary Criminal Proceedings: A Study of Six Sheriff Courts*, Scottish Office: Central Research Unit.
Bennett, R. (1993), 'Criminal justice', *London Review of Books*, 24 June, 15(12): 5.
Bentham, J. (1781), *An Introduction to the Principles of Morals and Legislation*, Oxford: Clarendon Press.
Bentham, J. (1840), *The Rationale of Judicial Evidence* in 'The Works of Jeremy Bentham now first collected; under the superintendence of his executor, John Bowring', Google Books.
Berger, M. (1976), 'The case against plea bargaining', *American Bar Association Journal,* 62: 621.
Bingham, Lord (2006), 'The rule of law', 6th David Williams Lecture, Centre for Public Law, University of Cambridge, 16 November, avail-

able at: http://www.cpl.law.cam.ac.uk/Media/THE%20RULE%20OF%20LAW%202006.pdf
Birkett, Lord (1961), *Six Great Advocates*, Harmondsworth: Penguin Books.
Blackstock J., E. Cape, J. Hodgson, A. Ogorodova and T. Spronken (2013), *Inside Police Custody: An Empirical Account of Suspects' Rights in Four Jurisdictions*, Cambridge: Intersentia Ltd.
Blackstone, W. (1765), *Commentaries on the Laws of England*, Vol. 1.
Blake, M. and A. Ashworth (1998), 'Some ethical issues in prosecuting and defending criminal cases', *Criminal Law Review*, 16.
Block, B., C. Corbett and J. Peay (1993a), *Ordered and Directed Acquittals in the Crown Court*, Royal Commission on Criminal Justice, Research Study No. 15, London: HMSO.
Block, B., C. Corbett and J. Peay (1993b), 'Ordered and directed acquittals in the Crown Court: A time of change?', *Criminal Law Review*, 95.
Blowe, K. (2011), 'Policing the police', *Red Pepper*, 9 March.
Blumberg, A. (1967), *Criminal Justice*, Chicago IL: Quadrangle.
Blume, J. (2007), *The Dilemma of the Criminal Defendant with a Prior Record – Lessons from the Wrongfully Convicted*, Cornell: Cornell Law School Legal Studies Research Paper Series No. 83.
Bonomy, Lord (2002), *Improving Practice: The 2002 Review of the Practices and Procedure of the High Court of Justiciary*, available at: http://www.scotland.gov.uk/Publications/2002/12/15847/14122
Borrie, G. and J. Varcoe (1970), *Legal Aid in Criminal Proceedings: A Regional Survey*, Birmingham: Institute of Judicial Administration.
Bottoms, A. and J. McClean (1976), *Defendants in the Criminal Process*, London: Routledge.
Boulton, W.W. (1953, 1957, 1961, 1965, 1971, 1975), *A Guide to Conduct and Etiquette at the Bar of England and Wales*, London: Butterworths.
Bourke, S. (1970), *The Springing of George Blake*, London: Cassell.
Bowers, J. (2008), 'Punishing the innocent', *University of Pennsylvania Law Review*, 156: 1117.
Bowles, R. and A. Perry (2009), *International Comparison of Publicly-funded Legal Services and Justice Systems*, London: Ministry of Justice, Research Series 14/09, October.
Bowling, B. and C. Phillips (2002), *Racism, Crime and Justice*, Harlow: Longman.
Boyle, K., T. Hadden and P. Hillyard (1975), *Law and State: The Case of Northern Ireland*, London: Martin Robertson.
Brabin, Justice (1966), *The Case of Timothy John Evans: Report of an Inquiry*, Cmnd. 3101, London: HMSO.

Bridges, L. (1975), 'The Dialectics of Legal Repression', *Race and Class*, 17: 83.
Bridges, L. (1994), 'Normalizing injustice: The Royal Commission on Criminal Justice', *Journal of Law & Society*, 21: 20.
Bridges, L. (2006), 'The ethics of representation on guilty pleas', *Legal Ethics*, 9(1): 80.
Bridges, L. (2012), 'Four days in August: the UK riots', *Race & Class*, 54(1): 1.
Bridges, L. and T. Bunyan (1983), 'Britain's new urban policing strategy – The Police and Criminal Evidence Bill in context', *Journal of Law & Society*, 10(1): 85.
Bridges, L. and E. Cape (2008), *CDS Direct: Flying in the Face of the Evidence*, London: Centre for Crime and Justice Studies.
Bridges, L. and S. Choongh (1998), *Improving Police Station Advice: The Impact of the Accreditation Scheme for Police Station Legal Advisers*, London: Law Society's Research and Policy Planning Unit/Legal Aid Board.
Bridges, L. and M. McConville (1997), 'Keeping faith with their own convictions: The Royal Commission on Criminal Justice', in M. McConville and L. Bridges (eds), *Criminal Justice in Crisis*, Cheltenham, UK and Lyme, NH, USA: Edward Elgar.
Bridges, L., E. Cape, P. Fenn, A. Mitchell, R. Moorhead and A. Sherr (2007), *Evaluation of the Public Defender Service in England and Wales*, London: HMSO.
Bridges, L., S. Choongh and M. McConville (2000), *Ethnic Minority Defendants and the Right to Elect Jury Trial*, London: Commission for Racial Equality.
Bridges, L., J. Hodgson, M. McConville and A. Pavlovic (1997), 'Can critical research influence policy?' *British Journal of Criminology*, 37: 378.
Brogden, A. (1981), 'Sus is dead: What about "SAS"?', *New Community*, 9: 44.
Brogden, M. (1982), *Police, Autonomy and Consent*, London: Academic Press.
Brogden, M. (1991), *On the Mersey Beat*, Oxford: Oxford University Press.
Brown, G. (2013), 'Sentence discounting in England and Scotland – some observations on the use of comparative authority in sentence appeals', *Criminal Law Review*, 8: 673.
Bryan, I. (1997), *Interrogation and Confession: A Study of Progress, Process and Practice*, Dartmouth: Ashgate.
Bull, R. (2011), 'The investigative interviewing of children and other vulnerable witnesses: psychological research and working/professional practice', *Legal and Criminological Psychology*, 15(1): 5.

Burney, E. (1979), *Magistrate, Court and Community*, London: Hutchinson.
Burton, F. and P. Carlen (1979), *Official Discourse: On Discourse Analysis, Government Publications, Ideology and the State*, London: Routledge and Kegan Paul.
Butler, T. and M. Garsia (1969), *Archbold, Pleading, Evidence & Practice in Criminal Cases*, 37th edn, London: Sweet & Maxwell.
Butler, T. and S. Mitchell (1973), *Archbold, Pleading, Evidence & Practice in Criminal Cases*, 38th edn, London: Sweet & Maxwell.
Cain, M. (1979), 'The general practice lawyer and the client: towards a radical conception', *International Journal of the Sociology of Law*, 7: 331.
Callander, I. (2013), 'The pursuit of efficiency in the reform of the Scottish fiscal fine: should we opt out of the conditional offer?', *Scots Law Times*, 5: 37–43; 6: 47–53.
Cape, E. (2004), 'The rise (and fall?) of a criminal defence profession', *Criminal Law Review*, 72.
Cape, E. (2013), 'The counter-terrorism provisions of the Protection of Freedoms Act 2012: preventing misuse or a case of smoke and mirrors?', *Criminal Law Review*, 5: 385.
Carlen, P. (1976), *Magistrates' Justice*, London: Martin Robertson.
Carlile, Lord (2010), *Report on the Operation in 2009 of the Terrorism Act 2000 and of Part 1 of the Terrorism Act 2006*, July. London: TSO.
Carter, Lord (2006), *Legal Aid: A Market-Based Approach to Reform*, London, available at: http://www.lccsa.org.uk/assets/documents/consultation/carter%20review%2013072006.pdf
Casale, S. (2013), *Report of the Independent External Review of the IPCC Investigation into the Death of Sean Rigg* (May), available at: http://www.ipcc.gov.uk/sites/default/files/Documents/investigation_commissioner_reports/Review_Report_Sean_Rigg.PDF
Chibnall, S. (1977), *Law and Order News: An Analysis of Crime Reporting in the British Press*, London: Tavistock Publishing.
Choongh, S. (1997), *Policing as Social Discipline*, Oxford: Clarendon Press.
Christian, L. (1985), 'Restriction without conviction: the role of the courts in legitimising police control in Nottinghamshire', in B. Fine and R. Millar (eds), *Policing the Miners' Strike*, London: Lawrence & Wishart.
Clarkson, C., A. Cretney, G. Davis and J. Shepherd (1994), 'Assaults: the relationship between seriousness, criminalisation and punishment', *Criminal Law Review*, 4.
Clough, J. and A. Jackson (2012), 'The game is up: proposals on incorporating effective disclosure requirements into criminal investigations', *Criminal Lawyer*, 211: 3.

Cluss, P.A., J. Boughton, E. Frank, B.D. Stewart and D. West (1983), 'The rape victim: psychological correlates of participation in the legal process', *Criminal Justice and Behavior*, 10: 342.

Cockburn, A.W. (1952), 'In lumine: an address on advocacy', Faculty of Law, Southampton.

Cohen, S. (1979), 'The punitive city: notes on the dispersal of social control', *Contemporary Crises*, 3: 339.

Cookson, G. (2011), *Unintended Consequences: The Cost of the Government's Legal Aid Reforms*, London: King's College London.

Council of Circuit Judges (2013), *Response to the Ministry of Justice Transforming Legal Aid Consultation, June 2013*, available at: http://www.judiciary.gov.uk/Resources/JCO/Documents/Consultations/cocj-response-transforming-legal-aid-june-2013.pdf

Cox, B., J. Shirley and M. Short (1977), *The Fall of Scotland Yard*, London: Penguin Books Ltd.

Cretney, A. and G. Davis (1995), *Punishing Violence*, London: Routledge.

Cretney, A. and G. Davis (1997), 'Prosecuting domestic assault: victims failing courts or courts failing victims?', *Howard Journal*, 32(2): 146.

Criminal Law Revision Committee (1972), *Eleventh Report, Evidence (General)*, Cmnd 4991, London: HMSO.

Crown Office Notice (1980), *Journal of the Law Society of Scotland*, 25(4): April.

Crown Prosecution Service (CPS) (2009), *Annual Report and Resource Accounts for the Period April 2008–March 2009*, London: Stationery Office, available at: http://www.cps.gov.uk/publications/reports/2008/index.html

Crown Prosecution Service (CPS) (2013), *Response to the Ministry of Justice Transforming Legal Aid Consultation*, 4 June, available at: http://www.cps.gov.uk/consultations/cps_response_to_legal_aid_consultation.pdf

Curran, P. (1991), 'Discussions in the judge's private room', *Criminal Law Review*, 79.

David, Judge (1978), 'In the Crown Court', *The Magistrate*, 34: 74.

Dawes, W., P. Harvey, B. Mackintosh, F. Nunney and A. Phillips (2011), *Attitudes to Guilty Plea Reductions*, Sentencing Council Research Series 02/11, London: Sentencing Council.

De Burgh, H. (2000), *Investigative Journalism: Context and Practice*, London: Routledge.

Dell, S. (1971), *Silent in Court*, London: Bell.

Dempsey, M. (2009), *Prosecuting Domestic Violence*, Oxford: Oxford University Press.

Demuth, C. (1978), *Sus: A Report of the Vagrancy Act of 1824*, London: Runnymede Trust.

Denning, Lord (1963), *The Circumstances Leading to the Resignation of the Former Secretary for War, Mr. J. D. Profumo*, Cmnd. 2152, London: HMSO.

Denyer, R. (2008), *Case Management in the Crown Court*, Oxford: Hart Publishing.

Denyer, R. (2012), *Case Management in Criminal Trials*, 2nd edn, Oxford: Hart Publishing.

Department for Communities and Local Government (2013), *Response to the Riots: Communities and Victims Panel's Final Report*, 12 July.

Department for Constitutional Affairs (2006a), *Judicial Statistics: England and Wales for the Year 2005*, CM 6799, May.

Department for Constitutional Affairs (2006b), *Delivering Simple, Speedy, Summary Justice*, 13 July.

Dervan, L. (2012), 'Bargained justice: plea bargaining's innocence problem and the Brady safety-valve', *Utah Law Review*, 51.

Dervan, L. and V. Edkins (2012), 'The innocent defendant's dilemma: an innovative empirical study of plea bargaining's innocence problem', available at: http://ssrn.com/abstract=2071397

Devlin, J.D. (1960), *Criminal Courts and Procedure*, London: Butterworth.

Devlin, Lord (1979), *The Judge*, Oxford: Oxford University Press.

Devlin, Lord (1991), 'The conscience of the jury', *Law Quarterly Review*, 107: 398.

Devlin, P. (1956), *Trial by Jury*, London: Stevens.

Devlin, P. (1960), *The Prosecution Process in England*, Oxford: Oxford University Press.

Dicey, A.V. (1885), *Introduction to the Study of the Law of the Constitution*, 1st edn, Macmillan.

Dignan, J. and A. Whynne (1997), 'A microcosm of the local community? Reflections on the composition of the magistracy in a Petty Sessional Division in the North Midlands', *British Journal of Criminology*, 37: 184.

Dixen, B. (2012), 'The record of the House of Lords in Strasbourg', *Law Quarterly Review*, 128 (July), 354.

Dixon, D., A.K. Bottomley, C.A. Coleman, M. Gill and D. Wall (1989), 'Reality and rules in the construction and regulation of police suspicion', *International Journal of the Sociology of Law*, 17: 185.

Doob, A. and C. Webster (2003), 'Sentence severity and crime: accepting the null hypothesis', in M. Tonry (ed.), *Crime and Justice: A Review of Research*, Vol. 30, Chicago: University of Chicago Press.

Doughty Street Chambers (2013), 'Response to the Ministry of Justice Transforming Legal Aid Consultation', 4 June, available at: http://www.doughtystreet.co.uk/documents/uploaded-documents/Transforming_Legal_Aid_-_Doughty_Street_Chambers_Response_(2).pdf

Downes, D. and R. Morgan (2002), 'The skeletons in the cupboard: the politics of law and order at the turn of the millennium', in M. Maguire, R. Morgan and R. Reiner (eds), *The Oxford Handbook of Criminology*, Oxford: Oxford University Press.

Du Cann, R. (1964), *The Art of the Advocate*, London: Penguin Group.

Duff, P. (1996a), 'The not proven verdict: jury mythology and "moral panics"', *Juridicial Review*, 1: 1.

Duff, P. (1999b), 'The Scottish criminal jury: a very peculiar institution', *Law and Contemporary Problems*, 62: 73.

Duff, P. (1999c), 'The Prosecution Service: independence and accountability', in P. Duff and N. Hutton (eds), *Criminal Justice in Scotland*, Aldershot: Ashgate.

Dworkin, R. (1985), 'Principle, policy, procedure', in R. Dworkin, *A Matter of Principle*, Cambridge, MA: Harvard University Press.

East, R. and P. Thomas (1985), 'Freedom of movement: Moss v McLachlan', *Journal of Law & Society*, 12(1): 77.

Eastwood, N., M. Shiner and D. Bear (2013), *The Numbers in Black and White: Ethnic Disparities in the Policing and Prosecution of Drug Offences in England and Wales*, Release (LSE consulting), August.

Edwards, A. (2010), 'Do the defence matter?', *International Journal of Evidence and Proof*, 14: 119.

Eisenstein, J. and H. Jacob (1977), *Felony Justice*, Boston: Little, Brown.

Ellis, R. and S. Biggs (2013), 'Simple cautions', *Archbold Review*, 5: 6.

Ellison QC, M. (2014),'The Stephen Lawrence Independent Review – Possible Corruption and the role of undercover policing in the Stephen Lawrence case (summary of findings)', (Ellison Report), UK: HMSO, HC1094, 6 March.

Equalities and Human Rights Commission (EHRC) (2010), *Stop and Think: A Critical Review of the Use of Stop and Search Powers in England and Wales*, London: EHRC.

Equalities and Human Rights Commission (EHRC) (2012), *Race Disproportionality in Stops and Searches under Section 60 of the Criminal Justice and Public Order Act, 1994*, available at: http://www.equality humanrights.com/uploaded_files/research/bp_5_final.pdf

Faulkner, D. (2010), *Criminal Justice and Government at a Time of Austerity: An Extended Review*, London: Criminal Justice Alliance.

Feeley, M. (1976), 'The concept of laws in social science: a critique and notes on an expanded view', *Law and Society Review*, 10: 497.

Feeley, M. (1977, 1979), *The Process is the Punishment*, New York: Russell Sage.

Feeley, M. (1982), 'Plea bargaining and the structure of the criminal process', *Journal of Justice Systems*, 73: 338.

Feinberg, J. (1992), 'In defence of moral rights', *Oxford Journal of Legal Studies*, 12: 149.
Fenwick, H. (1997), 'Procedural "rights" of victims of crime: public or private ordering of the criminal process?', *Modern Law Review*, 60(3): 317.
Ferguson, G. and D. Roberts (1974), 'Plea bargaining: directions for Canadian reform', *Canadian Bar Review*, 52: 498.
Fields, P. (2008), 'Case comment. Clarke and McDaid: a technical triumph', *Criminal Law Review*, 8: 612–24.
Fine, B. and R. Millar (eds) (1985), *Policing the Miners*, London: Lawrence & Wishart.
Finkelstein, M. (1975), 'A statistical analysis of guilty plea practices in the Federal Courts', *Harvard Law Review*, 89: 293.
Fisher, Sir Henry (1977), *Report of an Inquiry by the Hon. Sir Henry Fisher into the circumstances leading to the trial of three persons on charges arising out of the death of Maxwell Confait and the fire at 27 Doggett Road, London SE 6*, London: HMSO.
Fitzgerald, M. (1993), *Ethnic Minorities and the Criminal Justice System*, Royal Commission on Criminal Justice Research Study No. 20, London: HMSO.
Flanagan, R. (2008), *The Review of Policing: Final Report*, London: Home Office.
Foot, P. (1986), *Murder at the Farm*, London: Sidgwick & Jackson.
Foucault, M. (1978), *The History of Sexuality* (ed. Robert Hurley), London: Allen Lane.
Franey, R. (1983), *Poor Law*, London: CHAR, CPAG, CDC, NAPO, NCCL.
Frey, R. (1980), *Interests and Rights: The Case Against Animals*, Oxford: Clarendon Press.
Fuller, L. (1961), 'The adversary system', in H.J. Berman (ed.), *Talks on American Law*, New York: Vintage Books.
Fuller, L. (1978), 'The forms and limits of adjudication', *Harvard Law Review*, 92(2): 353.
Garden Court Chambers (2012), 'Sean Rigg Inquest report', 2 August, available at: http://www.gardencourtchambers.co.uk/news/news_detail.cfm?iNewsID=759
Garfinkle, H. (1955), 'Conditions of successful degradation ceremonies', *American Journal of Sociology*, 61: 420.
Garrett, B. (2008), 'Judging Innocence', *Columbia Law Review*, 108: 55.
Gee, J. and M. Button (2013), *The Financial Cost of Fraud Report 2013*, University of Portsmouth: Centre for Counter Fraud Studies.
Genders, E. (1999), 'Reform of the Offences Against the Person Act: Lessons from the Law in Action', *Criminal Law Review*, 689.

Gibson, J. (2006), 'Judicial institutions', in R. Rhodes, S. Binder and B. Rockman (eds), *The Oxford Handbook of Political Institutions*, Oxford: Oxford University Press.

Golding, P. and S. Middleton (1982), *Images of Welfare: Press and Public Attitudes to Poverty*, Oxford: Martin Robertson.

Gordon, G. (1970), 'Plea Bargaining', *The Scots Law Times*, 2 October: 153.

Goriely, T. et al. (2001), *The Public Defence Solicitors Office in Edinburgh: An Independent Evaluation*, Scottish Executive Council Research Unit/TSO.

Grayling, C. (2013), 'UK set to host 2015 Global Law Summit', Government Press Release, 6 October, available at: https://www.gov.uk/government/news/uk-set-to-host-2015-global-law-summit

Green, P. (1990), *Policing the Miners' Strike*, Milton Keynes: Open University Press.

Greer, S. (1995), *Supergrasses: A Study in Anti-Terrorism Law Enforcement in Northern Ireland*, Oxford: Clarendon Press.

Gregory, J. (1976), *Crown Court or Magistrates' Court*, Office of Population and Censuses and Surveys, London: HMSO.

Gregory, W., J. Mowen and D. Linder (1978), 'Social psychology and plea bargaining', *Journal of Personality and Social Psychology*, 36: 1521.

Gross, Rt Hon LJ and Treacy, Rt Hon LJ (2012), *Further Review of Disclosure in Criminal Proceedings*, Judiciary of England and Wales.

Gross, S., R. Jacoby, K. Matheson and D.J. Montgomery (2005), 'Exonerations in the United States, 1989 through 2003', *Journal of Criminal Law & Criminology*, 95: 523.

*Guardian*/LSE (2011), *Reading the Riots: Investigating England's Summer of Disorder*, London: *Guardian*/LSE.

Guest, S. (2009), 'How to criticize Dworkin's Theory of Law', *Analysis*, 69(2): 1.

Hall, A. (2010), 'Where do the advocates stand when the goalposts are moved?', *International Journal of Evidence & Proof*, 14: 107.

Hamlyn, B., A. Phelps, J. Turtle and G. Sattar (2004), *Are Special Measures Working? Evidence from Surveys of Vulnerable and Intimidated Witnesses*, Home Office Research Study No. 283, Home Office, Research Development and Statistics Directorate.

Harman, H. and J. Griffith (1979), *Justice Deserted: The Subversion of the Jury*, London: National Council for Civil Liberties.

Harper, R. and A. McWhinnie (1983), *The Glasgow Rape Case*, London: Hutchinson.

Harries, R. (1999), *The Cost of Criminal Justice*, Home Office Research Directorate, No. 103.

Harris, J. and S. Grace (1999), *A Question of Evidence? Investigating and*

*Prosecuting Rape in the 1990s*, Home Office Research Study No. 196, London: Home Office.

Hedderman, C. and D. Moxon (1992), *Magistrates' Court or Crown Court? Mode of Trial Decisions and Sentencing*, Home Office Research Study No. 125, London: HMSO.

Heilbroner, D. (1990), *Rough Justice: Days and Nights of a Young D.A.*, New York: Pantheon Books.

Henham, R. (1999), 'Bargain justice or justice denied? Sentence discounts and the criminal process', *Modern Law Review*, 62(4): 515.

Henham, R. (2002), 'Further evidence on the significance of plea in the crown court', *Howard Journal of Criminal Justice*, 41: 151.

Heumann, M. (1975), 'A note on plea bargaining and case pressure', *Law and Society Review*, 9: 515.

Heumann, M. (1978), *Plea Bargaining*, Chicago: University of Chicago Press.

Heydon, J. (2013), 'Threats to judicial independence: the enemy within', *Law Quarterly Review*, 129: 205.

Hilbery, M. (1975), *Duty and Art in Advocacy*, London: Stevens.

Hillyard, P. (1994), 'The politics of criminal justice: the Irish dimension', in M. McConville and L. Bridges (eds), *Criminal Justice in Crisis*, Aldershot, UK and Brookfield, VT, USA: Edward Elgar.

HM Crown Prosecution Service Inspectorate (HMCPSI) (2003), *Thematic Review of Attrition in the Prosecution Process (the Justice Gap)*, London: HMCPSI.

HM Crown Prosecution Service Inspectorate (HMCPSI) (2004), *Violence at Home: A Joint Thematic Inspection of the Investigation and Prosecution of Cases Involving Domestic Violence*, London: HMCPSI.

HM Crown Prosecution Service Inspectorate (HMCPSI) (2007), *Discontinuance (Thematic Review)*, London: HMCPSI.

HM Crown Prosecution Service Inspectorate (HMCPSI) (2012a), *CPS London: Follow-up Report*, London: HMCPSI.

HM Crown Prosecution Service Inspectorate (HMCPSI) (2012b), *CPS Gwent and CPS South Wales: Follow-up Inspection*, March, available at: http://www.hmcpsi.gov.uk/documents/reports/AEI/GWSW/WALS_FU_GWN_SWA_Mar12_rpt.pdf

HM Crown Prosecution Service Inspectorate (HMCPSI) (2012c), *CPS Core Quality Standards Monitoring Scheme: Thematic Review of the CPS Core Quality Standards Monitoring Scheme*, London: HMCPSI.

HM Crown Prosecution Service Inspectorate (HMCPSI) (2012d), *Follow Up Report of the Thematic Review of the Quality of Prosecution Advocacy and Case Presentation*, London: HMCPSI.

HM Inspectorate of Constabulary (HMIC) (2013a), *Stop and Search Powers: Are the Police Using Them Effectively and Fairly?* 9 July.

HM Inspectorate of Constabulary (HMIC) (2013b), *South Yorkshire Police's Response to Child Sexual Exploitation*, 11 November.

HM Inspectorate of Constabulary (HMIC) (2013c), *Crime Recording in Kent: A Report Commissioned by the Police and Crime Commissioner for Kent*, 17 June.

HM Inspectorate of Constabulary and HM Crown Prosecution Service Inspectorate (2011), *A New Approach to Tackling Offending in Communities Needed*, London: Criminal Justice Joint Inspection.

Home Affairs Committee (2013), *Eleventh Report, 2012–2013 on the Independent Police Complaints Commission*, HC 494, 1 February.

Home Office (1963), *Sheffield Police Appeal Inquiry*, Cmnd 2176, London: HMSO.

Home Office (1992), *Costs of the Criminal Justice System 1992*, Vol. 1, London: Home Office.

Home Office (2002), *Justice for All*, Cm 5563, London: Home Office.

Home Office (2004), *Analysis of Ethnic Minority Deaths in Police Custody*, London: HMSO.

Home Office (2011), *An Overview of Recorded Crimes and Arrests Resulting from Disorder Events in August 2011*, October.

Home Office (2012), *Police Powers and Procedures, England and Wales 2010/11: Second Edition (Stop and Searches)*, 19 April.

Hodgson, J. (2005), *French Criminal Justice*, Oxford: Hart Publishing.

Hodgson, J. (2006), 'The Role of the Criminal Defence Lawyer in an Inquisitorial Procedure: Legal and Ethical Constraints', *Legal Ethics*, 9(1): 125.

Hodgson, J. (2010), 'The future of adversarial criminal justice in 21st century Britain', *North Carolina Journal of International Law and Commercial Regulation*, 35: 319.

Hoffman, L. (1964), 'The Judges' Rules', *Lawyer*, 7: 23.

Hohl, K. (2011), 'The role of mass media and police communication in trust in the police: new approaches to the analysis of survey and media data', PhD thesis, LSE, available at: http://etheses.lse.ac.uk/213/

Honess, T., M. Levi and E. Charman (1998), 'Juror competence in processing complex information: implications from a simulation of the Maxwell Trial', *Criminal Law Review*, 763.

Honess, T., M. Levi and E. Charman (2003), 'Juror competence in serious frauds since Roskill: a research-based assessment', *Journal of Financial Crime*, 11(1): 17.

Hood, R. (1992), *Race and Sentencing*, Oxford: Oxford University Press.

Houlden, P. and S. Balkin (1985), 'Quality and cost comparisons of private bar indigent defense systems: contract vs. ordered assigned counsel', *Journal of Criminal Law and Criminology*, 76: 177.

House of Commons (1995), Hansard, *First Scottish Standing Committee*, Col. 556, 4 April.

House of Commons (2005), 'Terrorism and community relations, sixth report of sessions 2004–2005', *Home Affairs Select Committee*, Vol.1, HC 165–1, London: TSO.

House of Commons (2013a), Hansard (Debate), Col. 116, 5 February.

House of Commons (2013b), Hansard (Debate), Col. 523, 27 June.

House of Commons (2013c), Hansard (Debate), Cols 75–77WH, 4 September.

Howitt, D. (1998), *Crime, the Media and the Law*, West Sussex: Wiley.

Hucklesby, A. (1997), 'Remand decision makers', *Criminal Law Review*, 269.

Hughes, E. (1971), *The Sociological Eye*, Chicago: Aldine-Atherton.

Human Rights Watch (2010), *Without Suspicion: Stop and Search Under the Terrorism Act 2000*, London: Human Rights Watch.

Hyde, D. (2010), 'Tax evasion costs the Treasury 15 times more than benefit fraud', *Citywire Money*, available at: http://citywire.co.uk/money/tax-evasion-costs-treasury-15-times-more-than-benefit-fraud/a378274

Hyde, J. (2013), 'Grieve: legal aid cuts hurt, but bar is just too big', *Law Society Gazette*, 30 September.

Independent Police Complaints Commission (IPCC) (2012), *Corruption in the Police Service in England and Wales: Second Report – a report based upon the IPCC's experience from 2008 to 2011*, London: The Stationery Office.

Independent Police Complaints Commission (IPCC) (2013), *Southwark Sapphire Unit's Local Practices for the Reporting and Investigation of Sexual Offences, July 2008–September 2009 – Independent Investigation Learning Report*, February.

Institute of Race Relations (1987), *Policing Against Black People*, London: Institute of Race Relations.

Ip, J. (2013), 'The reform of counterterrorism stop and search after *Gillan v. United Kingdom*', *Human Rights Law Review*, 13(1): 1.

Jackson, J. (1993), 'Trial procedures', in C. Walker and K. Starmer (eds), *Justice in Error*, London: Blackstone Press.

Jackson, J. (1996), 'Judicial responsibility in criminal proceedings', *Current Legal Problems*, 49(1): 59.

Jackson, J. and S. Doran (1995), *Judge Without Jury*, Oxford: Oxford University Press.

James Committee (1975), *The Distribution of Criminal Business between the Crown Court and the Magistrates' Court*, Cmnd. 6323.

Jeremy, D. (2008), 'The prosecutor's rock and hard place', *Criminal Law Review*, 925.

Jones, R. (2009), 'From Orgreave to the City', *Red Pepper*, June.
Judge, Lord (2011), 'Summary justice in and out of court', John Harris Memorial Lecture, available at: http://www.judiciary.gov.uk/media/speeches/2011/lcj-speech-john-harris-memorial-lecture-07072011
Judicial Executive Board (2013), *Response to the Ministry of Justice Transforming Legal Aid Consultation*, June, available at: http://www.judiciary.gov.uk/Resources/JCO/Documents/Consultations/jeb-response-reform-legal-aid-june-2013.pdf
Judiciary of England and Wales (2013), *Response of the Judicial Executive Board to the Government's Consultation Paper CP14/2013, Transforming Legal Aid: Delivering a More Credible and Efficient System*, June.
JUSTICE (1971), *The Unrepresented Defendant in Magistrates' Courts*, London: Stevens & Sons.
Kalsi, S. (2011), 'August riots – the legal aftermath', 3 October, available at: http://www.law.ac.uk/august-riots/
Kee, R. (1986), *Trial and Error*, London: Hamish Hamilton.
Kelly, L., J. Lovett and L. Regan (2005), *Gap or Chasm? Attrition in Reported Rape Cases*, Home Office Research Study No. 293, London: Home Office.
Kemp, V. (2010), *Transforming Legal Aid: Access to Criminal Defence Services*, London: Legal Services Research Centre.
Kennedy, L. (1990), *On My Way to the Club*, London: Fontana.
Kettle, M. and L. Hodges (1982), *Uprising*, London: Pan Books.
King, M. (1971), *Bail or Custody*, London: The Cobden Trust.
King, M. and C. May (1985), *Black Magistrates*, London: Cobden Trust.
Kipnis, K. (1979), 'Plea bargaining: a critic's rejoinder', *Law & Society Review*, 13(2): 555.
Labour Party (2005), *Tackling Crime: Forwards Not Back*, Labour Party, UK.
Lacey, N. (1994), 'Missing the wood ... pragmatism versus theory in the Royal Commission', in M. McConville and L. Bridges (eds), *Criminal Justice in Crisis*, Aldershot, UK and Brookfield, VT, USA: Edward Elgar.
Langer, M. (2005), 'The rise of managerial judging in international criminal law', *American Journal of Comparative Law*, 835.
Law Society (2013), *Response to the Ministry of Justice Transforming Legal Aid Consultation*, June, available at: http://www.lawsociety.org.uk / representation / policy-discussion / transforming-legal-aid-consultation-law-society-response/
Lea, J. and S. Hallsworth (2012), 'Understanding the riots', *Criminal Justice Matters*, 87(1): 30.
Lea, S., U. Lanvers and S. Shaw (2003), 'Attrition in rape cases', *British Journal of Criminology*, 43: 583.
Lefstein, N. (1982), *Criminal Defense Services for the Poor: Methods and*

*Programs for Providing Legal Representation and the Need for Adequate Financing*, Chicago, IL: American Bar Association.

Leigh, L. (2013), 'Cautioning – whatever happened to common sense?', *Criminal Law & Justice*, 177: 269.

Leipond, A. (2005), 'How the pre-trial process contributes to wrongful convictions', *American Criminal Law Review*, 42: 1123.

Leishman, F. and P. Mason (2003), *Policing and the Media: Facts and Fictions*, Cullompton: Willan Publishing.

Leon, H.C. (1970), *The English Judge*, The Hamlyn Lectures, London: Stevens and Sons.

Leverick, F. (2004), 'Tensions and balances, costs and rewards: the sentence discount in Scotland', *Edinburgh Law Review*, 8(3): 360.

Leverick, F. (2006), 'Plea and confession bargaining in Scotland', *Electronic Journal of Comparative Law*, 10(3) December, available at: http://www.ejcl.org/103/art103-8.pdf

Leverick, F. (2012), 'Sentence discounting for guilty pleas: a question of guidelines', *Edinburgh Law Review*, 16(2): 233.

Leveson Report (2012), 'An Inquiry into the Culture, Practice and Ethics of the Press', UK: TSO, 29 November, available at: http://www.officialdocuments.gov.uk/document/hc1213/hc07/0780/0780.asp

Levi, M. (1993), *The Investigation, Prosecution and Trial of Serious Fraud*, Royal Commission on Criminal Justice, Research Study No.14.

Levitt, A. and the Crown Prosecution Service Equality and Diversity Unit (2013), *Joint Report – Charging Perverting the Course of Justice and Wasting Police Time in Cases Involving Allegedly False Rape and Domestic Violence Allegations*, March.

Lewis, P. and R. Evans (2013), *Undercover: The True Story of Britain's Secret Police*, London: Faber and Faber.

Lippke, R. (2011), *The Ethics of Plea Bargaining*, Oxford: Oxford University Press.

Lloyd-Bostock, S. (2007), 'The Jubilee Line jurors: does their experience strengthen the argument for judge-only trial in long and complex fraud cases?', *Criminal Law Review*, 255.

Lord Chancellor's Department (2001), *Code of Conduct for Employees of the Legal Services Commission who Provide Services as Part of the Criminal Defence Service*, London: The Stationery Office.

Lynch, D. (1994), 'The impropriety of plea agreements: a tale of two counties', *Law and Social Inquiry*, 19(1): 115.

Mack, K. and S. Anleu (1997), 'Sentence discount for a guilty plea: time for a new look', *Flinders Journal of Law Reform*, 1: 123.

*Magistrate* (2011), 'Stop delaying justice! A new training programme', 67(9): 6.

Mansfield, M. (2009), *Memoirs of a Radical Lawyer*, London: Bloomsbury Press.
Mark, Sir Robert (1973), *Minority Verdict*, London: BBC Publications.
Martin, R. (2013), 'The recent supergrass controversy: have we learnt from the troubled past?', *Criminal Law Review*, 4: 273.
McBarnet, D. (1978), 'The Fisher Report on the Confait case: four issues', *Modern Law Review*, 41: 455.
McBarnet, D. (1983), *Conviction: Law, the State and the Construction of Justice*, 2nd edn, London: Macmillan.
McCabe, S. and R. Purves (1972), *By-passing the Jury: A Study of Changes of Plea and Directed Acquittals in Higher Courts*, Oxford: Blackwell for the Oxford University Penal Research Unit.
McConville, M. (1992), 'Videotaping interrogations: police behaviour on and off camera', *Criminal Law Review*, 532.
McConville, M. and J. Baldwin (1981), *Courts, Prosecution and Conviction*, London: Oxford University Press.
McConville, M. and L. Bridges (1993a), 'Pleading guilty whilst maintaining innocence', *New Law Journal*, 143: 160.
McConville, M. and L. Bridges (1993b), 'Guilty pleas and the politics of research', *Legal Action*, 9 April.
McConville, M. and C. Mirsky (1993a), 'The disordering of criminal justice', *New Law Journal*, 143: 1446.
McConville, M. and C. Mirsky (1993b), 'To plea or not to plea', *Legal Action*, February.
McConville, M. and C. Mirsky (1995), 'Guilty plea courts: a social disciplinary model of criminal justice', *Social Problems*, 42(2): 216.
McConville, M. and C. Mirsky (2005), *Jury Trials and Plea Bargaining*, Oxford: Hart.
McConville, M. and P. Morrell (1983), 'Recording the interrogation: have the police got it taped?', *Criminal Law Review*, 158.
McConville, M. and E. Pils (eds) (2013), *Comparative Perspectives on Criminal Justice in China*, Cheltenham, UK and Northampton, MA, USA: Edward Elgar.
McConville, M. and D. Shepherd (1992), *Watching Police Watching Communities*, London: Routledge.
McConville, M., J. Hodgson, L. Bridges and A. Pavlovic (1994), *Standing Accused*, Oxford: Clarendon Press.
McConville, M., A. Sanders and R. Leng (1991), *The Case for the Prosecution*, London: Routledge.
McConville, M. et al. (2011), *Criminal Justice in China: An Empirical Inquiry*, Cheltenham, UK and Northampton, MA, USA: Edward Elgar.

McEwan, J. (2011), 'From adversarialism to managerialism: criminal justice in transition', *Legal Studies*, 31(3): 519.
McEwan, J. (2013), 'Truth, efficiency, and cooperation in modern criminal justice', *Current Legal Problems*, 66(1): 203–32.
McEwan, J. and F. Garland (2012), 'Embracing the overriding objective: difficulties and dilemmas in the new criminal climate', *International Journal of Evidence and Proof*, 16(3): 233.
McInnes Report (2004), *Report of the Summary Justice Review Committee: Report to Ministers*, 16 March.
McKenna, Mr Justice (1970), 'Police interrogation', *New Law Journal*, 16 July, 120.
Metropolitan Police Service (2012), *Strategic Review into the Disorders of August 2011 – Final Report*, London.
Mill, J.S. (1861), *On Representative Government*, London: Parker, Son and Bourn.
Miller, J. (2003), *Police Corruption in England and Wales: An Assessment of Current Evidence*, Home Office, Online Report 11/03.
Miller, J., N. Bland and P. Quinton (2000), *The Impact of Stops and Searches on Crime and the Community*, Home Office Research Paper No. 127, London: Home Office.
Ministry of Justice (2005), *The Criminal Procedure Rules and Criminal Practice Directions*, London: Ministry of Justice, available at: http://www.legislation.gov.uk/uksi/2013/1554/contents/made
Ministry of Justice (MoJ) (2011a), *Statistical Bulletin on the Public Disorder of 6th to 9th August 2011*, London: Ministry of Justice.
Ministry of Justice (MoJ) (2011b), *Judicial and Court Statistics 2010, 30 June, 2011 (revised July 2011)*, London: Ministry of Justice.
Ministry of Justice (MoJ) (2012a), *Statistical Bulletin on the Public Disorder of 6th to 9th August 2011 – February 2012 Update*, London: Ministry of Justice.
Ministry of Justice (MoJ) (2012b), *Judicial and Court Statistics 2011*, 28 June, London: Ministry of Justice.
Ministry of Justice (MoJ) (2012c), *Swift and Sure Justice: The Government's Plans for Reform of the Criminal Justice System*, Cm8388, 12 July, London: HMSO.
Ministry of Justice (MoJ) (2013a), *Criminal Justice Statistics, Quarterly Update to December 2012*, 30 May, London: Ministry of Justice.
Ministry of Justice (MoJ) (2013b), *Consultation Paper CP 14/2013. Transforming Legal Aid: Delivering a More Credible and Efficient System*, 9 April, London: Ministry of Justice.
Ministry of Justice (MoJ) (2013c), *Statistics on Race and the Criminal Justice System 2012*, November, London: Ministry of Justice.

Ministry of Justice (MoJ) (2013d), *Annual Reports and Accounts 2012–13*, 25 June, London: Ministry of Justice.

Ministry of Justice (MoJ) (2013e), *Her Majesty's Court and Tribunal Service Statistics*, September, London: Ministry of Justice.

Mitchell, B. (2011), 'Sentencing riot-related offending: considering Blackshaw and others', *Archbold Review*, 10: 4.

Moody, S. and J. Tombs (1982), *Prosecution in the Public Interest*, Edinburgh: Scottish Academic Press.

Morton, J. (1977), 'Trial by blacklist', *New Law Journal*, 127: 280.

Morton, J. (1993), *Bent Coppers*, London: Warner Books.

Moss, N. (2013), *Every Case, A Managed Case: Using The Criminal Procedure Rules Speech to London CPS*, 5 March, available at: http://www.judiciary.gov.uk/Resources/JCO/Documents/Speeches/nicholas-moss-speech-cps-london-050313.pdf

Moxon, D. (1988), *Sentencing Practice in the Crown Court*, Home Office Research Study No. 103, London: HMSO.

Mulcahy, A. (1994), 'The justifications of "Justice"', *British Journal of Criminology*, 34: 411.

Mullin, C. (1986), *Error of Judgement: The Truth about the Birmingham Bombings*, London: Chatto & Windus.

Murray, K. (2014), 'Stop and search in Scotland: an evaluation of police practice', The Scottish Centre for Crime & Justice Research, University of Edinburgh, January.

Nardulli, P. (1979), 'The caseload controversy and the study of criminal courts', *Criminal Law & Criminology*, 70: 89.

National Audit Office (2009), *The Procurement of Criminal Legal Aid in England and Wales by the Legal Services Commission*, 27 November, London: The Stationery Office.

National Audit Office (1992), *The Ministry of Justice's Language Service Contract, Memorandum*, 10 September 1992, available at: http://www.nao.org.uk/

Naughton, M. (ed.) (2010), *The Criminal Cases Review Commission: Hope for the Innocent?*, Basingstoke: Palgrave.

Neuberger, Lord (2013), 'Justice in an Age of Austerity', JUSTICE: Tom Sargant Memorial Lecture 2013, 15 October, available at: http://www.justice.org.uk/data/files/resources/357/Neuberger-2013-lecture.pdf

Newburn, T., M. Shiner and S. Hayman (1994), 'Race, crime and injustice: strip search and the treatment of suspects in police custody', *British Journal of Criminology*, 34: 677.

*New Law Journal* (1970), 'Comment. Plea bargaining – conflicts of interest', *New Law Journal*, 19 March.

*New Law Journal* (1970), 'Guilty pleas: counsel's role', *New Law Journal*, 30 April.
*New Law Journal* (1975), 'Right to counsel', *New Law Journal*, 13 February.
Newman, D. (2013), *Legal Aid Lawyers and the Quest for Justice*, Oxford: Hart Publishing.
Nicholson, D. (2013), 'Taking epistemology seriously: "truth, reason and justice" revisited', *International Journal of Evidence & Proof*, 17(1): 1.
Ormerod, D. (2012), *Blackstone's Criminal Practice*, 22nd edn, 2011, Oxford: Oxford University Press.
Orwell, G. (1945), 'Notes about nationalism', first published, London: Polemic.
Oxford Economics (2014), *Forecasting Criminal Legal Aid Expenditure*, January, Oxford, UK.
Padfield, N. (2013), 'Transforming legal aid', *Archbold Review*, 5: 5.
Parnas, R.I. and R.J. Atkins (1978), 'The elimination of plea bargaining: a proposal', *Criminal Law Bulletin*, 14: 101.
Pattenden, R. and L. Skinns (2010), 'Choice, privacy and publicly-funded legal advice at police stations', *Modern Law Review*, 73: 349.
Percy-Smith, J. and P. Hillyard (1985), 'Miners in the arms of the law: a statistical analysis', *Journal of Law and Society*, 12(3): 345.
Phillips, C. and D. Brown (1998), *Entry into the Criminal Justice System: A Survey of Police Arrests and their Outcomes*, Home Office Research Study No. 185, London: Home Office Research and Statistics Directorate.
Poland, Sir H.B. (1898), *Short History of the Criminal Evidence Act*, Mr. Baugh Allen's edition of the Act [originally cited in Rogers (1899)].
Ponting, C. (1987), 'R v Ponting', *Journal of Law and Society*, 14(3): 366.
Rauxloh, R. (2012), *Plea Bargaining in National and International Law*, Abingdon: Routledge.
Rawls, J. (1972), *A Theory of Justice*, Cambridge: Harvard University Press.
Reiner, R. (1985), *The Politics of the Police*, Brighton: Wheatsheaf Books.
Rhodes, D. (2013), 'Life in Crime: "Degrees of separation"', *Solicitor's Journal*, 157(12), 26 March.
Richards, P., E. Richards, C. Devon, S. Morris and A. Mellows-Facer (2011a), *Summary Justice Reform: Evaluation of Fiscal Work Order Pilots*, Scottish Government Social Research, available at: http://www.scotland.gov.uk/Publications/2011/01/24140850/0
Richards, P., E. Richards, C. Devon, S. Morris and A. Mellows-Facer (2011b), *Summary Justice Reform: Evaluation of Direct Measures*, Scottish Government Social Research, Morris Richards Ltd.

Richardson, J. (2011), 'A "just" outcome: losing sight of the purpose of criminal procedure', *Journal of Commonwealth Criminal Law*, 105.

Richardson, J. (2013), 'Is the criminal appeal system fit for purpose?', *Criminal Law Week*, Issue 19, 20 May.

Risinger, D. (2007), 'Innocents convicted: an empirically justified factual wrongful conviction rate', *Journal of Criminal Law & Criminology*, 97: 761.

Roberts, A. (2012), 'Case comment: Nunn v Chief Constable of Suffolk Constabulary: evidence – prosecution evidence – disclosure', *Criminal Law Review*, 12: 968.

Roberts, D. (1993), 'Questioning the suspect: the solicitor's role', *Criminal Law Review*, 368.

Roberts, J. (2012), 'Points of departure: reflections on sentencing outside the definitive guidelines ranges', *Criminal Law Review*, 6: 439.

Robertson, G. (2013), *Stephen Ward Was Innocent OK: The Case for Overturning His Conviction*, London: Biteback Publishing.

Robson, G. (2012), 'Swift and sure justice? Here we go again', *Criminal Law & Justice Weekly*, 7 September.

Roche, M. (1992), *Rethinking Citizenship: Welfare, Ideology and Change in Modern Society*, Cambridge: Polity Press.

Rogers, S. (1899), 'The ethics of advocacy', *Law Quarterly Review*, 15: 259.

Romily, S. (1810), *Observations on the Criminal Law of England*, Note D.

Rose, G. (1967), *Special Statistical Survey, Table 22, in Royal Commission on Assizes and Quarter Sessions, 1966–1969*, (1971) Cmnd. 4153.

Rose, G. (1971), *Royal Commission on Assizes and Quarter Sessions 1966–69. Special Statistical Survey*, London: HMSO.

Roskill, Lord (1986), *Fraud Trials Committee*, London: HMSO.

Rowntree, S. (1901), *Poverty: A Study in Town Life*, London: Macmillan.

Royal Commission on Criminal Justice (RCCJ) (1993), *Report*, Cm 2263, London: HMSO.

Royal Commission on Criminal Procedure (RCCP) (1981), *Report*, Cmnd. 8092, London: HMSO.

Royal Commission on Police Powers and Procedure (RCPPP) (1929), *Report*, Cmd. 3297.

Rozenberg, J. (2014), Lord Chief Justice elps politicians grasp courts' 'hot potato',' *The Guardian*, 4 March, 2014).

Rumney, P. (2006), 'False allegations of rape', *Cambridge Law Journal*, 65(1): 12.

Sanders, A. (1979), 'Guilt, innocence and jury acquittals', *Howard Journal of Criminal Justice*, 24: 76.

Sanders, A. and R. Young (2007), *Criminal Justice*, 3rd edn, Oxford: Oxford University Press.

Sanders, A. and R. Young with M. Burton (2010), *Criminal Justice*, 4th edn, Oxford: Oxford University Press.
Sanders, A., L. Bridges, A. Mulvaney and G. Crozier (1989), *Advice and Assistance at Police Stations and the 24-Hour Duty Solicitor Scheme*, London: Lord Chancellor's Department.
Sandham, J. (1983), 'Operation Major: a backward glance', *Probation Journal*, 30: 29.
Scanlon, T.M. (1999), *What We Owe to Each Other*, Cambridge MA: Belknap Press.
Scarman, Lord (1981), *The Brixton Disorders, 10–12th April*, London: HMSO.
Scheck, B., P. Neufeld and J. Dwyer (2000), *Actual Innocence: Five Days to Execution and Other Dispatches from the Wrongly Convicted*, New York: Doubleday.
Schulhofer, S. (1986), 'Effective assistance on the assembly line', *New York University Review of Law and Social Change*, 14: 137.
Schulhofer, S. (1992), 'Plea bargaining as disaster', *Yale Law Journal*, 101: 1979.
Scott, R. and W. Stuntz (1992), 'Plea bargaining as contract', *Yale Law Journal*, 101: 1909.
Scottish Executive (2003), *Modernising Justice in Scotland: The Reform of the High Court of Justiciary*, Edinburgh: Scottish Government.
Scottish Office (1993), *Improving the Delivery of Justice in Scotland: 1993 Review of Criminal Evidence and Procedure*, Great Britain: Scottish Office.
Scottish Office (1994), *Firm and Fair*, CM 2600, Edinburgh: HMSO.
Scraton, P. (1985), *The State of the Police*, London: Pluto Press.
Scraton, P. (2012), *The Report of the Hillsborough Independent Panel*, HC 581, London: The Stationery Office.
Scraton, P. (2013), 'The legacy of Hillsborough: liberating truth, challenging power', *Race & Class*, 55(2): 1.
Seabrook, R. (1992), *The Efficient Disposal of Business in the Crown Court*, London: The General Council of the Bar.
Sedley, S. (2011), *Ashes and Sparks: Essays on Law and Justice*, Cambridge: Cambridge University Press.
Seifman, R. (1980), 'Plea bargaining in England', in W. McDonald and J. Cramer (eds), *Plea Bargaining*, Lexington Books: D.C. Heath.
Sentencing Guidelines Council (2007), *Reduction in Sentence for a Guilty Plea: Definitive Guideline* (Sentencing Guidelines Secretariat, revised July).
Shapiro, D. (1984), 'Should a guilty plea have preclusive effect?', *Iowa Law Review*, 70: 27.

Shattuck, P. (1974), 'Law as politics', *Comparative Politics*, 7(1) (October): 127.

Shead, C. (2013), 'The decision in Murray v HM Advocate', *Scottish Criminal Law*, February: 93.

Shearing, C. (1981), 'Subterranean processes in the maintenance of power: an examination of the mechanisms coordinating police action', *Canadian Review of Sociology and Anthropology*, 18(3): 283.

Sheskin, A. (1981), 'Trial courts on trial: examining dominant assumptions', in J.A. Cramer (ed.), *Courts and Judges*, Beverly Hills, CA: Sage Publications.

Shiner, M. (2012), *Report on the Use of Section 60 of the Criminal Justice and Public Order Act 1994 by the Police*, February, available at: http://www.stop-watch.org/uploads/documents/Shiner_expertwitnessstatement_s60.pdf

Singh, D., S. Marcus, H. Rabbatts and M. Sherlock (2012), *After the Riots – the Final Report of the Riots Communities and Victims Panel*, March.

Skinns, L. (2009), '"I'm a detainee; get me out of here": predictors of access to custodial legal advice in public and privatized police custody areas in England and Wales', *British Journal of Criminology*, 49(3): 399.

Skinns, L. (2011), 'The right to legal advice in the police station: past, present and Future', *Criminal Law Review*, 19.

Slater, E. (2012), 'Scrutinising government – a case to answer: The return of the Supergrass', 7 October, The Bureau of Investigative Journalism, available at: http://www.thebureauinvestigates.com/2012/10/07/the-return-of-the-supergrass/

Smith, D. (1983), *Police and People in London: A Survey of Police Officers*, London: Policy Studies Institute.

Smith, P. and P. Thomas (1985), *Striking Back*, Cardiff: Welsh Campaign for Civil and Political Liberties.

Smith, R. (2011), 'Legal aid in England and Wales: entering the endgame', *ILAG Newsletter*, May, available at: http://www.ilagnet.org/newsletterstories.php?id=37

Smith, T. (2013a), 'The "quiet revolution" in criminal defence: how the zealous advocate slipped into the shadow', *International Journal of the Legal Profession*, 20(1): 111.

Smith, T. (2013b), 'Trust, choice and money: why the legal aid reform "u-turn" is essential for effective criminal defence', *Criminal Law Review*, 11: 906.

Spector, M. and J. Kitsuse (2001), *Constructing Social Problems*, New Brunswick, NJ: Transaction Publishers.

Stedman Jones, G. (1971), *Outcast London*, Oxford: Clarendon Press.

Stewart Committee Report (1983), *Keeping Offenders Out of Court: Further Alternatives to Prosecution*, 2nd Report, Cmnd. 8958, HMSO.

Steyn, Lord (1997), 'The Weakest and Least Dangerous Department of Government', *Public Law*, 84.

Storch, R. (1976), 'The policeman as domestic missionary: urban discipline and popular culture in northern England 1850–1880', *Journal of Social History*, IX: 4.

Tata, C. (2007), 'In the interests of commerce or clients? Legal aid, supply, demand, and ethical indeterminacy in criminal defence work', *Journal of Law and Society*, 34(4): 489.

Tata, C. (2010), 'Sentencing and penal decision-making: is Scotland losing its distinctive character?', in H. Croall, G. Mooney and M. Monro (eds), *Criminal Justice in Scotland*, Oxford: Willan Publishing.

Tata, C. and F. Stephen (2006), '"Swings and roundabouts": do changes to the structure of legal aid make a real difference to criminal case outcomes?', *Criminal Law Review*, 46: 722.

Thomas, G.C. (2010), 'Two windows into innocence', *Ohio State Journal of Criminal Law*, 7: 575.

Thomas, P.A. (1978), 'Plea bargaining in England', *The Journal of Criminal Law & Criminology*, 69(2): 170.

Thomas, P.A. (1982), 'Royal Commissions', *Statute Law Review*, Spring: 40.

Thomas, P.A. and G. Mungham (1976), *A Report on the Duty Solicitor Scheme Operating in the Cardiff Magistrates' Court*, Cardiff: University College.

Thomas, P.A. and G. Mungham (1977), 'Duty solicitor schemes: in whose interest?' *New Law Journal*, 127: 180.

Thomas, R.M. (1986), 'The British Official Secrets Acts 1911–1939 and the Ponting case', *Criminal Law Review*, 491.

Thomas of Cwmgiedd, Lord (2014), 'Reshaping Justice', Speech delivered to JUSTICE, 3 March, available at: http://www.judiciary.gov.uk/Resources/JCO/Documents/Speeches/lcj-speech-reshaping-justice.pdf

Thompson, E.P. (1971), 'The moral economy of the English crowd in the eighteenth century', *Past and Present*, 50(1): 76.

Thomson, D. (2004), 'Discount of sentencing following a guilty plea', *Scots Law Times*, 1.

Tonry, M. (2004), *Punishment and Politics*, Cullompton: Willan.

Travers, M. (1997a), 'Preaching to the converted? Improving the persuasiveness of criminal justice research', *British Journal of Criminology*, 37: 359.

Travers, M. (1997b), *The Reality of Law: Work and Talk in a Firm of Criminal Lawyers*, Aldershot: Ashgate.

Vennard, J. (1982), *Contested Trials in Magistrates' Courts*, Home Office Research Study No. 71, London: HMSO.

Verdun-Jones, S. and A. Hatch (1988), *Plea Bargaining and Sentence Guidelines*, Ottawa: Department of Justice Canada.

Von Hirsch, A., A. Bottoms, E. Burney and P-O. Wikstrom (1999), *Criminal Deterrence and Sentence Severity: An Analysis of Recent Research*, Oxford: Hart Publishing.

Walchover, D. (1989), 'Should judges sum up on the facts?', *Criminal Law Review*, 781.

Walker, C. (2002), 'Miscarriages of justice and the correction of error', in M. McConville and G. Wilson (eds), *The Handbook of the Criminal Justice Process*, Oxford: Oxford University Press.

Walker, C. (2006), 'Case comment: *R. (on the application of Gillan) v Commissioner of Police of the Metropolis* [2006] UKHL 12; [2006] 2 A.C. 307 (HL)', *Criminal Law Review*, August: 751.

Ward, T. (1986), *Death and Disorder*, London: Pluto Press.

White, R. (2008), 'Out of court and out of sight', *Edinburgh Law Review*, 12(3): 481.

Whitton, E. (1988), *The Cartel: Lawyers and their Nine Magic Tricks*, Australia: E & N Whitton.

Wigmore, J.H. (1940), *Treatise on the Anglo-American System of Evidence in Trials at Common Law*, 3rd edn, Boston: Little, Brown.

Williams, C. (2012), 'Britain's police forces: forever removed from democratic control?', available at: http://www.historyandpolicy.org/papers/policy-paper-16.html

Williams, G. (1960), 'Questioning by the police: some practical considerations', *Criminal Law Review*, 325.

Williams, G. (1961), 'England', *Journal of Criminal Law & Criminology*, 52: 50.

Williams, G. (2009), *Shafted: The Media, The Miners' Strike and the Aftermath*, London: Campaign for Press & Broadcasting Freedom.

Wilmore, G. (1850), *Is Trial By Jury Worth Keeping?*, 2nd edn, London

Woofinden, B. (1987), *Miscarriages of Justice*, London: Coronet Books.

Worrall, A. (1990), *Offending Women*, London: Routledge.

Wright, R. and M. Miller (2002), 'The screening/bargaining tradeoff', *Stanford Law Review*, 55: 29.

Young, J. (2011), 'Ours was a thankless task', *Law Society Gazette*, 3 November.

Young, R. (2008), 'Street policing after PACE: The drift to summary justice', in E. Cape and R. Young (eds), *Regulating Policing: The Police and Criminal Evidence Act 1984 Past, Present and Future*, Oxford: Hart Publishing.

Young, R. and D. Wall (1996), 'Criminal Justice, Legal Aid and the Defence of Liberty', in R. Young and D. Wall (eds), *Access to Criminal Justice*, London: Blackstone Press Ltd.
Zander, M. (1969), 'Unrepresented defendants in the criminal courts', *Criminal Law Review*, 632.
Zander, M. (1971a), 'Unrepresented defendants in magistrates' courts', *New Law Journal*, 122: 1042.
Zander, M. (1971b), 'A study of bail/custody decisions in London magistrates' courts', *Criminal Law Review*, 191.
Zander, M. (1972a), 'Unrepresented defendants in magistrates' courts, 1972', *New Law Journal*, 1041.
Zander, M. (1972b), 'Access to a solicitor in the police station', *Criminal Law Review*, 342.
Zander, M. (1974), 'Are too many professional criminals avoiding conviction? A study in Britain's two busiest courts', *Modern Law Review*, 87: 28.
Zander, M. (1978), 'The right to silence in the police station and the caution', in P. Glazebrook (ed.), *Re-shaping the Criminal Law*, London: Stevens.
Zander, M. (1991), 'What the annual statistics tell us about pleas and acquittals', *Criminal Law Review*, 252.
Zander, M. (2001), *Lord Justice Auld's Review of the Criminal Courts: A Response*, available at: http://www.lse.ac.uk/collections/law/staff%20publications%20full%20text/zander/auld_response_web.pdf
Zander, M. (2009), 'Zander on Woolf', *New Law Journal*, 13 March.
Zander, M. and P. Henderson (1993), *Crown Court Study*, Research Study No.19, The Royal Commission on Criminal Justice, London: HMSO.

## NEWS AND NEWSPAPER ARTICLES

Ahmed, K. (2000), 'Molester walks free', *The Observer*, 22 October.
Airs, T. (2012), 'Judge slams "blunders" in baby assault case', *Banbury Cake*, 9 April, available at: http://www.banburycake.co.uk/news/9638668. Judge_slams___blunders___in_baby_assault_case/
*BBC News* (2009), '[W]e accept that the wrong decision was made not to charge Mr Mannan at an earlier stage', 5 March.
*BBC News* (2010), 'CPS apologises to woman over assault case collapse', 7 October.
*BBC News* (2011a), 'Private detective axe murder case collapses 24 years on', 11 March.
*BBC News* (2011b), 'Ratcliffe power station protestors cleared on appeal', 19 July.

*BBC News* (2011c), 'Riot sentence "feeding frenzy" claims anger magistrates', 29 August.

*BBC News* (2011d), 'Police chiefs in misconduct probe over Kevin Nunes murder', 23 December.

*BBC News* (2012a), 'Nine men cleared of murdering UDA man Tommy English', 22 February.

*BBC News* (2012b), 'Met race claim victims "made to suffer," says retiring officer', 9 May.

*BBC News* (2012c), 'Lynette White: fresh concerns raised over investigation', 13 August.

*BBC News* (2012d), 'Mark Haddock UVF supergrass trial cost taxpayers £11.5m', 11 October.

*BBC News* (2012e), 'Attorney general "cannot review" GBH sentence', 20 January.

*BBC News* (2012f), 'Sex offenders in Yorkshire given police cautions', 18 May.

*BBC News* (2012g), 'Serco chief executive stands down after scandal', 25 October.

*BBC News* (2012h), 'David Leggatt jailed for rape and sex assaults on girls in Fife', 19 December.

*BBC News* (2013a), 'Police chief Dal Babu criticizes ethnic recruitment', 4 February.

*BBC News* (2013b), 'Timeline: Daniel Morgan axe murder', 21 May.

*BBC News* (2013c), 'Police corruption: criminals "give officers steroids"', 23 January.

*BBC News* (2013d), 'Undercover police "used dead children's identities"', 3 February.

*BBC News* (2013e), 'Colchester General Hospital: police probe cancer treatment', 5 November.

*BBC News* (2013f), 'Lord Neuberger, UK's most senior judge, voices legal aid fears', 5 March.

*BBC News* (2013g), 'Cleveland Police deputy chief constable Derek Bonnard sacked', 25 March.

*BBC News* (2013h), 'Former police officer admits selling stories to Sun', 26 April.

*BBC News* (2013i), 'Daniel Morgan murder: inquiry to examine "police corruption"', 10 May.

*BBC News* (2013j), 'Sir Norman Bettison smear claim shocks Lawrence witness', 5 July.

*BBC News* (2013k), 'Angela England jailed over Conwy false rape allegation', 10 August.

*BBC News* (2013l), 'Benefit fraud could lead to 10-year jail terms, says DPP', 16 September.
*BBC News* (2013m), 'Courts failing child sex abuse victims, says NSPCC', 5 October.
*BBC News* (2013n), 'Stuart Lawrence race complaint against Met upheld', 12 October.
*BBC News* (2013o), 'Rape case referrals to CPS reach five-year low', 27 October.
*BBC News* (2013p), 'Crime victims to get voice in court under new code', 29 October.
*BBC News* (2013q), 'Orgreave miners strike handling referred to IPCC', 16 November.
*BBC News* (2013r), 'G4S £24.1m tagging offer rejected by ministers', 19 November.
*BBC News* (2013s), 'Police fix crime statistics to meet targets, MPs told', 19 November.
*BBC News* (2013t), 'Essex policewoman jailed for "rape" lie', 6 December.
*BBC News* (2014), 'Policing "damaged" after Stephen Lawrence report', 6 March.
Berlins, M. (1971a), 'Rules now helping guilty will soon go', *The Times*, 8 April.
Berlins, M. (1971b), 'Call to ease police questioning methods', *The Times*, 17 July.
Bowcott, O. (2013a), 'Legal aid cuts putting huge fraud trial at risk', *The Guardian*, 15 November.
Bowcott, O. (2013b), 'Criminal barristers announce half-day refusal to work in legal aid protest', *The Guardian*, 3 December.
Bowcott, O. (2013c), 'Solicitors to join walkout over MoJ plans to cut legal aid fees by up to 30%', *The Guardian*, 1 December.
Bowcott, O. (2013d), 'Critics of legal aid cuts force Law Society vote', *The Guardian*, 19 November.
Bowcott, O. (2013e), 'Lawyers to earn higher legal aid fees for early guilty pleas', *The Guardian*, 1 November.
Bowcott, O. (2014), 'Declining crime rates will "save £80m a year in legal aid"', *The Guardian*, 13 January.
Bowcott, O. and S. Bates (2011), 'Riots: magistrates advised to "disregard normal sentencing"', *The Guardian*, 15 August.
Bowcott, O., P. Walker and L. O'Carroll (2014), 'Courts close across England and Wales as lawyers protest at legal aid cuts', *The Guardian*, 6 January.
Brown, C. (1993), 'Howard seeks to placate "angry majority": Home

Secretary tells party that balance in criminal justice system will be tilted towards public', *The Independent*, 7 October.

Burrell, I. and J. Benetto (1999), 'Police unit to blame for "dozens more injustices"', *The Independent*, 1 November.

Carrell, S. (2014), 'Police stop and search rates in Scotland four times higher than in England', *The Guardian*, 17 January.

Clarke, K. (2011), 'Punish the feral rioters but address our social deficit too', *The Guardian*, 5 September.

Conn, D. (2012), 'Hillsborough investigation should be extended to Orgreave, says NUM leader', *The Guardian*, 21 October.

Davies, C. (1970), 'The innocent who plead guilty', *Law Guardian*, March, pp. 9–15.

Dodd, V. (2011), 'Asian people 42 times more likely to be held under terror law', *The Guardian*, 23 May.

Dodd, V. (2012), 'Police marksman was "absolutely certain" Mark Duggan was holding gun"', *The Guardian*, 26 September.

Dodd, V. (2013a), 'Minorities stopped disproportionally in decade after Macpherson report', *The Guardian*, 22 April.

Dodd, V. (2013b), 'Former judge to examine role of police corruption in murder investigation', *The Guardian*, 10 May.

Duffin, C. (2013), 'Woman who made a string of false rape allegations is jailed', *The Telegraph*, 9 July.

Dworkin, R. (2006), 'It is absurd to calculate human rights according to a cost-benefit analysis', *The Guardian*, 24 May.

Dyer, C. (2000), 'Making a pact with the devil', *The Guardian*, 30 October.

*Express & Star* (2009), 'Judge hits out over handling of raid case', 8 May.

Foley, C. (2009), 'Police violence and death: an old story', *The Guardian*, 26 April.

Gibb, F. (2005), 'Courts to reduce time-wasting', *The Times*, 5 April.

Gilligan, A. (2012), 'Have the men in blue crossed the line?', *The Telegraph*, 21 December.

Grice, A. and P. Peachey (2012), 'Lawrence murder: police "corruption" will be investigated', *The Independent*, 10 March.

Halliday, J. (2014), 'Plebgate row: police officer pleads guilty', *The Guardian*, 10 January.

Halpin, T. (1994), 'Judge outraged by CPS plea-bargain', *Daily Mail*, 23 June.

Harper, T. (2014a), 'Revealed: how gangs used the Freemasons to corrupt police', *The Independent*, 13 January.

Harper, T. (2014b), 'The corruption of Britain: UK's key institutions infiltrated by criminals', *The Independent*, 10 January.

Harper, T. (2014c), 'Scotland Yard's rotten core: police failed to address Met's "endemic corruption"', *The Independent*, 10 January.

*Hexham Courant* (2008), 'Judge criticizes knife case charge', 28 July.
Higham, N. (2014), 'Cabinet papers reveal "secret coal pits closure plan"', *BBC News*, 3 January.
Howard, M. (1993), *The Daily Telegraph*, 7 October.
Hunter, N. (2013), 'Soldier tells how false rape claims ruined his life', *The Northern Echo*, 24 June.
Jennings, A. and P. Lashmar (1990), 'The wall of silence that refuses to fall', *The Guardian*, 13 August.
Kamal, A. (2000), 'Move to ban plea bargains after molester walks free', *The Observer*, 22 October.
Kennedy, H. (2014), 'The David Miranda judgement has chilling implications for press freedom, race relations and basic justice', *The Guardian*, 19 February.
King, M. (2011), 'Crackdown on tax evasion leads to rise in criminal convictions', *The Guardian*, 27 August.
Lakhani, N. (2012), 'Night the row about riot sentencing was reignited', *The Independent*, 16 June.
*Law Society Gazette* (1970), Comment, March.
Leake, C., M. Delgado and G. Arbuthnott (2010), 'Police have shot dead 33 people since 1995 – only two marksmen have ever been named', *Mail Online*, 26 September.
Lewis, P. (2010), 'Blair Peach killed by police at 1979 protest, Met report finds', *The Guardian*, 27 April.
Lissaman, C. (2011), 'Birmingham Six Release Remembered', *BBC News*, 14 March.
*Liverpool Echo* (2012), 'Judge blasts CPS for "undercharging" thug who smashed glass over drinker's head in Southport pub', 22 August.
MacPherson, H. (1970), 'Is it backroom British justice?', *The Guardian*, 24 February.
*Mail Online* (2010), 'Police killed Blair Peach during riot three decades ago then launched a cover-up', 28 April.
*Mail Online* (2012), 'Eleven Met firearms officers deny collusion after admitting writing their statements together in the same room after Mark Duggan shooting', 28 September.
*Mancunian Matters* (2012), 'Rochdale child sex ring: Crown Prosecution Service apologises to teenage sex victim for "not taking her seriously"', 9 May.
McLagan, G. (2004), 'The last old-style fit-up?', *The Guardian*, 2 November.
Mullins, A. (2000), 'Elite police squad are jailed for drug deals', *The Independent*, 5 August.
Narain, J. (2011), 'Judge attacks "absurd" deal that saved serial thief from 4 years' jail', *Mail Online*, 28 April.

*News & Star* (2011), 'Carlisle judge criticizes CPS over danger driver charge', 9 July.
*News & Star* (2012), 'Cumbrian man jailed for brutal attack on his own mum', 5 May.
*News of the World* (1984), 'Godfather Scargill's mafia mob', 7 October.
Norton-Taylor, R. (2000), 'Pat Pottle', *The Guardian*, 3 October.
Owers, A. (2014), 'Police co-operation lacking in Mark Duggan probe by IPCC', *The Guardian* (Letters), 14 January.
Payne, T. (2014), 'Brothel-running, child abuse images, and selling firearms among nearly 200 crimes committed by police in last three years', *The Independent*, 16 January.
Peachey, P. (2013), 'Collapse of Britain's biggest police corruption trial: "No misconduct involved" in Cardiff Three fit-up case', *The Independent*, 16 July.
Peirce, G. (2011), 'The Birmingham Six', *The Guardian*, 12 March.
Porter, H. (2013), 'Police corruption is now so rife that radical reform is the only answer', *Observer*, 20 October.
Rawstorne, T. (2003), '£1.7m crook walks free after plea-bargain deal', *The Daily Mail*, 24 April.
Rogers, S. (2012), 'Homelessness jumps by 14% in a year', *The Guardian*, 8 March.
Rozenberg, J. (2000), 'Plea bargaining ban angers trial judge', *The Telegraph*, 21 November.
Rozenberg, J. (2012), 'Chris Grayling, Justice Secretary: non-lawyer and "on the up" politician', *The Guardian*, 4 September.
Rozenberg, J. (2014), 'Lord Chief Justice helps politicians grasp courts' "hot potato"', *The Guardian*, 4 March.
Ryder, M. (2014), 'Why so many find the Mark Duggan verdict hard to accept', *The Observer*, 19 January.
*Scots Law Times* (1980), 15 February.
Shaw, D. (2013a), 'Police chief Dal Babu criticises ethnic recruitment', *BBC News*, 4 February.
Shaw, D. (2013b), 'Lawrence friend Dwayne Brooks "bugged by police"', *BBC News*, 25 June.
Slater, E. (2012), 'Special report: the return of the supergrass', *The Independent*, 8 October.
Syal, R. (2013), 'Britain's £35bn tax gap is "tip of iceberg", says Margaret Hodge', *The Guardian*, 28 October.
*The Daily Mail* (1970a), 'MPs protest at "rigged trials"', 23 February.
*The Daily Mail* (1970b), 'The case of Stephen Carver', 13 April.
*The Daily Mail* (1970c), 'The case of Ronald Price', 13 April.
*The Daily Mail* (1970d), 'Are innocent persuaded to plead guilty?', 13 April.

*The Daily Mail* (1970e), 'Lawyers to probe plead-guilty court deals', 14 April.

*The Daily Telegraph* (1970), 'When a judge makes a deal with a barrister', 2 April.

*The Daily Telegraph* (2010), 'Criminals escape justice due to CPS flaws, says judge', 10 March.

*The Guardian* (1969), '"Plea bargains" on the way?', 14 October.

*The Guardian* (2000), 'DPP inquiry into collapse of drugs case', 5 November.

*The Guardian* (2010), 'DPP apologises to woman failed by courts after sexual assault', 20 September.

*The Guardian* (2012), 'Police forces confess 944 officers have a criminal record', 2 January.

*The Guardian* (2013a), 'Welfare fraud and error: how much is the UK losing?', 13 May.

*The Guardian* (2013b), 'MoJ's misleading evidence on the cost of the legal system', 3 October.

*The Guardian* (2013c), 'Barristers threaten strike action over cuts to legal aid', 16 November.

*The Guardian* (2013d), 'PlebGate: police, camera, action', 27 November.

*The Independent* (2000), 'Elite police squad are jailed for drug deals', 5 August.

*The Independent* (2013), 'Five police forces investigated over alleged Stephen Lawrence smear campaign', 6 July.

*The London Gazette* (1990), 'State intelligence', 22 February.

*The Observer* (2012), 'Justice must be seen to be done in South Wales police scandal', 28 January.

*The Sun* (1984), 'Scargill's real aim is war', 5 April.

*This is Cornwall* (2009), 'Judge blasts CPS over savage gang attack case', 24 July.

Tomlinson, S. (2013), 'Britain's newest "underworld king" unmasked after he loses libel claim against Sunday newspaper that labelled him violent and dangerous', *Mail Online*, 5 July.

Townsend, M. (2012), 'Criminal records of striking miners "should be erased"', *The Observer*, 1 December.

Tyler, R. (1970), 'Lord Parker bans court deals', *The Daily Mail*, 25 April.

*Wales Online* (2011), 'Judge attacks CPS over sentence for wife beater', 13 June.

*Wales Online* (2012), 'CPS issues apology after collapse of assault trial', 12 April.

Walker, P. and V. Dodd (2012), 'Cleveland police chief sacked for "shameful" misconduct', *The Guardian*, 5 October.

*Western Telegraph* (2010), 'Judge slams Haverford magistrates for "shambolic" case', 26 May.
White, C. (1973), 'I pleaded guilty after court "deal"', *The Daily Mail*, 13 August.
Young, H. (1992), 'In tune with the times', *Guardian Weekly*, 2 August.

## TELEVISION PROGRAMMES

BBC Television, *Braden's Week*, 21 February 1970.
BBC Television, *Police* (Producer: Roger Graef), 1982.
BBC Television, *Police: Operation Carter: A Different World* (Producer: Roger Graef), 1982.

## WEBSITES

CRISIS website, available at: http://www.crisis.org.uk/
'Insurance Fraud Bureau and City of London case collapses', 5 December, 2011, available at: http://www.cisionwire.com/rms/r/insurance-fraud-bureau-and-city-of-london-case-collapses,c9196130
'Prosecutors criticized for not levelling a more serious charge in racism case', 24 March, 2011, available at: http://www.foreignersinuk.co.uk/news-sos_racism-prosecutors_criticized_for_not_levelling_a_more_serious_charge_in_racism_case_2738.html
Tooks Chambers website, available at: http://www.tooks.co.uk/

# Index

Adams, J. 71
Administrative Directions 40, 53
adversary system
 advantages of 82–3, 220–21
 dangers to 48–9, 216, 253–4
 factual *vs.* legal guilt 5, 47
 purpose of 4–6, 82, 220–21
 shadow system, implications of 216–18, 253–4
Alge, Daniele 159, 187–8
Alschuler, Albert 3
Ashworth, A. 23–4, 55, 97, 178, 244
Asian minorities *see* black and ethnic minorities
*Attorney-General's Guidelines on the Acceptance of Pleas and the Prosecutor's Role in the Sentencing Exercise (2009)* 134
Auld Report on Criminal Courts (2001)
 on advance indication of sentencing 120, 128
 on 'cracked' trials 93–4, 116–18
 on defence role 165, 167–70, 173–5
 on innocent defendant problem 118–19
 on judicial miscarriages of justice 241
 on plea bargaining
  cost savings from 113, 222–6
  justifications for 221–6
  and over-charging or charge reductions 137
  sentencing discounts 91–4, 116
 political influences on 93–4
 on prosecution role 128–9, 154
 purpose 90–93, 221
 recommendations 90–92
 and rights of suspects 249–51
 on standard of proof 92–3

Balbus, Isaac 7, 10, 24, 252

Baldwin, John 109
Ball, R. 18
Bar Council
 disciplinary functions 168
 on legal aid costs 183
 on public defender reform proposals 185
barristers *see also* defence counsel
 discipline 168
 judicial relationships 217
 Masonic influences on 218–19
 shadow structure, implications for 217–18
 technical competence challenges 163–5
benefits fraud
 and denigration of innocence 231–2
Bentham, Jeremy 199–201
Bentley, Derek 48
Birkett, Lord 172
Birmingham, public disorder *see* Urban Disorder (2011)
*Birmingham Six* 50–52, 57–8
black and ethnic minorities
 innocence, derogation of 230–32
 and institutional racism 119–20
 jury trials, choice of 119–20
 police stop and search trends 17–18, 32, 34–5, 120, 250
 sentencing discounts 119
Blackstock, J.E. 157, 159, 161
Block, B. 109
Blumberg, A. 244–5, 252
Bonomy, Lord 195–6
Bottoms, A. 62–4
Boulton, William 166
Bowcott, Owen 124
*Braden's Week* (TV programme) 66–9

*287*

Bridges, Lee 24, 99, 117–18, 124–5, 185, 220–21
*Bridgewater Four* 51–2, 58
Brooks, Dwayne 231
burden of proof
  beyond reasonable doubt 5–6
  principle 5–6, 46–7
  and right to silence 46–7
  in road traffic offences 167
  and state-induced guilty pleas 223–4
Burton, F. 53, 247

Cape, E. 124
*Cardiff Three* 52
Carlen, P. 53, 247
Carter Inquiry on legal aid (2006) 123–4
case-load hypothesis 223
case management 178–9, 181
caution rule
  abolition, basis for 48–9
  conditional cautions 131
  and public interest 131
  purpose of 38
Cecil Leon, Henry 78
Central Fraud Group 127
Choongh, S. 159
*Conduct and Etiquette at the Bar (1953)* 166
Confait, Maxwell 40–41, 53–4, 233
confessions
  admissibility of
    and access to legal representation 40–41
    under *Judges' Rules* 38–9, 49
  extorted, protection from 37, 49–51
  and Police coercion 37–8, 43, 49–51, 64
  untrue confessions
    and Bentham's theory of punishment 200–201
    guilty-plea sentence discounts, influence on 199–201
conspiracy *see* corruption and conspiracy
Cook, Donald 73
corruption and conspiracy, in Police procedure
  alarm signals 242–3
  code of silence 239

criminal infiltration 240–41
and failure to act 237–9
investigations 44, 234, 240–41
judicial treatment of 239–40
non-disclosure 239–40, 243
perjury 42–3, 48, 50–51, 56, 218, 232, 237–40
protected witnesses, treatment 236–7
quashed convictions 241
systemic corruption 234–9
whistleblowers 240
Court of Appeal
  appeal delays and miscarriages of justice 51–2
  'clean hands' approach 219
  empty protestations 76
  sentencing practices, compared with lower courts 249
'cracked' trials
  Auld Report on 93–4, 116–18
  causes of 98–103
    deliberate 121–2, 159
    HMCPSI evidence of 107–8, 110
    late plea notification 100–101
    prosecutorial errors and inefficiency 105–10
  and cost-efficiency 104–10
  *Crown Court Study* on 101–6, 109–10
  definition 98
  influences on
    defendant decision-making 100–103
    prosecution case preparation 103–4
    state-induced guilty pleas 98–110
  problems caused by 89
  and time wasting 103–10
  trends 98–100, 106–7
criminal inquiries
  appeal delays and miscarriages of justice 52–3
criminal justice system, generally *see also* criminal process, theory of
  adversary system
    advantages of 82–3, 220–21
    dangers to 48–9, 216, 253–4
    factual *vs.* legal guilt 5, 47
    purpose of 4–6, 82, 220–21
    shadow system, implications of 216–18, 253–4

criminal offences, law reform
      proposals 45–6
   political purpose 53
Criminal Law Revision Committee
   Eleventh Report (1972) 28, 45, 49
Criminal Procedure Rules Committee
   94
criminal process, theory of
   bureaucratic justice 244–5, 252
   courtroom workshops model 245,
      252–3
   disciplinary justice model 247–51
   *Judges' Rules,* influence on 244–5
   and judicial dissent 248–9
   managerialism 245–6
   perspectives on 244
   quasi-inquisitorial justice 246–7
criminals
   infiltration of Police by 240–41
   profiling 28–9
   stereotyping
      innocence, denigration of
         230–32
      and institutional racism 119–20
      jury trials, choice of 119–20
      police stop and search trends
         17–18, 32, 34–5, 120, 250
   stigmatisation 116
cross-examination
   under *Judges' Rules* 38–9
   and Police collaboration 42–4
   purpose 42, 82
   restrictions on 167–8, 243
   and right to fair trial 2–3
*Crown Court Study* (1993) 88–9
   on costs of trials and inefficiency
      112–14
   on 'cracked' trials 101–6, 109–10
Crown Prosecution Service
   and guilty-plea development 154
      Attorney General's guidelines on
         pleas and sentencing 134
      challenges 129–32
      and factual basis of bargain
         143–6
      independence of 147–8
      over-charging 136–7
      political context 129–32
      and public interest 131
      technical competence 132–6

under-charging 136–43
organisation structure 127–8
role of 128–9

Dawes, W. 101–2
de Menezes, Jean Charles 233
defence counsel
   challenges for
      contempt of court 175, 180
      guilt, presumption of 158–9
      legal aid funding restrictions 159
      prosecution gaps 176–8
      technical competence 173–5
   general principles 156–7
      attitudes and behaviour towards
         clients 158–62
      case management 178–9, 181
      'Charter for Counsel' 180
      persuasion, role of 172
   obligations
      historical position 166–7
      reform proposals 165, 167–70,
         173–5
   role restructuring 165–81
      Auld Report proposals 165,
         167–70, 173–5
      background 165–7
      truth-seeking role development
         170–74
defendants, innocent 118–19
Dell, S. 63
Denning, Lord 119, 172, 233
Devlin, Mr Justice 230
Director of Public Prosecutions (DPP)
   127–8
Drury, J. 18
Du Cann, R. 156
Duggan, Mark 16–17, 43–4
Dworkin, Ronald 5–6, 222

Edwards, A. 246
Eisenstein, J. 245, 252
Ellison Report on death of Stephen
   Lawrence (2014) 58, 230–31, 235,
   238, 240–41
ethnic minorities *see* black and ethnic
   minorities
*Evaluation of the Public Defender
   Service (2007)* 185
Evans, Timothy 52

fair trial *see* right to fair trial
*Firm and Fair* (White Paper, Scotland, 1994) 195
fiscal fines 213–14
Fisher Inquiry (1977) 40–41, 52–3, 233
Flying Squad
  corruption in 235–6
formal legal rationality
  abnormal situations, legal treatment during
    legal principles 6–7
    media role in 12–13, 16, 19
    Miners' Strike (1984) 13–16
    normal cases, courts' responses to 24–5
    Operation Major (1980s) 8–12
    and restoring order 7
    Urban Disorders (2011) 16–24
    US Black Ghettos (1960s) 7
  adversary system
    advantages of 82–3, 220–21
    dangers to 48–9, 216, 253–4
    factual *vs.* legal guilt 5, 47
    purpose of 4–6, 82, 220–21
    shadow system, implications of 216–18, 253–4
  principles, generally 5–6
  rights and principles 2
    historical development 27–8
    judicial limitation of 48–9
Foucault, M. 251
Francis, Peter 231
Franey, R. 11
Fraud Trials Committee (1986) 45
freedom of access to judiciary
  and state-induced guilty pleas
    and defendants' choice 120–24, 218–19
    legitimacy 70–71, 73, 219–20
freedom of individual
  infringement
    and anti-terrorism 29
    justification for 3–5
    and Police collaboration 42–4
    and Police rights of seizure 41–2
    prohibition 4
  principles, generally 36–7
Frey, Ronald 2
Fuller, L. 65, 156

*The Gateway to Justice (2011)* 131
Genders, E. 99
Goddard, Lord 48
*Goodyear* guidelines 94–8, 123–4
Grayling, Chris 183–6
Gross, Rt Hon LJ 177–8
*Guildford Four* 52, 57–8, 235
guilt, generally *see also* burden of proof
  admission of, first reasonable opportunity for 115, 207
  factual *vs.* legal guilt 5, 47
  and moral harm 5–6
guilty pleas, generally *see also* state-induced guilty pleas
  in Court Martial cases 124
  definition 62
  purpose 10
  trends 62–3, 217

Hall, A. 226, 246
Hallsworth, S. 18–19
Halpin, Tony 139
Hamilton, Alexander 1
Harries, R. 112
Henderson, P. *see* Crown Court Study
Henham, R. 99, 217
Heumann, M. 245
Hillsborough Disaster 239
Hillyard, Paddy 14–15
HMCPSI Reports
  on case discontinuance trends 224
  on 'cracked' trials 107–8, 110
  on performance of prosecution advocates 103–4, 106–10, 129–30, 136
Hodgson, J. 6, 245–6
Hoffman, L. 48, 54
homelessness 1, 8, 11 *see also* Operation Major (1980s)
human rights, generally *see also* individual rights
  and stop and search powers 29–31
Hutchinson-Foster, Kevin 44
Hyde, J. 181

inconsistent pleaders 63–4
Independent Police Commission Investigations
  on CPS inefficiencies 130

limitations 55, 236
  on Police conspiracy and corruption 231, 234–5
  powers and resources 234–5
  witness refusal to answer during 44
ineffective trials
  cost-effectiveness, relevance of 111–12
  trends 110–11
innocence *see also* burden of proof; guilt
  'however innocent,' interpretation 117–18, 229–30
  inconsistent pleaders 63–4
  innocent defendants 117–19
  institutional denigration of 229–32
  and media stereotyping 230–31
  and punishment, justification for 229–32
  subjugation of risk to innocent 228–9
investigations
  into plea-bargaining
    by JUSTICE 69–70, 253
    by Law Society 69–70
  into Police corruption 44, 240–41
  profiling, role in 28–9
  into tax evasion 10–11

Jacob, H. 245, 252
James Committee on distribution of business between Crown Court and Magistrates' Court (1975) 45, 251
Jarrett, Cynthia 18, 43
John Harris Memorial Lecture (2011) 148–9
*Judges' Rules*
  Administrative Directions 40, 53
  arrest and custodial powers 38–9
  confessions, admissibility of 38–9, 49
  criticism of 48, 217–18
  cross-examination 38–9
  historical background 37, 53
  as implied recognition of Police authority 54
  influence of 59–60, 248–9
  interpretation 39–40, 53
  judiciary, influences on 248–9

  legitimacy of 53–4
  non-compliance, implications 38
  purpose 37–8, 248–9
  reasonable suspicion 38
  right to legal advice 39–41
  right to silence 39–41, 49
  suspects' rights, influences on 39–41, 49, 249
judiciary
  generally
    discourtesy 149–50
    independence of 148–9
    legal understanding, lack of 150–51
    public confidence in 1, 233–4, 247–8
  Police corruption, treatment of 239–40
  prosecution role
    adherence to rules 149–50
    judicial oversight, failure of 148–55
    misdirection 149–51
    as protection mechanism in 148–9
  sentencing practices
    dissent opportunities 248–9
  and state-induced guilty pleas
    and defendants' choice 120–24, 218–19
    judge-initiated bargaining 74–5
    judicial oversight, legal failures during 148–54
    legitimacy of 70–71, 73, 219–20
    in Scotland, role of judicial discretion 194–5
Junius 251
JUSTICE
  plea-bargaining investigations 69–70, 253
*Justice for All* (White Paper, 2002) 93–4, 116–17

Kaldor-Hicks economic efficiency theory 203–4
Kennedy, Ludovic 51
King, M. 11
Kiszco, Stefan 52

Lacey, Nicola 233–4
Laity, Louis Paul 66–8

Law Society
  plea-bargaining investigations 69–70
  on public defender reform proposals 185
Lawrence, Stephen 58, 230–31, 235, 238, 240–41
Lea, J. 18–19
legal advice/ representation
  and confessions, admissibility of 40–41
  in Operation Major (1980s) 9–10
  right to 46–7
    extension of 61
    under *Judges' Rules* 39–41
Legal Aid
  income thresholds 186–7
  as market product, implications of 187–8
  reforms
    competitive tendering, challenges of 184–6
    criticisms of 184–7
    financial implications 183–4, 186–8
    guilty plea trends, potential impact on 187–8
    implications for justice 181–3, 186–8
    as managed consolidation 184–5
    purpose 181–2
legitimacy
  moral basis 2
  need for 220–21
  of Police, *Judges' Rules* role in establishment 37–8, 53–4
  and purpose of criminal courts 6–7
Leigh, L. 131m, 163
Levitt, Alison 227
Lippke, Richard 3
Liverpool, public disorder *see* Urban Disorder (2011)
*Luton Post Office Murder* case 51

McBarnet, Doreen 39, 42, 54
McClean, J. 62–4
McEwan, Jenny 175, 178, 245, 247
Magistrates Courts
  charge-bargaining trends 136
*Maguire Six* 52

Manchester, public disorder *see* Urban Disorder (2011)
Martin-Sperry, David 242–3
Masons, influences of 218–19
media
  institutional denigration by 230–31
  Miners' Strike (1984), role in 13, 16
  Operation Major (1980s), role in 12
  plea bargaining, disclosure of 66–9
  public relations role 12
  Urban Disorders (2012), role in 19
Miller, J. 112, 234
Millhench, Ronald 40
Miners' Strike (1984)
  intercept policy 13–14
  media role 13, 16
  prosecution strategies 13–16
  state-induced guilty please, role of 15–16
miscarriages of justice
  Auld Report on 241
  court distancing from 59
  and Court of Appeal delays 51–2
  and criminal inquiries 52–3
  displacement practices 57
  individuation practices 57
  legitimation practices 56
  and public confidence 1, 233–4, 247–8
  and Royal Commission on Criminal Justice (1993) 87–8, 233–4
  treatment challenges 56–7
Mitchell, B. 21
*Modernising Justice in Scotland* (2003) 196
Moody, S. 191–2
moral rights
  infringement, justification for 3–4
  moral harm and guilt 5–6
  and right to fair trial 2–3
Morgan, Daniel 239–40
Morton, J. 42–3
Mungham, Geoff 64

Neuberger, Lord 187–8
*A New Approach to Tackling Offending in Communities Needed (2011)* 131
Newman, Daniel 157, 159–62

*Newton* hearings
 and sentencing discounts 96, 113, 115, 136, 225
NHS Care Quality Commission 130–31
Nicholson, D. 171
not proven verdicts, in Scotland 230

open-door policy 70–71
Operation Major (1980s)
 arrest, legal basis for 9
 emergency court procedures 9–10
 impact on law enforcement reputation 11–12
 legal justifications 12
 legal representation, access to 9–10
 media role 12
 sentencing strategies 9–10
Operation Swamp 81 29
Orwell, G. 123

Padfield, Nicola 185
Peach, Blair 218, 232
Percy-Smith, Janie 14–15
perjury
 by Police 42–3, 48, 50–51, 56, 218, 232, 237–40
plea bargaining, generally *see also* state-induced guilty pleas
 counsel-initiated bargaining 74
 definition 1
 judge-initiated bargaining 74–5
 justifications for 221–2
Pleas and Case Management Hearings 112–13
*Plebgate* 182
Police, generally
 corruption and conspiracy
  alarm signals 242–3
  code of silence 232, 239
  collaboration 42–4
  criminal infiltration 240–41
  failure to act 237–9
  illegality, attitudes to 27–8, 50–51
  investigations into 44, 234–5, 240–41
  judicial treatment of 233–4, 239–40
  non-disclosure 239–40, 243
  oversight mechanisms, limitations of 55
  perjury 42–3, 48, 50–51, 56, 218, 232, 237–40
  protected witnesses, treatment 236–7
  and public confidence 58, 233–4
  quashed convictions 241
  to secure convictions, justifications for 233–4
  systemic causes 57–8, 234–9
  whistleblowers 240
 discretion, role of 27–8
 Masonic influences on 218–19
 political power of 182
 profiling, role of 28–9
 and public confidence 58, 233–4
Police powers
 cross-examination 42, 82, 167
 and collaboration 42–4
 custodial detention 60–61
 generally
  background 36–7
  caution, purpose of 38
  as justification for new law 54–5
  legitimacy 53–4
  political influences on 60–61
  as sources of law 54
 *Judges' Rules*
  Administrative Directions 40, 53
  arrest and custodial powers 38–9
  confessions, admissibility of 38–9, 49
  criticism of 48, 217–18
  cross-examination 38–9
  historical background 37, 53
  influence of 59–60
  interpretation 53
  interpretative guidance 39–40
  judiciary, influences on 248–9
  legitimacy of 53–4
  non-compliance, implications 38
  and Police authority, implied recognition of 54
  purpose 37–8, 54, 248–9
  reasonable suspicion 38
  right to legal advice 39–41
  right to silence 39–41, 49
  suspects' rights, influences on 39–41, 49, 249

necessity for 55
and prevention of terrorism
  influence of 60–61
  reasonable suspicion 29, 60
search and seizure 41–2
stop and search 28–36
  amongst black and ethnic
    minorities 17–18, 32, 34–5,
    120
  and anti-terrorism 29–30
  concerns regarding 34–6
  and ECHR 30, 33–4
  excessive and indiscriminate use
    of 29–30
  illegal use of 30
  and public safety 31–2
  and reasonable suspicion 29, 60
  and right to liberty 33–4
  and right to privacy 33
  safeguards, limitations of 30–32
  trends 17–18, 32, 34–6
Price, Ronald 69
profiling, role in Police investigations
  28–9
prosecution
  CPS role in guilty-plea bargains
    development 154
    Attorney General's guidelines on
      pleas and sentencing 134
    challenges 129–32
    and factual basis of bargain 143–6
    general role of 128–9
    independence of 147–8
    organisation structure 127–8
    over-charging 136–7
    political context 129–32
    and public interest 131
    and technical competence 132–6
    under-charging 136–43
  Director of Public Prosecutions
    (DPP) role 127–8
  Judicial role in guilty-plea bargains
    development
    adherence to rules 149–50
    judicial oversight, failure of
      148–55
    misdirection 149–51
    as protection mechanism in 148–9
public confidence
  in judiciary 1, 233–4, 247–8

and Police malpractice 58
reasons for 1–2
public interest justification
  caution rule 131
  for guilty-plea bargaining, in
    Scotland 202
punishment, generally
  Bentham's theory of 200–201
  justification for 4–5, 199, 229–32
  principles of 200–201
  untrue confessions, influence of
    199–201

rape, false allegations 227–8
reasonable suspicion
  and prevention of terrorism 29, 60
  and stop and search powers 29, 60
Redmayne, M. 55, 97, 178, 244
Reid, Lord 166
remorse, relevance in 72, 84–5, 120
  in Scotland 201
Rhodes, D. 124
Richardson, James 152, 172, 248
right to equal treatment 5–6
right to fair trial 220
  and case-load hypothesis 223
  general principle under ECHR 2–3
  and trial by jury 3–4
right to legal advice/ representation
  46–7
  extension of 61
  under *Judges' Rules* 39–41
right to liberty
  general legal principles 36–7
  and stop and search powers 33–4
right to privacy 33
right to silence 220
  and burden of proof 46–7
  under *Judges' Rules* 39–41
  law reform proposals 45, 48–9
Roberts, Andrew 59
Roberts, J. 21, 23, 59
Robertson, G. 72, 254
Romily, S. 91
Rose, G. 63
Royal Commission on Criminal Justice
  (1993)
  on defendant-decision making
    influences on choice of guilty
      pleas 100–102

on miscarriages of justice 233–4
proposals for restrictions on state-induced guilty pleas 88–9
purpose 87–8
on sentencing system injustices 117
Royal Commission on Criminal Procedure (1981) 75
Royal Commission on Police (1962) 53
Royal Commission on Police Powers and Procedure (1929) 36–7
  balance strategy 54–5
  and right to silence 48–9
Rozenberg, J. 76

Sanders, Alison 182, 244
Scanlon, T.M. 65
Scotland
  not proven verdicts, trends 230
  sentencing practices, generally 249
  state-induced guilty pleas
    case cost comparisons, relevance of 201–4
    as charge bargaining 191
    comparative role of 25–6, 190
    discretion *vs.* policy debate 204–208, 210–12, 214–15
    fiscal fines 213–14
    fixed fees system, impact 192
    guidelines, need for 207–8
    higher court criticisms of 193–5
    informal procedures 190–92
    judicial discretion, role of 194–5
    Lord Justice General's Practice Notes 196–7
    in lower courts 190–92, 212–14
    in minor cases, as alternatives to prosecution 212–14
    official promotion of 192–9
    partial pleas 191
    policy development 197–9, 201–4, 206–7, 209–12
    practical aspects, emphasis on 208–10
    public interest justification 202
    remorse, relevance of 201
    risks, judicial management of 206–208
    sentence discount recording 197
    statutory basis for 190, 195–9
    time of plea, relevance of 207
    trends 192
    utilitarian justification 198–201
    withdrawal conditions 193
  stop and search trends 34
Scraton, P. 231
Seabrook Committee on Crown Court Business (1992) 98, 101, 104, 225
search and seizure 41–2
Seifman, R. 64
sentence discountS
  and *Newton* hearings 96, 113, 115, 136, 225
  Royal Commission on Criminal Justice (1993) on 88–9
  Scottish court views on 206–208
  state-induced guilty pleas as 72–3, 84–5
    admission of guilt, time of 115, 207
    advantages, evidence of 112
    burden of proof, influence on 223–4
    case-load hypothesis 223
    cost-efficiency justification 112–15, 222–6, 228–9, 245–6, 251
    as lowest possible sentence 228–9
    victims and witnesses, impact on 226–8
Sentencing Council 94, 113
Sentencing Guidelines
  on custodial sentences for non guilty pleas 135
  departure from, in abnormal circumstances 22–3
  lower courts development of 23
  on the reduction of sentences for guilty pleas 94, 114–15, 197, 223
  on time of admission of guilt 115
Sentencing Guidelines Council 94, 113
Serious Crime Group 127
Shattuck, Petra 24
Sheskin, A. 252
silence *see* right to silence
solicitors *see also* defence counsel
  attitudes and behaviour towards clients 158–62
  presumption of guilt by, trends 158–9

technical competence challenges 157–62
Special Demonstration Squad 231
standard of proof
  Auld Review on 92–3
  civil standard of 5, 52–3, 233
  role of 2–3
*Standing Accused (1994)* 158–62
state-induced guilty pleas
  burden of proof, influence on 223–4
  choice
    admission of guilt, first reasonable opportunity 115, 207
    coercion, relevance of 116–17
    and freedom of access to judge 120–24, 218–19
    inconsistent pleaders 63
    influences on 64
    and innocent defendant problem 118–19
    pre-trial procedure, potential influences on 105–6
    studies of 63–4
    tactical motives 115–18
  cost-efficiency justification 112–15, 222–6, 228–9, 245–6, 251
  and case-load hypothesis 223
  committal proceedings, abolition of 223–5
  legitimacy 83–5, 94
  counsel-initiated bargaining 74
  defence lawyers status, influence on 125
  emergence of
    Auld Report (2001), influence on 90–94
    and 'cracked' trials 98–110
    'culture change,' influence *of* 95
    and denigration of defendant 114–20, 251
    *Goodyear* guidelines 94–8
    and 'ineffective' trials 110–12
    *Justice for All* (White Paper 2002) 93–4
    Royal Commission on Criminal Justice (1993), influence on 87–9
    Seabrook Committee (1992) 98, 225
  and trial cost efficiency 112–15, 222–6
  importance 65–6
  judicial oversight
    distancing 120–24
    freedom of access to judge 70–71, 73, 219–20
    judge-initiated bargaining 74–5
    legal failures during 148–54
    refuge from judicial coercion 72
  late notification 100–101
  legitimacy
    as administrative efficiency 83–5, 94
    and balance of interests 222–6
    challenges of 65–6
    as contradiction of adversarial justice 82–3
    Court of Appeal protestations 76
    as customary practice 75–6
    and defendant's freedom of choice 72–3
    and defendants' justice, challenges to 80–82
    developments in 83–6
    five consequences approach 73
    four deceptions approach 71–2
    and freedom of access to judge 70–71, 73, 120–24, 218–20
    media focus on 68–70
    procedural challenges 77–80
    as refuge from judicial coercion 72
    remorse, relevance of 72, 84–5, 120
    and sentence discounting 72–3, 84–5
    three freedoms approach 70–71
  as lowest possible sentence 228–9
  media focus on 66–9
  in Scotland
    case cost comparisons, relevance of 201–4
    as charge bargaining 191
    comparative role of 25–6, 190
    discretion *vs.* policy debate 204–208, 210–12, 214–15
    and fiscal fines 213–14
    fixed fees system, impact 192
    guidelines, need for 207–8
    higher court criticisms of 193–5

informal procedures 190–92
judicial discretion, role of 194–5
Lord Justice General's Practice
    Notes 196–7
in lower courts 190–92, 212–14
in minor cases, as alternatives to
    prosecution 212–14
official promotion of 192–9
partial pleas 191
policy development 197–9, 201–4,
    206–7, 209–12
practical aspects, emphasis on
    208–10
public interest justification 202
remorse, relevance of 201
risks, judicial management of
    206–208
sentence discount recording 197
statutory basis for 190, 195–9
time of plea, relevance of 207
trends 192
utilitarian justification 198–201
withdrawal conditions 193
as sentence discounting 72–3, 84–5
    admission of guilt, time of 115,
        207
    advantages, evidence of 112
    burden of proof, influence on
        223–4
    case-load hypothesis 223
    cost-efficiency justification
        112–15, 222–6, 228–9, 245–6,
        251
    as lowest possible sentence 228–9
    victims and witnesses, impact on
        226–8
    trends 62–3, 217
    in Scotland 192
    utilitarian justification 198–201
    victims and witnesses, impact on
        226–8
Stephen, F. 192
Steyn, Lord 1, 59, 157
stop and search
    powers
        and anti-terrorism 29–30
        concerns regarding 34–6
        and ECHR 30
        excessive and indiscriminate use
            of 29–30
        illegal use of 30
        and public safety 31–2
        and racial discrimination 32–3,
            120
        and reasonable suspicion 29, 60
        and right to liberty 33–4
        and right to privacy 33
        safeguards, limitations of 30–32
    trends
        in black and ethnic minorities
            17–18, 32, 34–5, 120
        generally 34–6
supergrasses 236
*Swift and Sure Justice: The
    Government's Plans for Reform
    of the Criminal Justice System*
    (White Paper, 2012) 228

Tata, C. 192
tax evasion, investigation trends
    10–11
terrorism, prevention of
    Police stop and search powers 29–32,
        60–61
Thomas, Phil 64
Thomson, D. 112
Tombs, J. 191–2
Tomlinson, Ian 230–31
*Tottenham Three* 52, 57–8
*Transforming Legal Aid: Delivering
    a More Credible and Efficient
    System (2013)* 184
Treacy, Rt Hon LJ 177–8
trial by jury
    ethnic minorities choice of 119–20
    guilty pleas, influence on 62
    jury nobbling 45–6
    principles behind 3–4
    reform of 251
trials, generally *see also* 'cracked' trials
    case discontinuance trends 224
    committal proceedings, proposed
        abolition 223–5
    cost-efficiency arguments 112–15,
        222–6, 228–9, 245–6
    costs of, in serious crime cases 183
    fraud trials, law reform 45–6
    ineffective trials 110–12
    judge-only trials, law reform
        proposals 45–6

Police evidence, faith in 50–51
as public events 6
summing-up 50–51

UK Global Law Summit (2015) 186
United States
  plea bargaining, State prohibition policy influences on 112
Urban Disorder (2011)
  background 16–18
  media role 19
  prosecution strategies 17–18, 21–3
  public protection emphasis 17–19
  public support 21–2
  sentencing strategies 19–22
  stop and search in ethnic communities 17–18

victims and witnesses
  'cracked' trials, impact on 89
  pressures on 227–8
  state-induced guilty pleas, impact on 226–8
  symbolism of 227–8

Walker, C. 32
Wallis, Keith 182
warrants
  search and seizure restrictions 41–2
West Midlands Serious Crime Squad
  survey of wrongful convictions by 242–3
Williams, Glanville 38–9
Wilmore, G. 223
witnesses *see* victims and witnesses
Woolf Reforms of Civil Justice (1996) 94, 169
Wright, R. 112

Young, R. 244–5

Zander, Michael 39–40 *see also Crown Court Study*